LE CORBUSIER REDRAWN
THE HOUSES
STEVEN PARK

Princeton Architectural Press   New York

Published by
Princeton Architectural Press
A McEvoy Group Company
202 Warren Street
Hudson, New York 12534

Visit our website at www.papress.com.

© 2012 Princeton Architectural Press
All Illustrations and captions © 2012 Soo Jin Park
All rights reserved
Printed and bound in China
20 19 18   5 4 3

No part of this book may be used or reproduced in any manner without written permission from the publisher, except in the context of reviews.

Every reasonable attempt has been made to identify owners of copyright. Errors or omissions will be corrected in subsequent editions.

Editors: Linda Lee and Sara Stemen
Designer: Jan Haux

Special thanks to: Bree Anne Apperley, Sara Bader, Nicola Bednarek Brower, Janet Behning, Fannie Bushin, Megan Carey, Carina Cha, Andrea Chlad, Russell Fernandez, Will Foster, Jan Hartman, Diane Levinson, Jennifer Lippert, Gina Morrow, John Myers, Katharine Myers, Margaret Rogalski, Elana Schlenker, Dan Simon, Andrew Stepanian, Paul Wagner, and Joseph Weston of Princeton Architectural Press
—Kevin C. Lippert, publisher

Library of Congress Cataloging-in-Publication Data
Park, Steven, 1975-
Le Corbusier redrawn : the houses / Steven Park. — First edition
240 pages : illustrations ; 26 cm
Includes bibliographical references.
ISBN 978-1-61689-068-1 (pbk. : alk. paper)
1. Le Corbusier, 1887-1965—Themes, motives. 2. Architectural drawing—France—20th century. 3. Architecture, Domestic—France—Designs and plans. I. Le Corbusier, 1887-1965. Works. Selections. 2012. II. Title.
NA2707.L4P37 2012
728'.37092—dc23
2012008172

Acknowledgments

I would like to thank Timothy Brown, John Kriegshauser, Peter Land, Robert Piotrowski, and Catherine Wetzel for encouraging me to pursue this documentation; Susan Augustine and her staff at the Ryerson and Burnham Libraries; Princeton Architectural Press for the insightful editorial comments; and especially my friend and colleague Nicolas Anderson for his continuous support from the very beginning of the project.

LE CORBUSIER REDRAWN

Contents

Preface 6

1 **MAISON-ATELIER OZENFANT** 8
2 **VILLA BESNUS** 14
3 **LA PETITE MAISON** 18
4 **VILLAS LIPCHITZ-MIESTCHANINOFF** 28
5 **VILLAS LA ROCHE-JEANNERET** 34
6 **MAISON TERNISIEN** 46
7 **PAVILLON DE L'ESPRIT NOUVEAU** 56
8 **MAISON PLANEIX** 68
9 **MAISON GUIETTE** 76
10 **VILLA COOK** 82
11 **VILLA STEIN-DE MONZIE** 90
12 **VILLA CHURCH NO. 1** 104
13 **VILLA CHURCH NO. 2** 114
14 **WEISSENHOFSIEDLUNG VILLA NO. 1** 124
15 **WEISSENHOFSIEDLUNG VILLA NO. 2** 132
16 **VILLA BAIZEAU** 140
17 **VILLA SAVOYE** 144
18 **VILLA DE MANDROT** 154
19 **MAISON DE WEEKEND (HENFEL)** 164
20 **VILLA LE SEXTANT** 172
21 **MAISON CURUTCHET** 178
22 **LE PETIT CABANON LE CORBUSIER** 186
23 **MAISONS JAOUL** 188
24 **VILLA SHODHAN** 200
25 **VILLA SARABHAI** 214
26 **MAISON DE L'HOMME** 228

Bibliography 240

PREFACE

This book presents sectional perspectives of twenty-two houses designed by Le Corbusier, as well as plans, sections, and elevations of these and four additional residences. Sectional perspectives—as opposed to orthogonal drawings of a building or an architectural idea—possess unique representational advantages. As pictorial projections, they allow viewers to easily visualize the three-dimensional shapes of exterior forms and interior spaces. Shade and shadows added to the outline perspectives facilitate this three-dimensional reading by emphasizing a structure's spatial depth, while the absence of color and texture highlight the basic form of spatial enclosures. By depicting in a single view multiple spaces within the building envelope, sectional perspectives create a sense of movement through a sequence of spaces and reveal their interrelationships within the overall spatial hierarchy.

Based on the original drawings from the Le Corbusier Foundation's archives, the plans, sections, and elevations were drawn at a 1:200 scale with a uniform graphic standard to accompany sectional perspectives (which vary in scale) as dimensional references. This consistency in scale and graphic representation underscores the book's thematic focus and chronological organization, which highlight the evolutionary development of Le Corbusier's changing philosophy about an ideal dwelling and facilitate a comparative analysis among different houses. This enables viewers to trace how Le Corbusier adapted design features or planning principles—such as the ramp or the concept of free plan—to different contexts and for various clients.

The primary aim of this book is to help architecture students develop and refine their visualization skills by studying Le Corbusier's houses in three dimensions. The illustrations, however, are not intended to re-create or replace the actual experience of the houses, and the readers are encouraged to visit the houses documented in the following pages. Walking through a building, measuring its dimensions with hands and arms, and observing how its forms and spaces are delineated by the changing shades and colors of light will all help readers to experience in reality what they have learned through study and to understand better the relationship between the representation and reality. Such an understanding will in turn be useful in visualizing, developing, and refining their own architectural ideas and in bringing them to fruition.

MAISON-ATELIER OZENFANT

LOCATION: Paris, France
DATE: 1922

The site for the studio of painter Amédée Ozenfant, Le Corbusier's friend and collaborator, is small and irregular but features an open corner. Internal programs are expressed in the design of enclosure systems: a working studio at the top is articulated by sawtooth skylights and double-height windows, and living spaces below by long strip windows. A sculptural spiral stair signals the start of a sequence of movement through the building from the entrance on the first floor to the domestic programs (kitchen, bedroom, bathroom, and gallery) on the second floor. An enclosing wall around interior stairs is partially open at the second-floor gallery, exposing the next sequence of ascent to the painting studio above.

    The quality of natural light defines the interior spaces. Strip windows on the second floor provide plenty of light and air to support daily activities. The double-height windows of the painting studio, on the north and east elevations, provide an expansive backdrop of light, while sawtooth skylights—which evoke industrial associations—bring in constant filtered light from above.

    When viewed from the inside, the painting studio appears to be an illuminated cube dissolved by the northern light. However, when seen from the outside, the profile of skylights accentuated by a projecting cornice defines the top of the building. This distinctive topography also offers a practical solution to the problem of draining a large glass area of roof.

    Within Le Corbusier's oeuvre, this house is significant because he employed certain notable components that repeatedly appeared in his later designs, such as a double-height space with a mezzanine, skylights to bring in natural light, strip windows to achieve flexible planning principles, and spiral stairs for planning efficiency and graceful upward movement.

CLIENT: Amédée Ozenfant
PROGRAM: Working and living studio
FEATURES: Double-height painting studio, sawtooth skylight, spiral stair, strip windows, handcrafted glazing details that intentionally resemble industrialized products

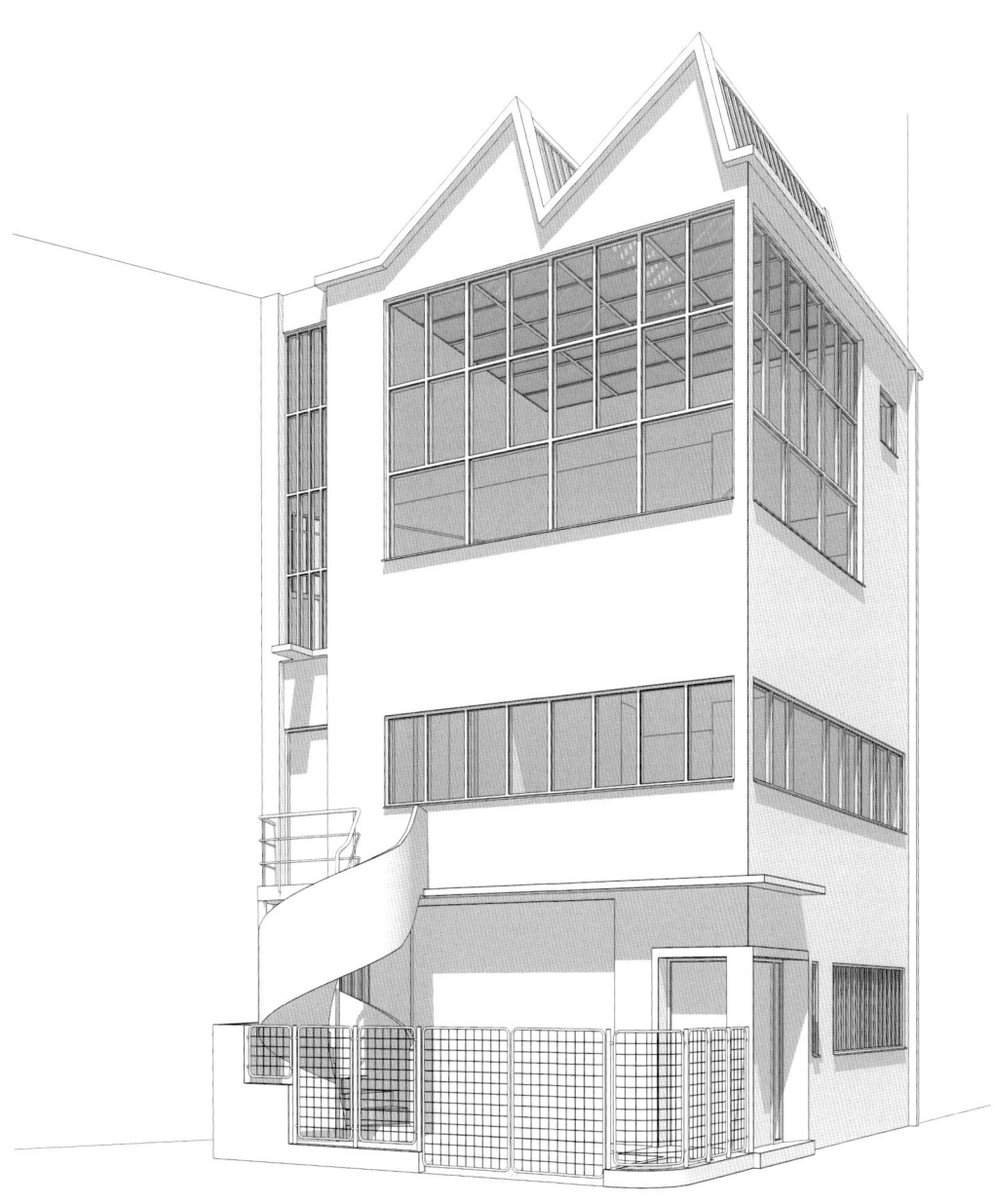

MAISON-ATELIER OZENFANT — Exterior perspective, northeast corner

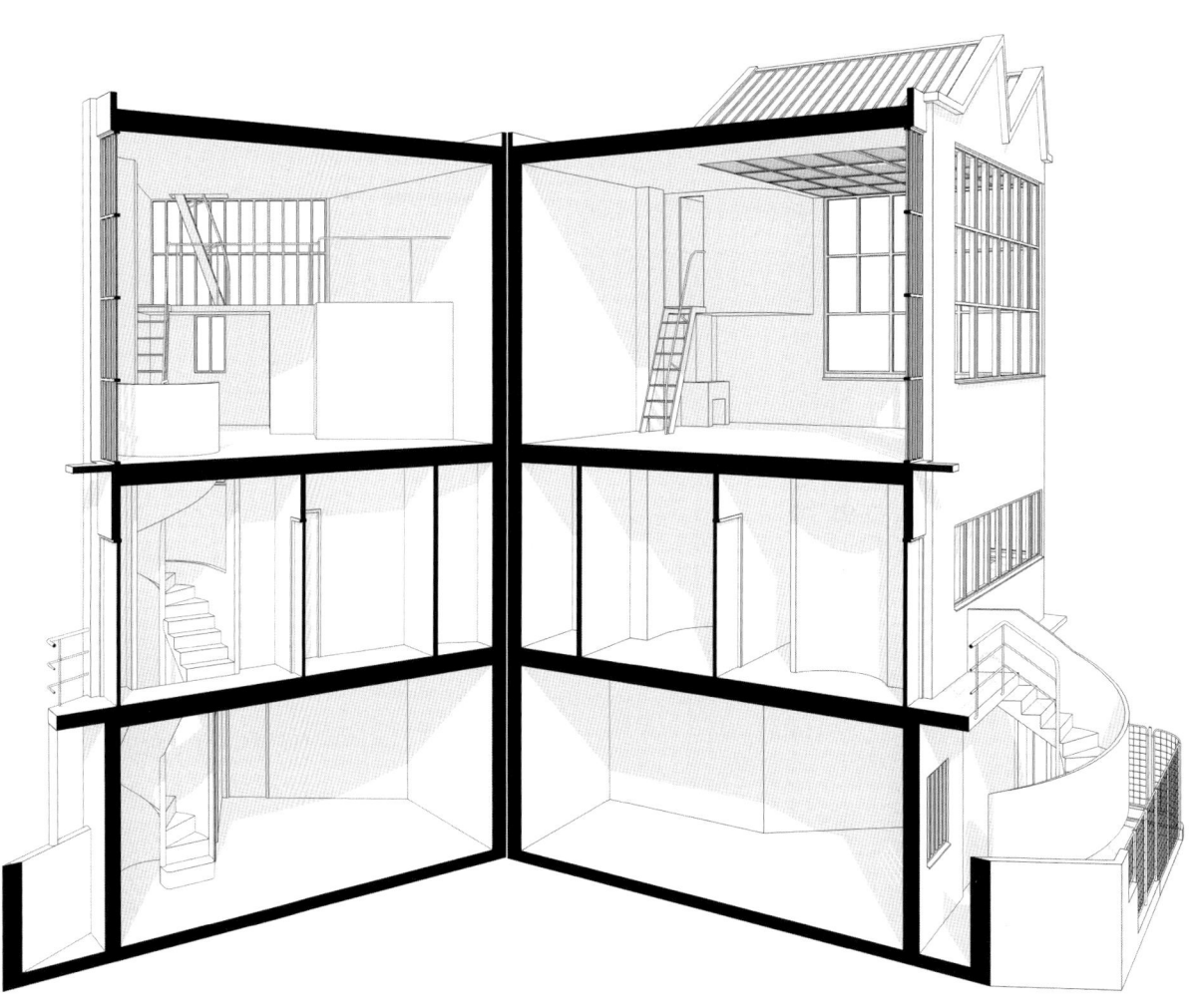

Composite of west–east and east–west sectional perspectives

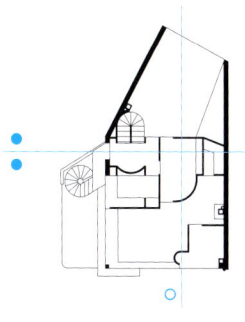

11 **MAISON-ATELIER OZENFANT** ◯ North–south sectional perspective

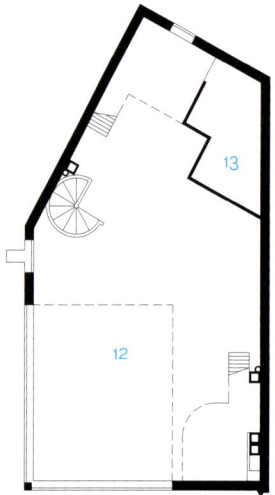
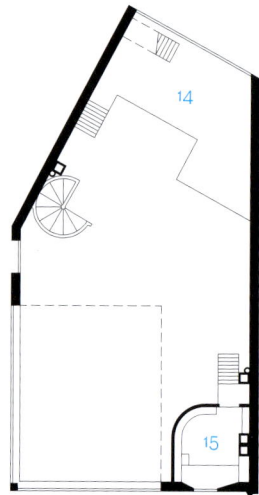
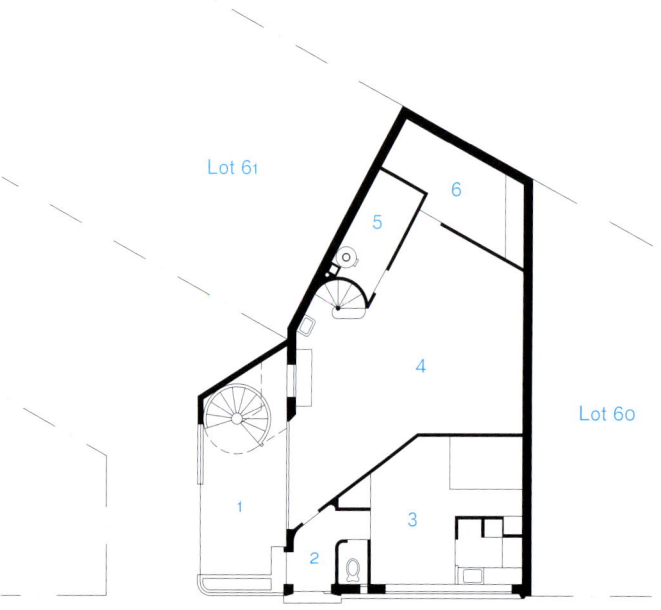
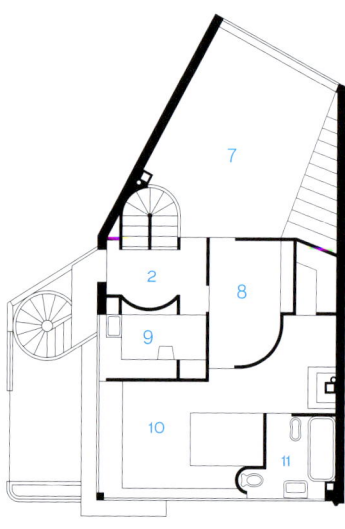

Third-floor plan   Fourth-floor plan
First-floor plan   Second-floor plan

1. Gated front yard
2. Vestibule
3. Caretaker's room
4. Garage
5. Mechanical room
6. Storage
7. Gallery
8. Showroom
9. Kitchen
10. Bedroom
11. Bathroom
12. Painting studio
13. Darkroom
14. Mezzanine
15. Library

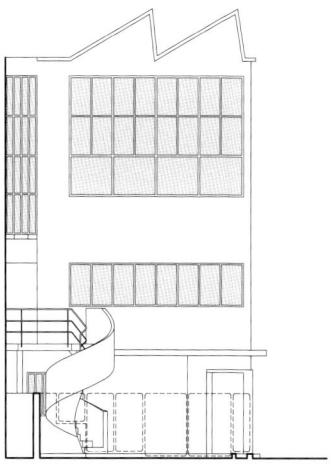

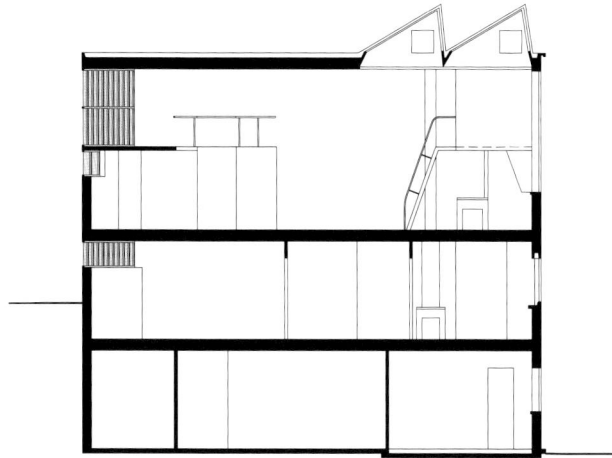
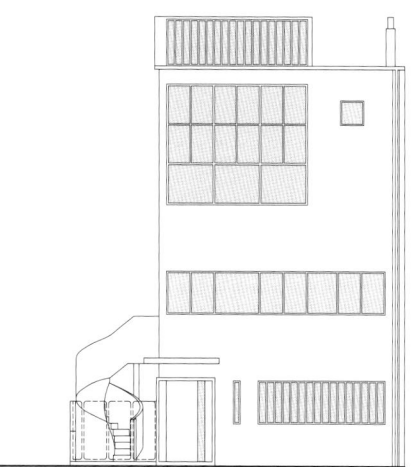

East elevation
South–north section

North elevation

13 **MAISON-ATELIER OZENFANT**

VILLA BESNUS

LOCATION: Vaucresson, France
DATE: 1922

Georges Besnus, who knew of Le Corbusier through the architect's writings in *L'Esprit Nouveau*, wanted a house similar in design to the Maison Citrohan, which he had seen at the Salon d'Automne in Paris in 1922. He commissioned Le Corbusier to design a modern villa with a modest budget.

Le Corbusier used regulating lines to lay out an asymmetrical street (north) elevation, which has a projecting window and a balcony. The garden (south) elevation is based on the neoclassical principle of tripartite symmetry. The design of the garden elevation is similar to that of Le Corbusier's Villa Schwob, except that Villa Besnus is rendered in a pure and abstract form, marking a transitional phase in Le Corbusier's work from classicism to the machine aesthetic.

In the interior, fixed elements such as a fireplace and bathroom occupy the center of the plan, and living spaces are organized around the fixed elements. After construction, the house was plagued by a series of problems, including excessive dampness in the staircase and living room, flooding in the garage and cellar, and fractures in load-bearing walls. Shortly after moving into his new modern house, Besnus sold it and moved to Brittany. Subsequent owners have made significant modifications to the residence.

CLIENT: Georges Besnus
PROGRAM: Working and living studio
FEATURES: Street elevation laid out using regulating lines, garden elevation with tripartite symmetry

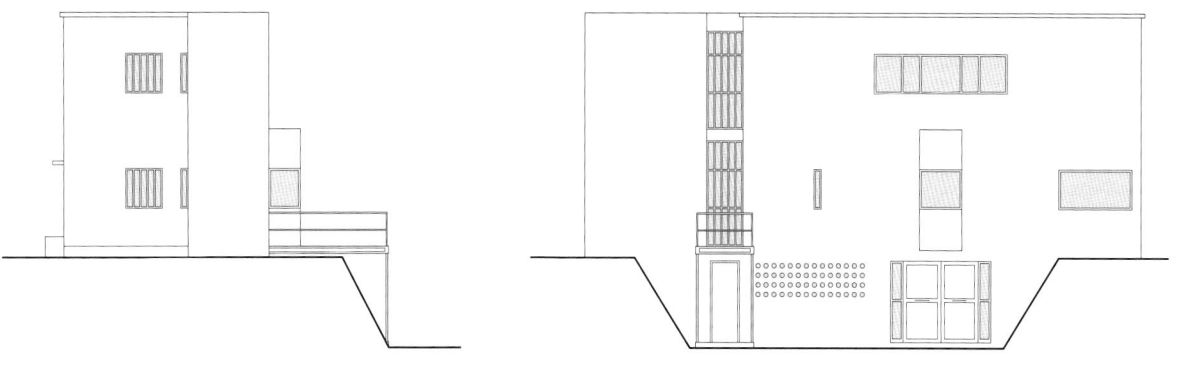
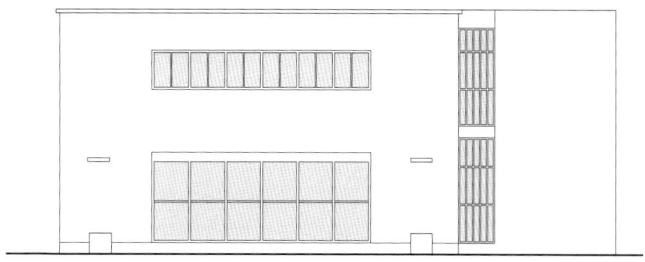

East elevation

North elevation
South elevation

15 **VILLA BESNUS**

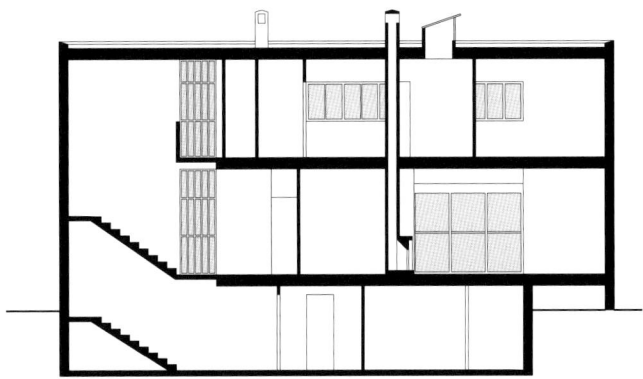

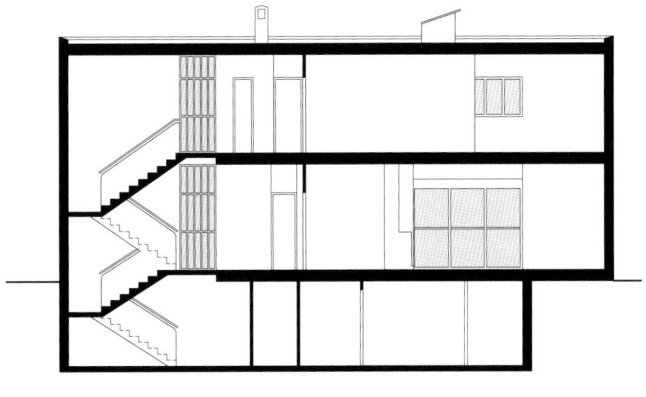

East–west sections

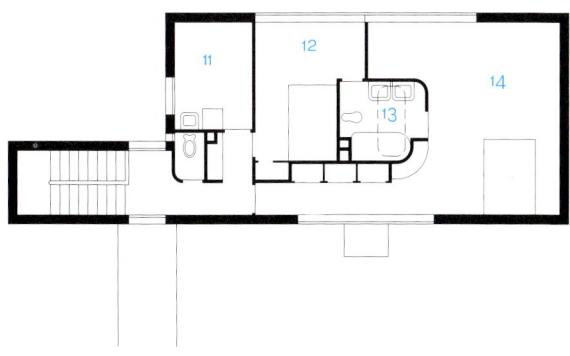

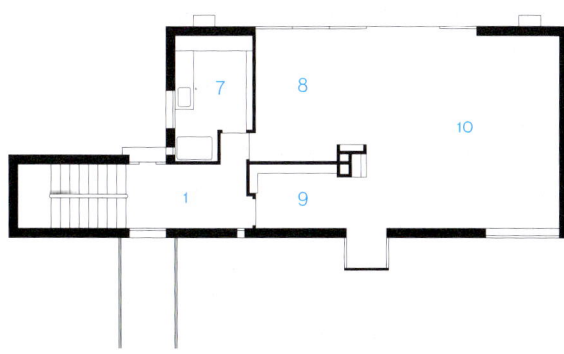

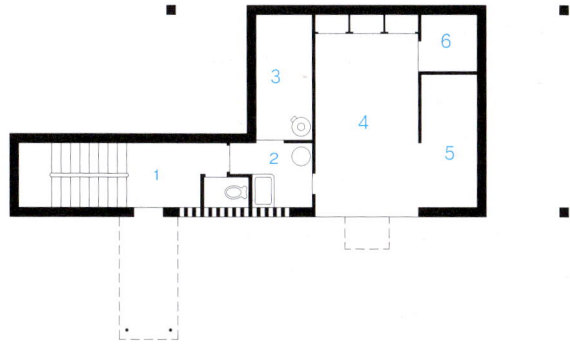

Third-floor plan
Second-floor plan
First-floor plan

1	Vestibule	8	Dining room
2	Laundry	9	Library
3	Mechanical room	10	Living room
4	Garage	11	Dressing room
5	Storage	12	Bedroom
6	Cellar	13	Master bathroom
7	Kitchen	14	Master bedroom

17 **VILLA BESNUS**

LA PETITE MAISON

LOCATION: Corseaux, Switzerland
DATE: 1923

Le Corbusier designed this small house for his parents. After his father's death, shortly after completion of the project, his mother and brother resided here. Similar to those of Le Corbusier's prototype-housing projects, the plan of this house was laid out purely on the basis of programmatic considerations before the selection of a site. Here in Corseaux, Le Corbusier demonstrated that a schematic plan developed without a site could be successfully integrated into specific local conditions.

A seemingly simple exterior belies the spatial complexities within. A multipurpose room with sliding walls and retractable beds doubles as a guest room. The living room also demonstrates flexible planning principles, through the design of a movable desk and rotatable lamp. Interior sliding partitions reinforce the concept of transformable spaces, which is extended outside with the incorporation of operable shutters around the patio.

An eleven-meter-long strip window on the south facade provides a panoramic view of Lake Geneva and the Alps and brings in natural light. The window also unifies interior spaces and gives a clear identity to the building, as its most visually prominent feature. The north elevation, facing the street, features punched windows that are small enough to preserve privacy. They limit street noise while providing constant northern light. Spaces that are more private receive natural light from small skylights in the roof.

The roof garden is in tune with nature and connects the house with the local landscape of lake and mountains. In a corresponding small outdoor garden on the ground level, Le Corbusier designed a viewing platform by punching a small opening in the south perimeter wall to frame a human-scaled view of the vast surrounding landscape. A perimeter wall steps down in height along the lakefront to allow for visual continuity between the house and the surrounding landscape. Exterior mounted shutters provide protection against strong sunlight, wind, and rain; the added component of a roller shutter protrudes from the wall. In Le Corbusier's more advanced later projects, shading devices are integrated within the depths of walls.

CLIENTS: Georges-Édouard Jeanneret and Marie-Charlotte-Amélie Jeanneret-Perret
PROGRAM: Family residence
FEATURES: Strip window, roof garden, roller shade, covered outdoor patio, movable partitions and furniture, multipurpose room, site-neutral schematic design

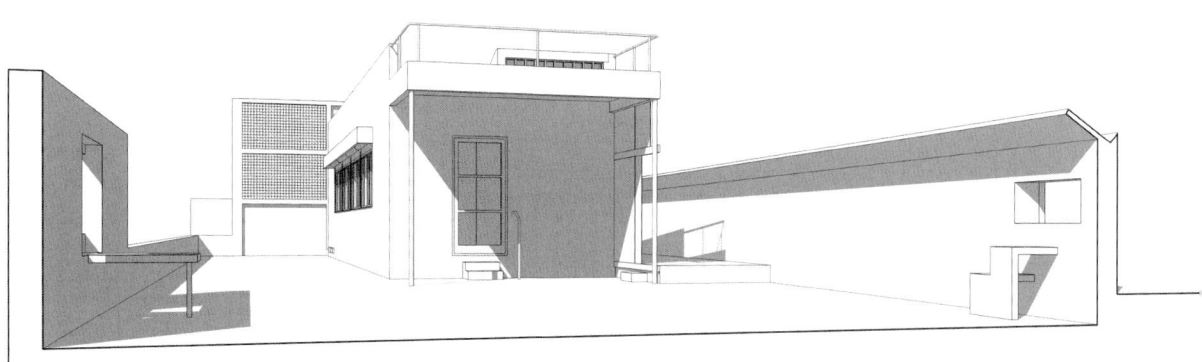

Exterior perspective, southeast corner

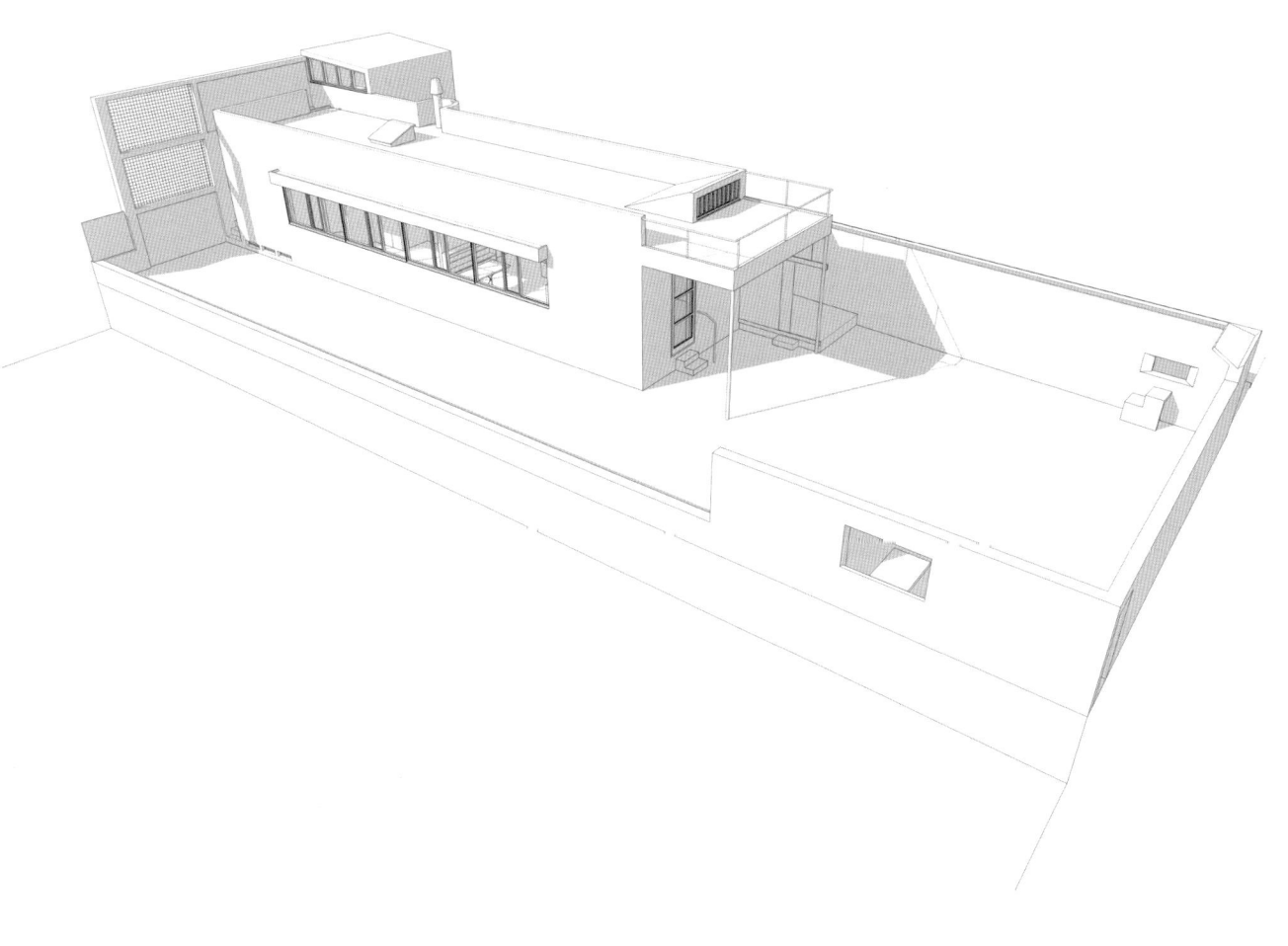

Aerial perspective, southeast corner

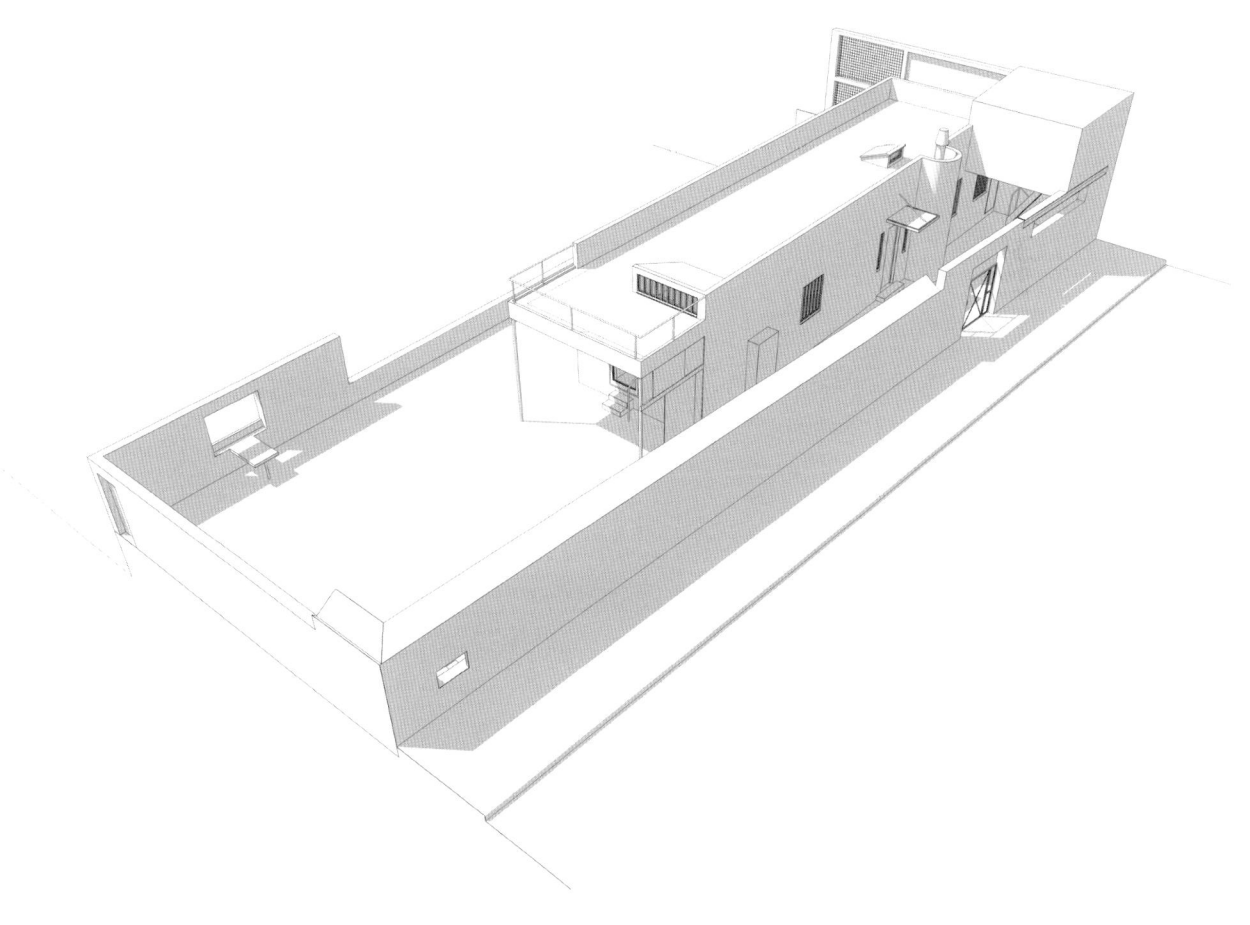

Aerial perspective, northeast corner

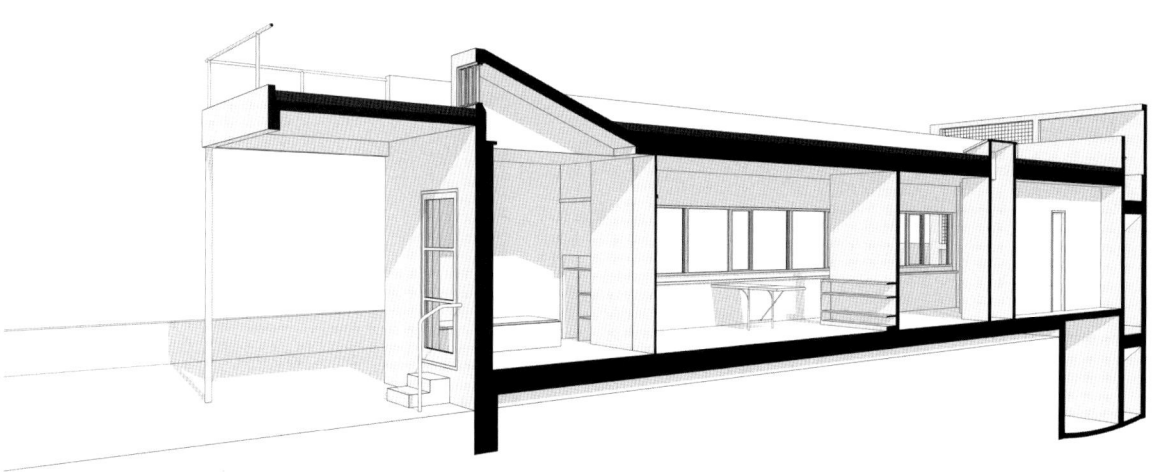

East–west sectional perspective

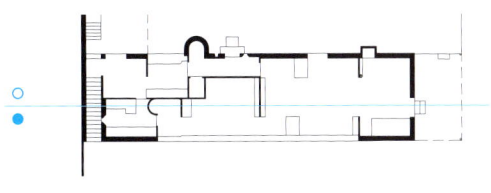

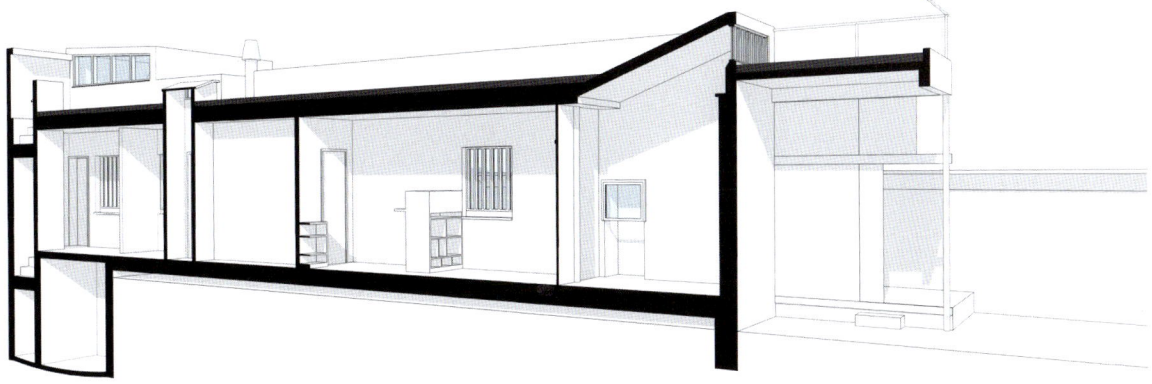

23 **LA PETITE MAISON**   ◯   West–east sectional perspective

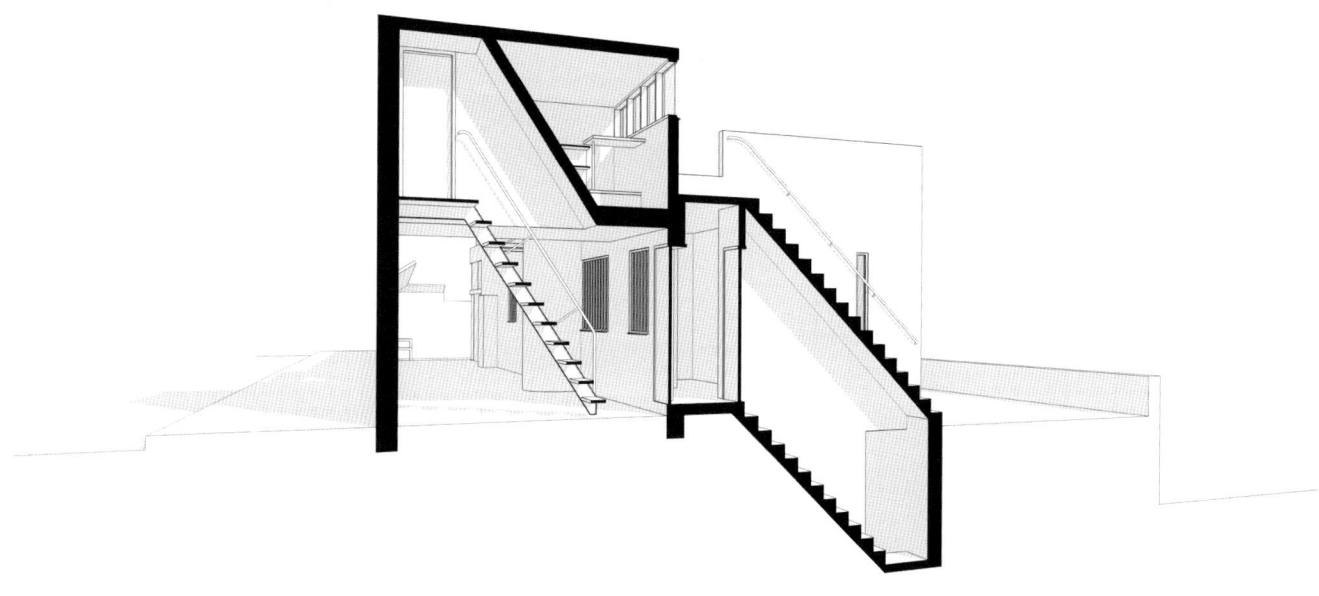

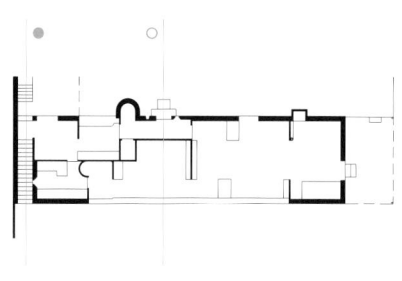

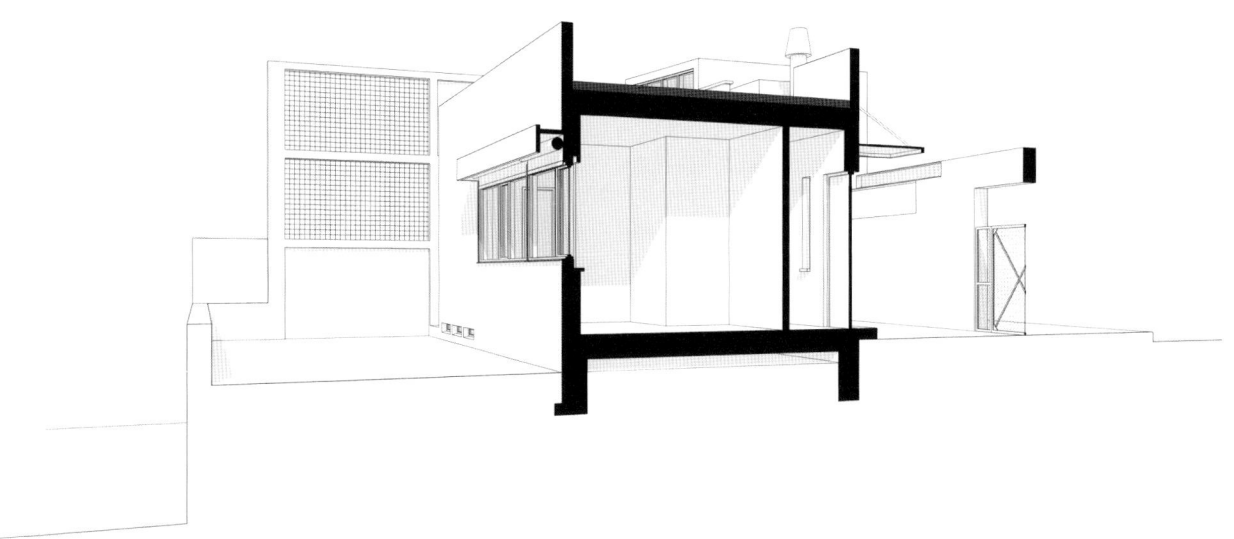

○ South–north sectional perspective at bedroom

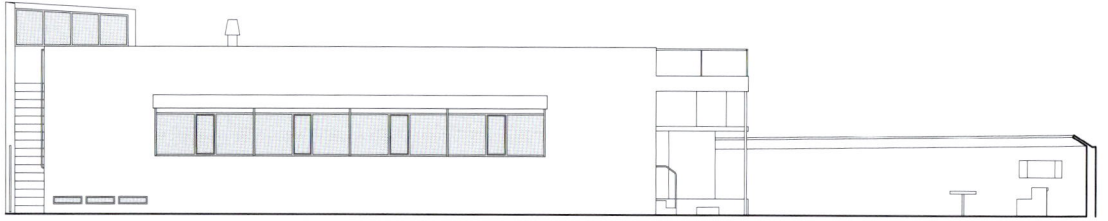
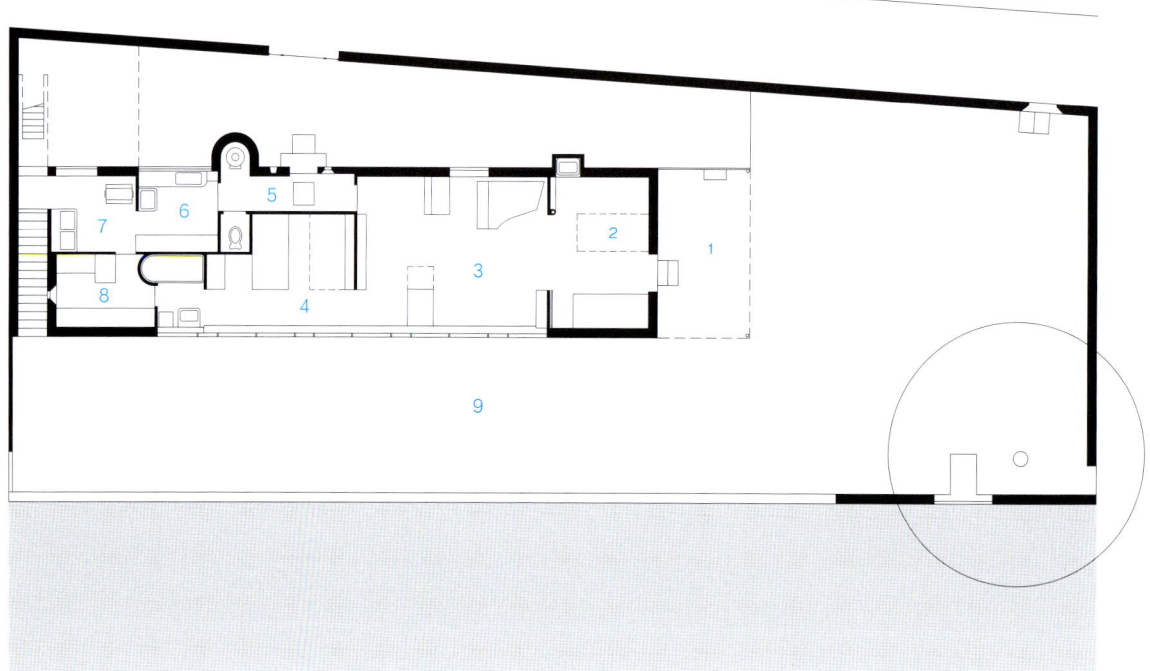

East elevation
South elevation
First-floor plan

1 Covered patio
2 Multipurpose room
3 Living room
4 Bedroom
5 Vestibule
6 Kitchen
7 Utility room
8 Closet
9 Garden

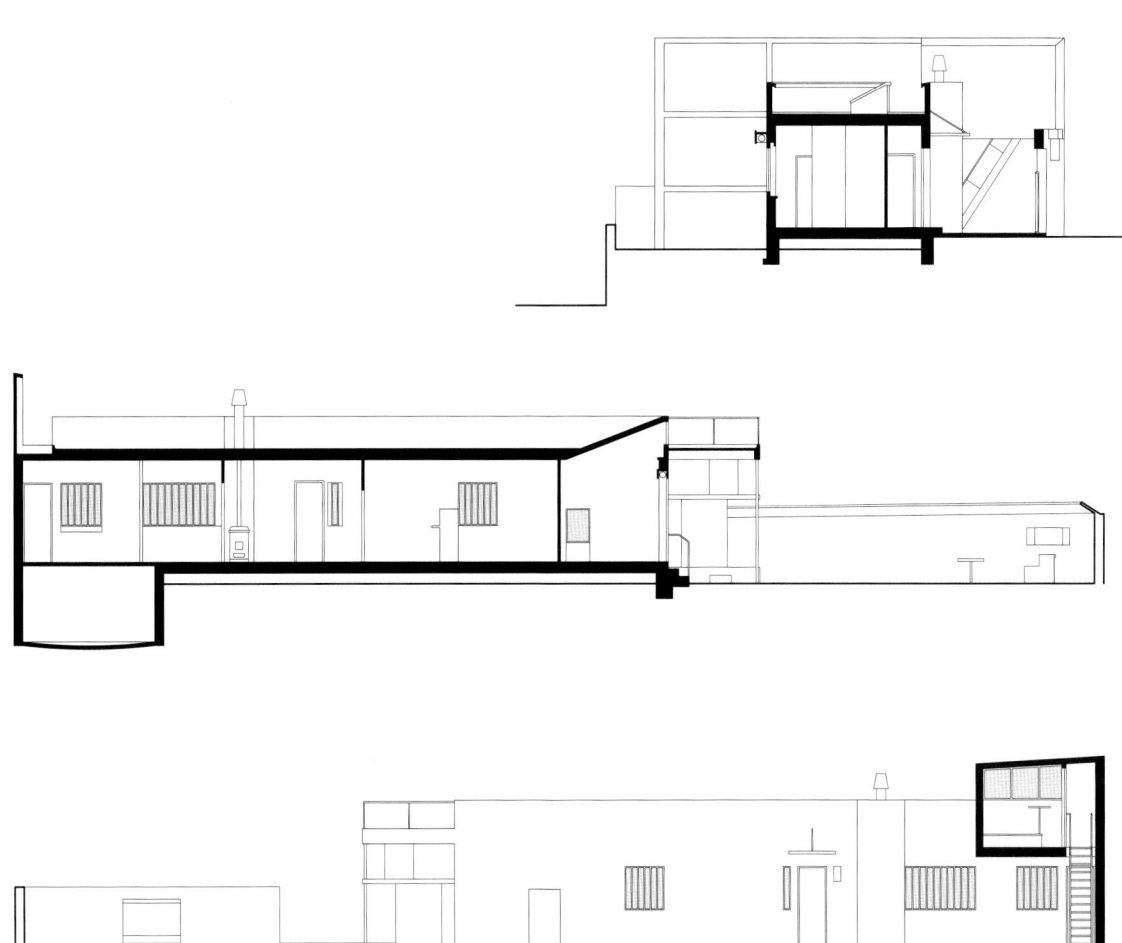

South–north section
West–east section
East–west section

4 VILLAS LIPCHITZ-MIESTCHANINOFF

LOCATION: Boulogne-sur-Seine, France
DATE: 1923

The clients for these residences were two sculptors who were Le Corbusier's close friends among the Parisian avant-garde. The sculptors commissioned the architect to design their studio-residences as part of a planned artists' colony. A third house that Le Corbusier designed for this site for Victor Canale was never built.

Double-height sculpture studios, similar in form to traditional Parisian workshops, are placed on the ground level, with oversized access doors to accommodate the large-scale projects that were to be created within. Despite differences in their detailed programs and the shapes of their plans, the houses were unified into a single ensemble by Le Corbusier's various techniques: articulating the repeated building components, such as the exterior staircases and clerestory windows, with similar architectural details; creating formal links, such as the bridge between Villa Miestchaninoff and Villa Canale; and providing visual references for symmetrical readings of the corresponding volumes across the site.

CLIENTS: Oscar Miestchaninoff and Jacques Lipchitz
PROGRAM: Two studio residences
FEATURES: Sculpture studios, roof terrace, outdoor courtyard, bridge

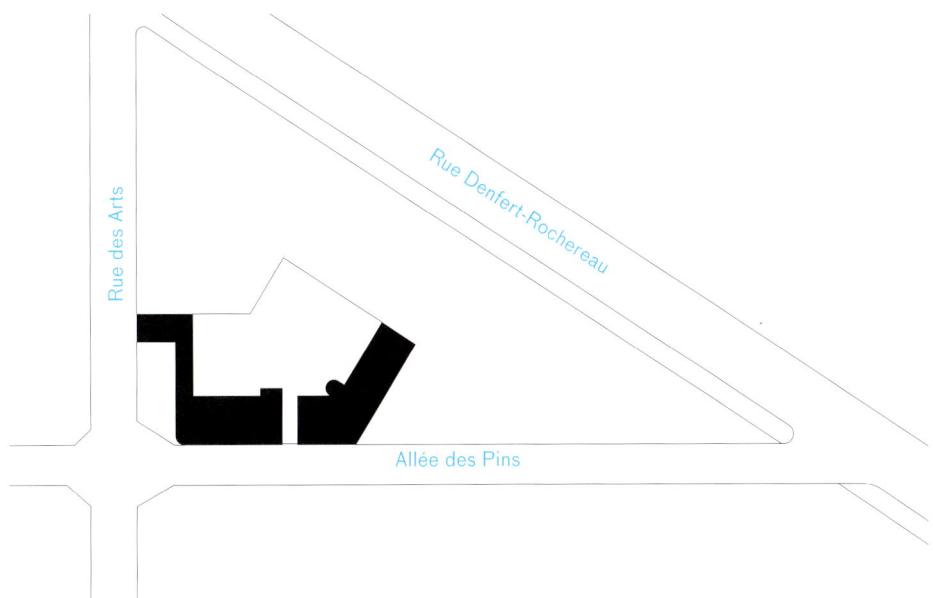
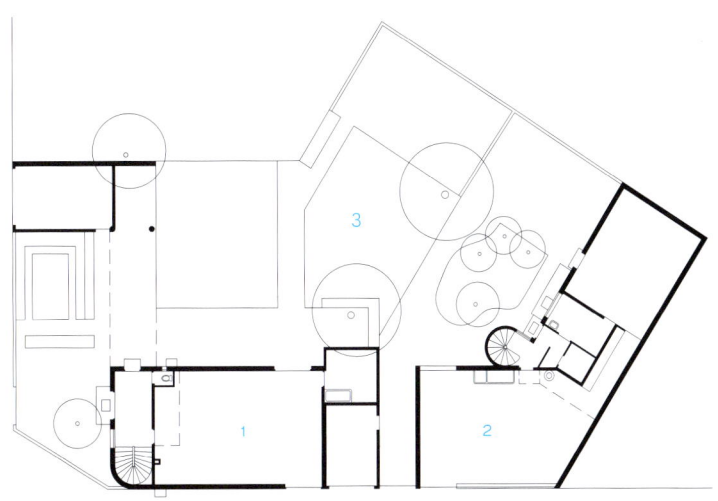

Site plan (1:1000)

Site plan (1:400)

1 Villa Miestchaninoff
2 Villa Lipchitz
3 Outdoor garden

29 **VILLAS LIPCHITZ-MIESTCHANINOFF**

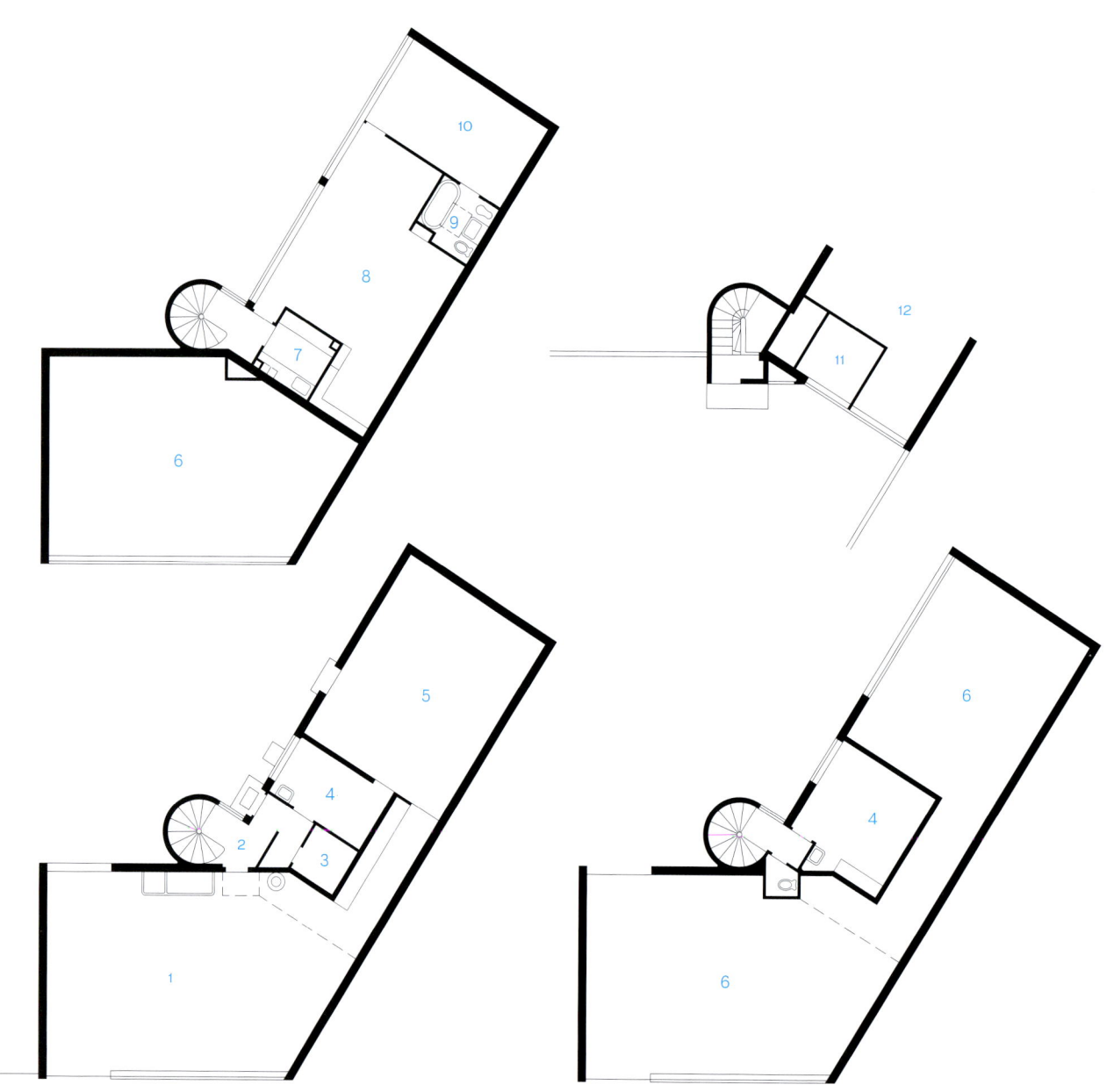

Villa Lipchitz:
Third-floor plan Fourth-floor plan
First-floor plan Second-floor plan

1. Large studio
2. Vestibule
3. Coal storage
4. Storage
5. Small studio
6. Open to studio below
7. Kitchen
8. Living room
9. Bathroom
10. Bedroom
11. Open to kitchen below
12. Open to living room below

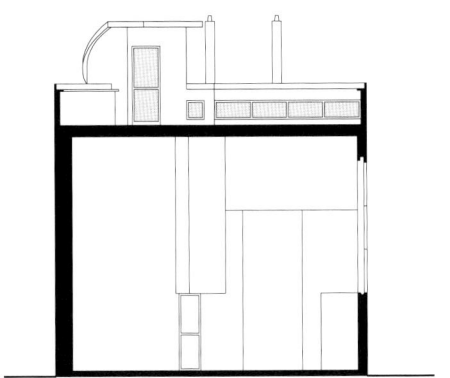

Villa Lipchitz:
South–north section

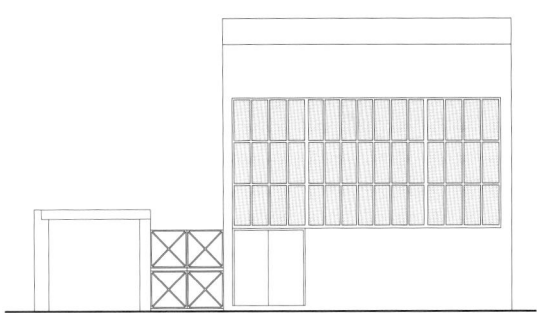

Villa Lipchitz:
South elevation
North elevation

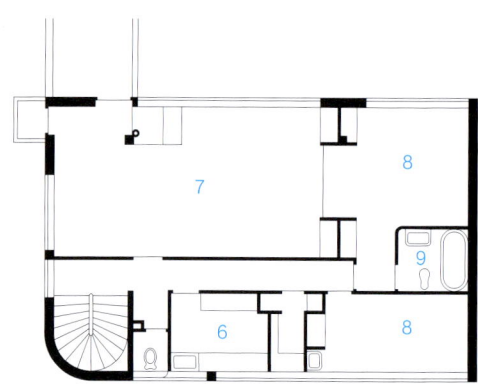

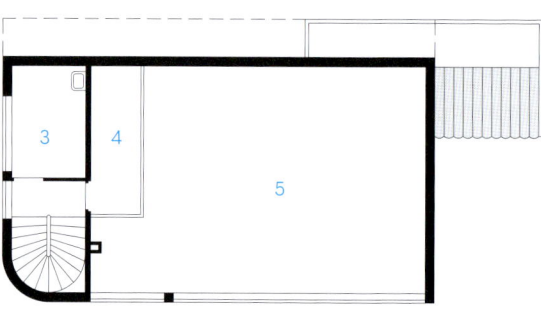

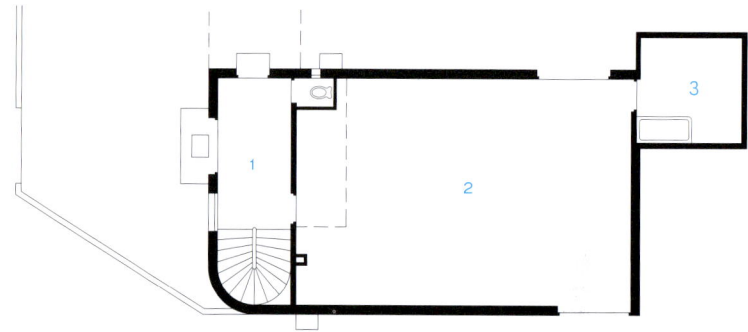

Villa Miestchaninoff:
Third-floor plan
Second-floor plan
First-floor plan

1. Vestibule
2. Studio
3. Storage
4. Loft
5. Open to studio below
6. Kitchen
7. Living room
8. Bedroom
9. Bathroom

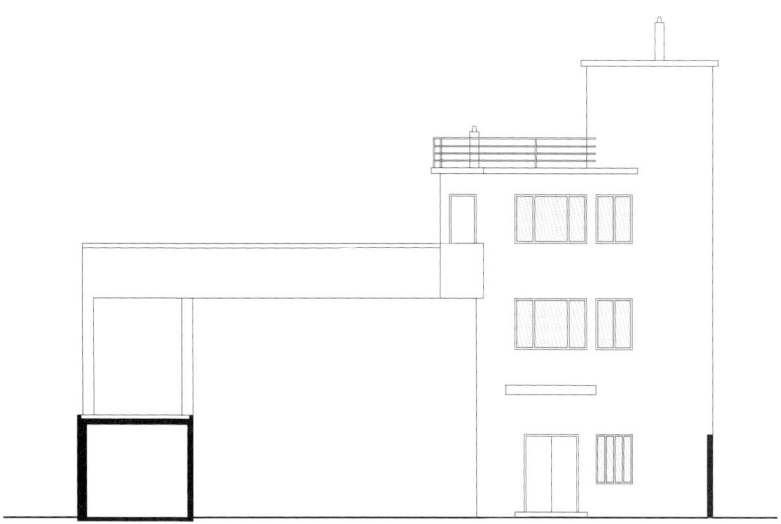

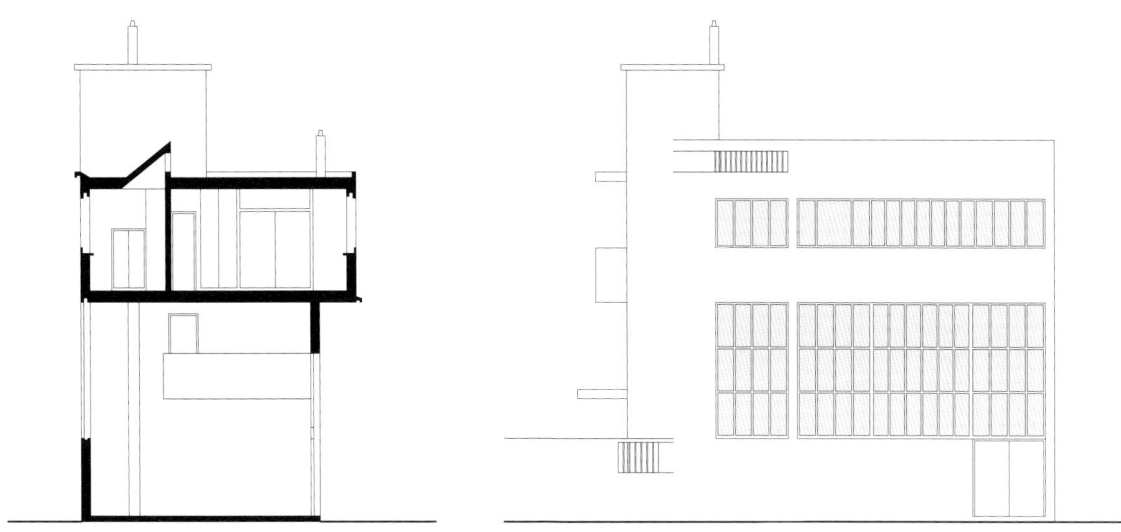

Villa Miestchaninoff:
North–south section

Villa Miestchaninoff:
East elevation
North elevation

5 VILLAS LA ROCHE-JEANNERET

LOCATION:	Paris, France
DATE:	1923

One of the of two houses of this complex was designed for Raoul La Roche, a Swiss banker whom Le Corbusier met at a dinner in Paris; the other was for Lotti Raaf, a patron of modern art, and her husband, Albert Jeanneret, Le Corbusier's cousin and collaborator.

Villas La Roche-Jeanneret was a speculative project on which Le Corbusier could test architectural and urban innovations such as *pilotis*—round and smooth concrete columns that raise a building up in the air, thereby freeing the ground level for an uninterrupted flow of pedestrian and vehicular circulation—and providing amenities at the roof level. Before fully taking on the responsibilities of architect, Le Corbusier worked as a broker to sell the land to prospective clients. The architect initially favored a south-facing site but ended up with an L-shaped, north-facing lot with zoning restrictions on the building's height, depth, and locations of windows facing adjoining lots, in accordance with French privacy laws. Despite these obstacles, Le Corbusier succeeded in creating a unified formal composition for two houses with programs that could not have been more different: one for a bachelor banker who wanted a gallery to display his large collection of paintings and the other for a couple with more domestic objectives.

Due to the small site, Le Corbusier could provide only an outdoor roof garden (aside from a ground-level entrance garden at Villa La Roche), where the occupants could retreat from urban life and enjoy a panoramic view of the city unobstructed by neighboring buildings.

The curved wall of Villa La Roche emphasizes the entry and draws visitors in. The concept of architectural promenade is important to the design, and the curvature of the wall also expresses the residence's interior ramp, which creates a gradual, smooth movement through the gallery. The large double-height window of Villa Jeanneret similarly underscores the importance of its internal program, as it marks both the entrance and the location of the main living space housed within.

CLIENTS:	Raoul La Roche, Lotti Raaf, and Albert Jeanneret
PROGRAM:	Bachelor and family residences
FEATURES:	Ramp, painting gallery, library, *pilotis*, triple-height lobby, roof terrace, architectural promenade

Exterior perspective, northeast corner showing east elevation

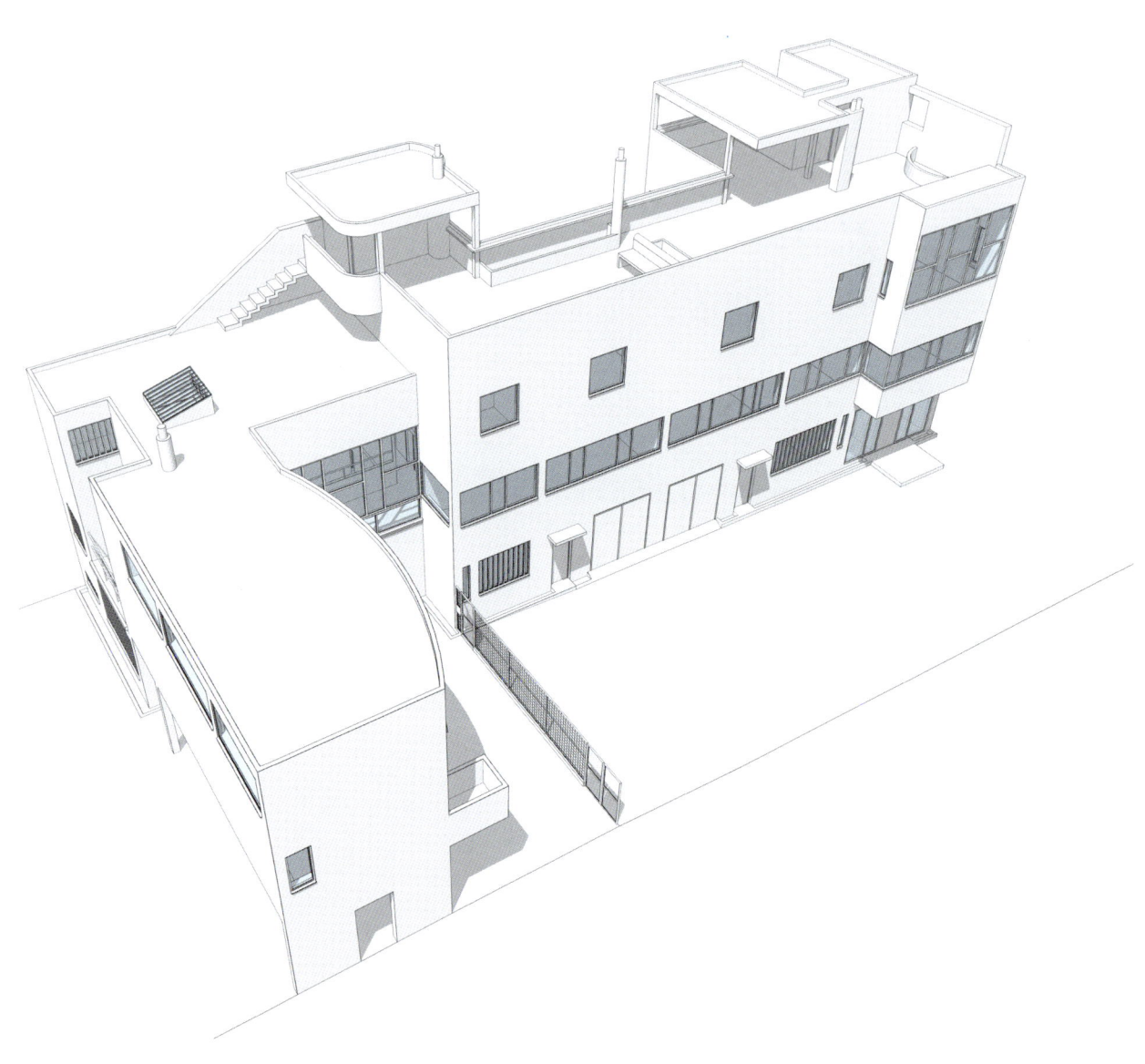

Aerial perspective, southeast corner, main entrance court

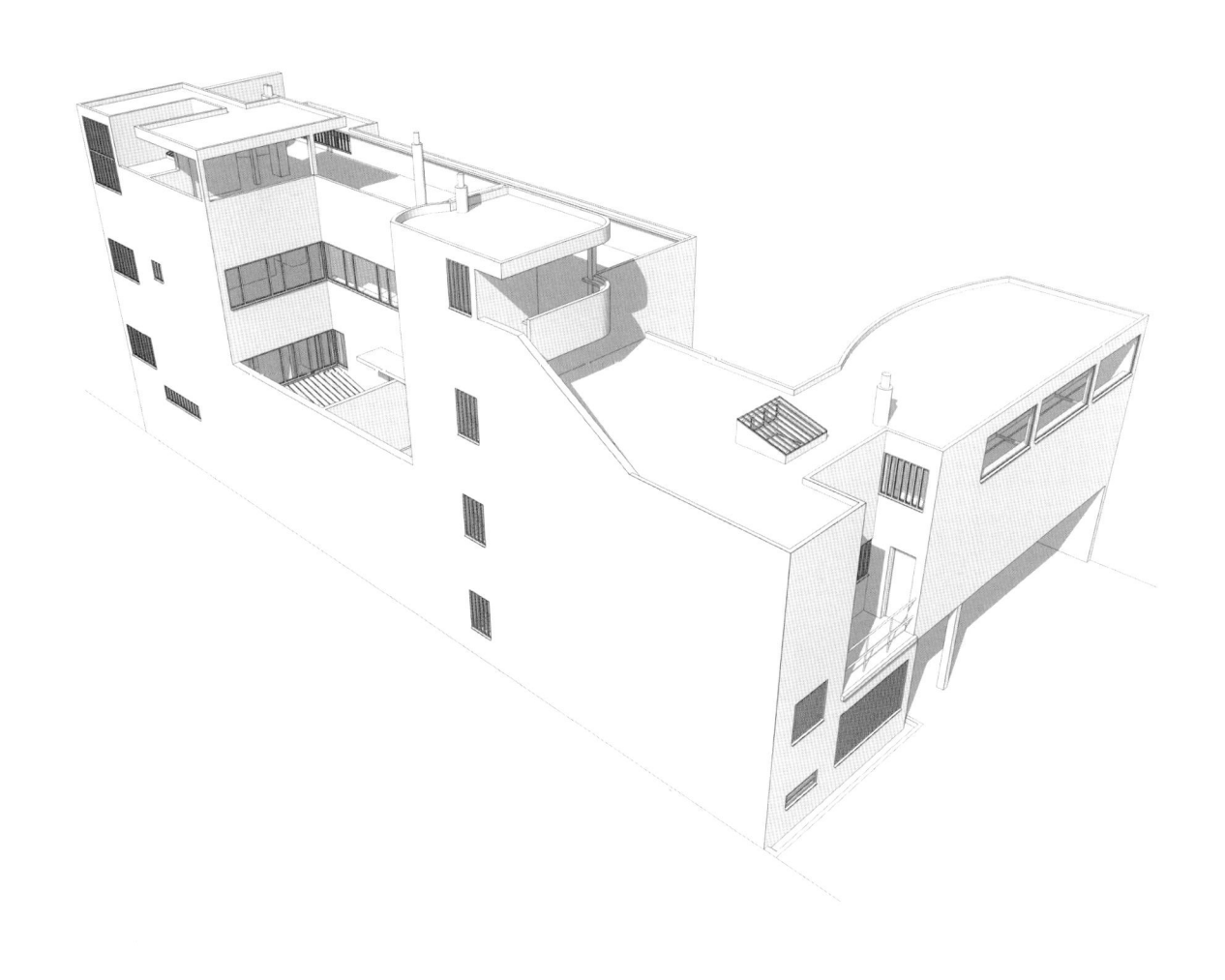

37 VILLAS LA ROCHE-JEANNERET Aerial perspective, southwest corner

East–west sectional perspective at stairs

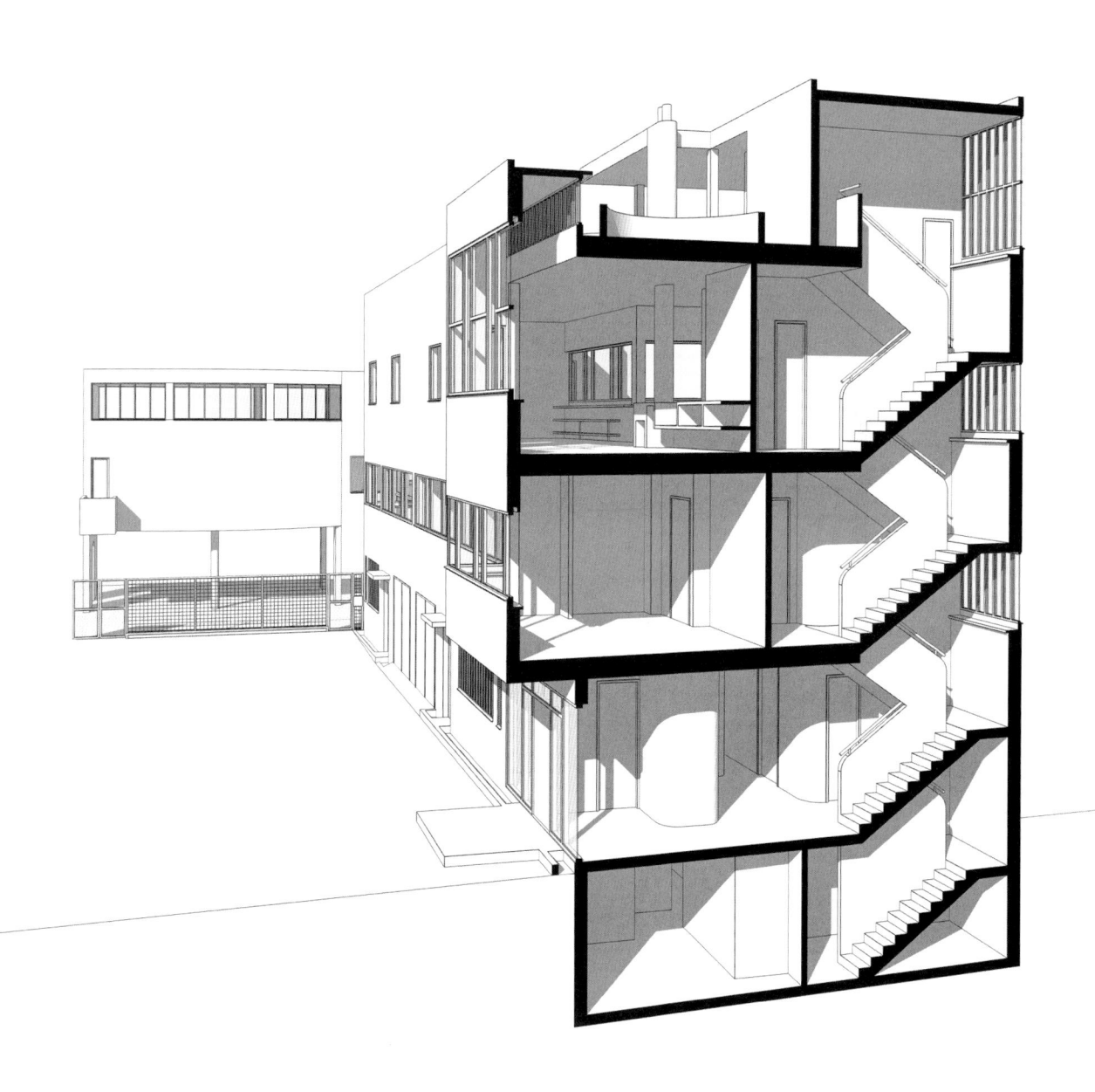

North–south sectional perspective at stairs

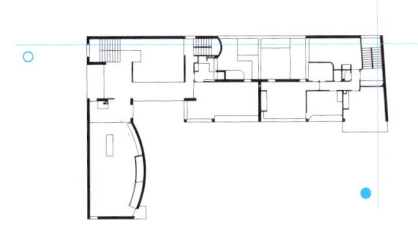

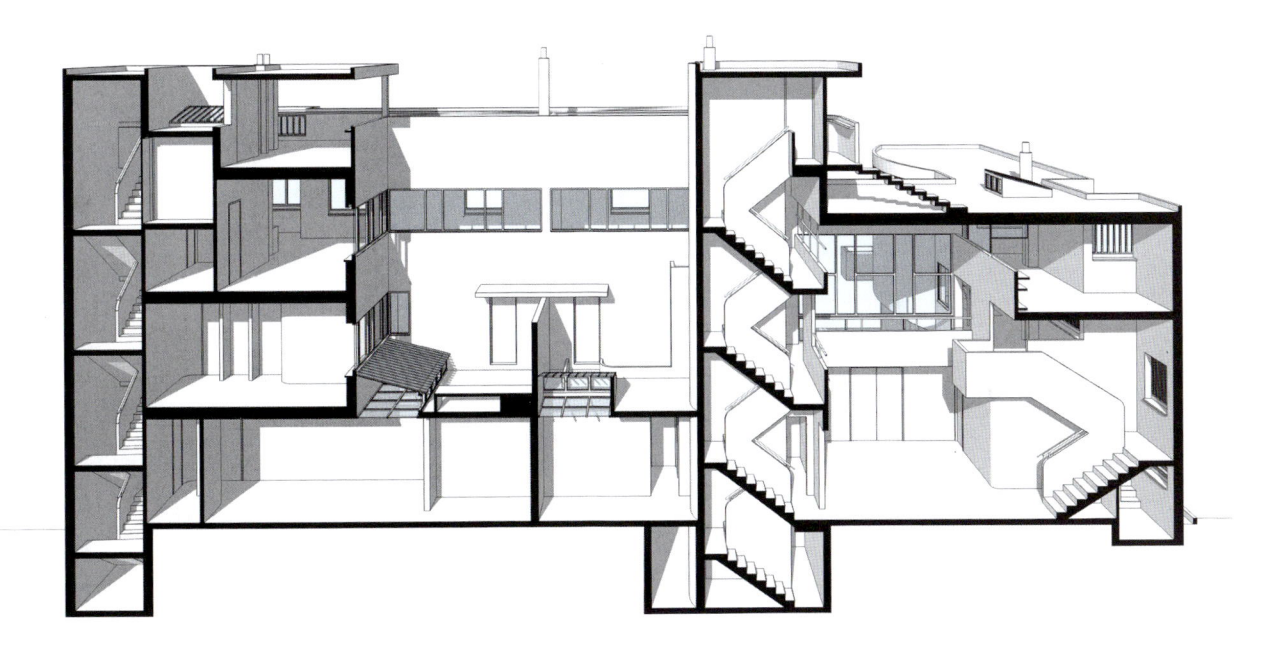

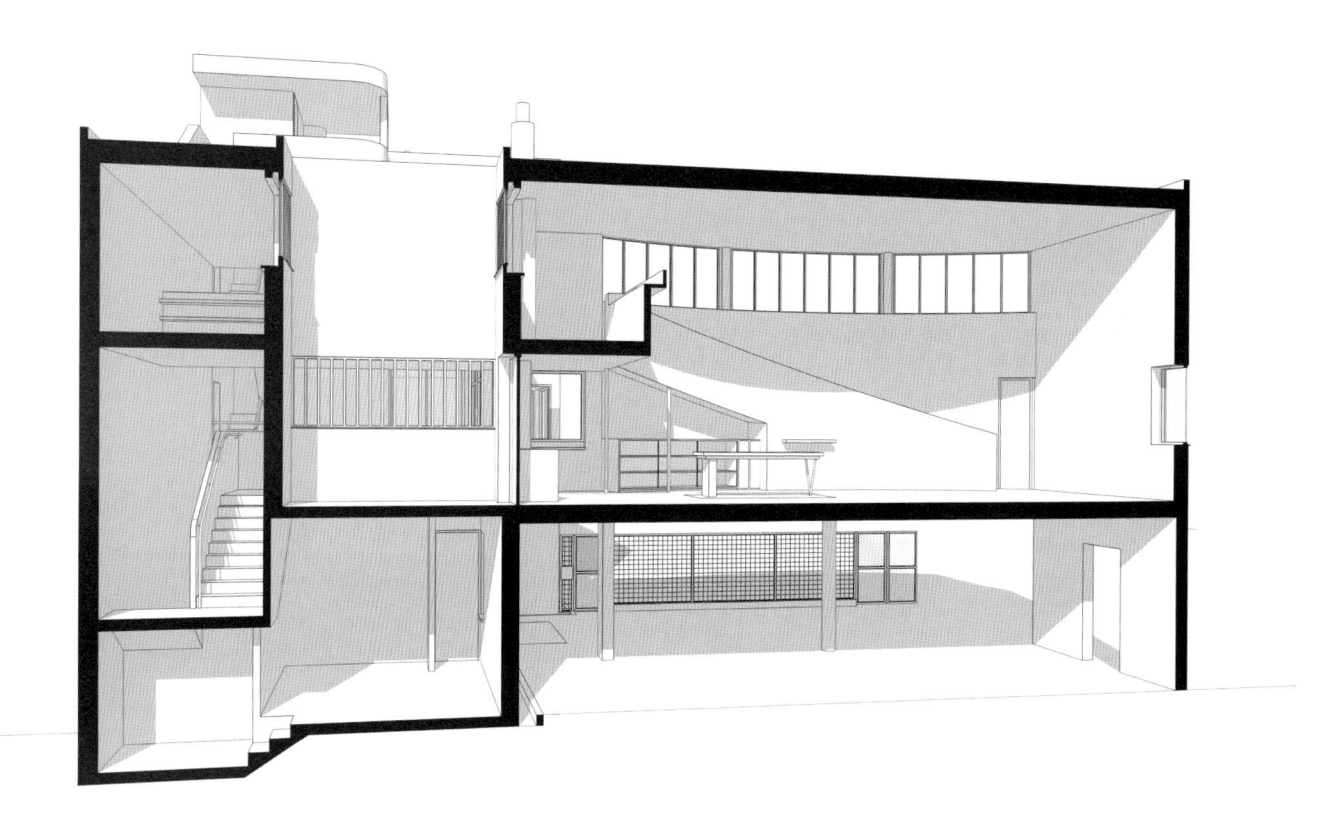

VILLAS LA ROCHE-JEANNERET West–east sectional perspective at Villa La Roche gallery

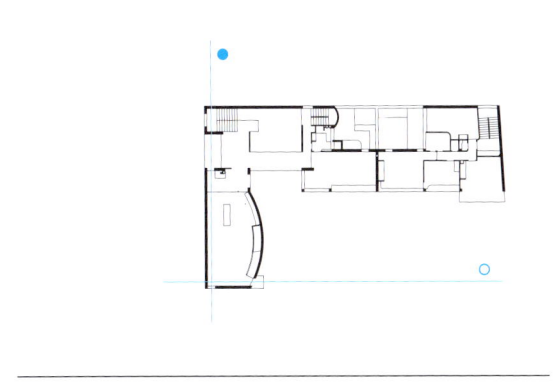

South–north sectional perspective at Villa La Roche gallery

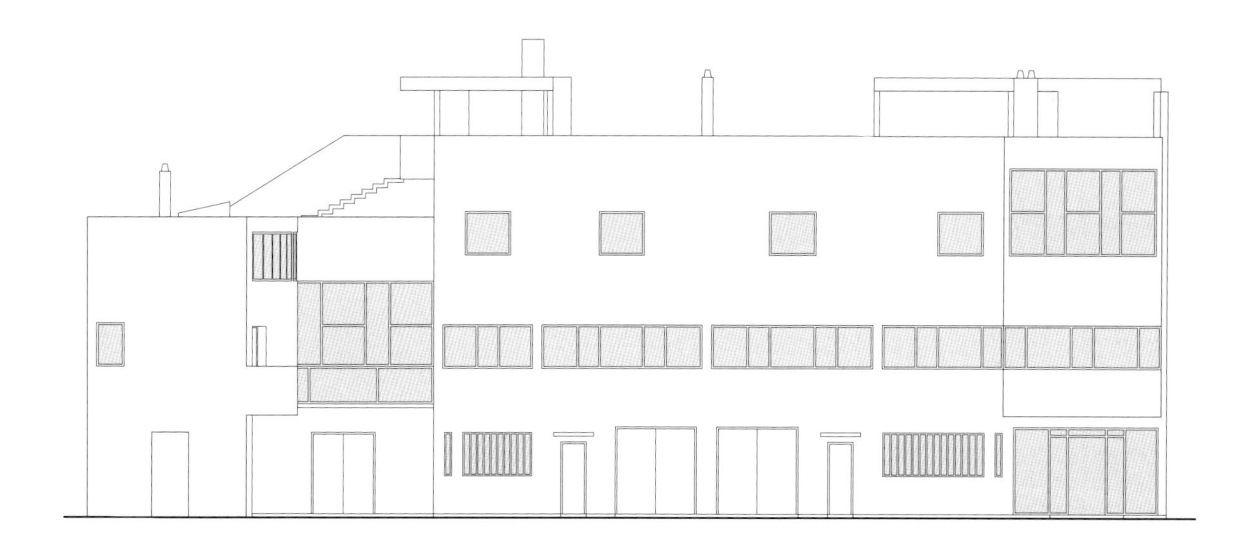

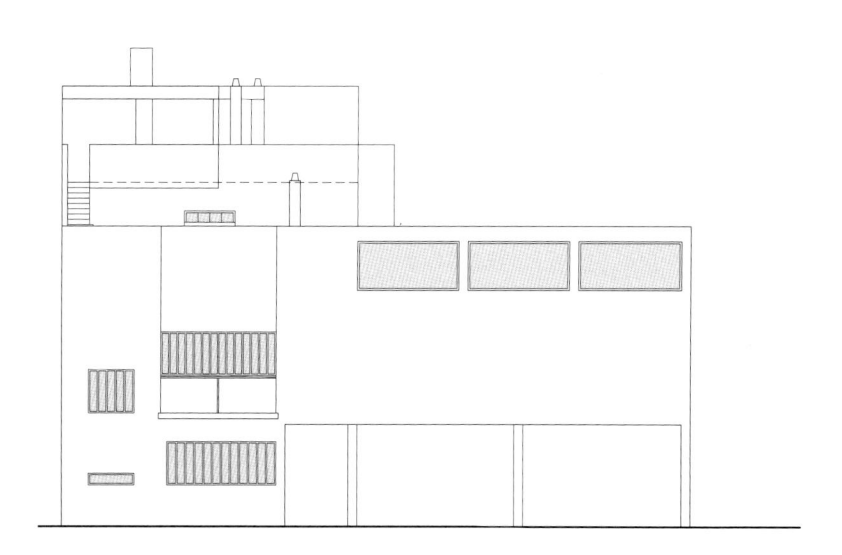

East elevation
South elevation

42 **VILLAS LA ROCHE-JEANNERET**

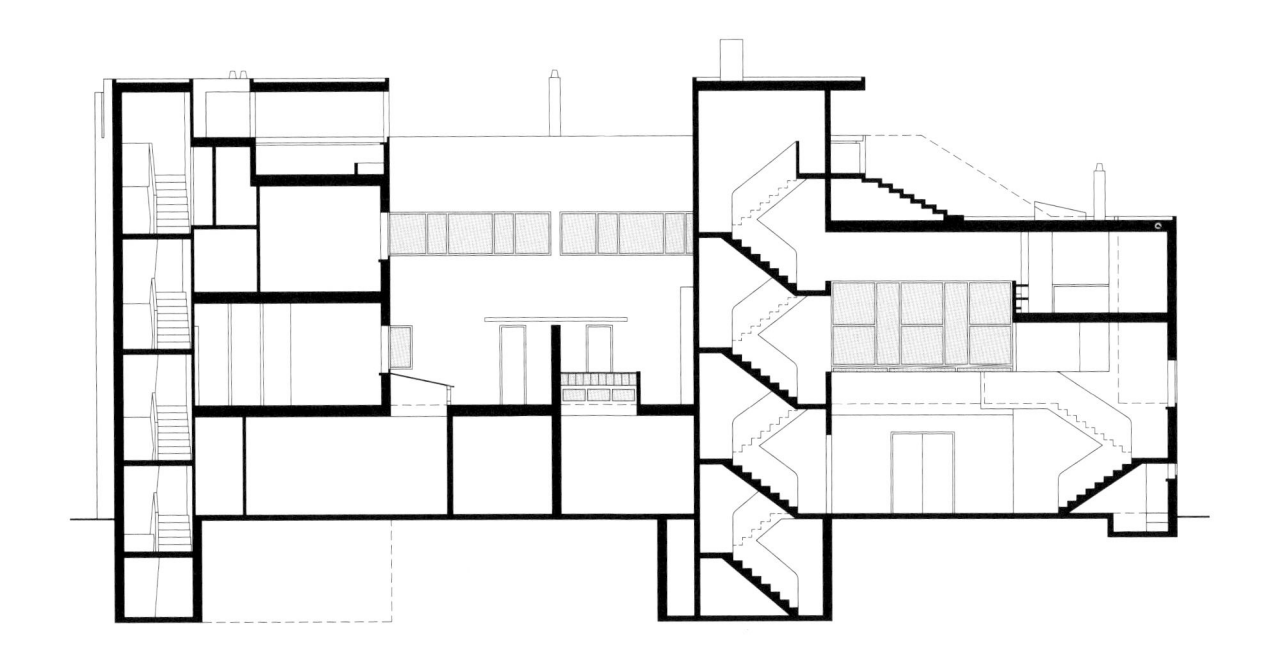

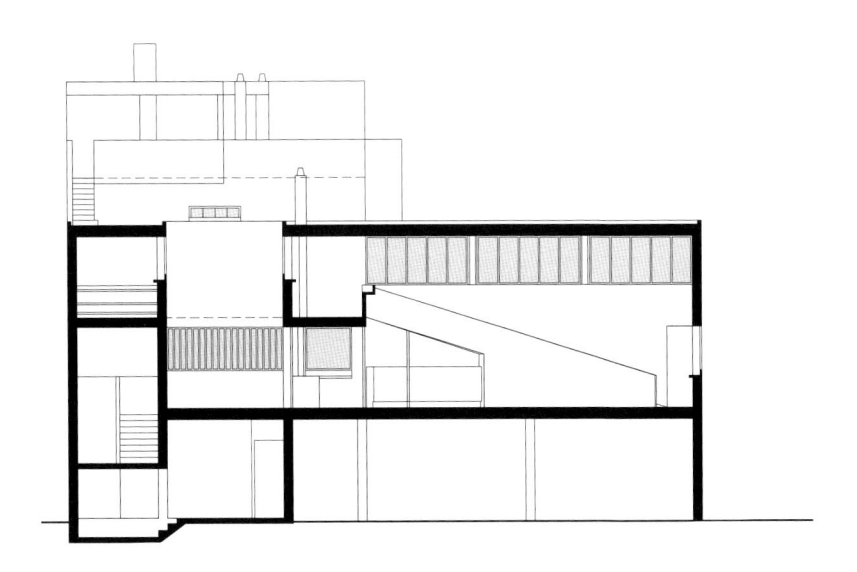

North–south section
West–east section

VILLAS LA ROCHE-JEANNERET

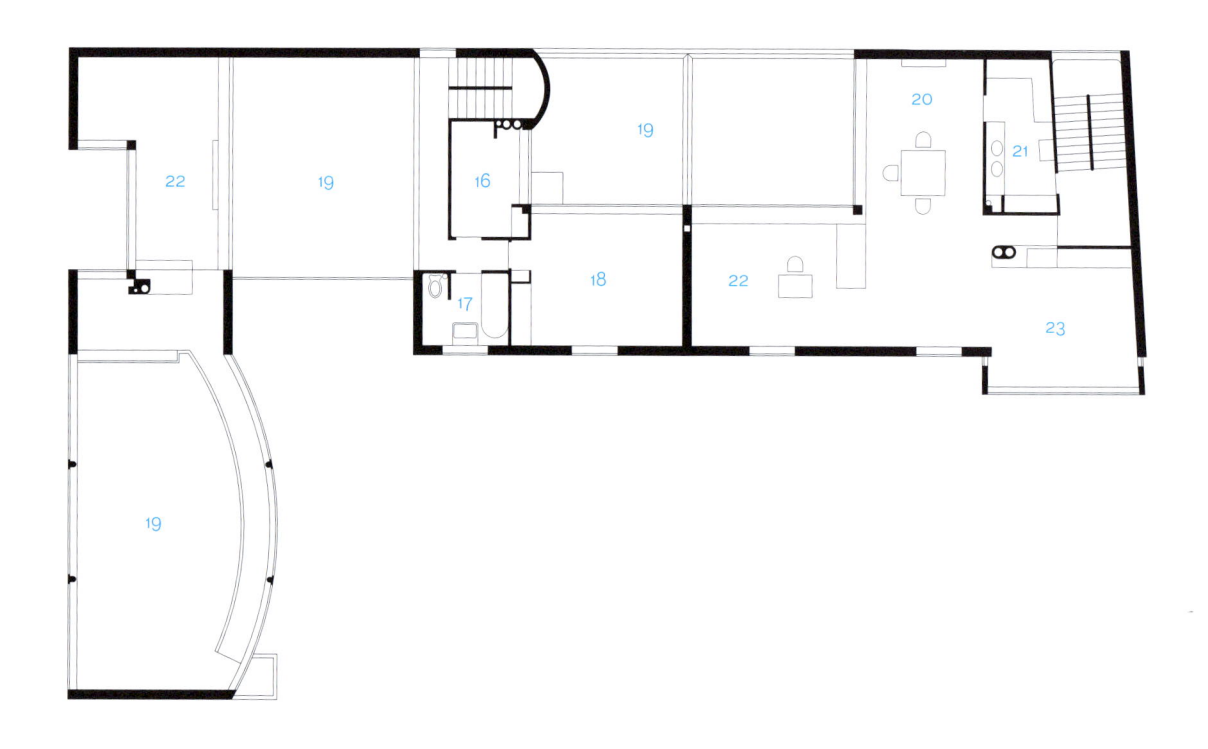

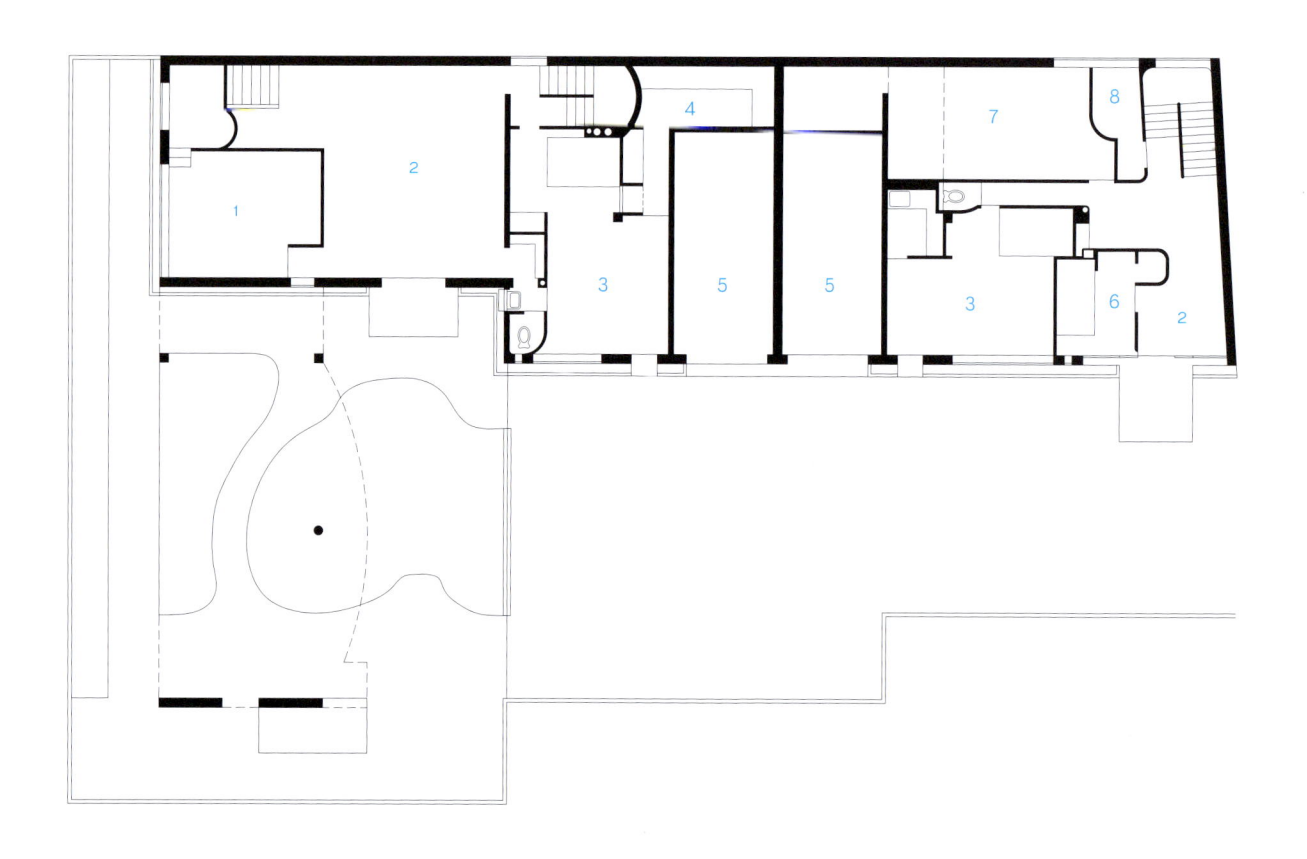

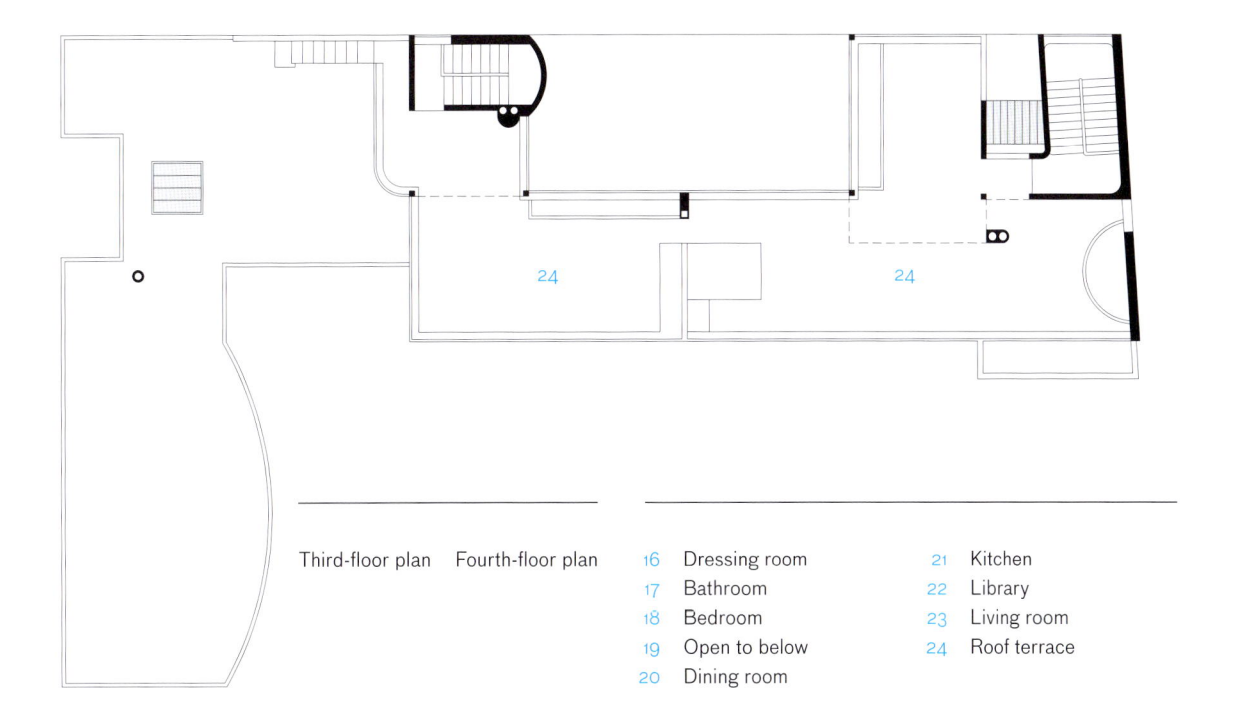

Third-floor plan   Fourth-floor plan

16	Dressing room	21	Kitchen
17	Bathroom	22	Library
18	Bedroom	23	Living room
19	Open to below	24	Roof terrace
20	Dining room		

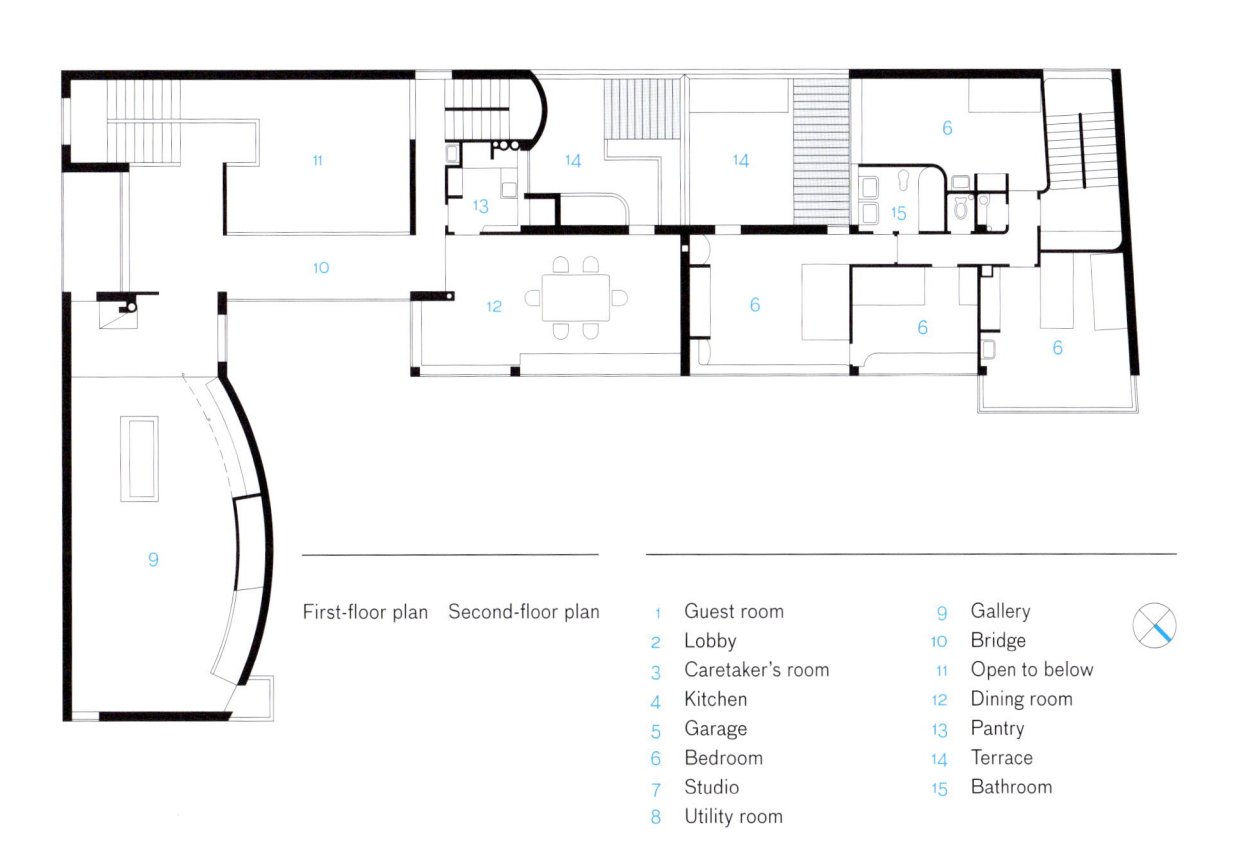

First-floor plan   Second-floor plan

1	Guest room	9	Gallery
2	Lobby	10	Bridge
3	Caretaker's room	11	Open to below
4	Kitchen	12	Dining room
5	Garage	13	Pantry
6	Bedroom	14	Terrace
7	Studio	15	Bathroom
8	Utility room		

MAISON TERNISIEN

LOCATION: Boulogne-sur-Seine, France
DATE: 1923

The house was designed for a couple who approached Le Corbusier after he lectured at the Sorbonne in 1924. The overall building form is influenced by the shape of the triangular site and the interior by the requirement of merging two different programs: a double-height space with a sleeping balcony for the wife's painting studio and a pie-shaped one-story space for the husband's music studio. The two studios come together in the middle with shared spaces, including an entrance foyer, bathroom, kitchen, and library. The recessed entry is the result of the architect's desire to preserve an existing tree by shaping the house around it. This volumetric offset, along with the tree and the curved wall of the music studio, announces the location of the entry and draws visitors in.

Despite its small size, the house is an important project in Le Corbusier's body of work because of its masterful resolution of complex programmatic requirements with rich spatial experiences. Carefully planned circulation through the house is achieved by sculpting the interior spaces with natural light. The initial scheme accounted for future expansion on top of the single-story volume. However, the clients experienced financial difficulties, causing legal disputes over building repair costs and unpaid design fees. This eventually led to the demolition of the house, and now a five-story apartment building designed by another architect stands in its place.

CLIENTS: Paul and Mme Ternisien
PROGRAM: Studio residence
FEATURES: Music studio, painting studio, library, roof terrace, vertical slot windows, double-height space with sleeping balcony, design using regulating lines

Exterior perspective, east elevation

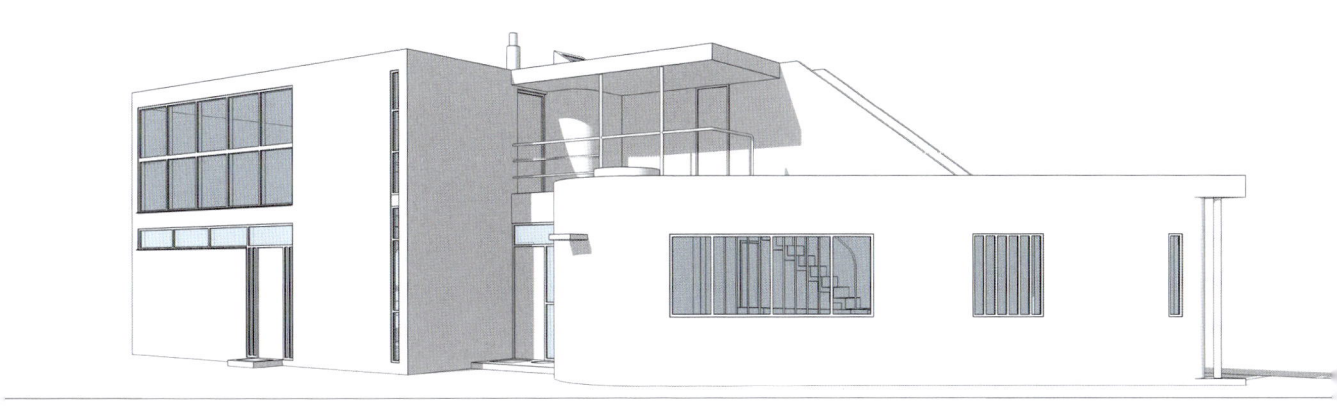

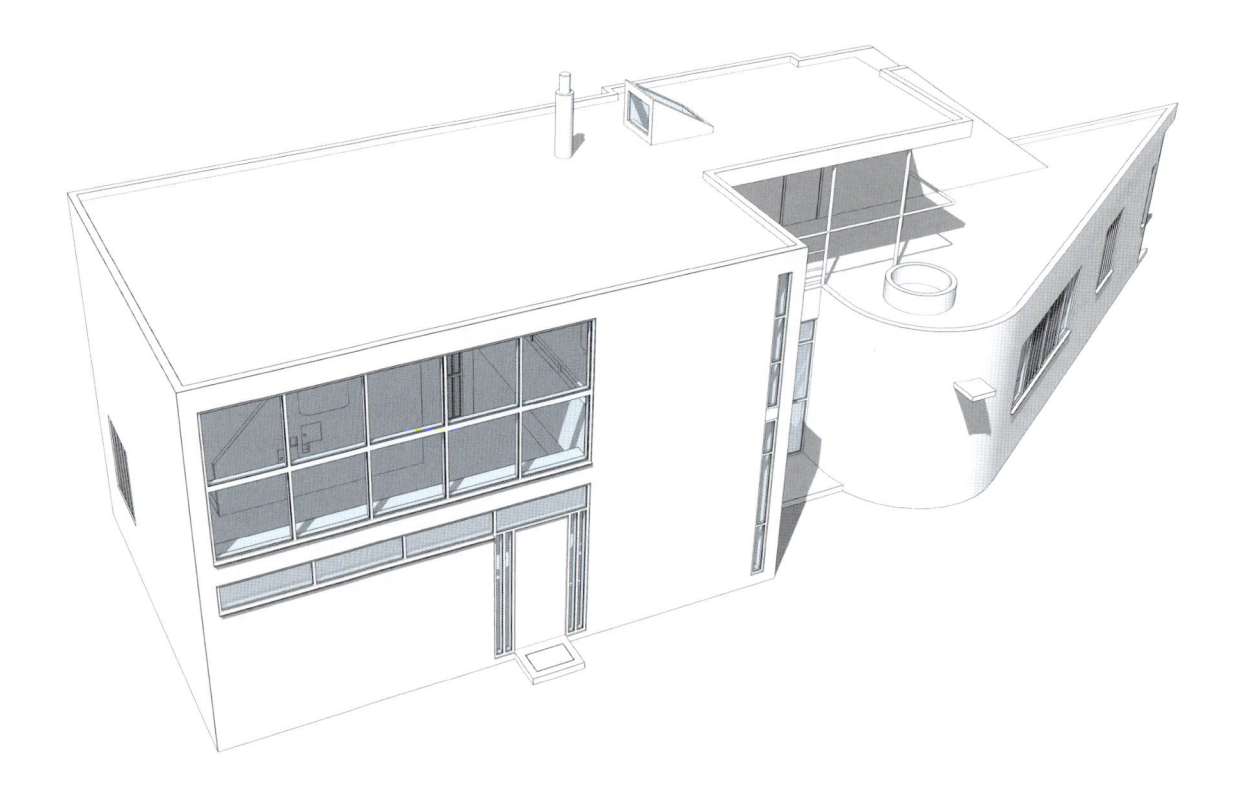

48 **MAISON TERNISIEN** — Aerial perspective, southeast corner

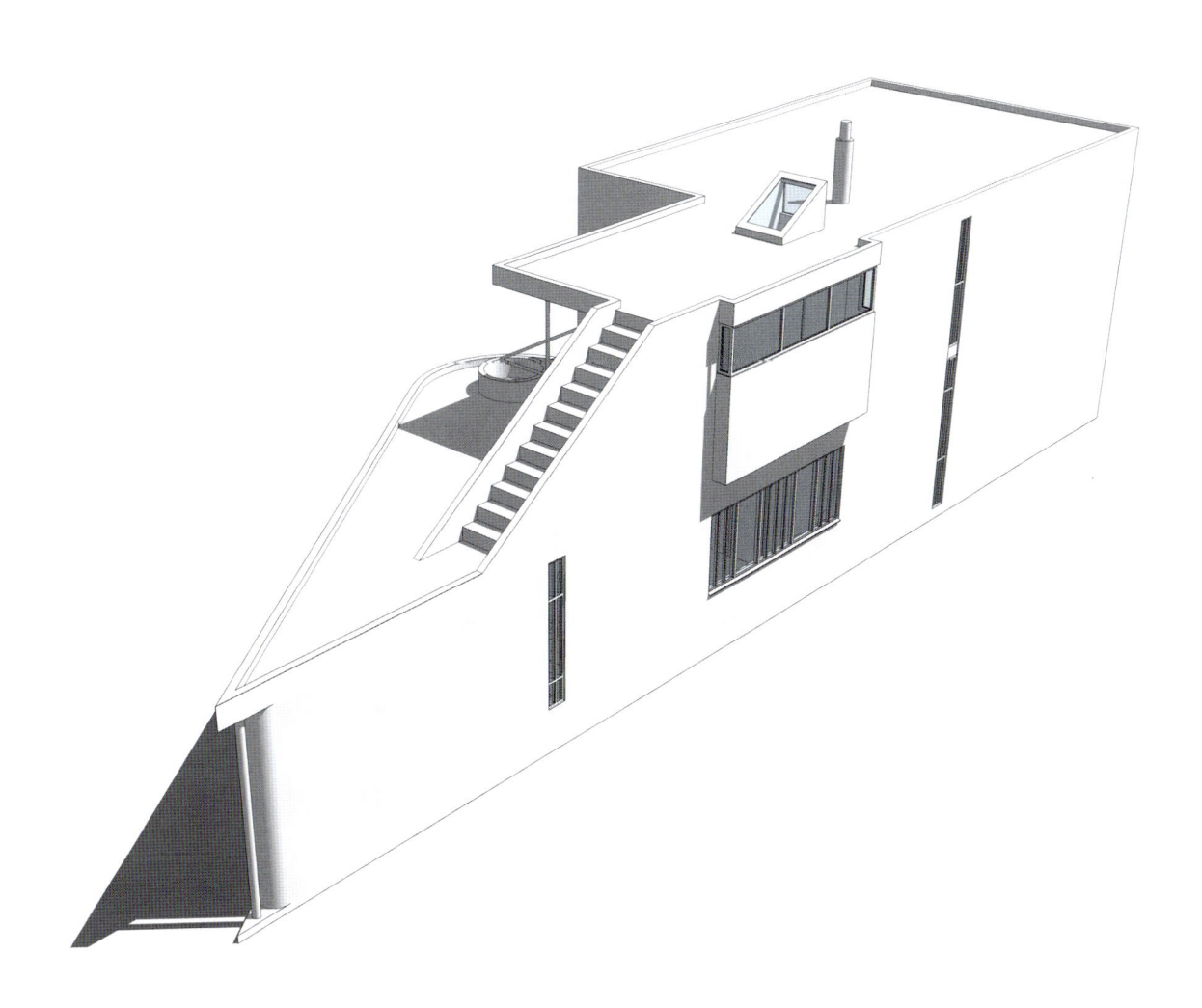

MAISON TERNISIEN — Aerial perspective, northwest corner

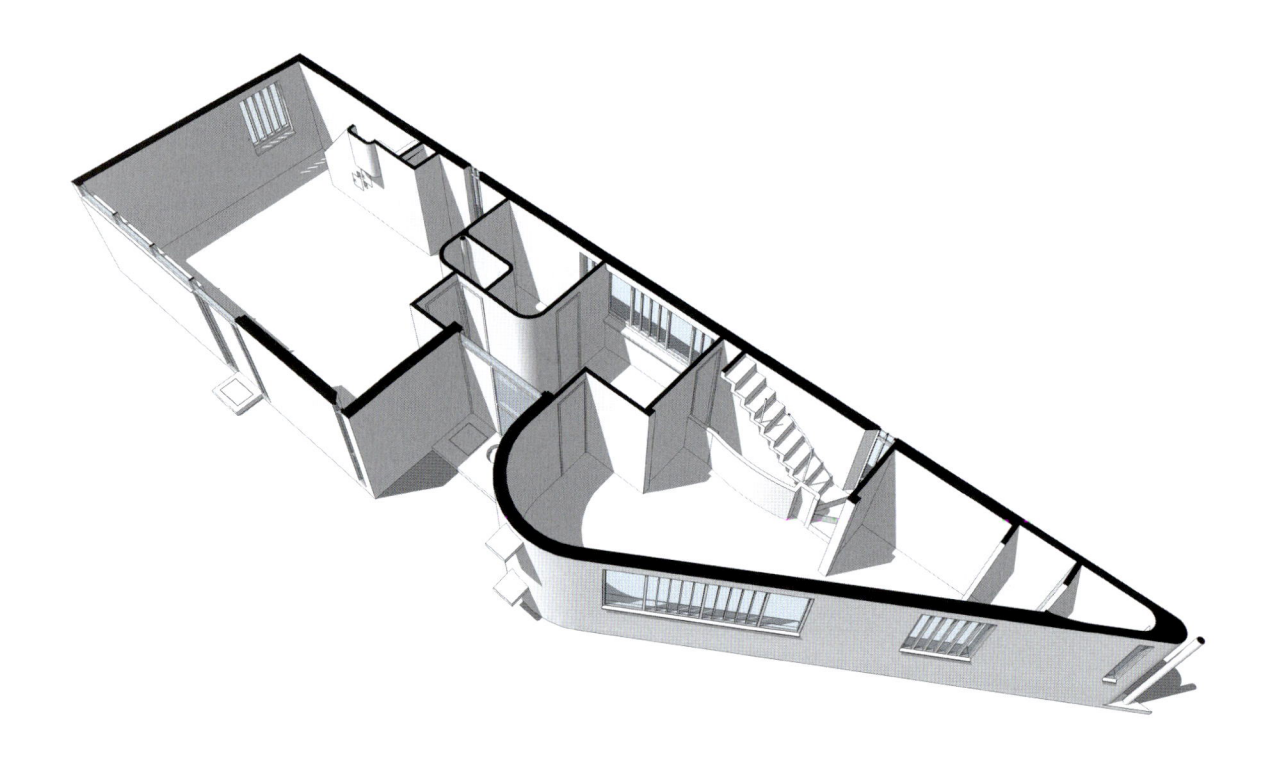

MAISON TERNISIEN First-floor planar perspective, northeast corner

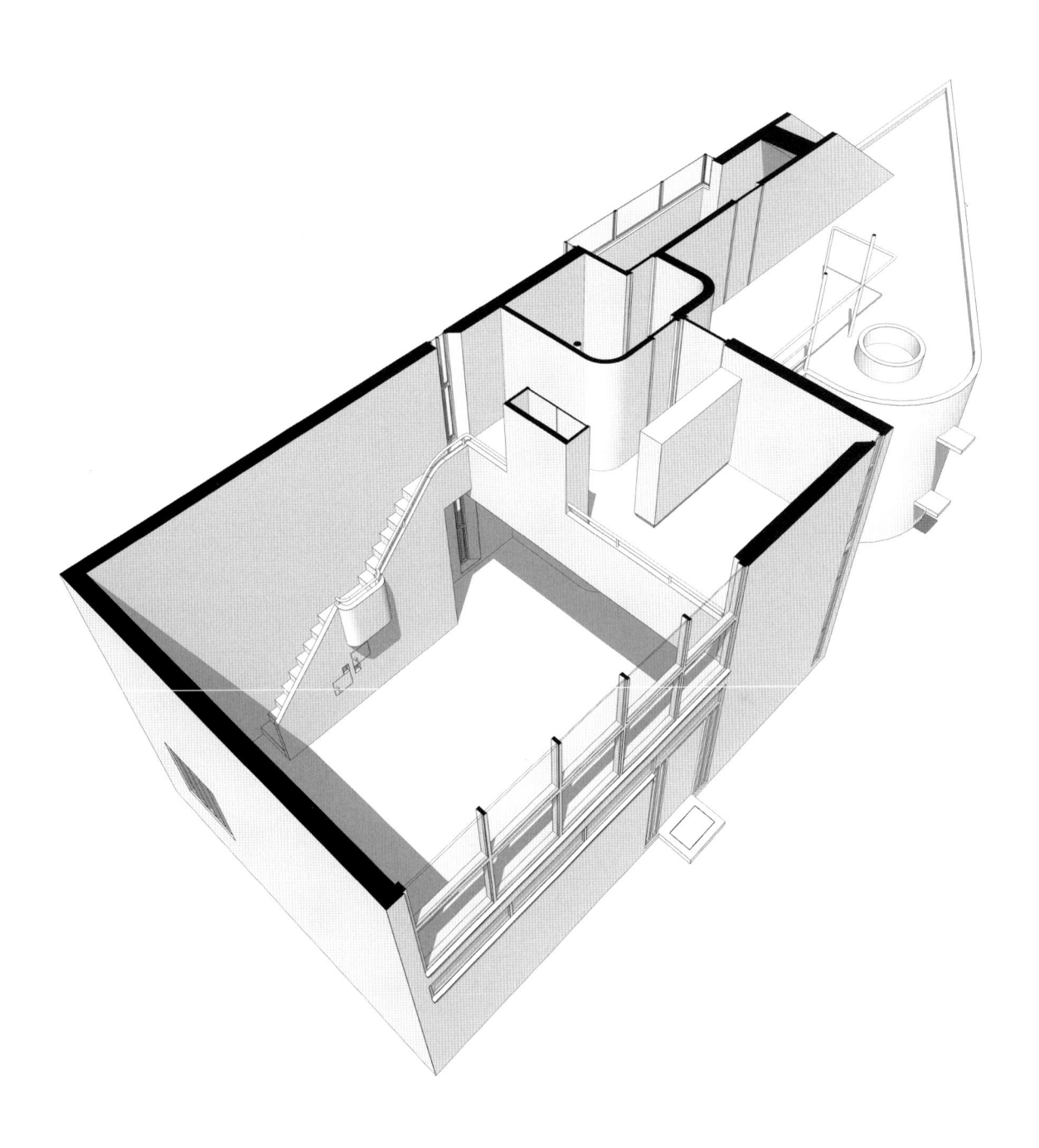

51 **MAISON TERNISIEN** Second-floor planar perspective, southeast corner

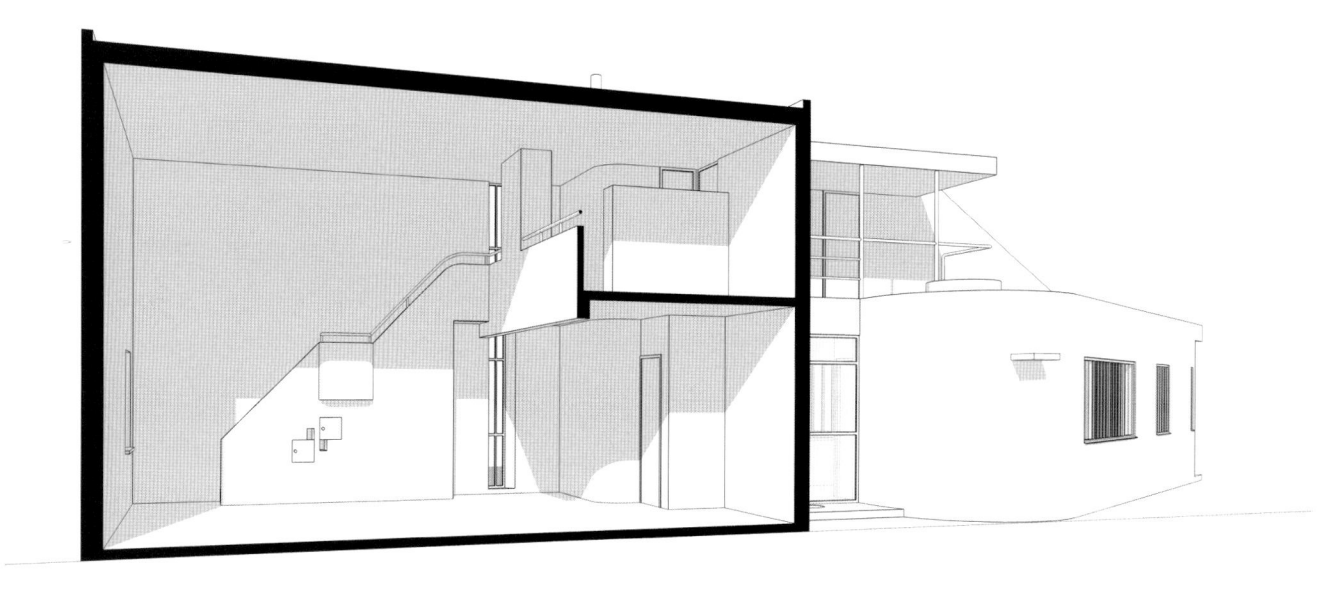

MAISON TERNISIEN South–north sectional perspective at art studio

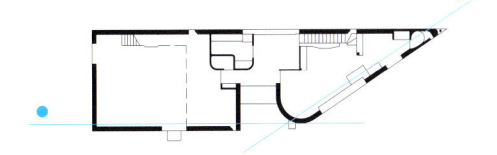

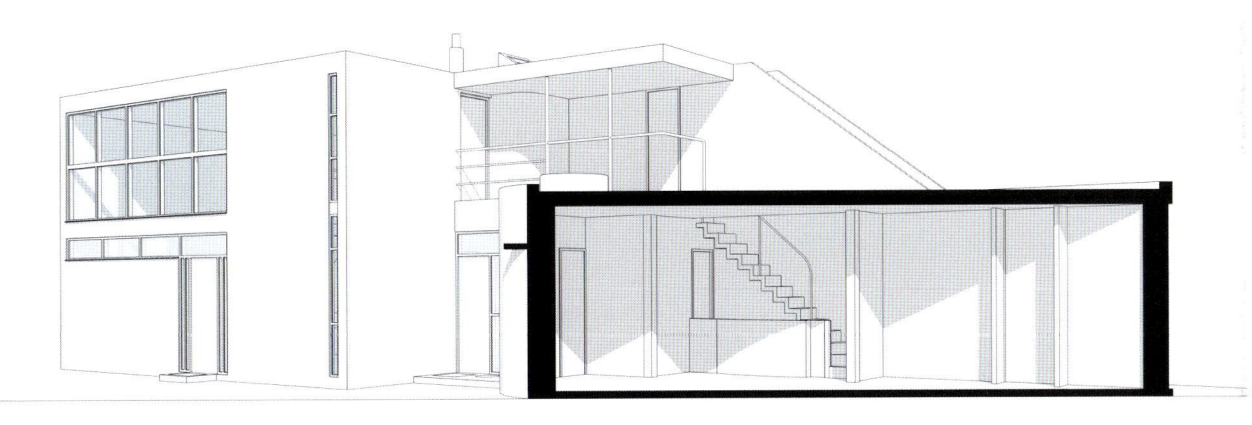

53 **MAISON TERNISIEN**   ○   Southeast–northwest sectional perspective at music studio

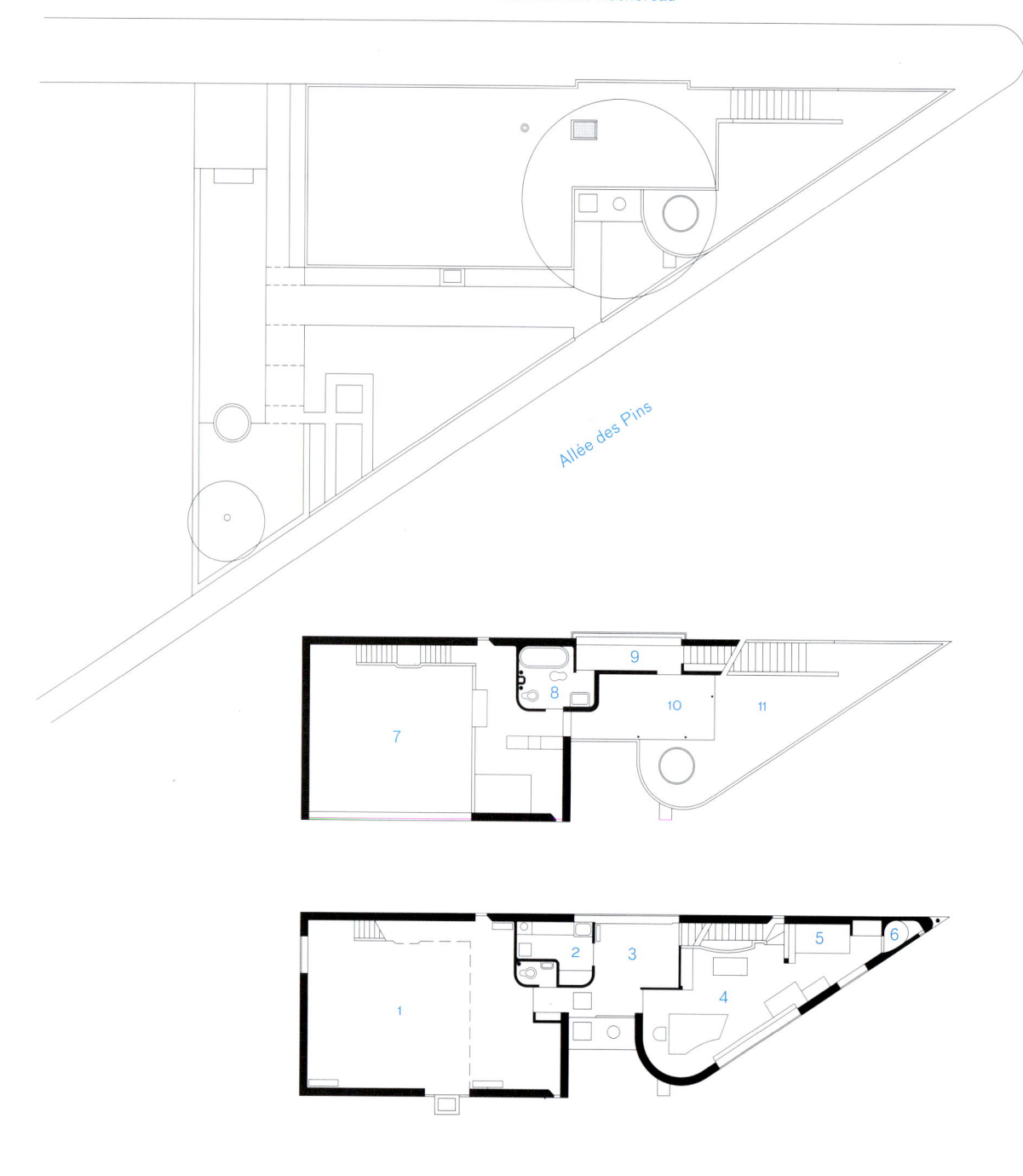

Site plan (1:200)
Second-floor plan
First-floor plan

1. Art studio
2. Kitchen
3. Dining room
4. Music studio
5. Bedroom
6. Shower
7. Open to below
8. Bathroom
9. Library
10. Covered patio
11. Roof terrace

54 MAISON TERNISIEN

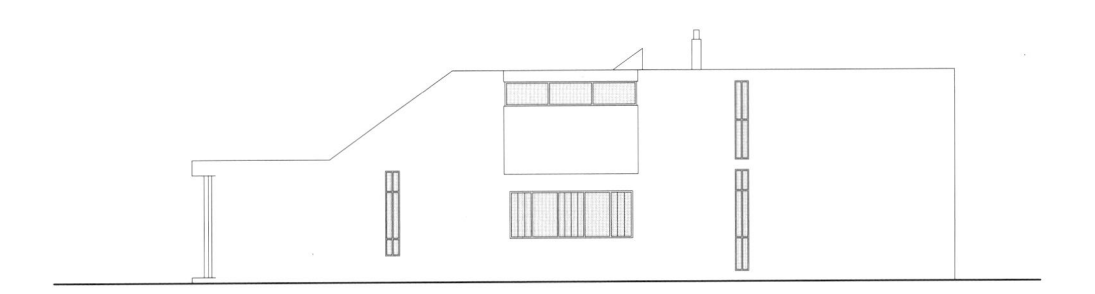

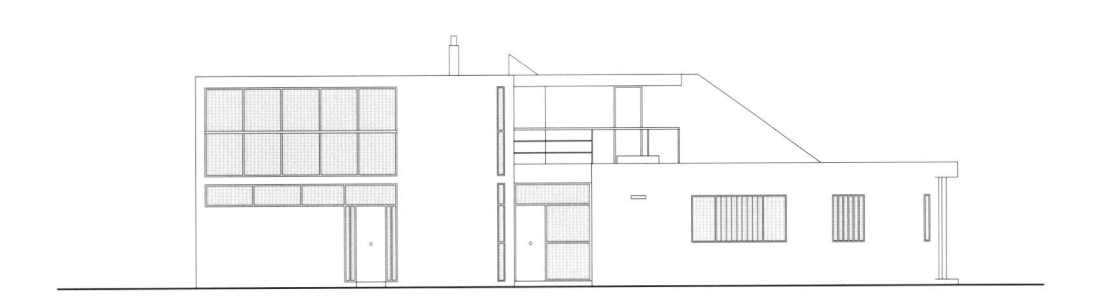

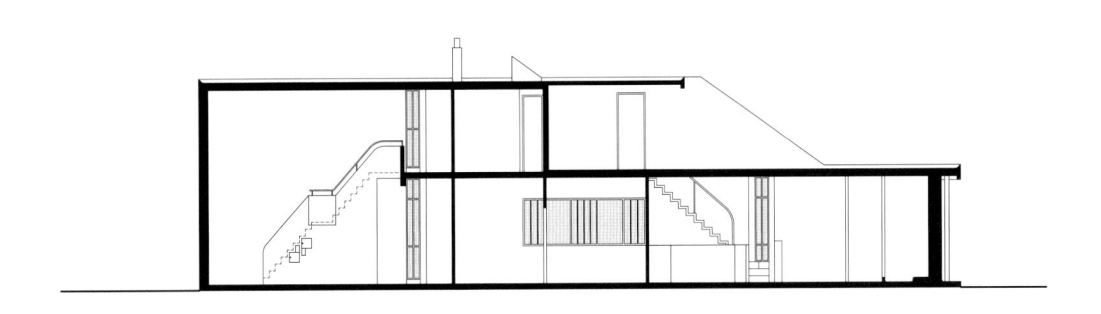

West elevation
East elevation
South–north section

55 **MAISON TERNISIEN**

7 PAVILLON DE L'ESPRIT NOUVEAU

LOCATION: Paris, France (original); Bologna, Italy (re-creation)
DATE: 1924; 1977

Le Corbusier designed this temporary pavilion for the International Exposition of Modern Decorative and Industrial Arts held in Paris in 1925. With this commission, he wanted to demonstrate how industrial standardization through mass production could create pure forms with an artistic value and how reinforced concrete and steel could be used to produce standardized houses, which he thought could solve housing shortages and were well suited for a modern life.

The pavilion consists of two main components: first, the rotunda, which exhibited dioramas of Le Corbusier's urban plans A Contemporary City for Three Million Inhabitants and the Plan Voisin; and second, a prototypical unit of the Immeubles-villas—an apartment block with superimposed villas, which the architect had designed in connection with A Contemporary City for Three Million Inhabitants.

The prototypical unit features a large outdoor terrace around which the living spaces are organized in an L-shaped plan. Such an arrangement is similar to the plan of a monk's cell at the monastery in Ema, near Florence, whose austerity and simplicity deeply impressed Le Corbusier and influenced his work throughout his life. Interior spaces are equipped with furniture prototypes designed for mass production, some of which were considered at the time to be too utilitarian for domestic use.

The event sponsors did not give much weight to Le Corbusier's earnest effort, although he was one of only a few architects who adhered to their requirement that the pavilions be modern without any historicist references. They gave him a site in a secluded section of the exhibition ground, obstructing a clear view of his pavilion with a screen, and they denied him the first prize for which he was nominated. Demolished against the architect's will in 1926, it was reconstructed as a French pavilion at the international building exhibition in Bologna in 1977.

CLIENT: French government
PROGRAM: Temporary pavilion
FEATURES: Furniture prototypes, oculus, rotunda, sliding panels

PAVILLON DE L'ESPRIT NOUVEAU — Exterior perspective, northwest corner

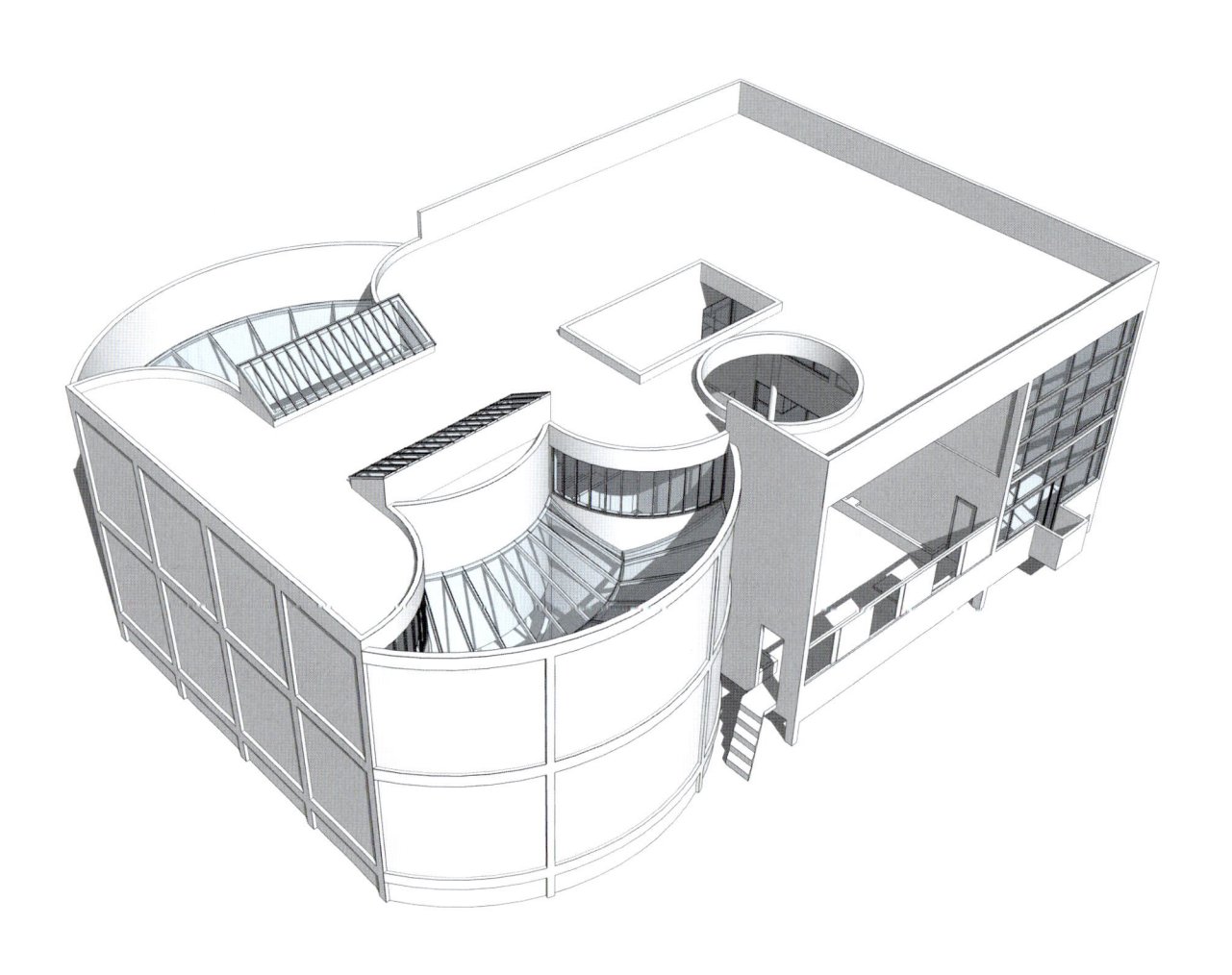

58 **PAVILLON DE L'ESPRIT NOUVEAU** Aerial perspective, northeast corner, rotunda and outdoor terrace

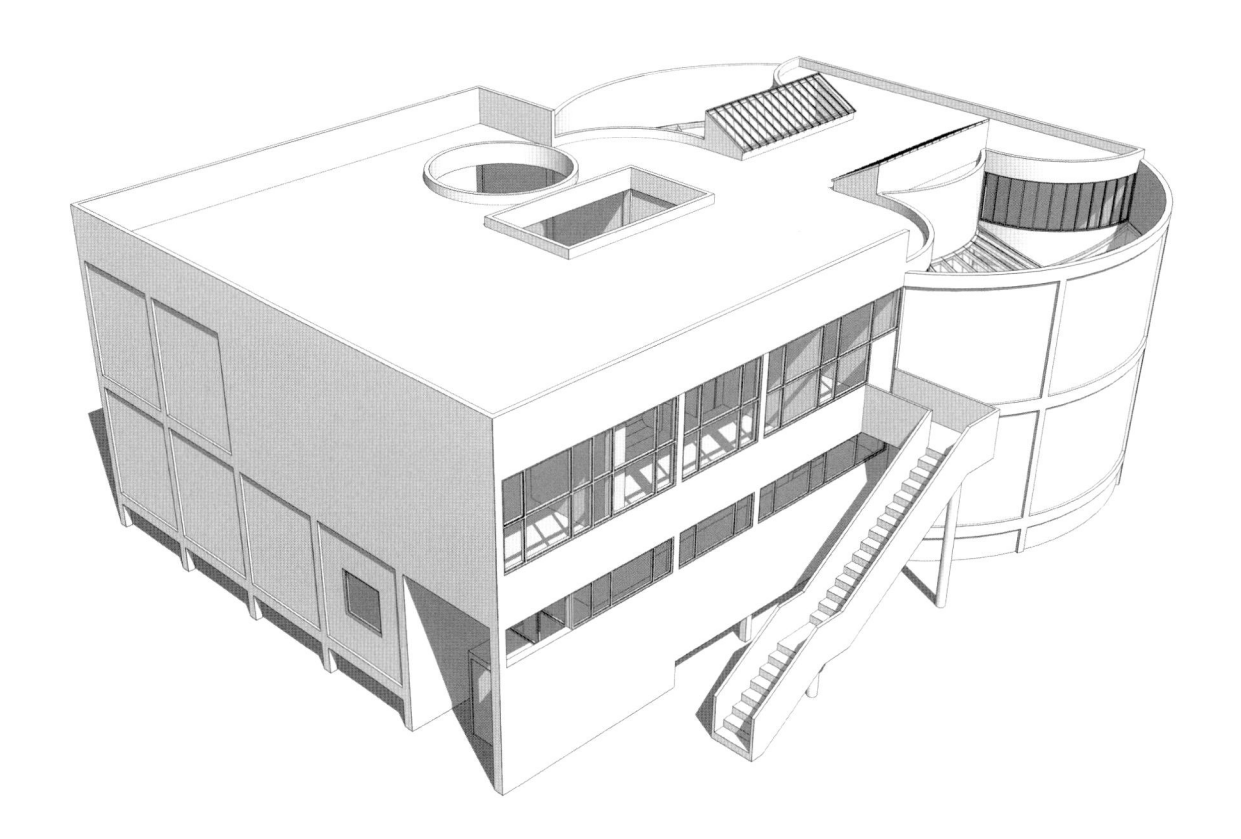

Aerial perspective, southwest corner, main entrance

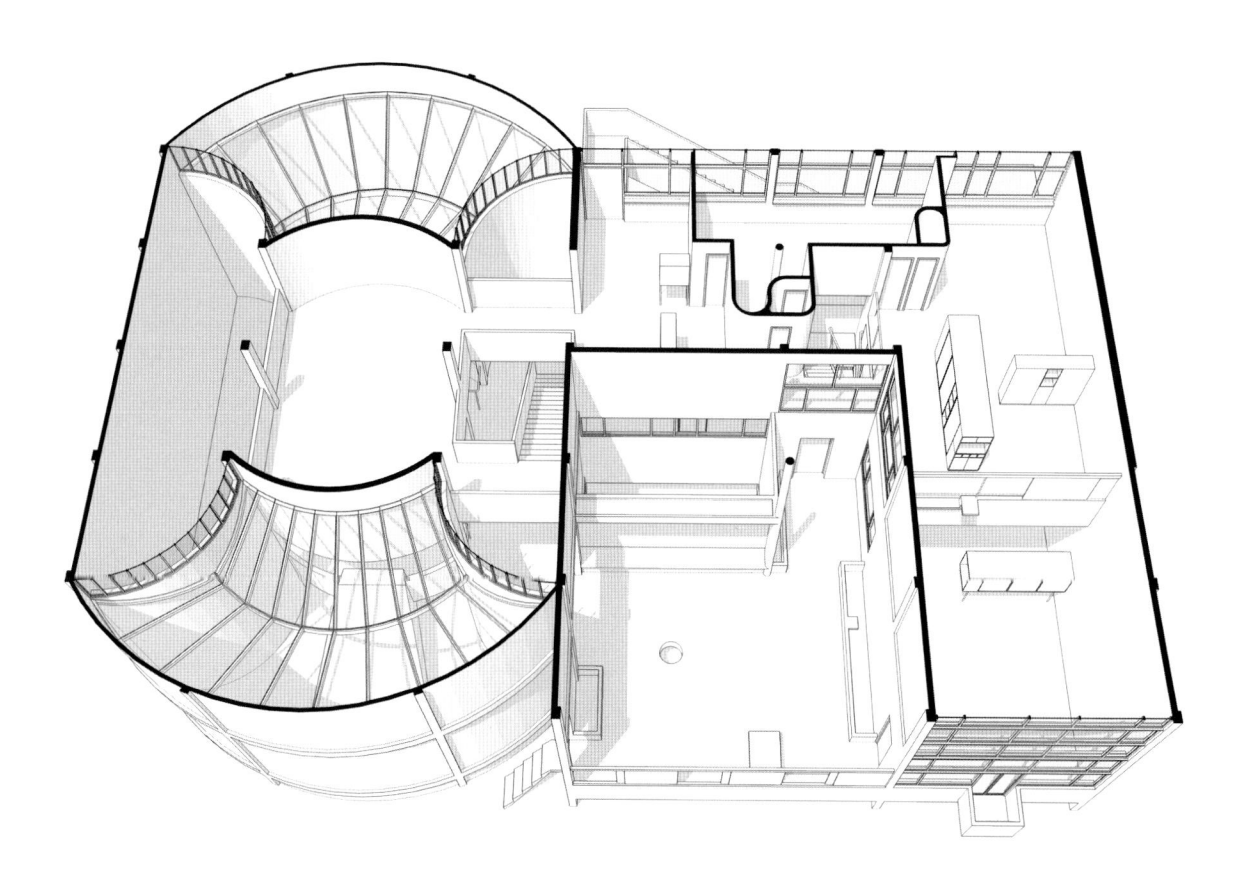

PAVILLON DE L'ESPRIT NOUVEAU — Second-floor planar perspective showing north elevation

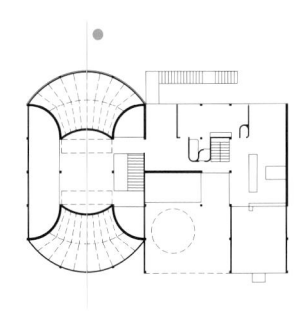

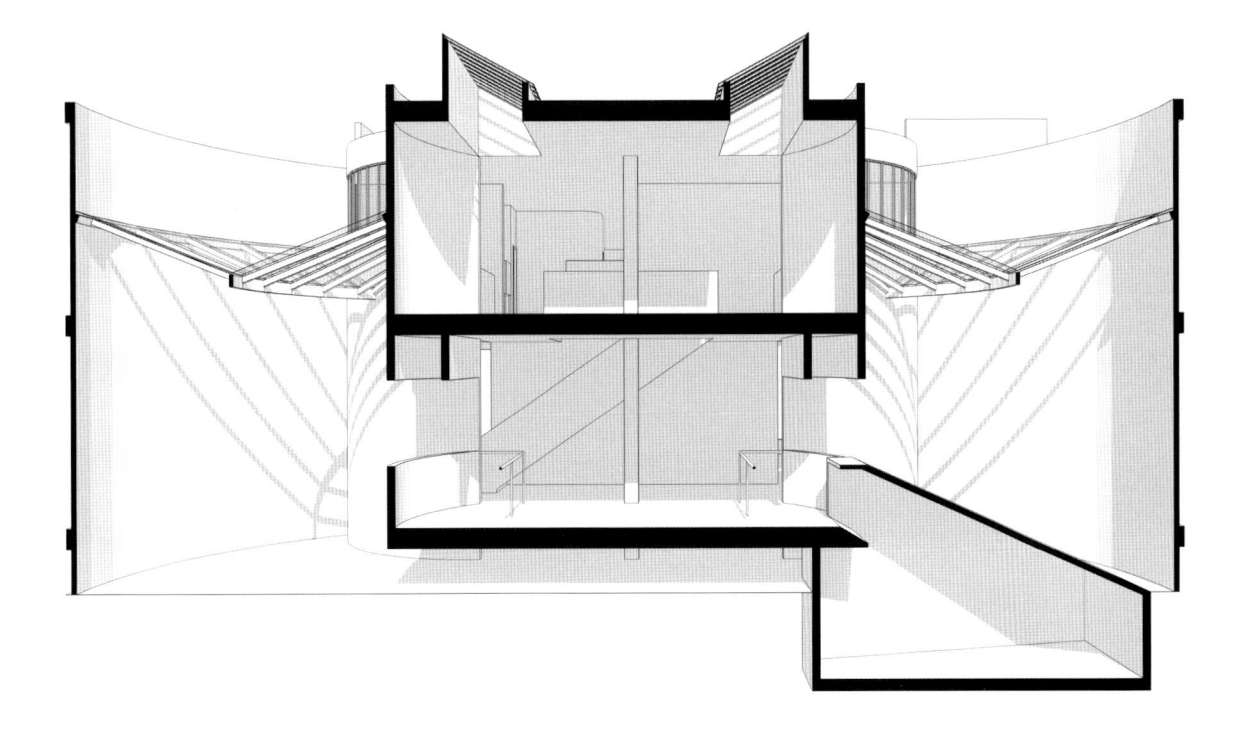

PAVILLON DE L'ESPRIT NOUVEAU South–north sectional perspective at rotunda

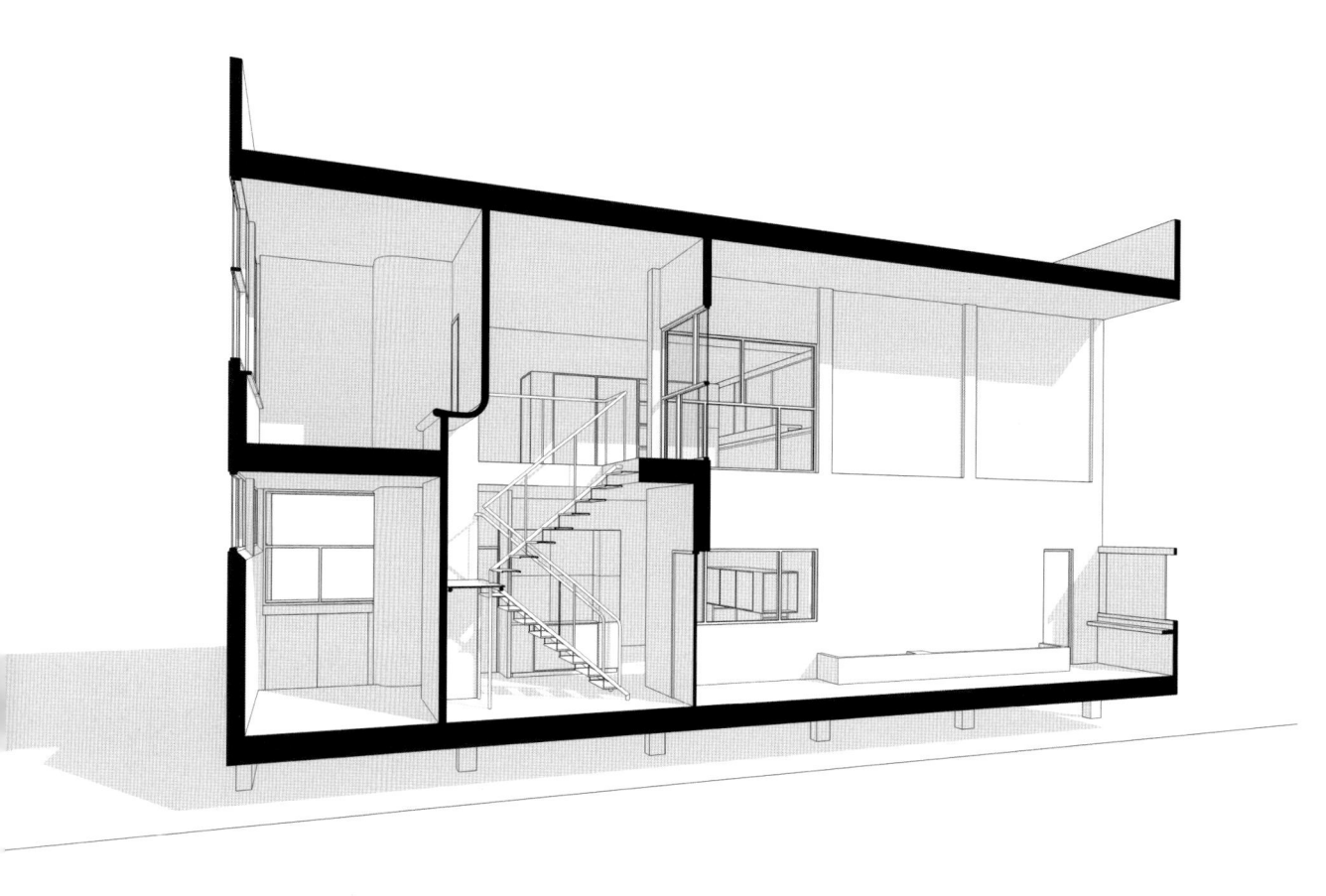

62 **PAVILLON DE L'ESPRIT NOUVEAU** ● South–north sectional perspective at stairs

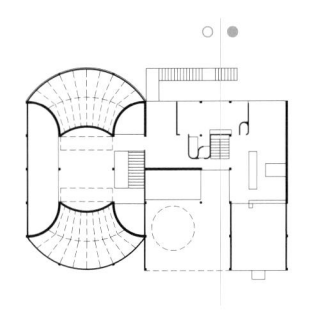

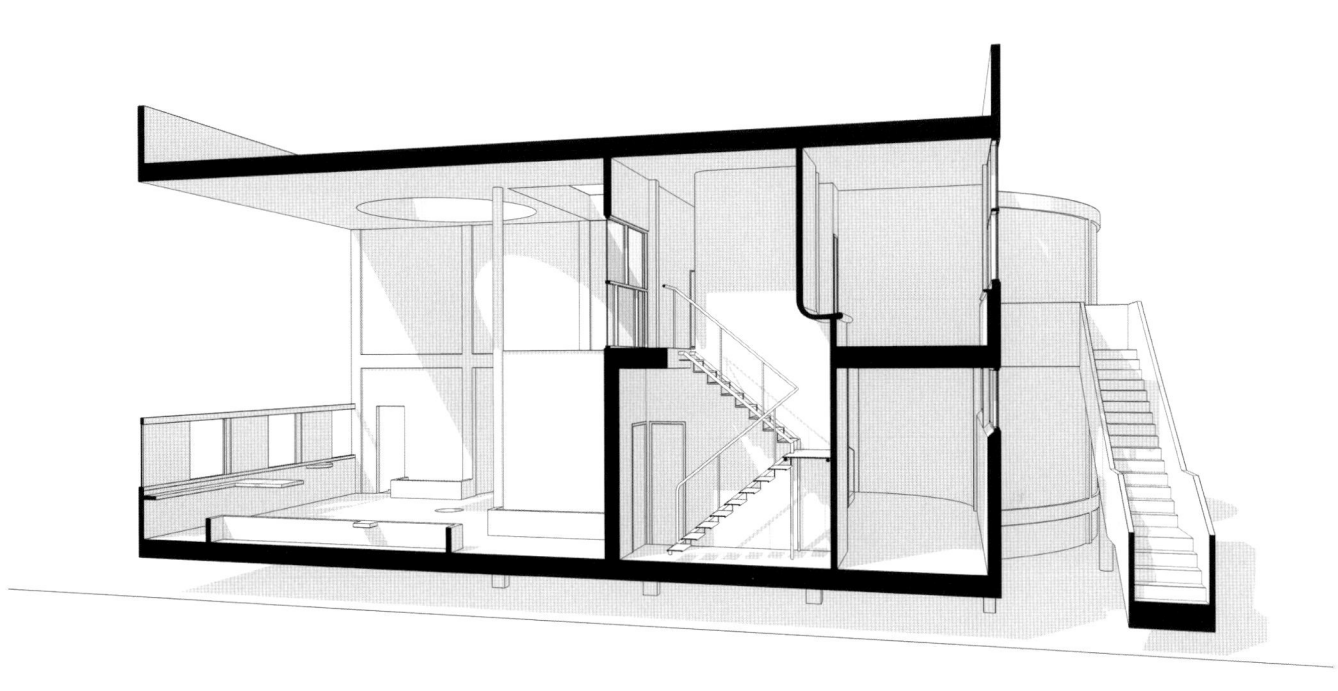

63 **PAVILLON DE L'ESPRIT NOUVEAU**   ○   North–south sectional perspective at stairs

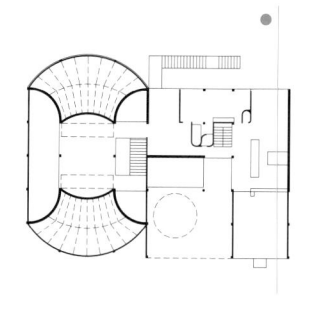

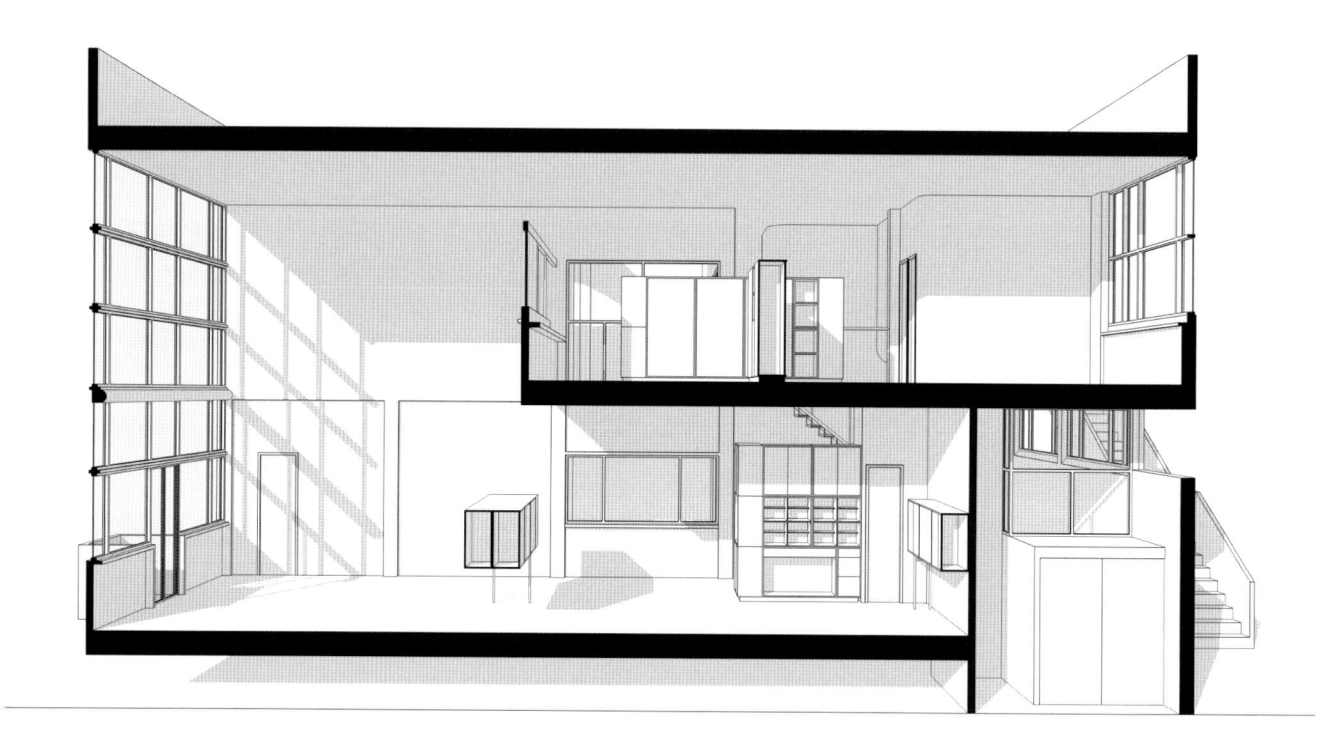

PAVILLON DE L'ESPRIT NOUVEAU   North–south sectional perspective at double-height living room

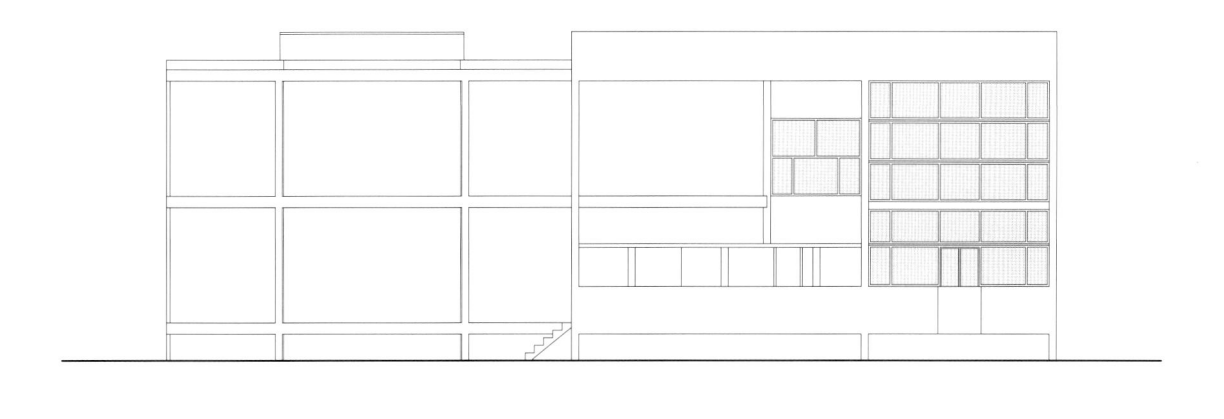

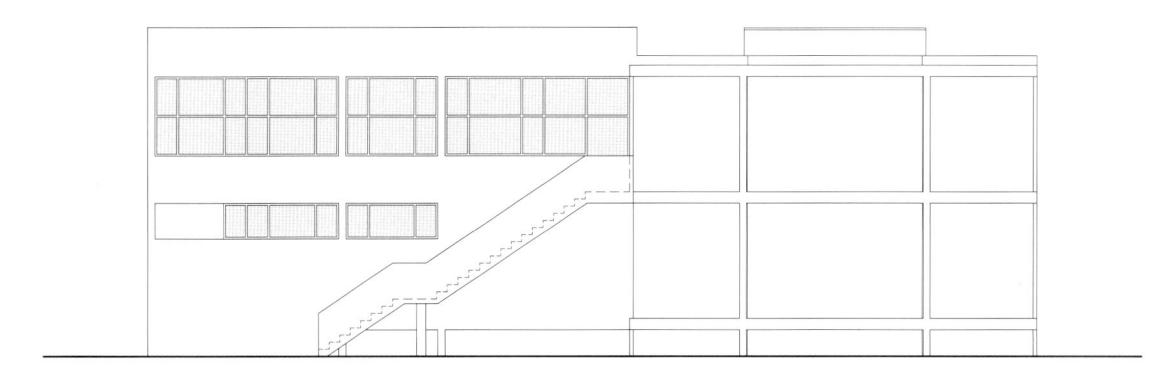

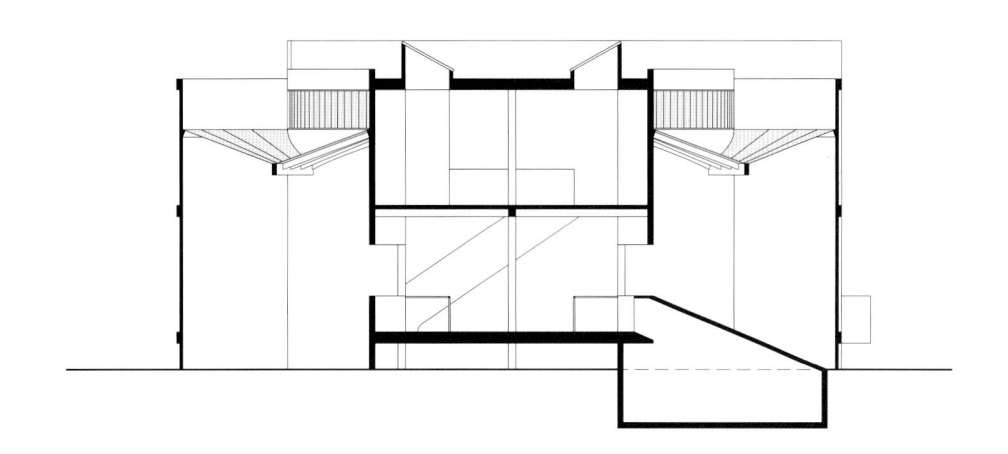

North elevation
South elevation
South–north section

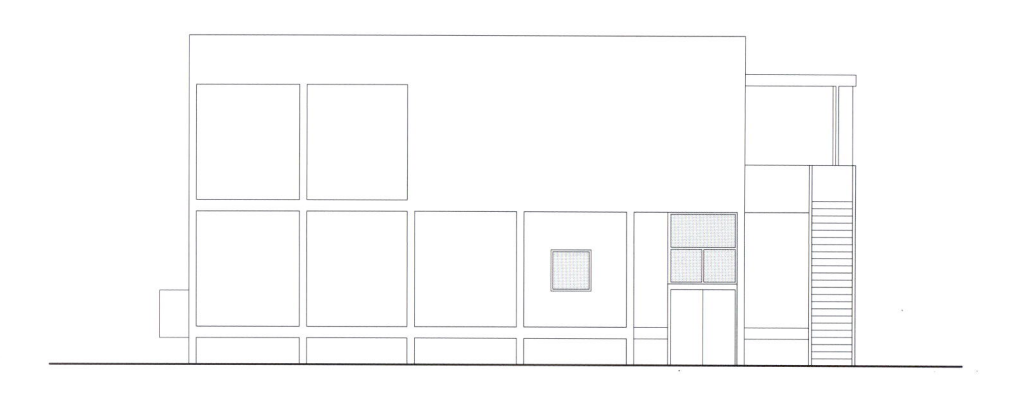

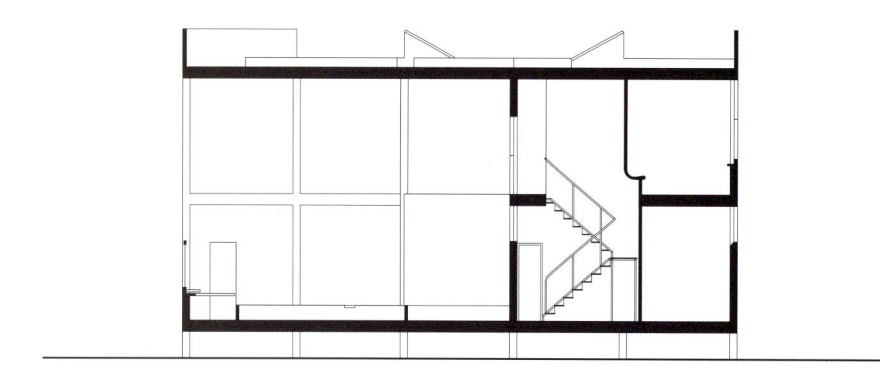

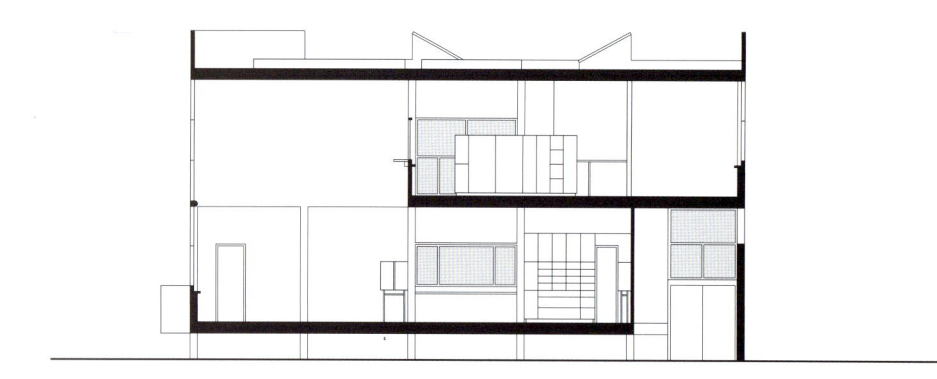

West elevation
North–south sections

Second-floor plan
First-floor plan

1 Exhibition hall
2 Gallery
3 Bedroom
4 Kitchen
5 Outdoor terrace
6 Library
7 Dining room
8 Living room
9 Exercise room
10 Sitting room
11 Open to below

66 PAVILLON DE L'ESPRIT NOUVEAU

PAVILLON DE L'ESPRIT NOUVEAU

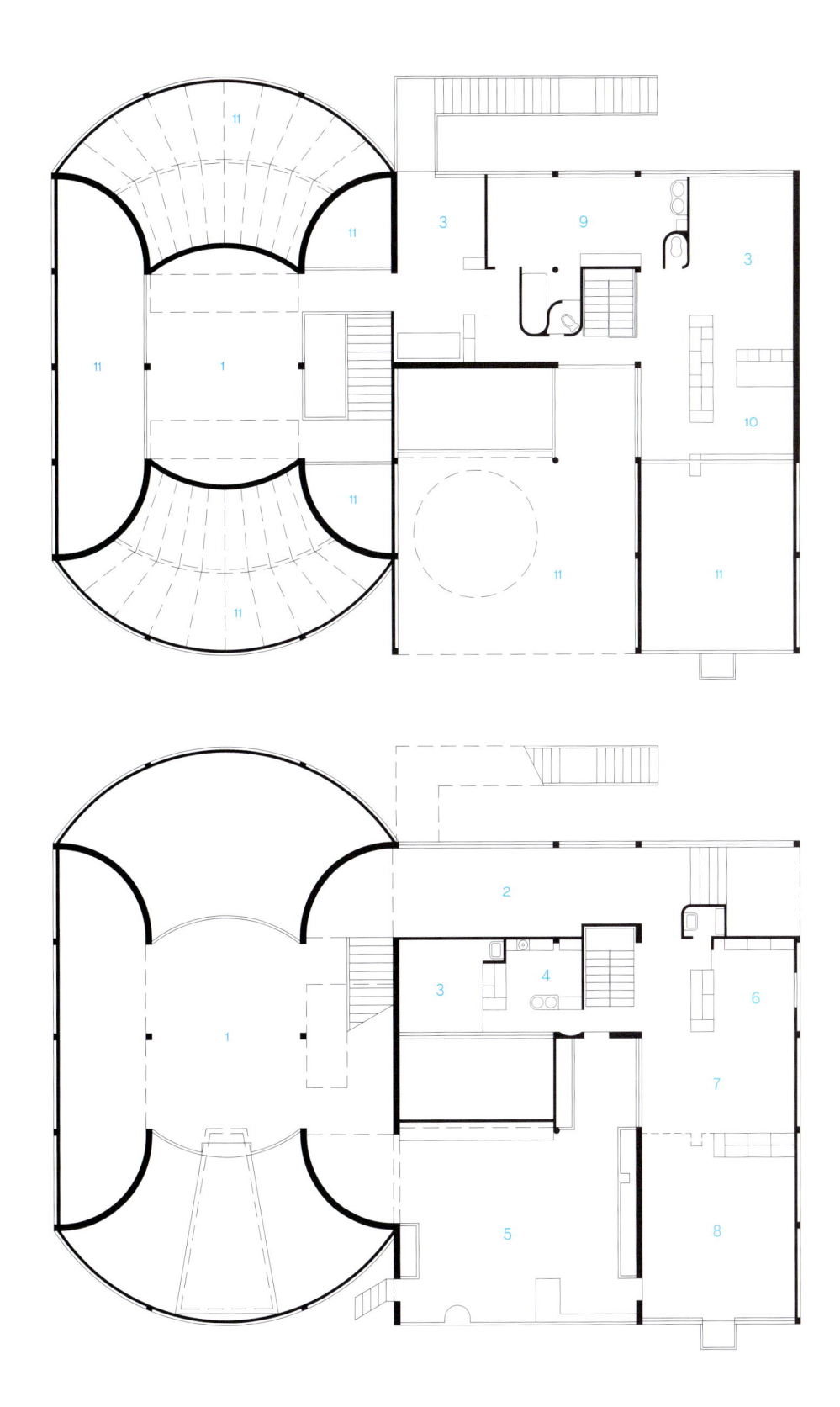

MAISON PLANEIX

LOCATION: Paris, France
DATE: 1924

This house is built on an urban-infill site for a client who made tomb monuments as his business. Le Corbusier addressed the client's complex requirements on a small, restricted site by using inventive spatial arrangements, most notably volumes that interlock in section. The entrance door to the garage, which is placed between two rental units on the ground level, provides a through-connection to the back of the house, where an exterior stair leads to the owner's living and working spaces above. Although each rental unit has a small floor area, double-height spaces give them a sense of grandeur. Suitable for artists' studios, the rental units open out to the urban life on the street through large glass windows.

Behind the symmetrical facade that adheres to a simple, three-bay spacing of the concrete structure, the interior of the house is more freely organized, with many of the basic design elements typical of Le Corbusier's architecture: double-height spaces with mezzanines that offer different vantage points, skylights that bring in natural light from above, outdoor terraces and gardens that extend the interior spaces to the outside, and carefully positioned windows that direct the occupants' movement through the house.

CLIENT: Antonin Planeix
PROGRAM: Rental apartments and owner's studio residence
FEATURES: Double-height space, sawtooth skylight, tripartite facade, exterior stairs, bridge, vertical slot windows

69 **MAISON PLANEIX** Exterior perspective, south elevation

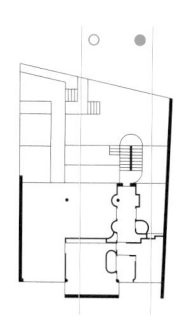

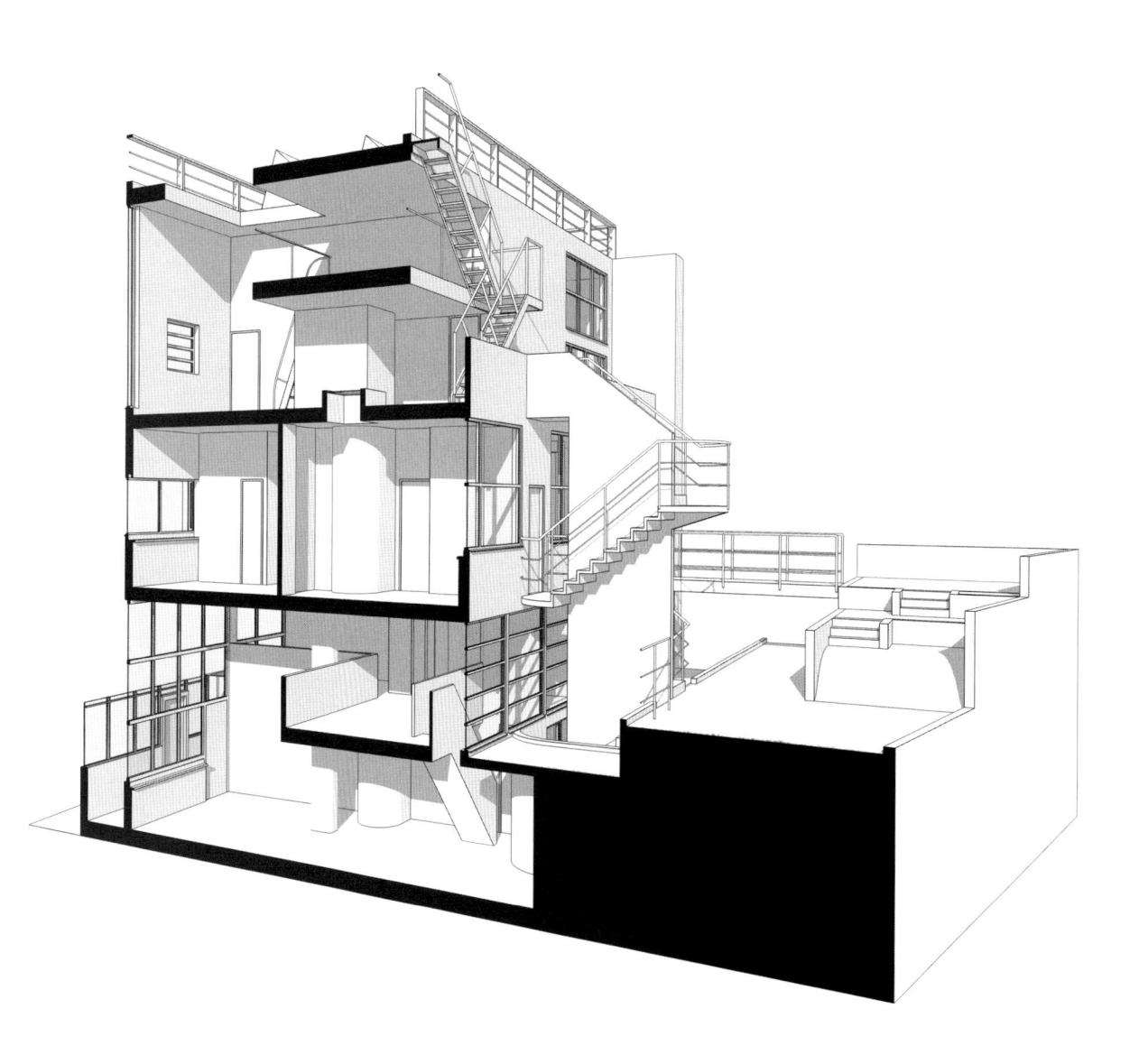

MAISON PLANEIX South–north sectional perspective at rental apartments

MAISON PLANEIX   North–south sectional perspective at studio

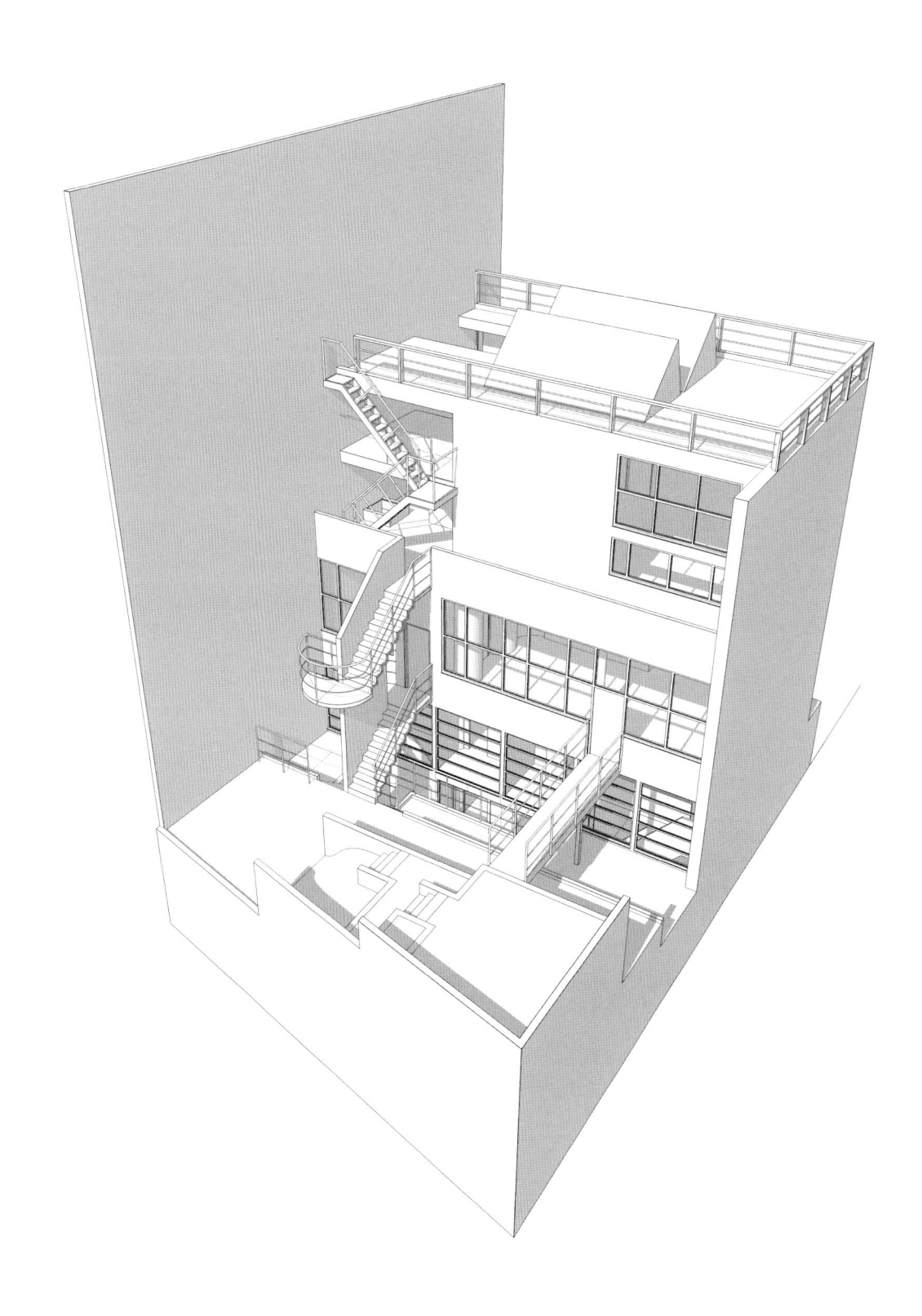

72 **MAISON PLANEIX** Aerial perspective, north elevation

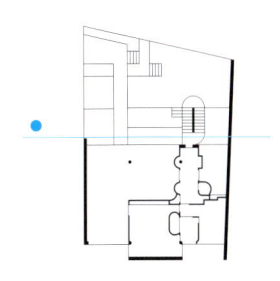

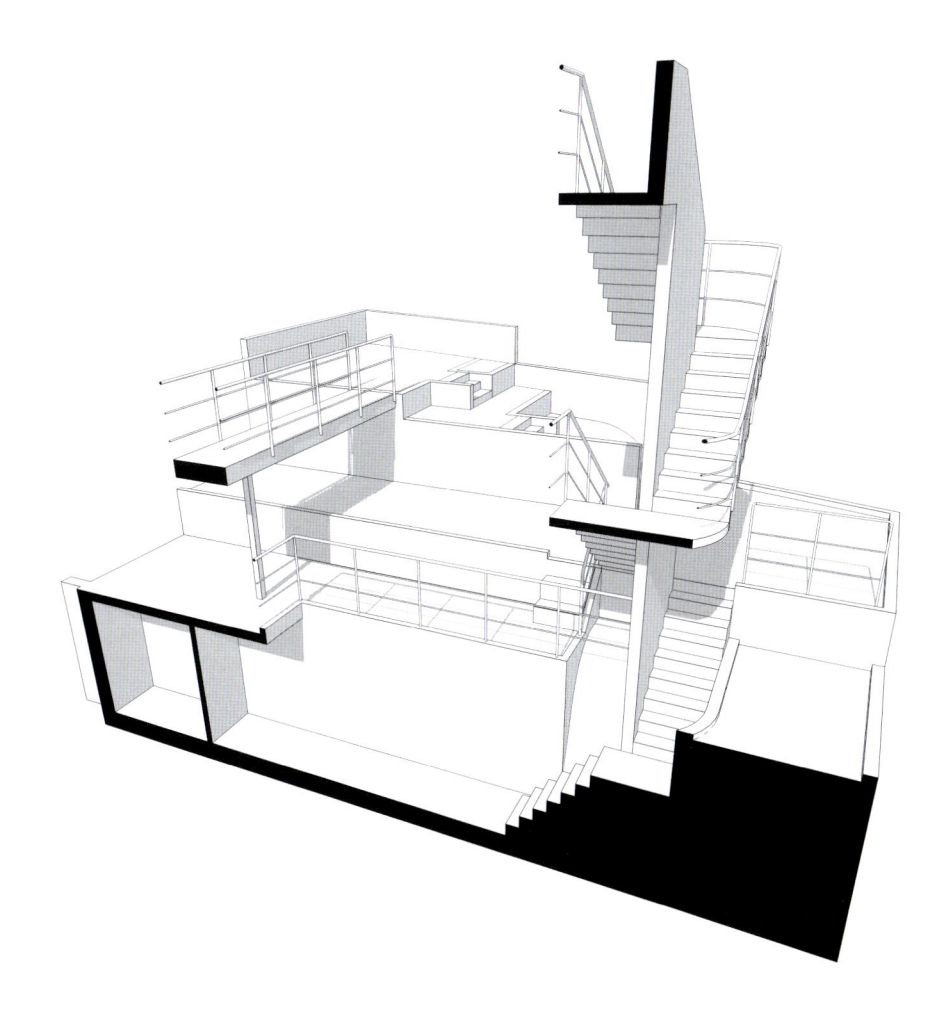

73 **MAISON PLANEIX**   West–east sectional perspective at stairs

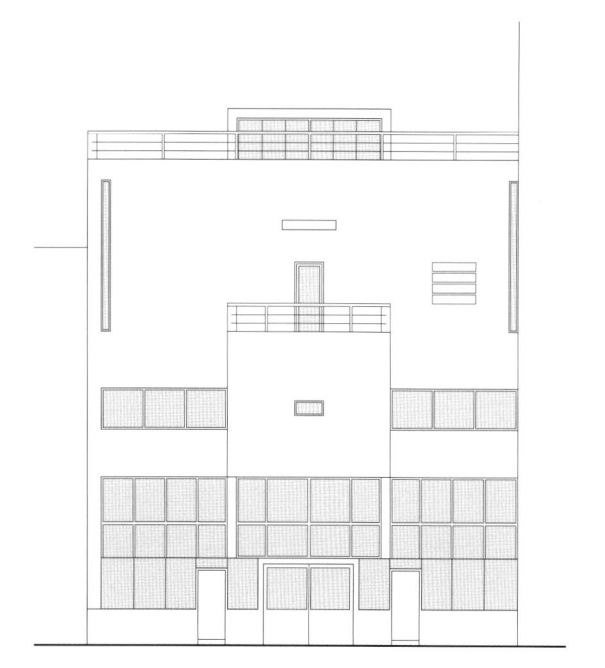

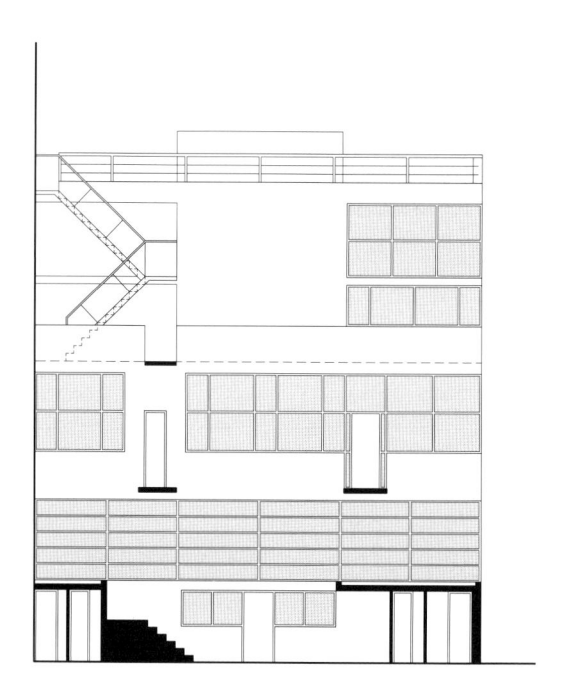

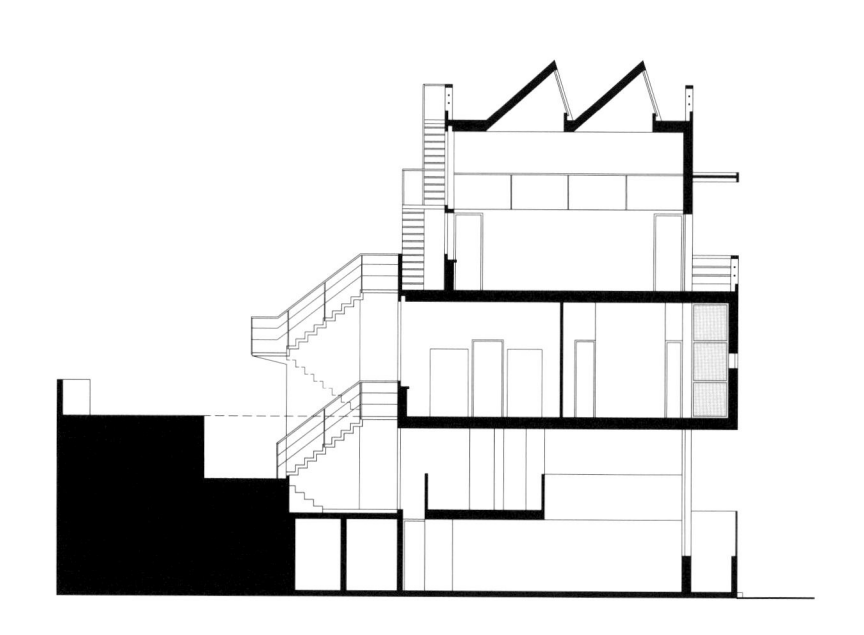

South elevation

North elevation
North–south section

74 **MAISON PLANEIX**

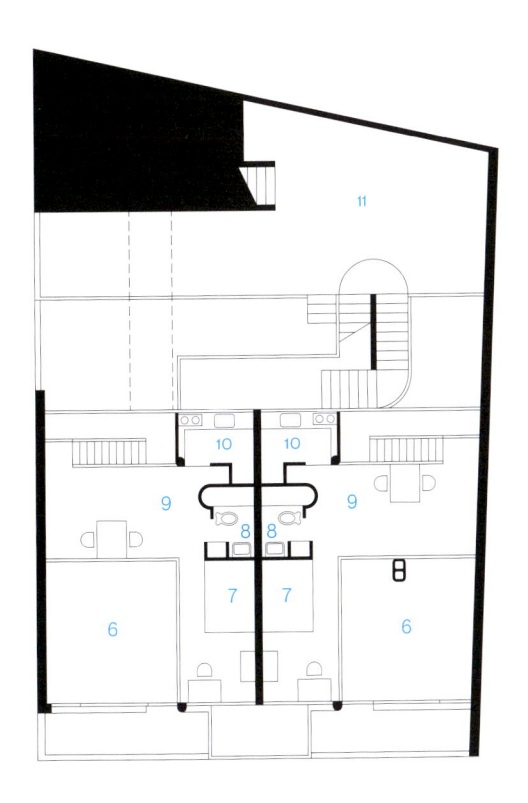

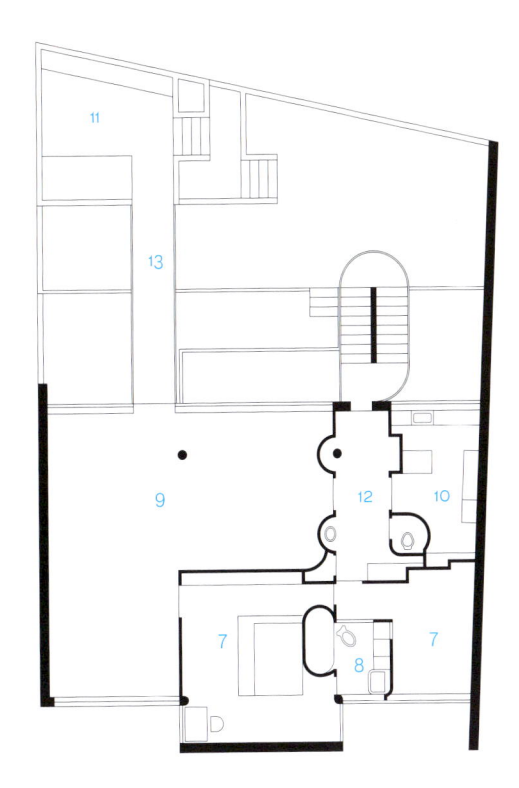

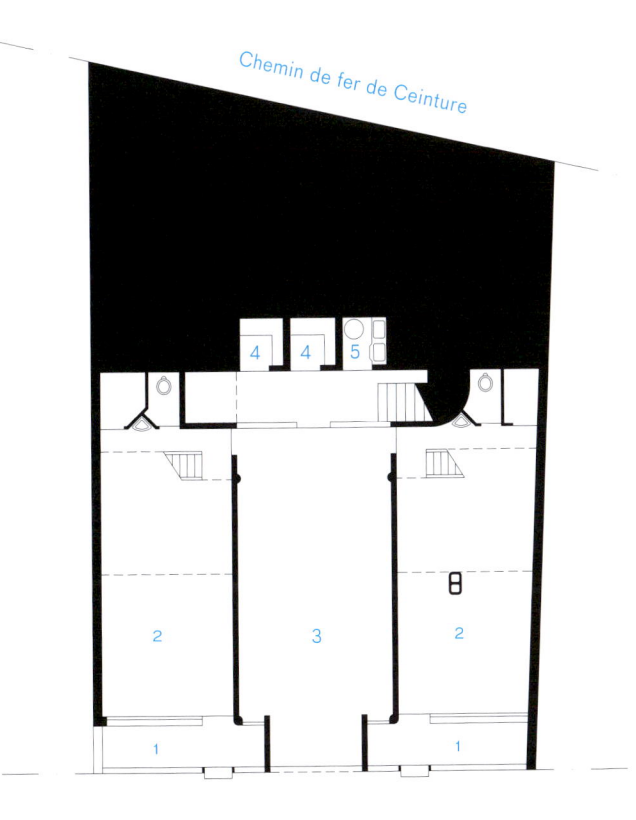

Chemin de fer de Ceinture

Second-floor plan   Third-floor plan
First-floor plan

1 Front yard
2 Studio
3 Garage
4 Cellar
5 Utility room
6 Open to below
7 Bedroom
8 Bathroom
9 Dining and living room
10 Kitchen
11 Outdoor garden
12 Vestibule
13 Bridge

Boulevard Masséna

MAISON PLANEIX

MAISON GUIETTE

LOCATION: Antwerp, Belgium
DATE: 1926

Designed for painter René Guiette and his family, this house offered the architect an opportunity to test the adaptability of his Maison Citrohan housing prototype, developed in the early 1920s. The most notable features of Maison Citrohan were an elongated rectangular volume, fully glazed front elevation, industrial windows, a mezzanine overlooking a double-height living room, and an outdoor terrace.

Maison Guiette is located along the southern edge of its site, providing space for a small yard on the ground level. Here, the double-height living room of the Citrohan model is reassigned a new program as a painting studio at the uppermost level, with a connection to the roof garden. Another difference from the Citrohan type is a reversal of the vertical circulation sequence. At Maison Citrohan, the living room becomes a circulation space with a straight-run stair embedded within, while at Maison Guiette the living room is isolated from the stair, which provides direct access from the vestibule to the upper levels. Unlike in the Citrohan prototype, the roof terrace at Guiette is enclosed by walls, which maintains the overall cubic form of the house while providing greater privacy. These differences contribute to the successful urban adaptation of the Citrohan prototype for a unique site, program, and client.

CLIENT: René Guiette
PROGRAM: Family residence with a painting studio
FEATURES: Double-height painting studio, elements from Maison Citrohan prototype

Exterior perspective, northeast corner

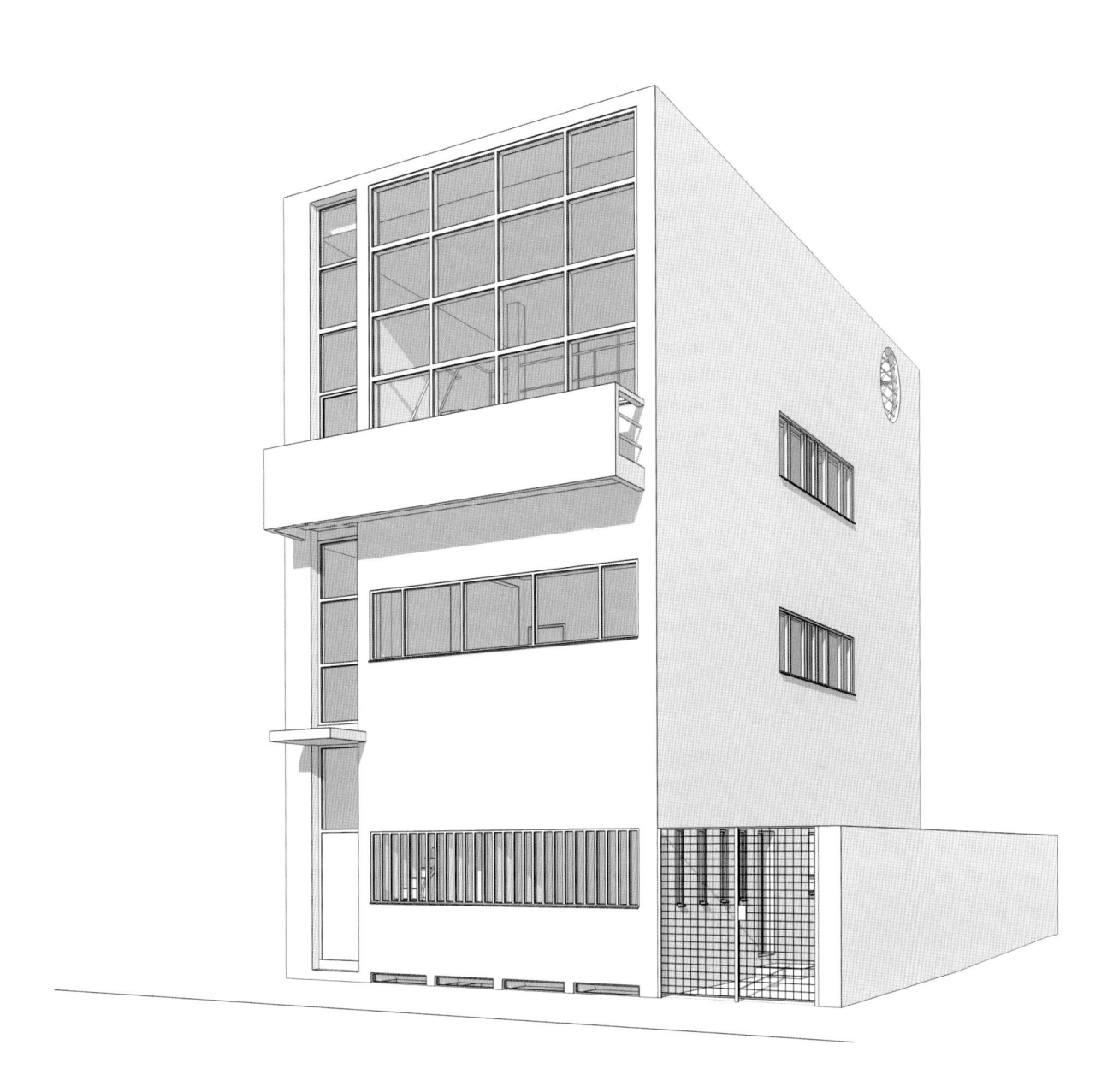

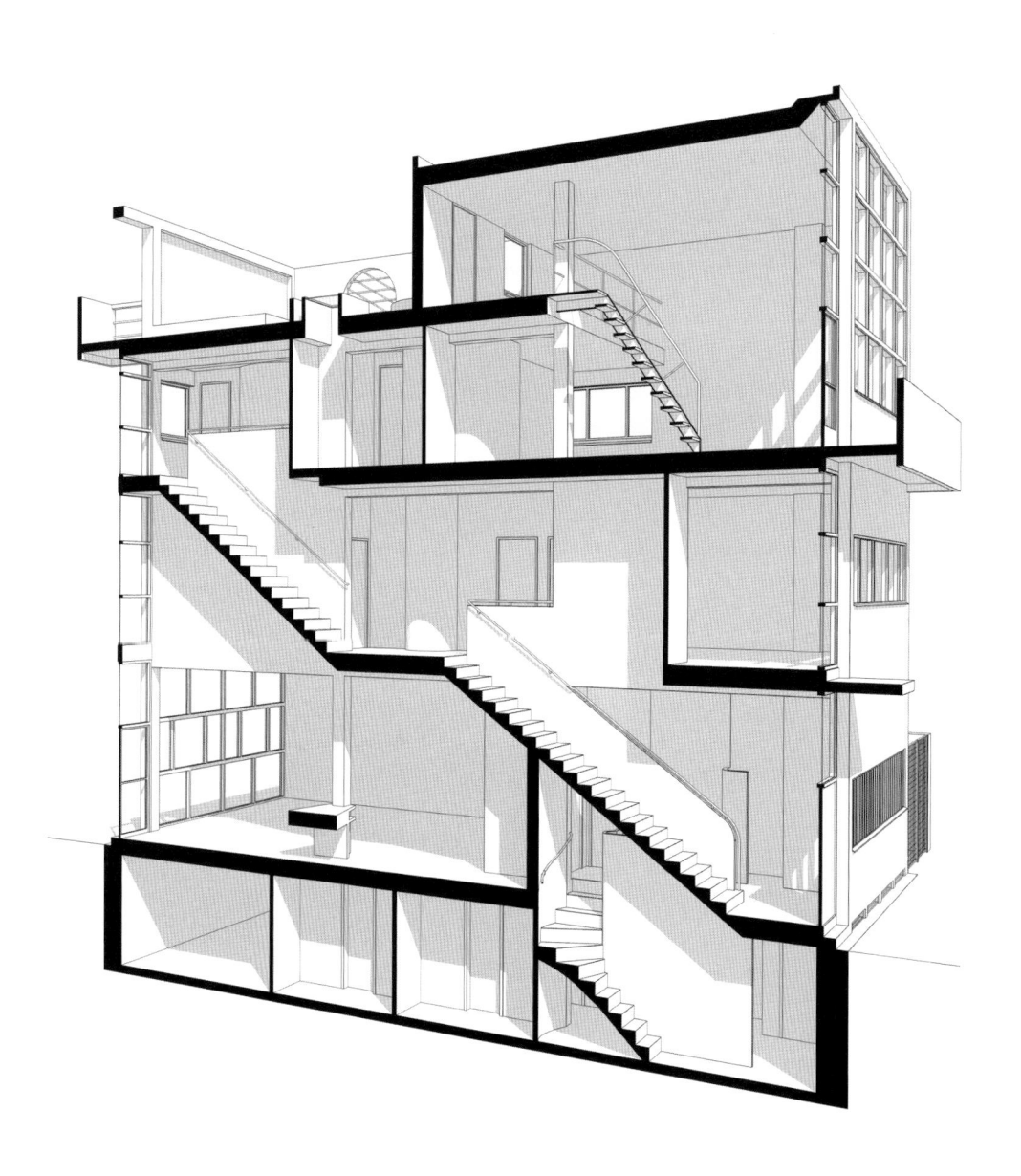

MAISON GUIETTE — West–east sectional perspective at stairs

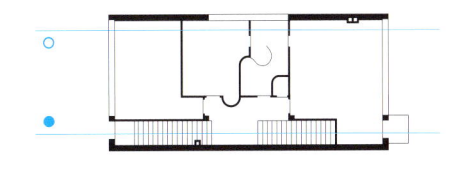

East–west sectional perspective at dining and living room

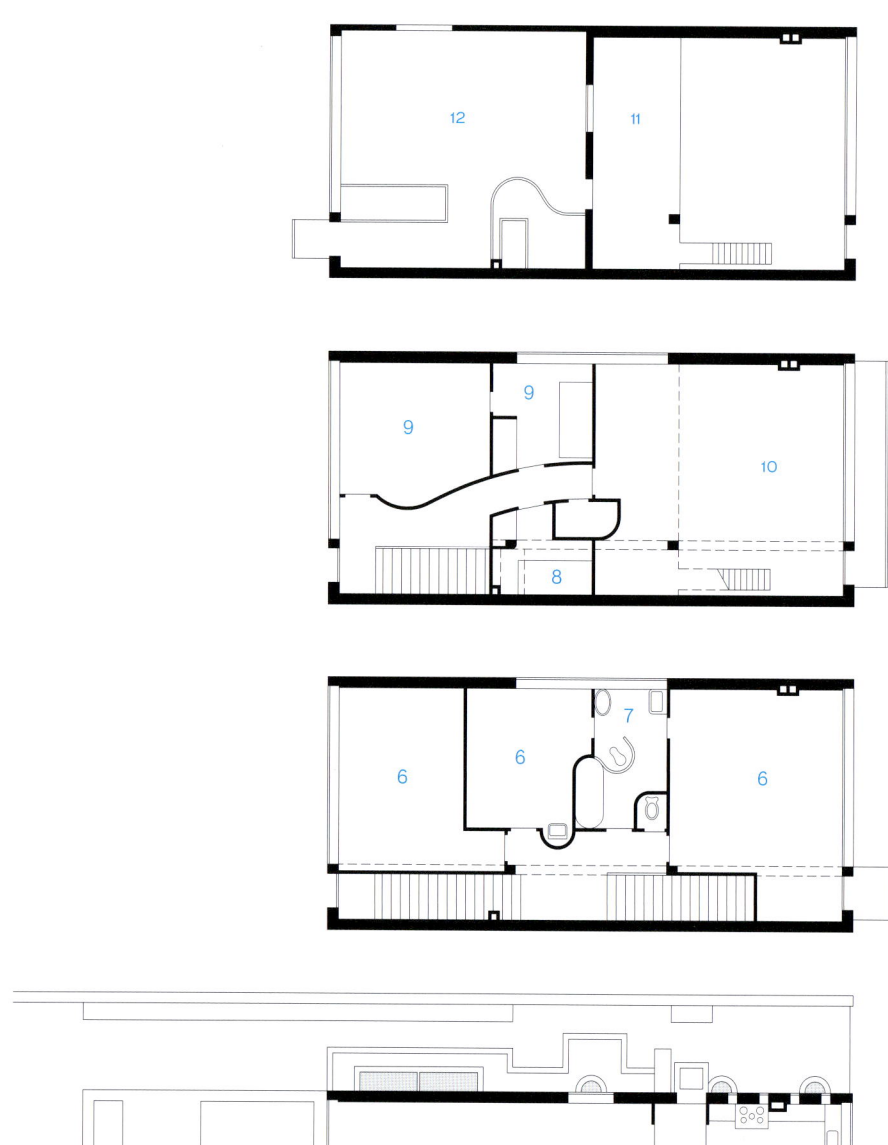

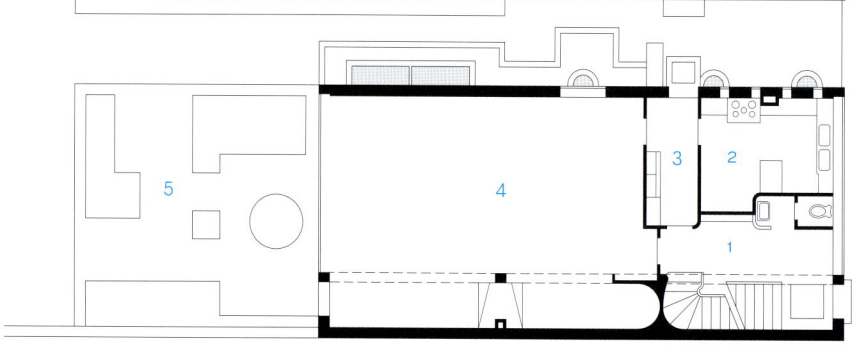

Fourth-floor plan
Third-floor plan
Second-floor plan
First-floor plan

1. Vestibule
2. Kitchen
3. Pantry
4. Dining and living room
5. Garden
6. Bedroom
7. Bathroom
8. Storage
9. Utility room
10. Art studio
11. Gallery
12. Roof terrace

80 **MAISON GUIETTE**

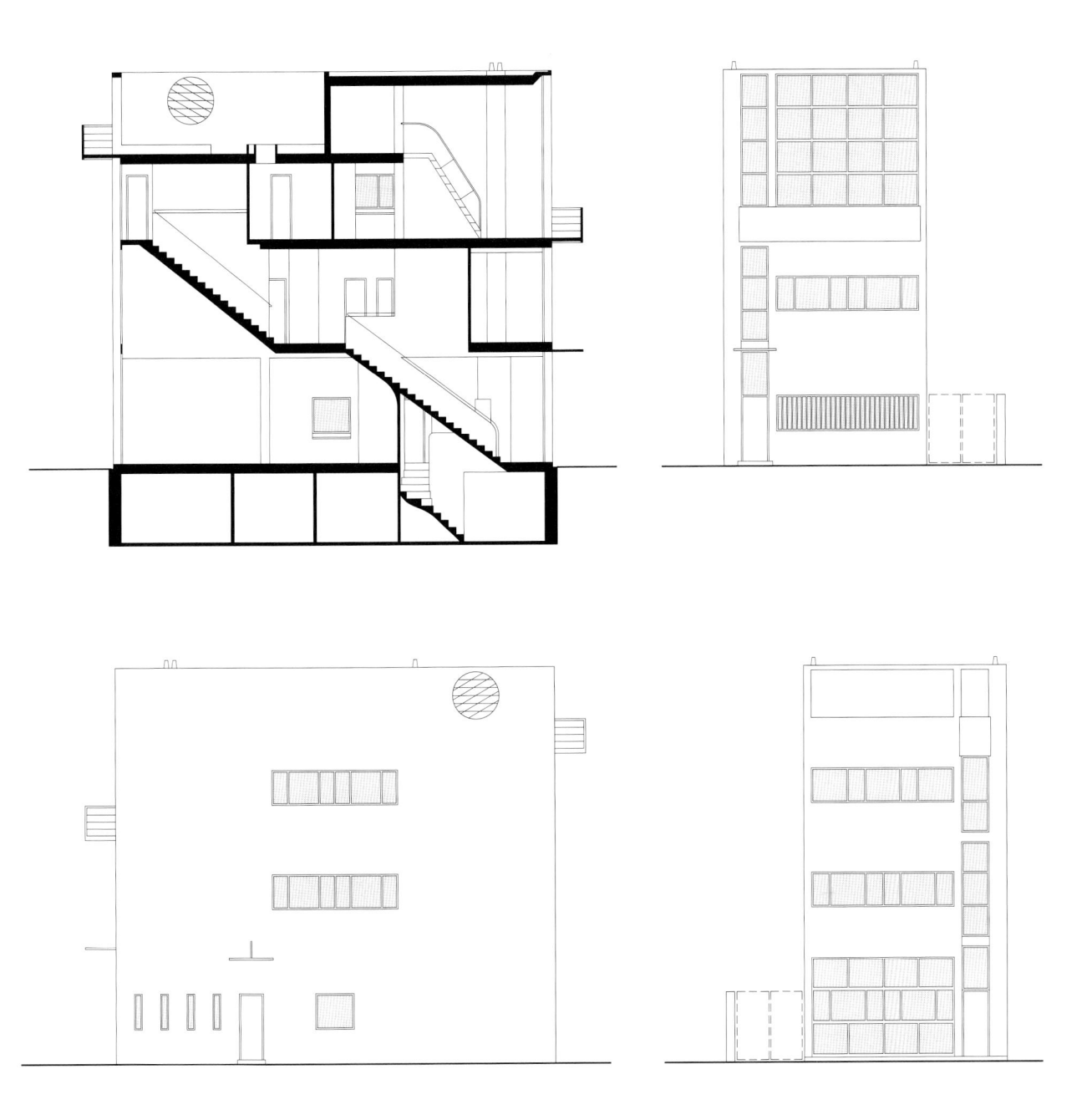

West–east section
North elevation

East elevation
West elevation

81 **MAISON GUIETTE**

10 VILLA COOK

LOCATION: Boulogne-sur-Seine, France
DATE: 1926

Villa Cook was the clearest expression of Le Corbusier's formulation of architectural principles to date, namely his Five Points of a New Architecture, developed in 1926: freestanding columns (*pilotis*); roof gardens; a free plan; long, horizontal windows; and a free facade. Built on an urban-infill site, the house is held in the air by slender concrete columns, freeing up the ground level for automobile access to the garage and uninterrupted pedestrian circulation from the front garden through the protected outdoor space to a private backyard. Non-load-bearing interior partitions could be positioned freely according to the architect's desires rather than the engineer's requirements. Strip windows span the full width of the building, and different types of operable panels, such as sliding, hopper, and casement windows, were incorporated to accommodate a wide range of internal functions, highlighting the planning flexibility afforded by a long horizontal window. The center column was held back from the main elevation to allow the latter to be arranged freely.

Programs that are most actively used during the day occupy the uppermost levels, to provide maximum access to light and air. Space flows from dining to living room, a two-story space that is connected to a library and finally opens out onto the roof garden. A large clerestory window in the living and dining rooms provides light and views while preserving privacy within. Villa Cook's overall volume is an almost-perfect cube, one of the ideal forms Le Corbusier mentioned in his 1923 book *Toward an Architecture*.

CLIENTS: William and Jeanne Cook
PROGRAM: Family residence
FEATURES: Adherence to the Five Points of a New Architecture, overall cubic volume

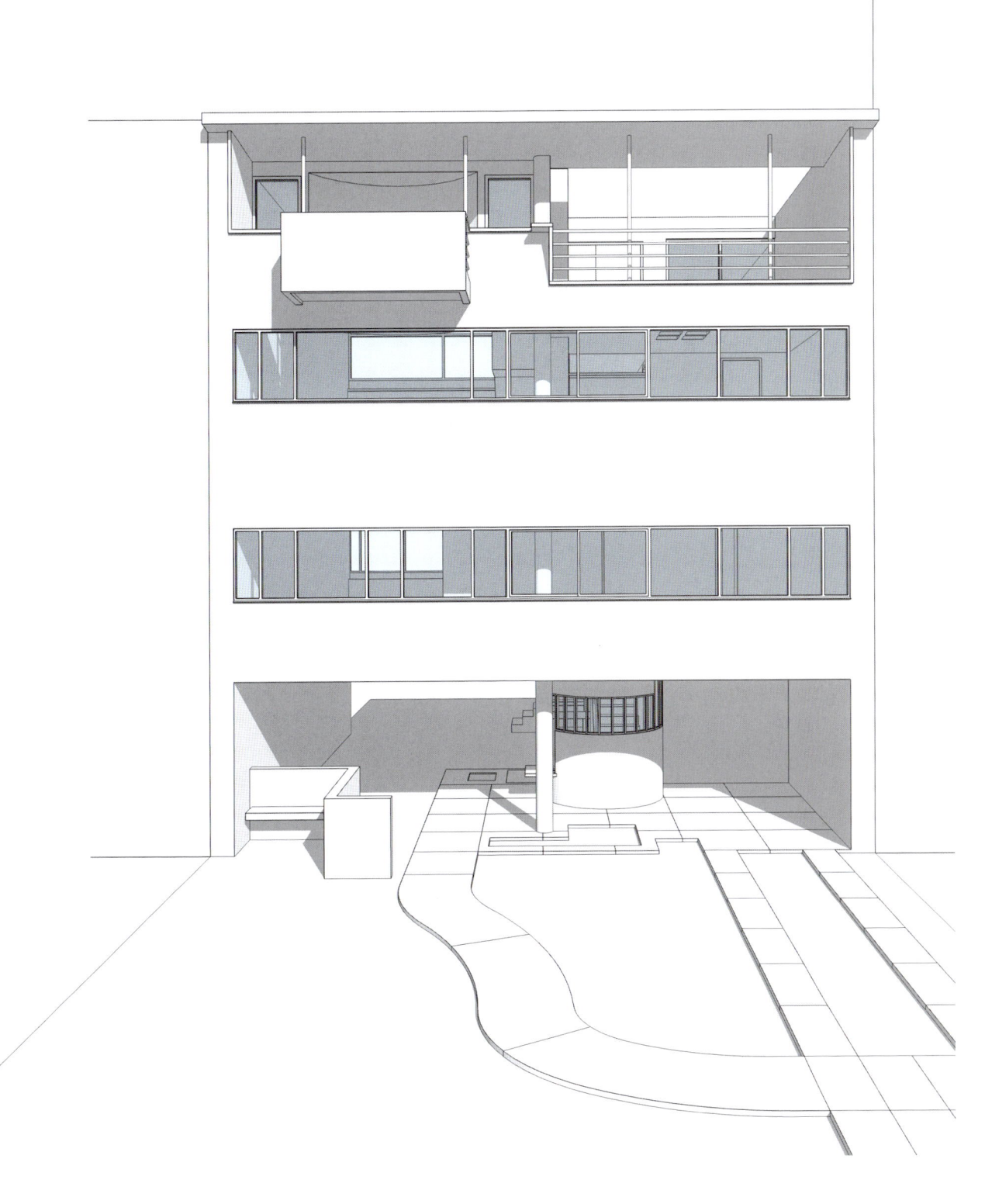

83 **VILLA COOK** Exterior perspective, north elevation

North–south sectional perspective at stairs

85　**VILLA COOK**　　○　South–north sectional perspective at stairs

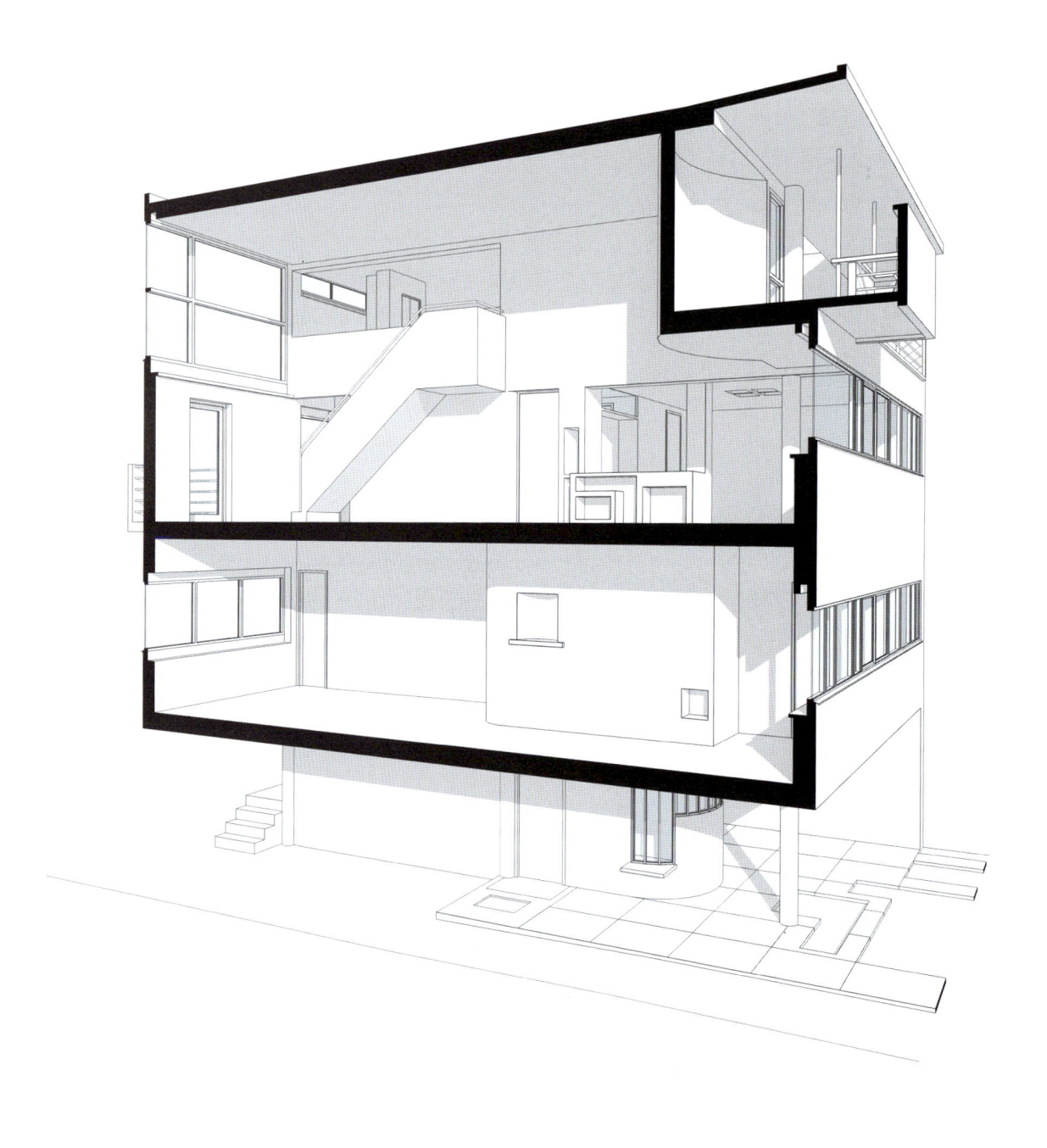

86   **VILLA COOK**   South–north sectional perspective at living room

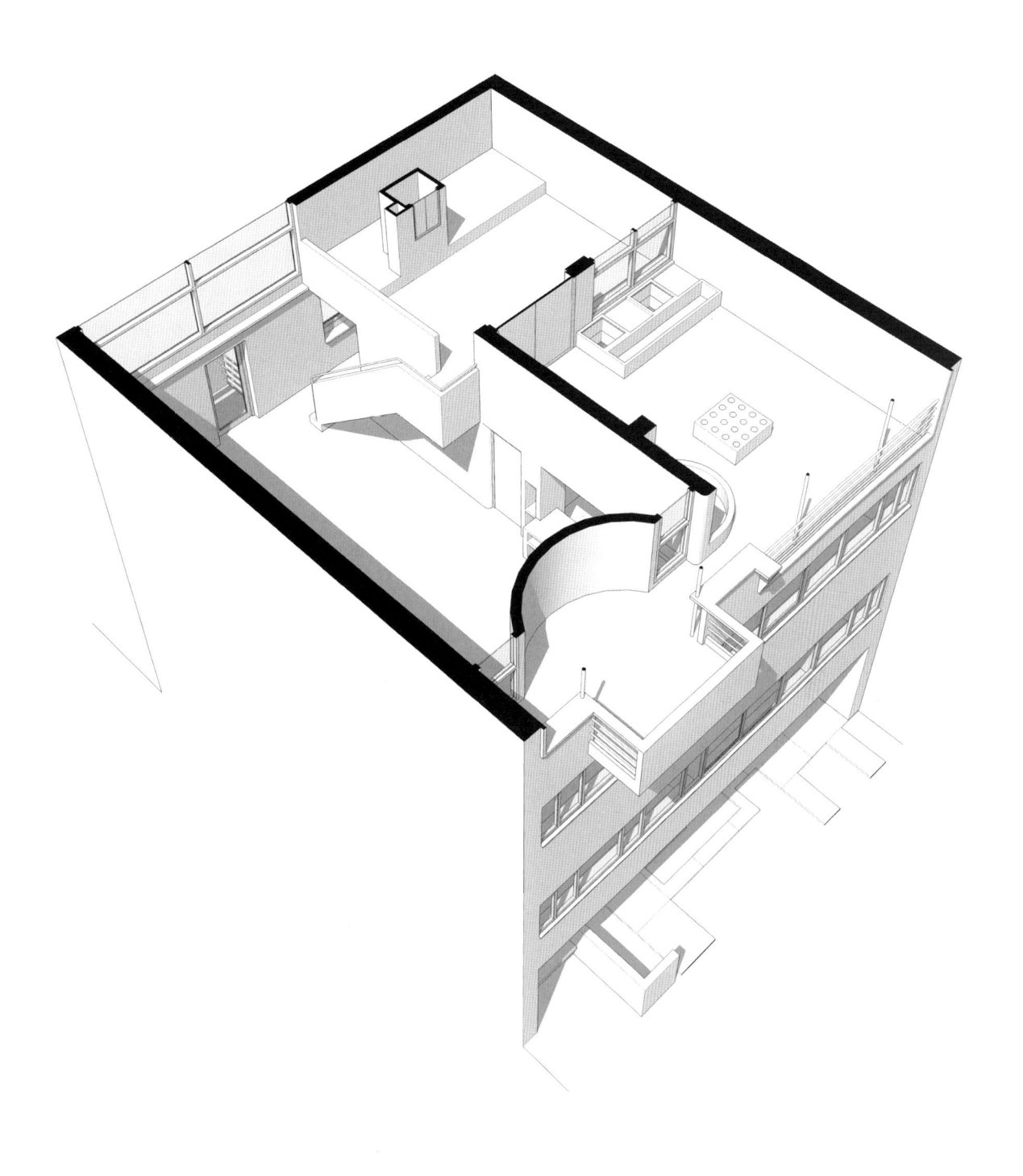

87　**VILLA COOK**　　　　　　　　　　　　　　　Fourth-floor planar perspective, northeast corner

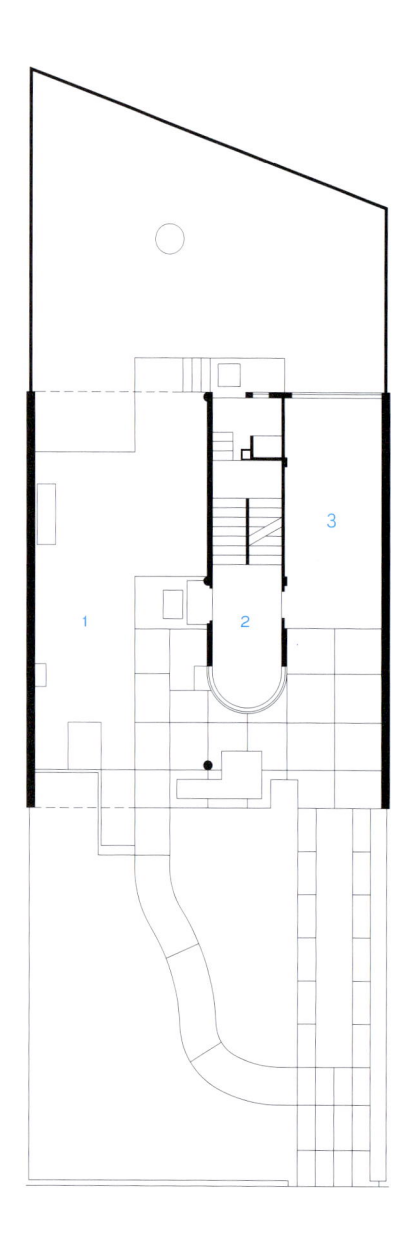

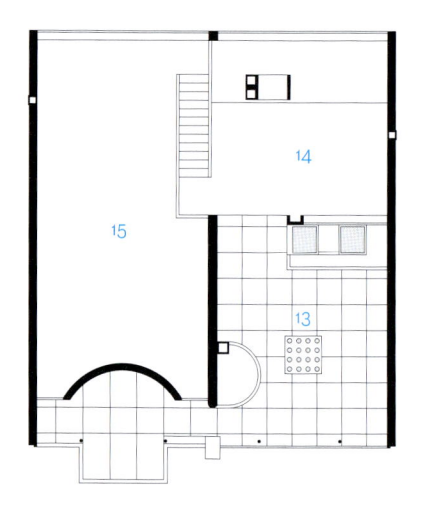

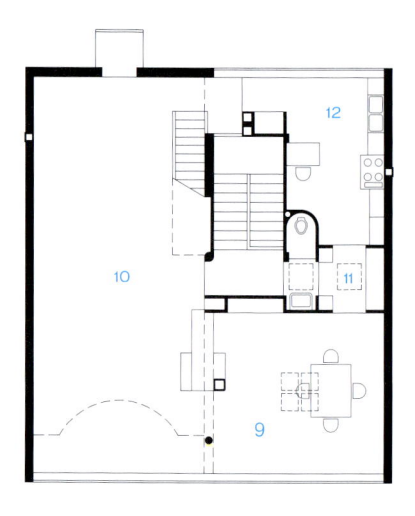

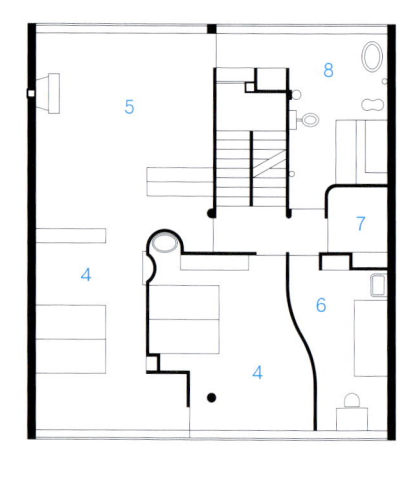

First-floor plan Fourth-floor plan
　　　　　　　　Third-floor plan
　　　　　　　　Second-floor plan

1. Covered outdoor garden
2. Vestibule
3. Garage
4. Bedroom
5. Sitting room
6. Maid's room
7. Utility room
8. Bathroom
9. Dining room
10. Living room
11. Pantry
12. Kitchen
13. Roof terrace
14. Library
15. Open to below

88 **VILLA COOK**

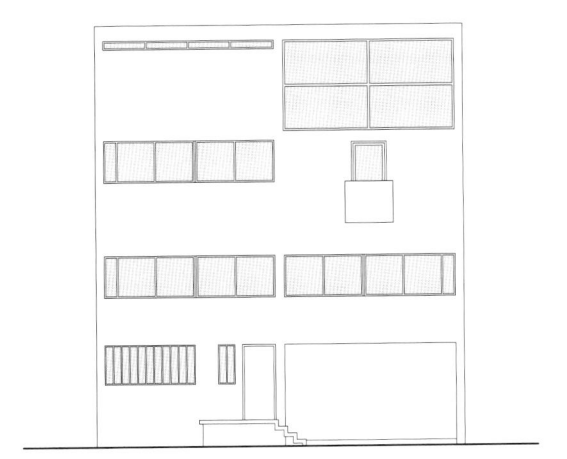

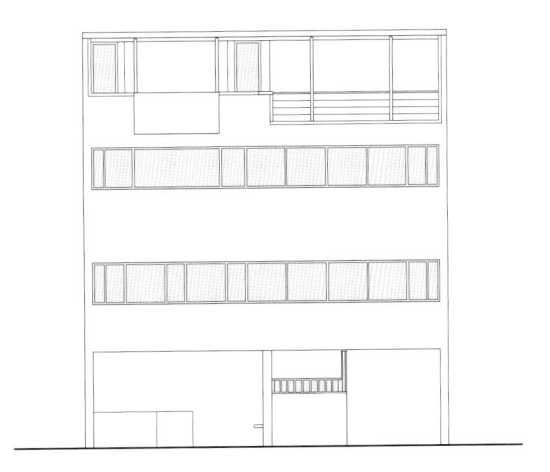

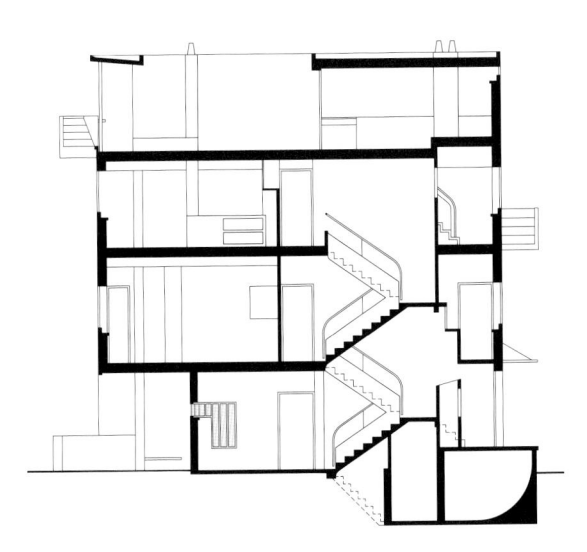

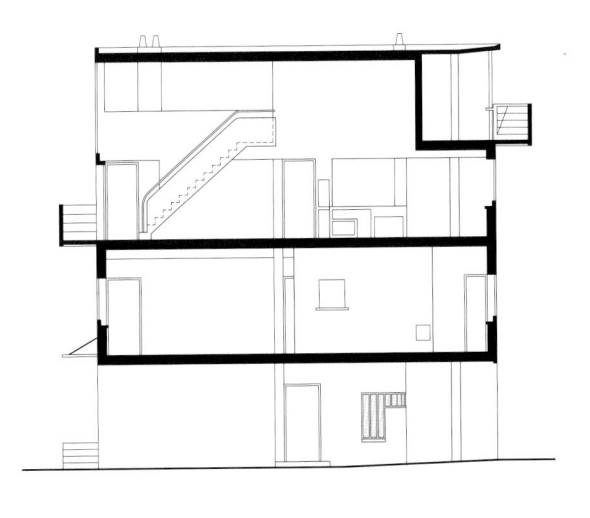

South elevation
North–south section

North elevation
South–north section

89 **VILLA COOK**

11 VILLA STEIN-DE MONZIE

LOCATION: Vaucresson, France
DATE: 1926

The clients for this house wanted to commission an architect who was among the pioneers of the modernist movement to create an exemplary building. Le Corbusier was involved in the project from the site selection. He went through a series of schematic design options with various siting configurations before reaching the final as-built solution, which occupies almost the full width of a long, narrow site. The most notable features of the house are the cascading outdoor terraces on its garden side. Their carefully detailed balustrades provide the house's occupants with access to light, views, and open space.

The house was built according to the Five Points of a New Architecture. Like many of Le Corbusier's villas from the 1920s, it appeared in its smooth, white finish to be an expression of a machine aesthetic as a consequence of industrial production, but ironically, it employed the most traditional methods of construction using concrete blocks and plaster finish.

CLIENTS: Gabrielle de Monzie and Michael and Sarah Stein
PROGRAM: Family residence
FEATURES: Terraces on multiple levels, adherence to the Five Points of a New Architecture

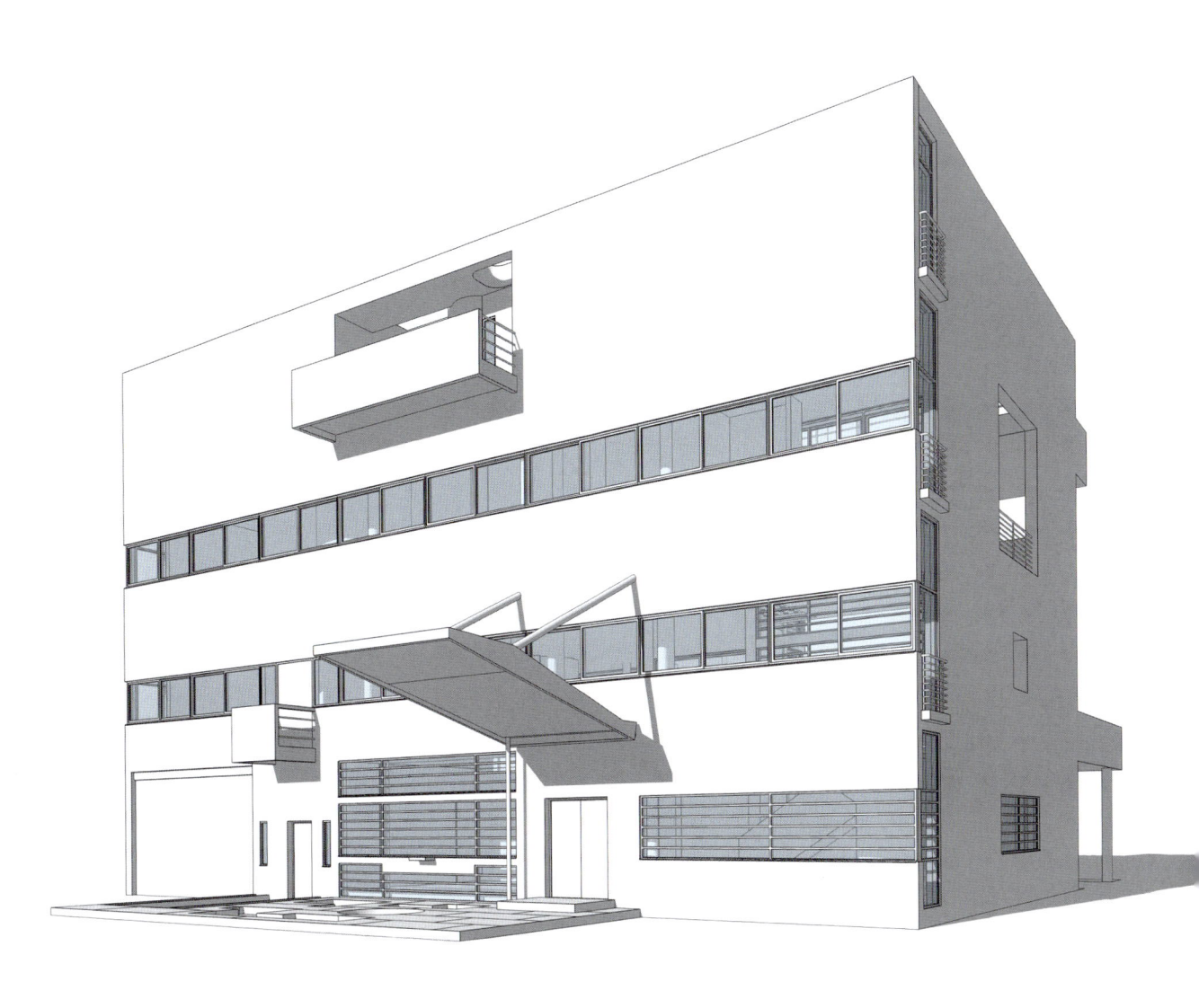

VILLA STEIN-DE MONZIE — Exterior perspective, northwest corner

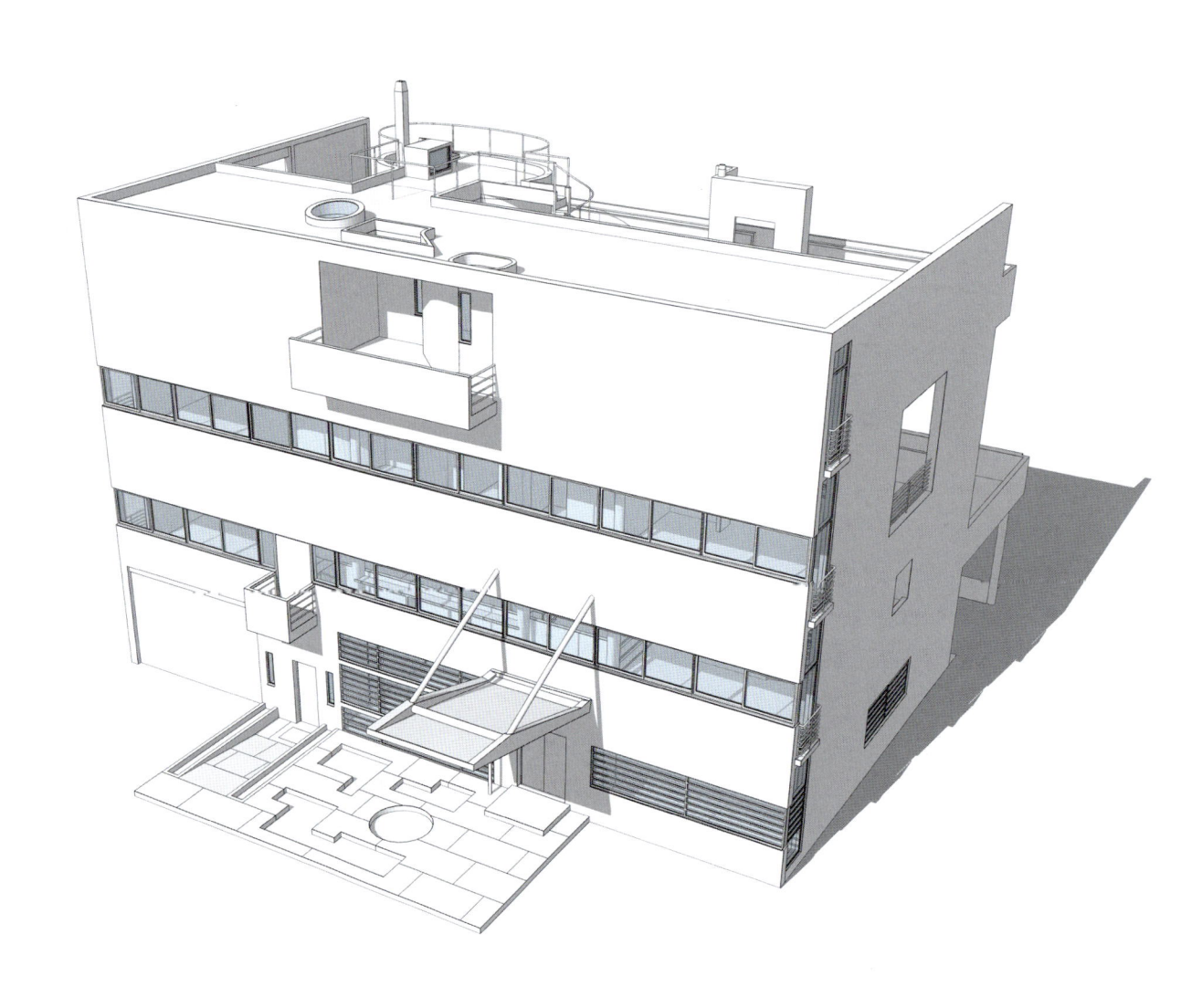

VILLA STEIN-DE MONZIE Aerial perspective, northwest corner

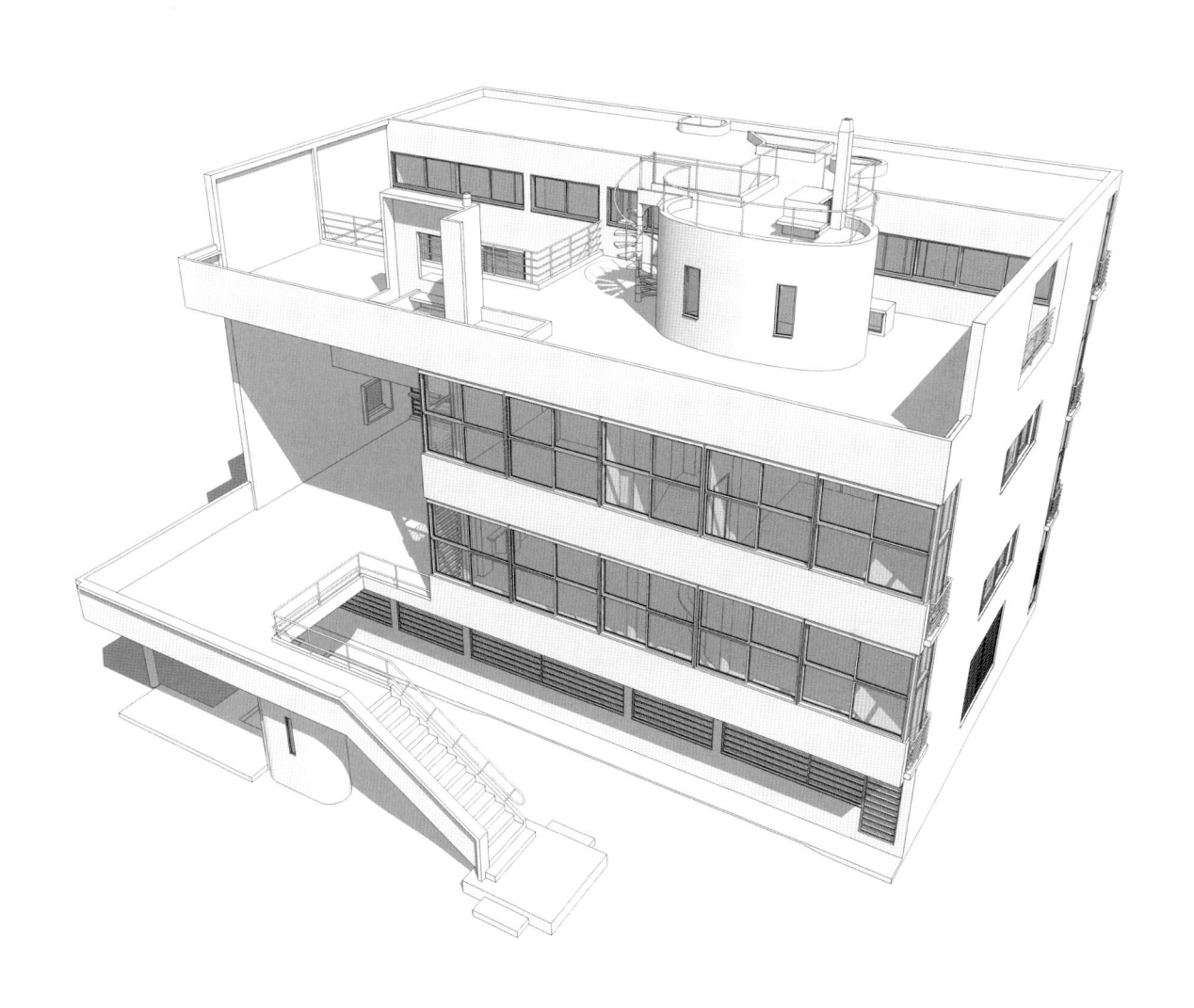

VILLA STEIN-DE MONZIE — Aerial perspective, southeast corner

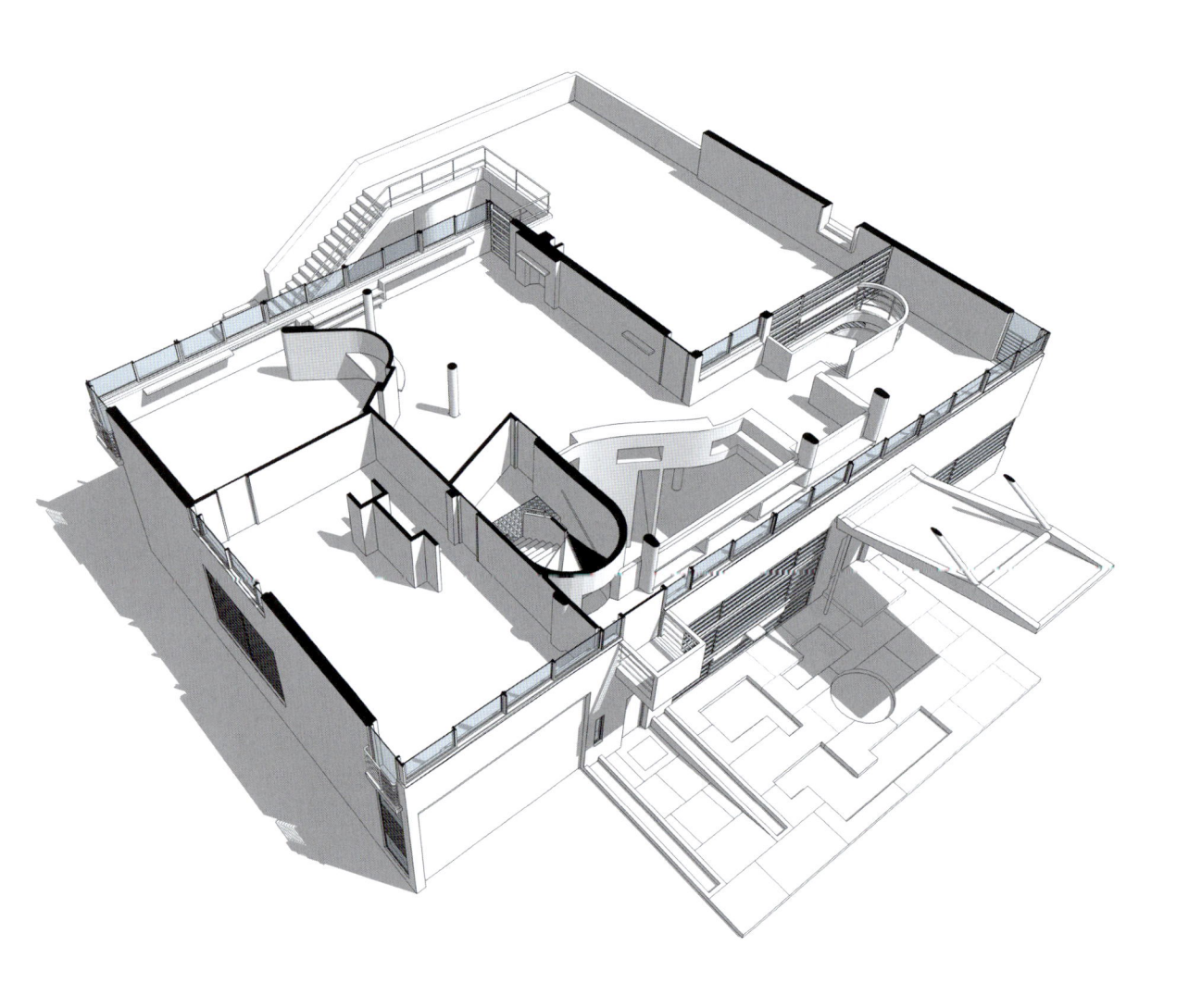

Second-floor planar perspective, northeast corner

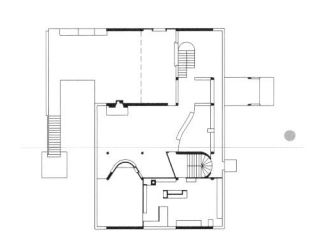

95 **VILLA STEIN-DE MONZIE**　　　　South–north sectional perspective at entrance hall

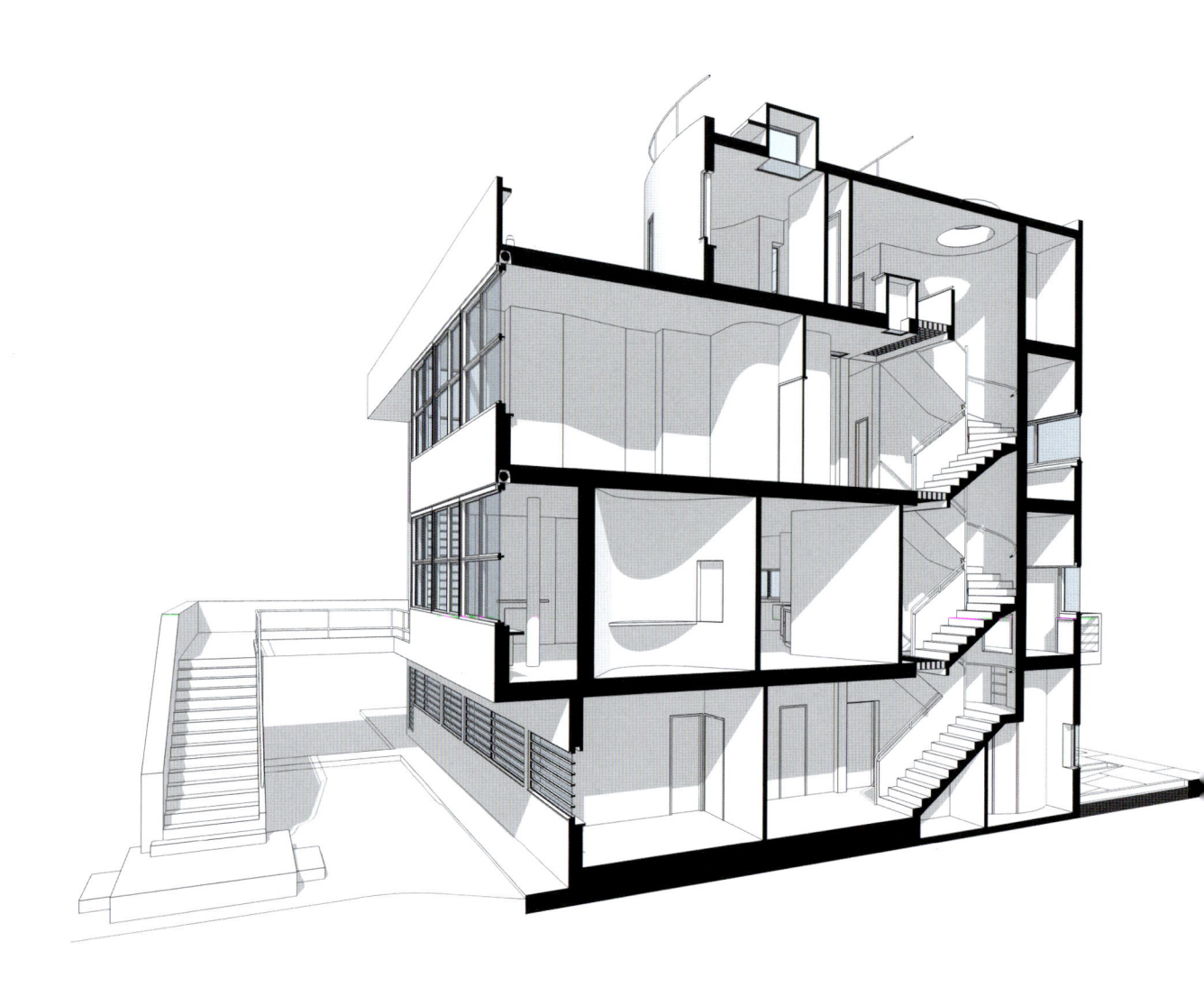

96 VILLA STEIN-DE MONZIE   South–north sectional perspective at stairs

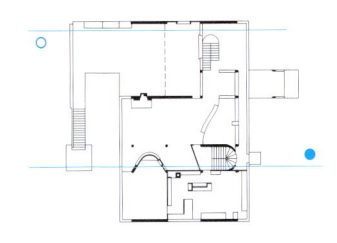

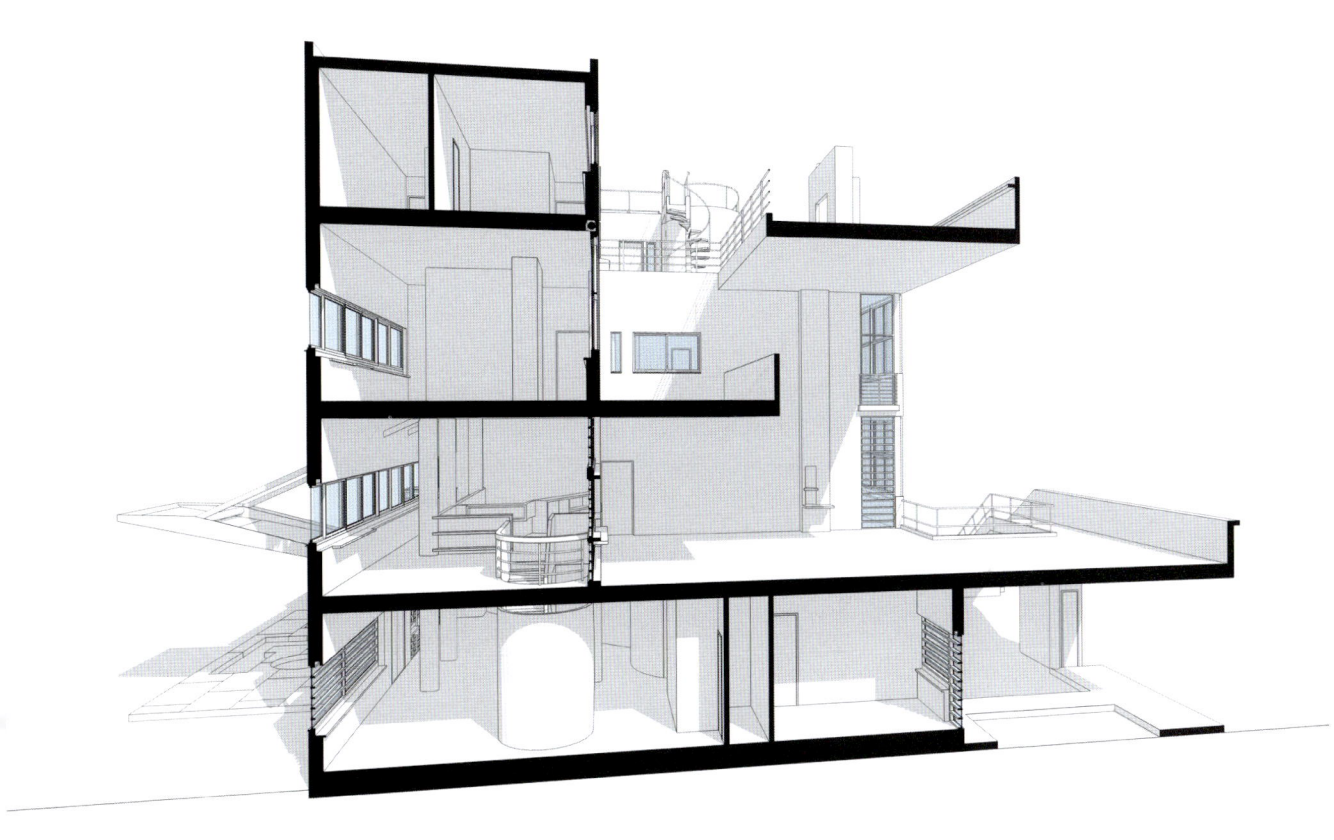

97　**VILLA STEIN-DE MONZIE**　　North-south sectional perspective at outdoor terraces

Third-floor plan
First-floor plan

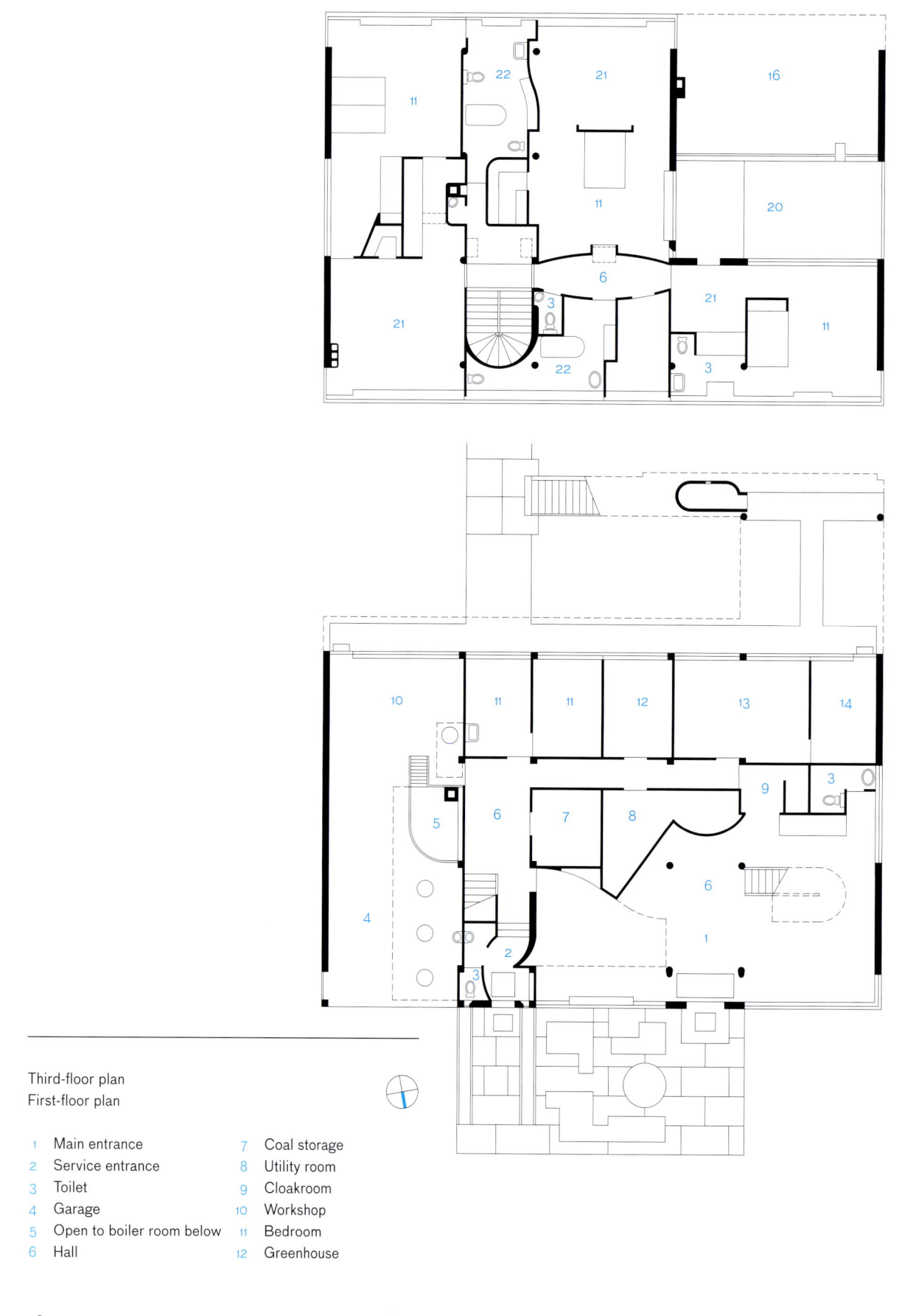

1. Main entrance
2. Service entrance
3. Toilet
4. Garage
5. Open to boiler room below
6. Hall
7. Coal storage
8. Utility room
9. Cloakroom
10. Workshop
11. Bedroom
12. Greenhouse

98 **VILLA STEIN-DE MONZIE**

Fourth-floor plan
Second-floor plan

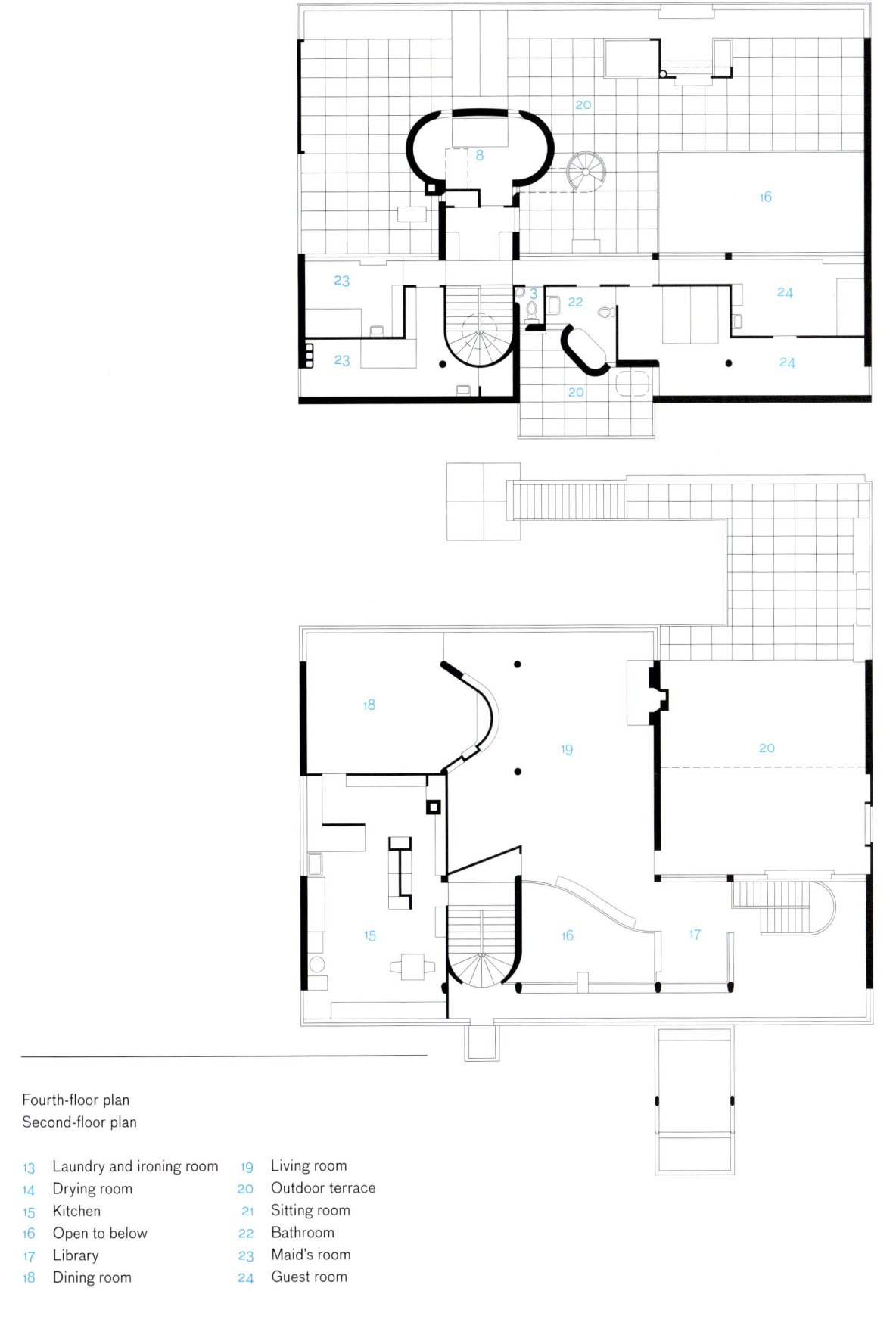

13	Laundry and ironing room	19	Living room
14	Drying room	20	Outdoor terrace
15	Kitchen	21	Sitting room
16	Open to below	22	Bathroom
17	Library	23	Maid's room
18	Dining room	24	Guest room

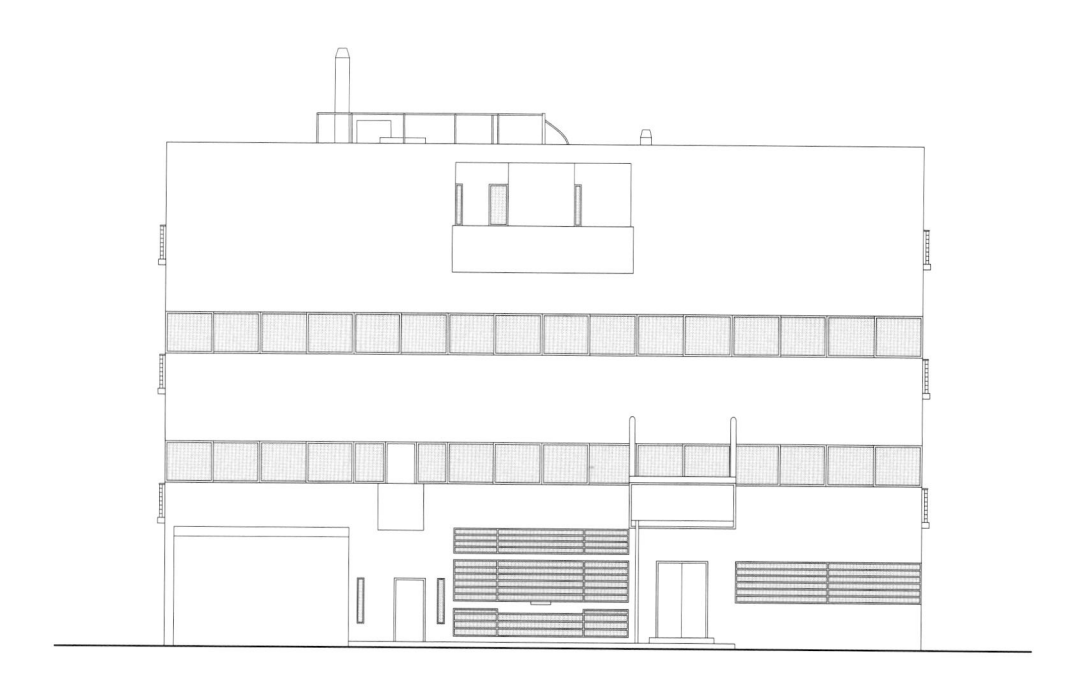

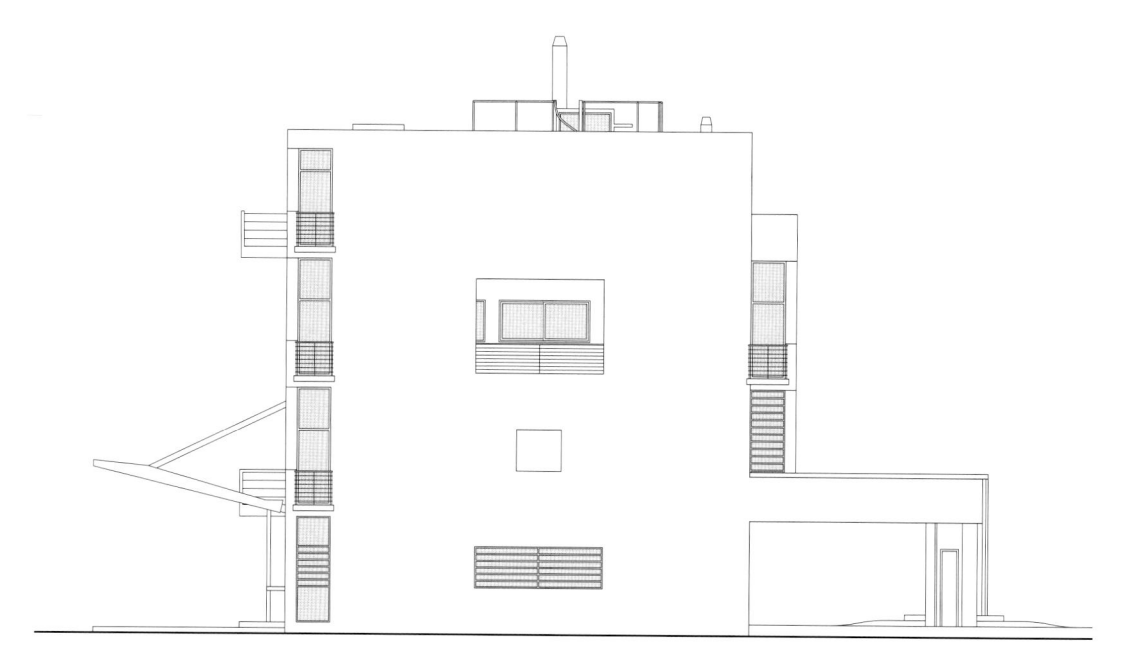

North elevation
West elevation

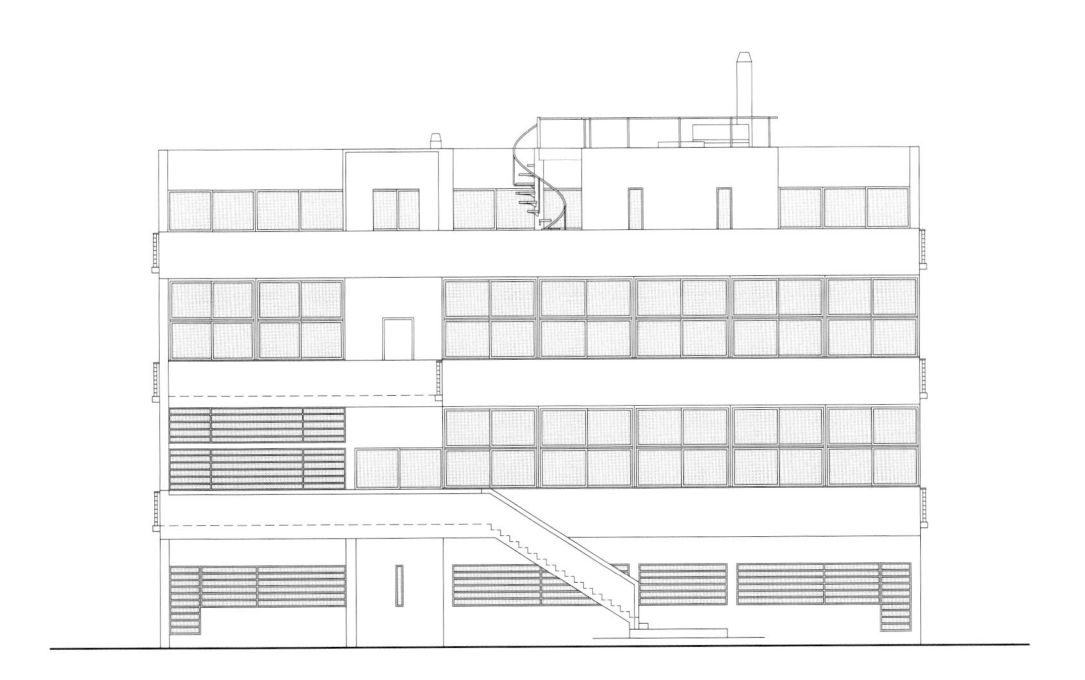

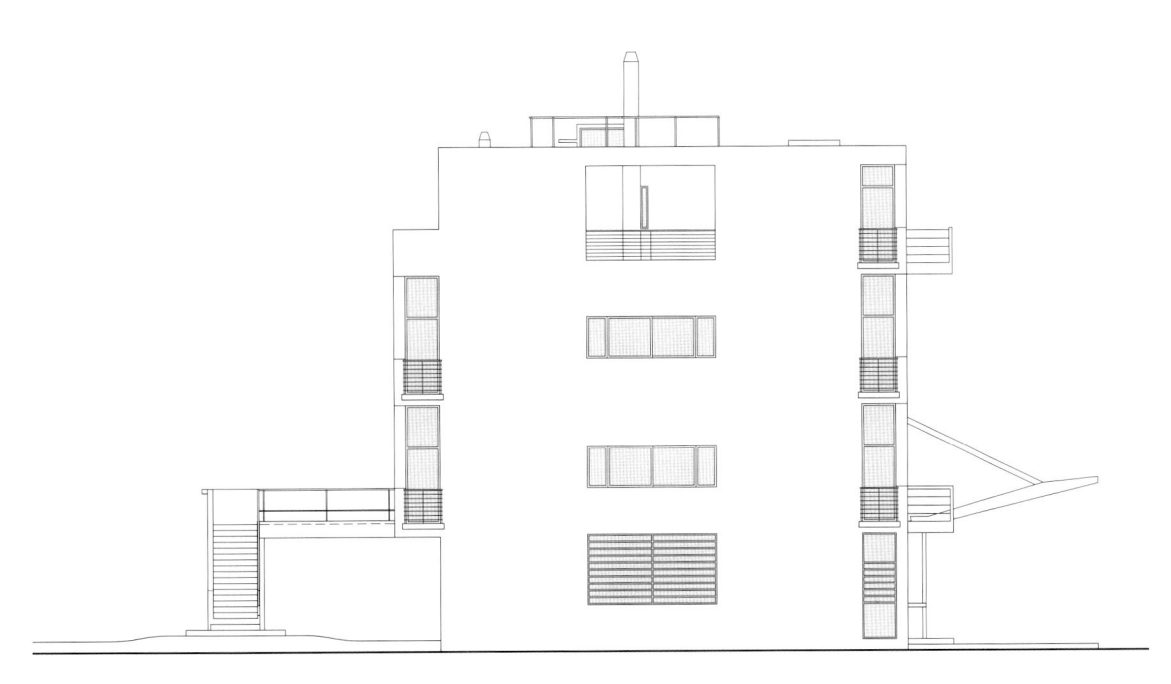

South elevation
East elevation

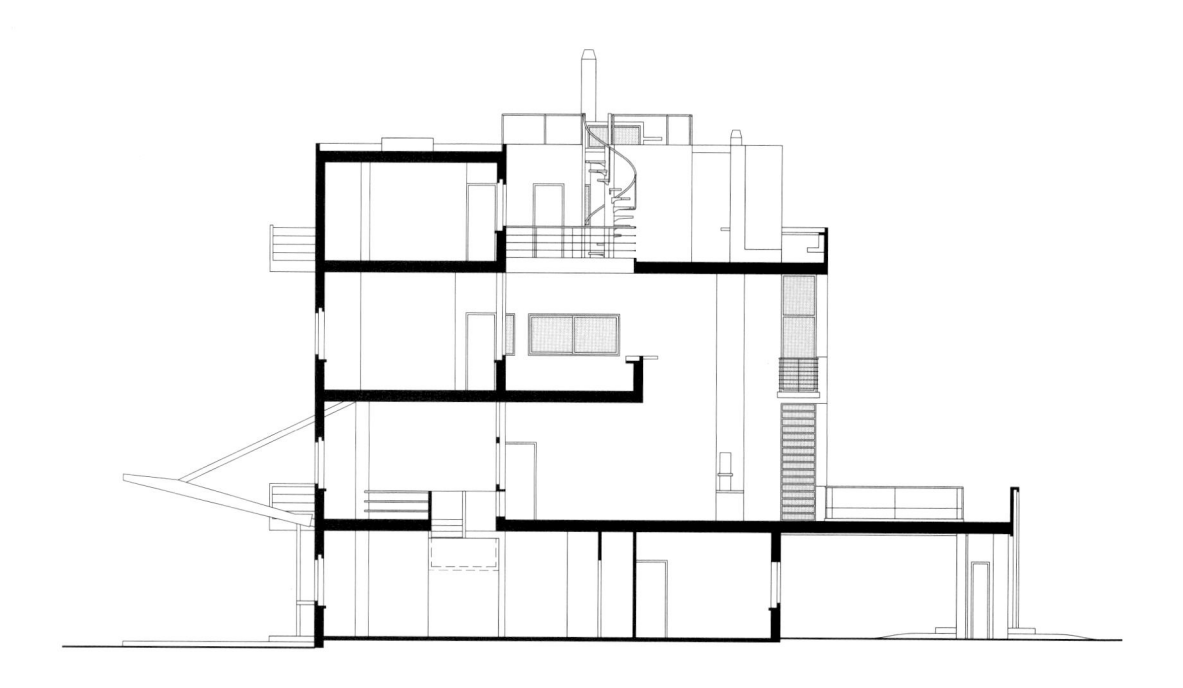

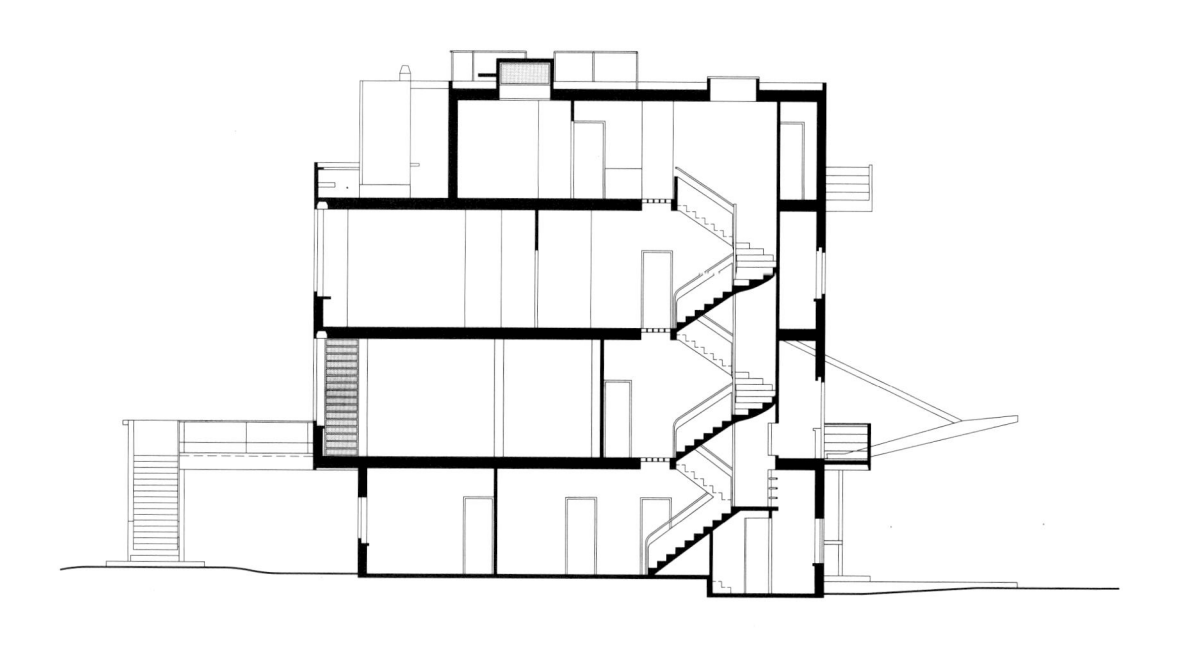

North–south section
South–north section

102 **VILLA STEIN-DE MONZIE**

Site plan (1:1000)

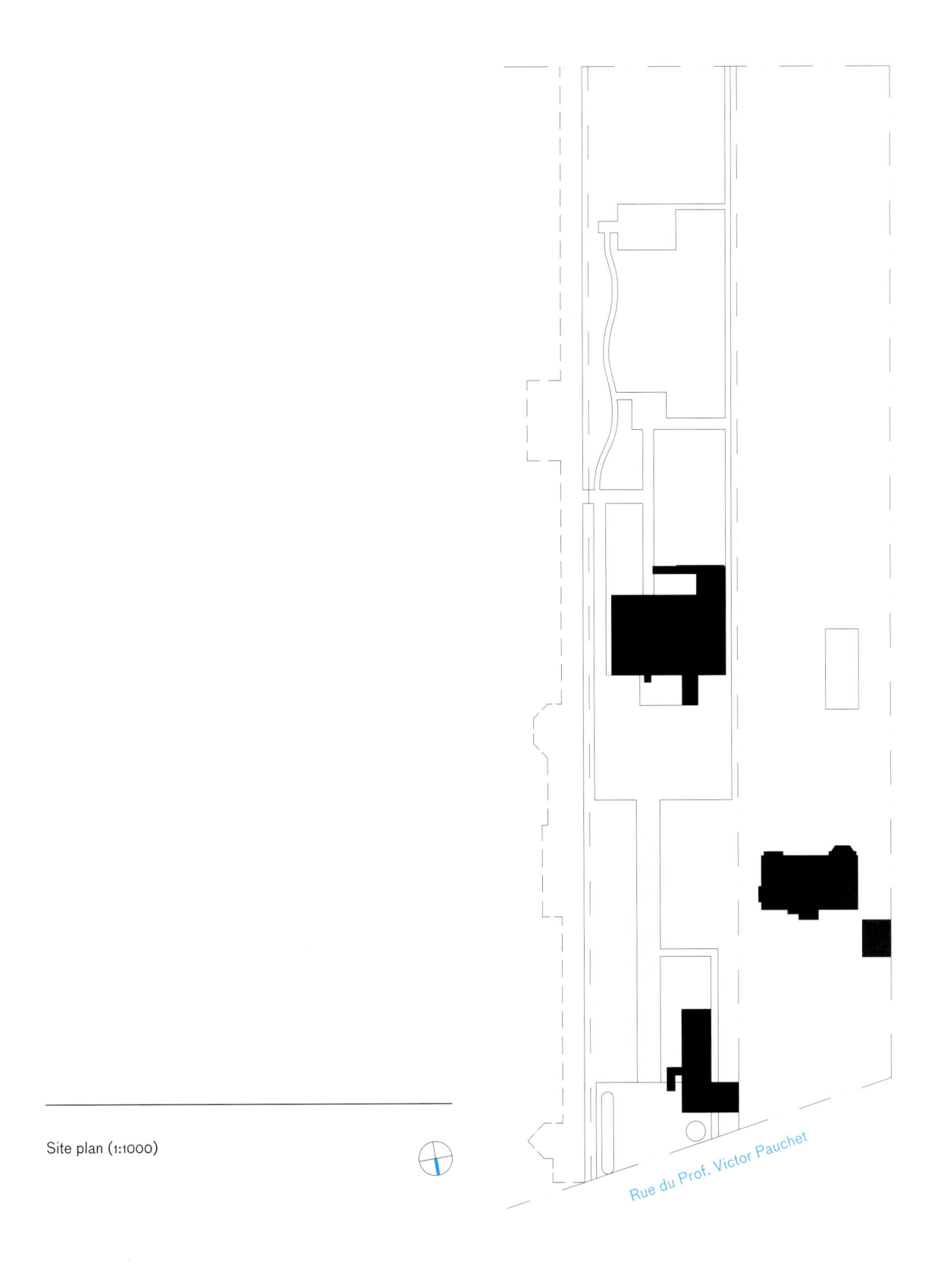

Rue du Prof. Victor Pauchet

103　**VILLA STEIN-DE MONZIE**

VILLA CHURCH NO. 1

LOCATION: Ville-d'Avray, a western suburb of Paris, France
DATE: 1927

A wealthy American couple who were tenants on a large estate commissioned Le Corbusier to design three separate projects as renovations of and additions to existing buildings. Villa Church No. 1, located near the main house, was the replacement of an existing stable with a summer house for guests. The stable was demolished and a new superstructure, following its existing L-shaped layout, was built on the remaining foundations. It conforms to and marks the western edge of the site with a fortresslike elevation along the property line; the interior spaces face an entrance court with views of the main house set within beautifully landscaped gardens.

Different programs are clearly articulated as distinct cubic volumes of white mass: a living room with a library on a mezzanine as a two-story volume at one end of the house, bedrooms as an elongated volume with roof trellis and an annex of maids' bedrooms at the other end, and kitchen and dining rooms as a recessed connecting volume in the middle. One of the most distinctive features of the house is its luxurious roof garden. With Villa Church No. 1, Le Corbusier successfully incorporated into existing settings all the elements of his Five Points of a New Architecture, demonstrating their flexibility and adaptability.

CLIENTS: Barbara and Henry Church
PROGRAM: Replacement of an existing stable with a guesthouse
FEATURES: Roof terrace, trellis, double-height space, strip windows

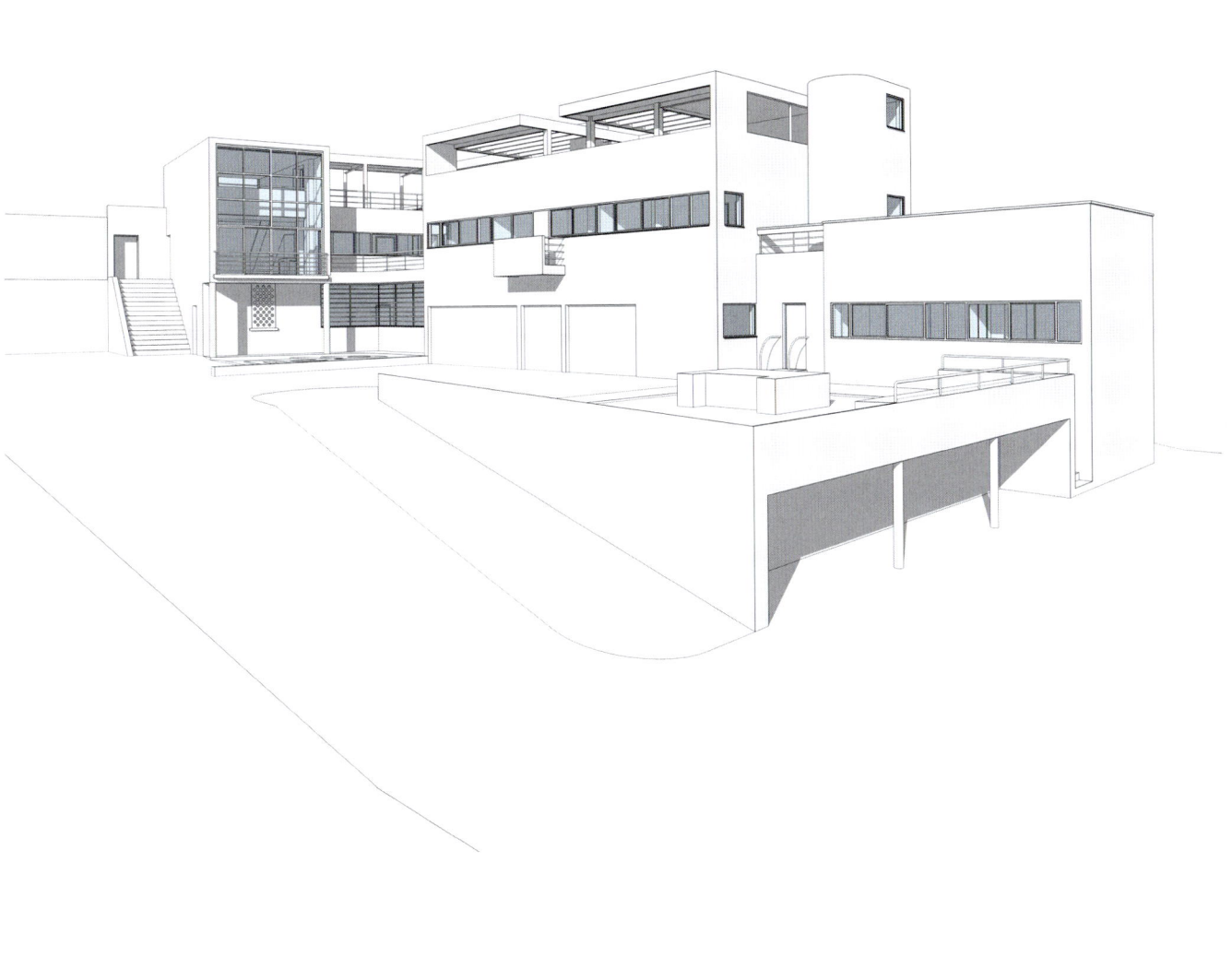

VILLA CHURCH NO. 1 — Exterior perspective, northeast corner

Aerial perspective, northeast corner

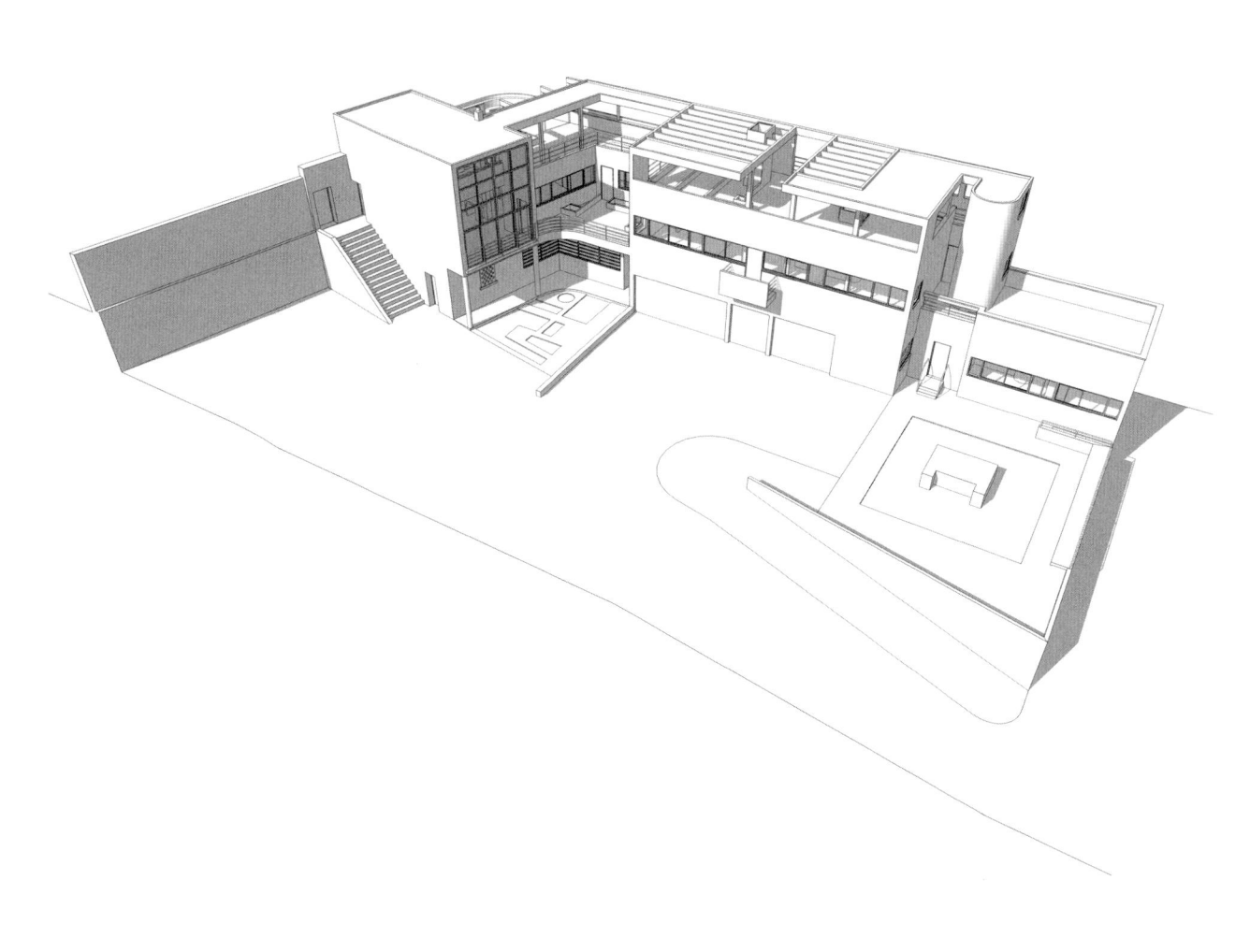

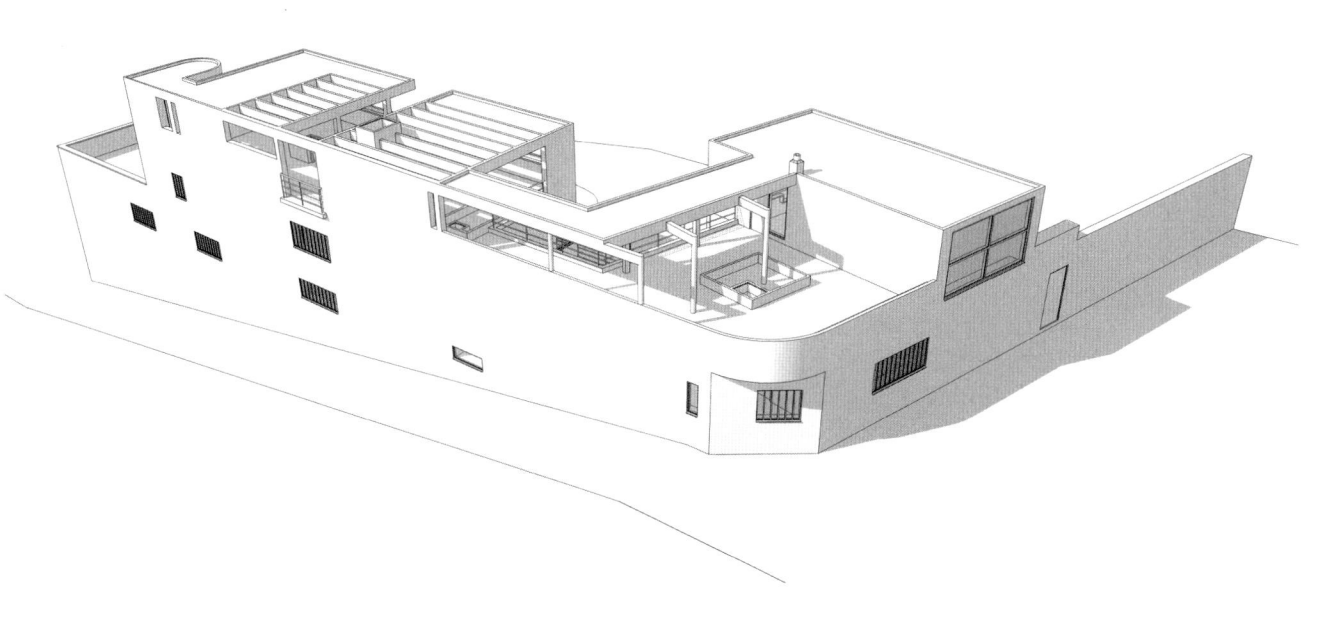

VILLA CHURCH NO. 1 — Aerial perspective, southwest corner

VILLA CHURCH NO. 1

East–west sectional perspective at entrance hall

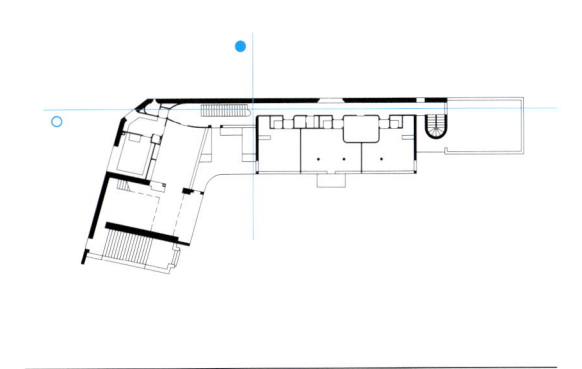

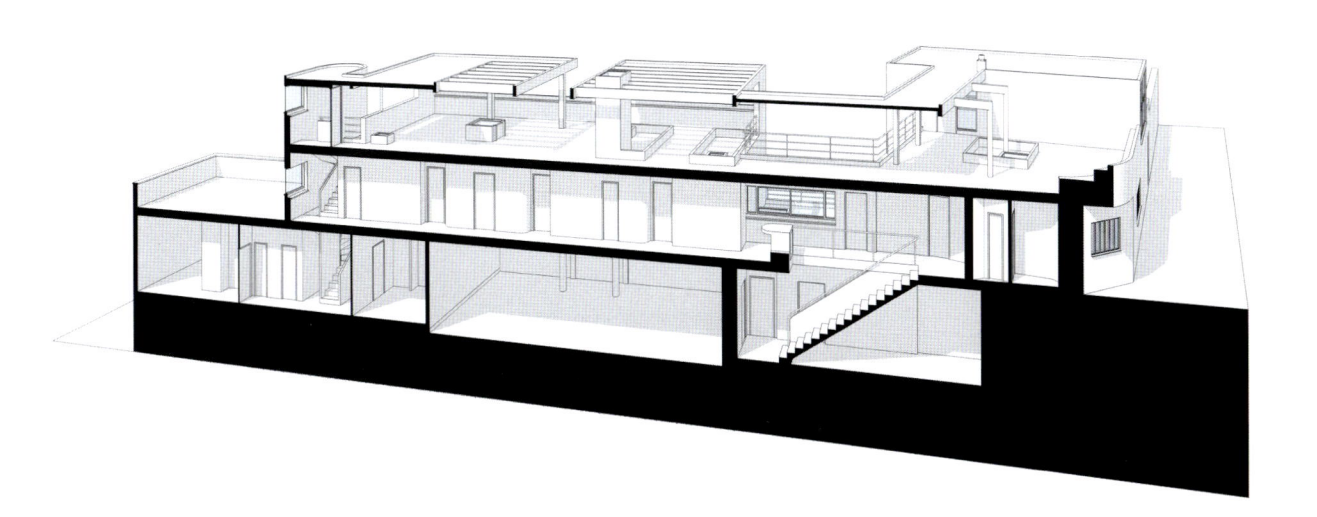

109 VILLA CHURCH NO. 1 — North–south sectional perspective at corridor

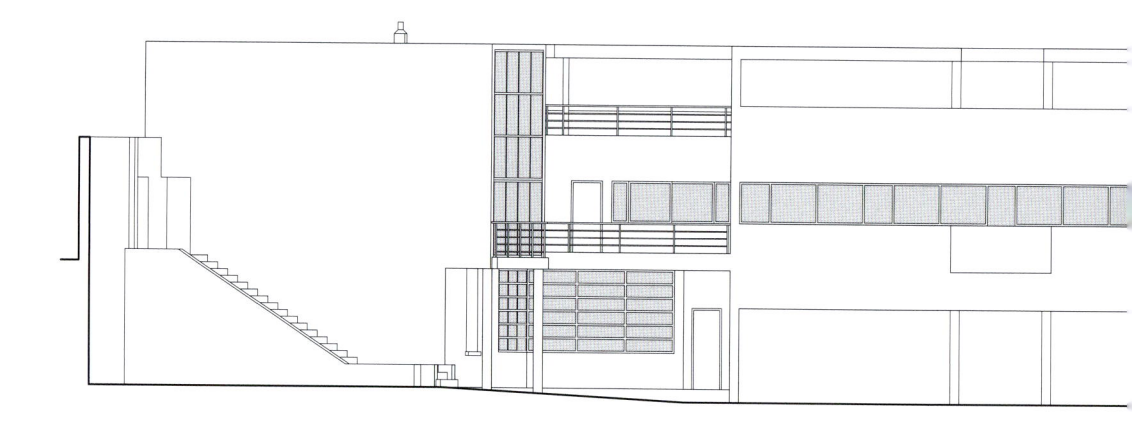

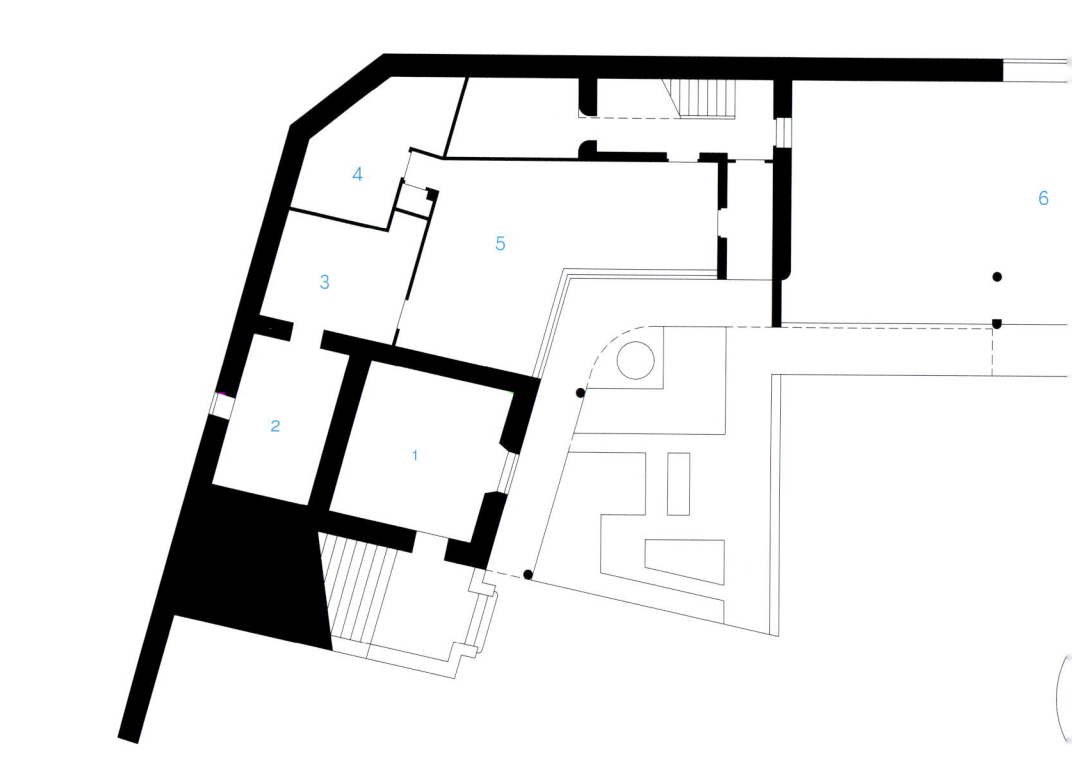

East elevation
First-floor plan

1. Cellar
2. Coal storage
3. Boiler room
4. Drying room
5. Laundry and ironing room
6. Garage
7. Chauffeur's room
8. Maid's room
9. Bathroom

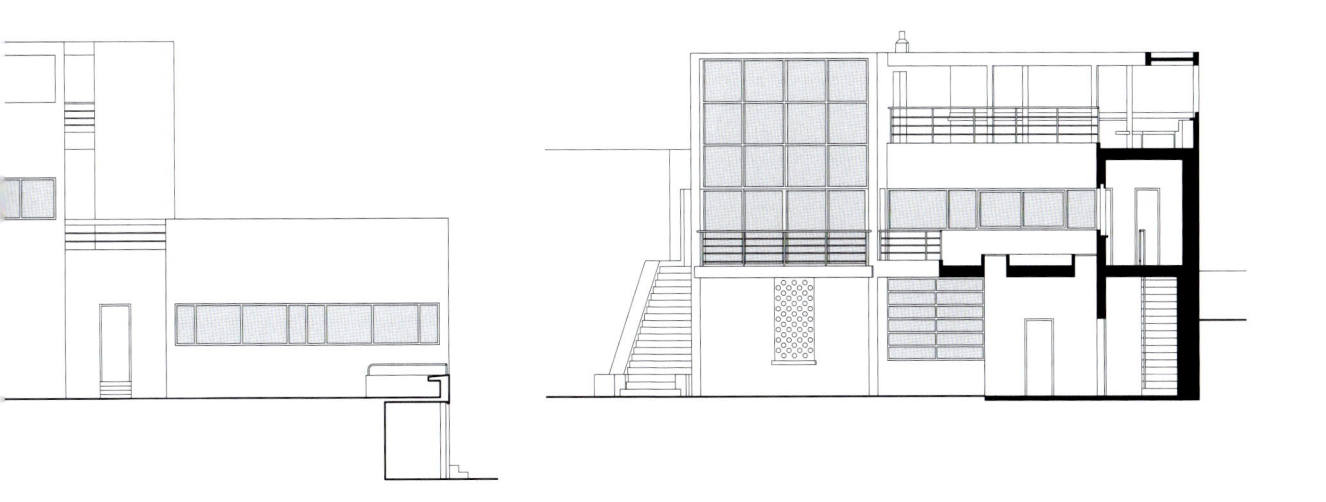

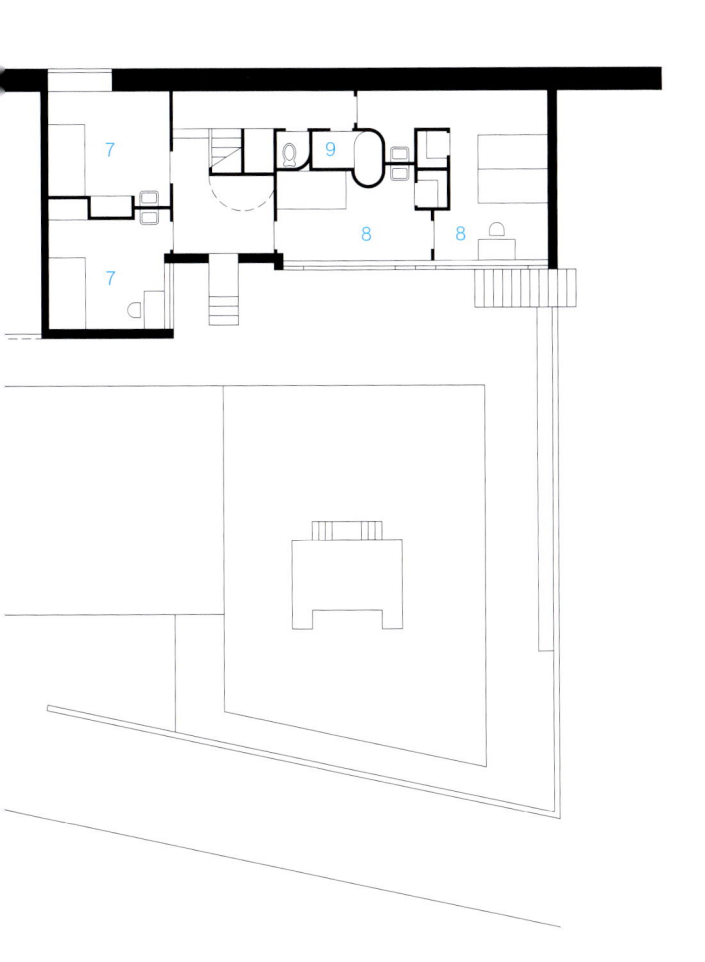

East–west section

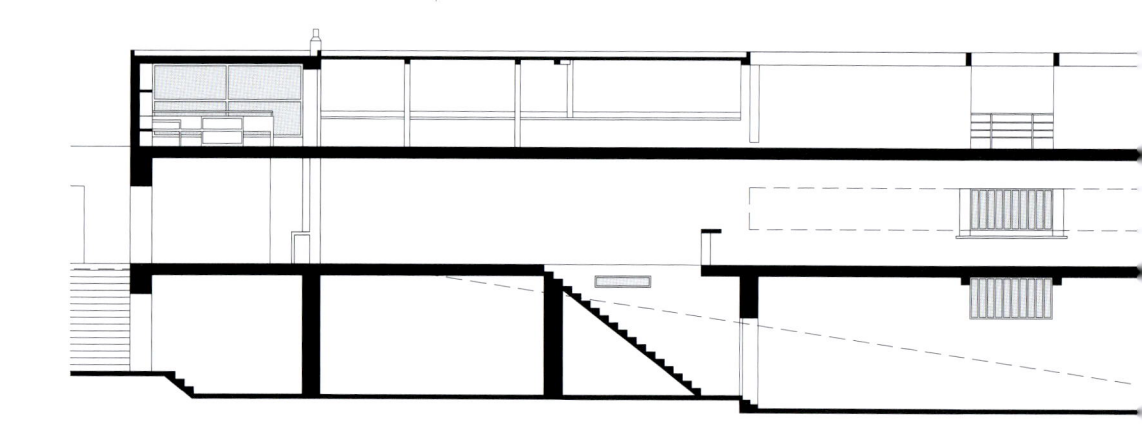

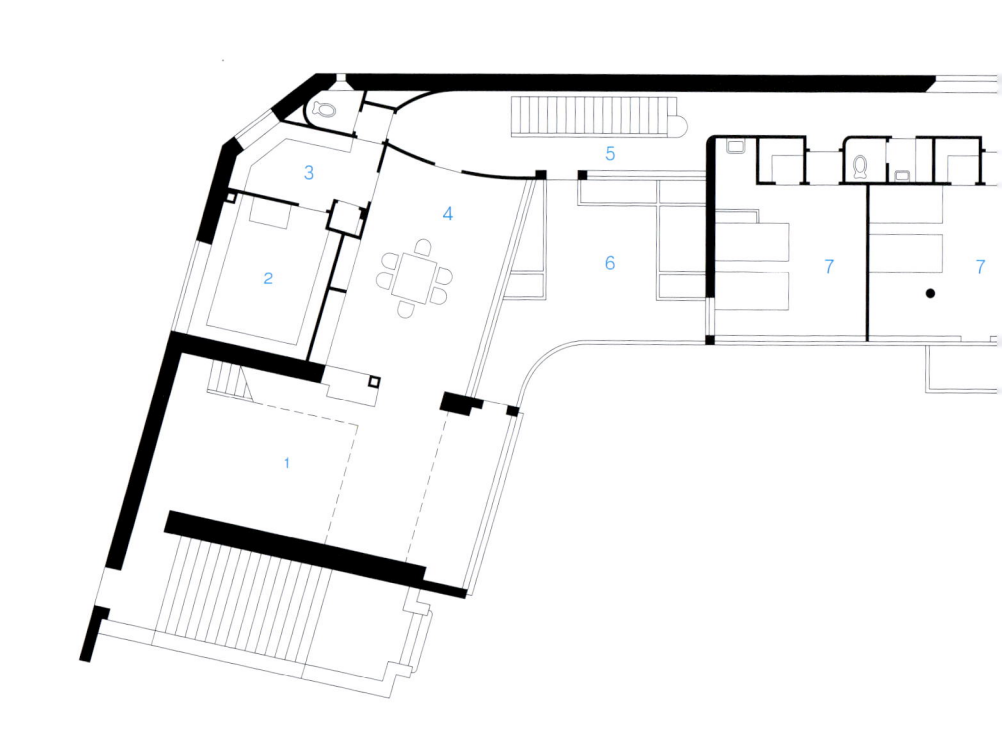

South–north section
Second-floor plan

1 Living room
2 Kitchen
3 Pantry
4 Dining room
5 Hall
6 Outdoor terrace
7 Bedroom
8 Bathroom

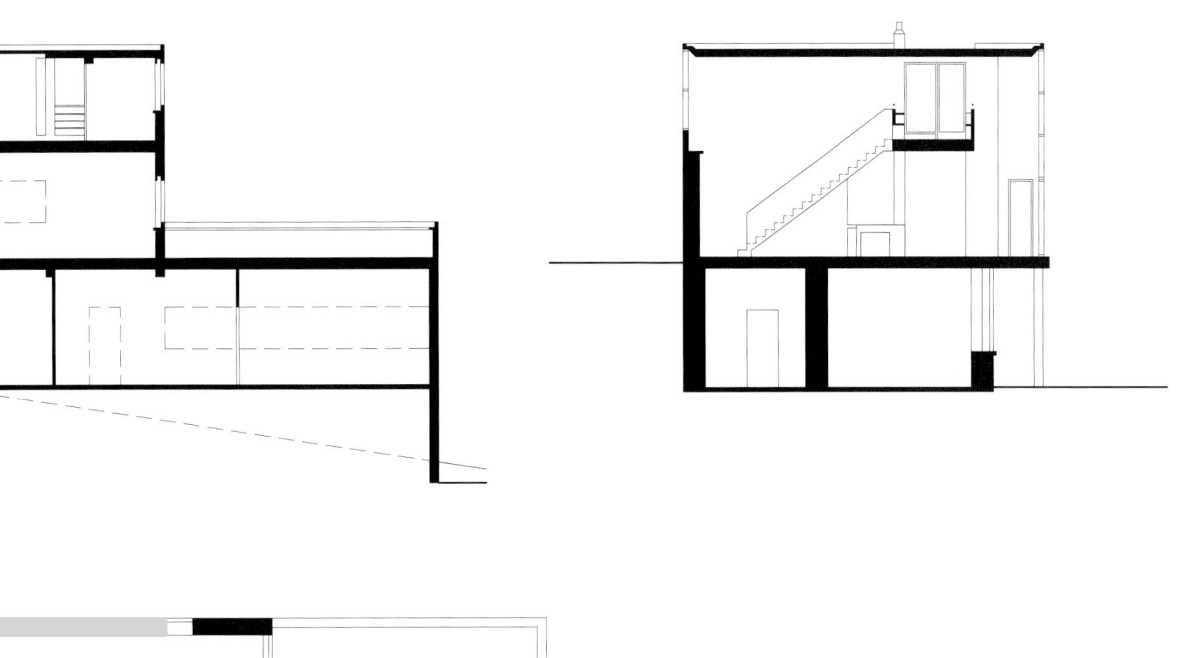

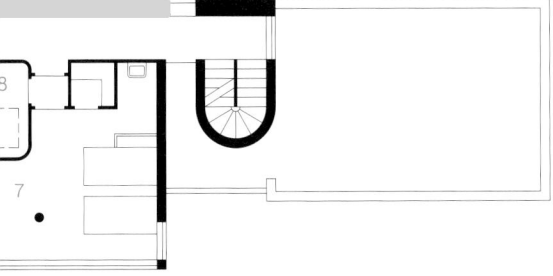

South–north section

VILLA CHURCH NO. 2

LOCATION: Ville-d'Avray, a western suburb of Paris, France
DATE: 1927

Villa Church No. 2 was a project to renovate an existing neoclassical villa into a music and dance pavilion for entertaining guests. Throughout much of the first floor, the existing exterior walls remained intact. Due to existing site conditions with irregular contours and a large elevational drop, the architect devised a bridge to connect the main house to the music pavilion. The entrance to the pavilion was on the second floor through a roof garden. By carefully selecting the size, shape, and location of openings, Le Corbusier directed natural light to interior spaces to define their unique characters and framed views to both inside and outside to direct the occupants' journey through the pavilion. The bridge provides panoramic views around the estate and creates a sensation of being suspended in the air with no barrier between man and nature, heightening one's awareness of the surrounding landscape.

Whereas Le Corbusier had failed to persuade his clients at the Villa Stein-de Monzie to equip their house with modern furniture, here he succeeded: the interior of the music pavilion housed the first group of chairs, tables, and cabinets completely designed by Le Corbusier and his onetime collaborator Charlotte Perriand. Although Le Corbusier's fruitful professional relationship with Perriand would last for nearly ten years, his relationship with Barbara and Henry Church became strained due to cost overruns and disagreements over fees.

CLIENTS: Barbara and Henry Church
PROGRAM: Renovation of an existing villa into a music and dance pavilion
FEATURES: Roof terrace, double-height space, bridge, grand stair, strip windows

VILLA CHURCH NO. 2 Exterior perspective, south elevation

Aerial perspective, southwest corner

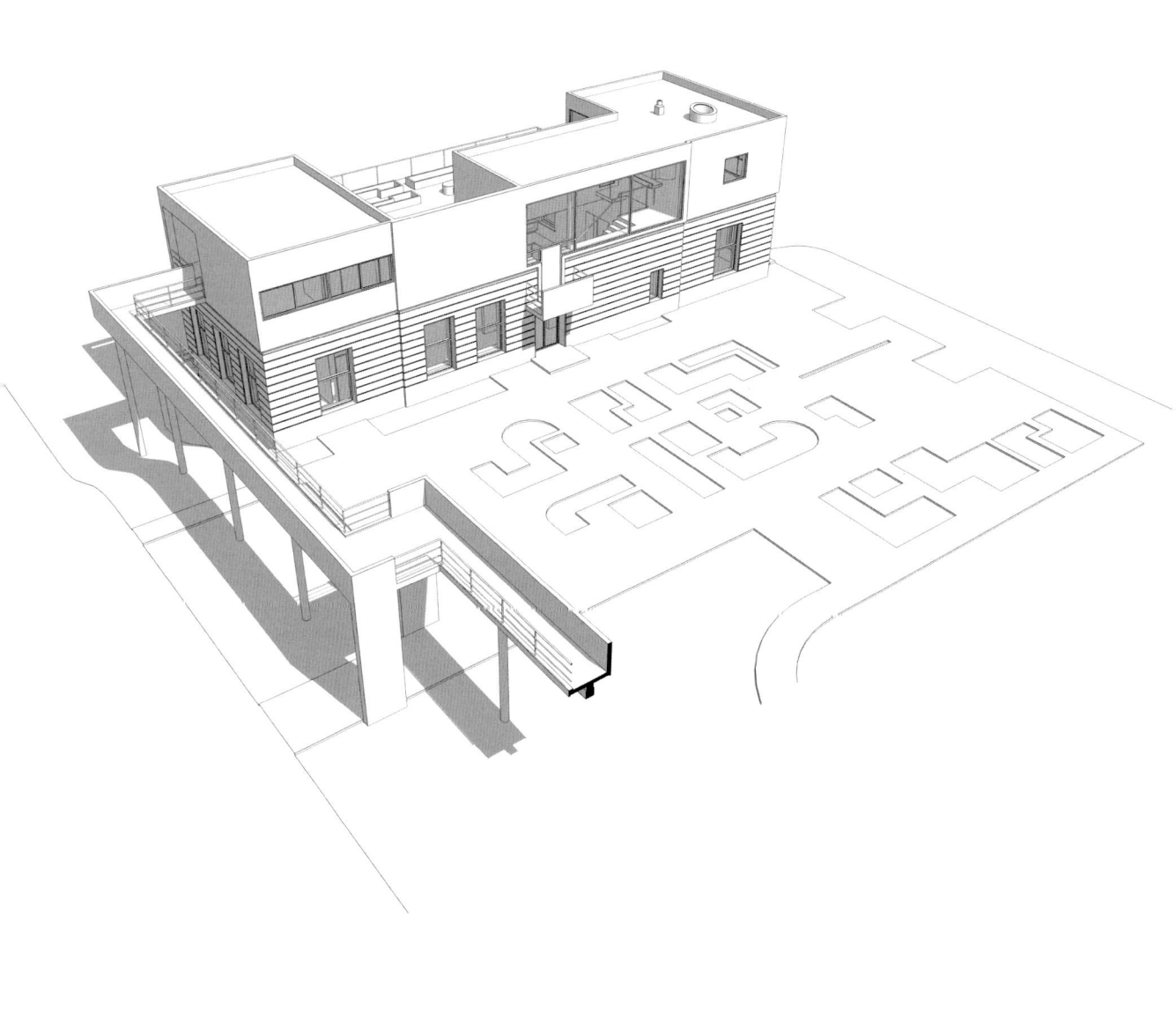

Aerial perspective, northwest corner

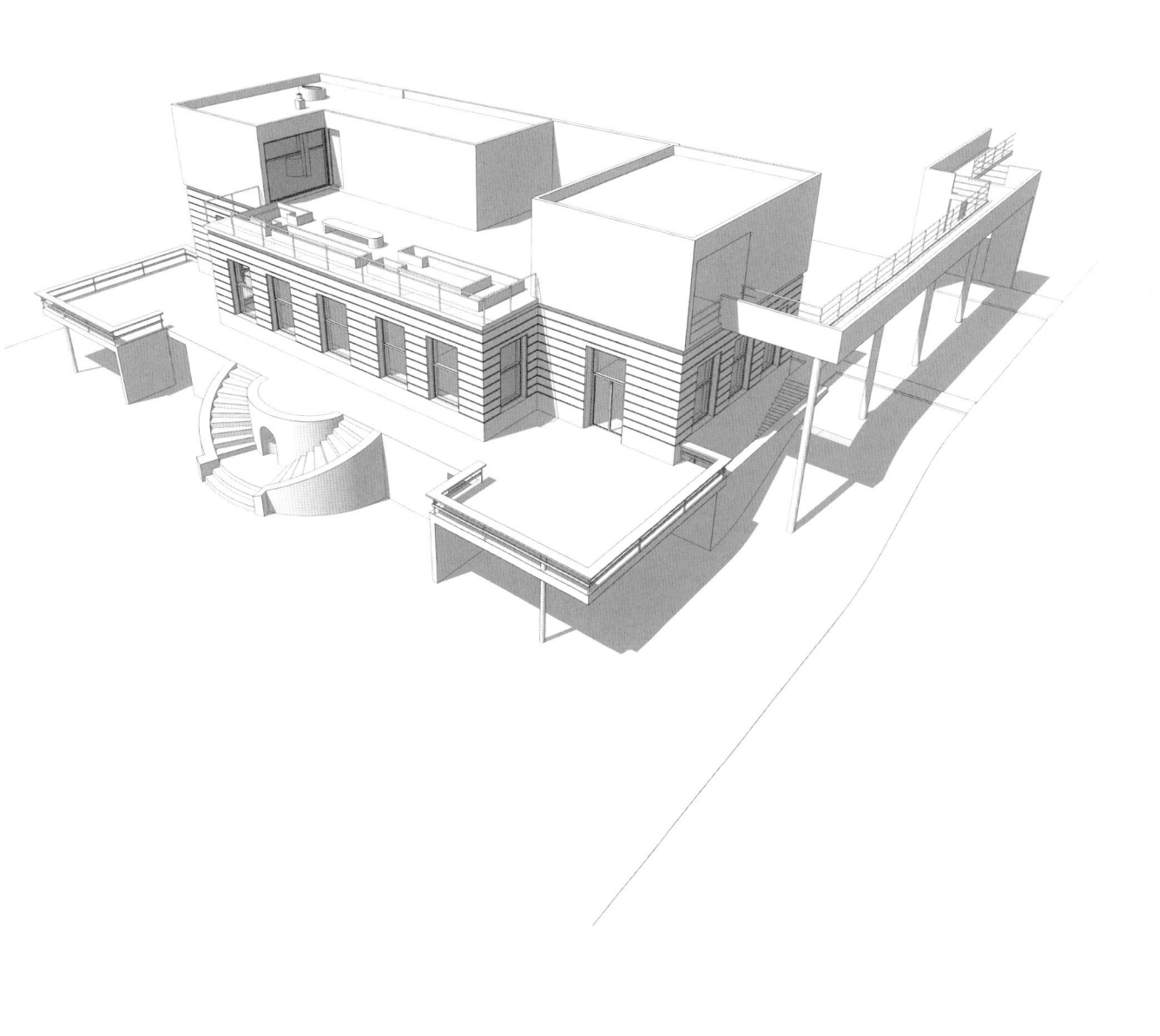

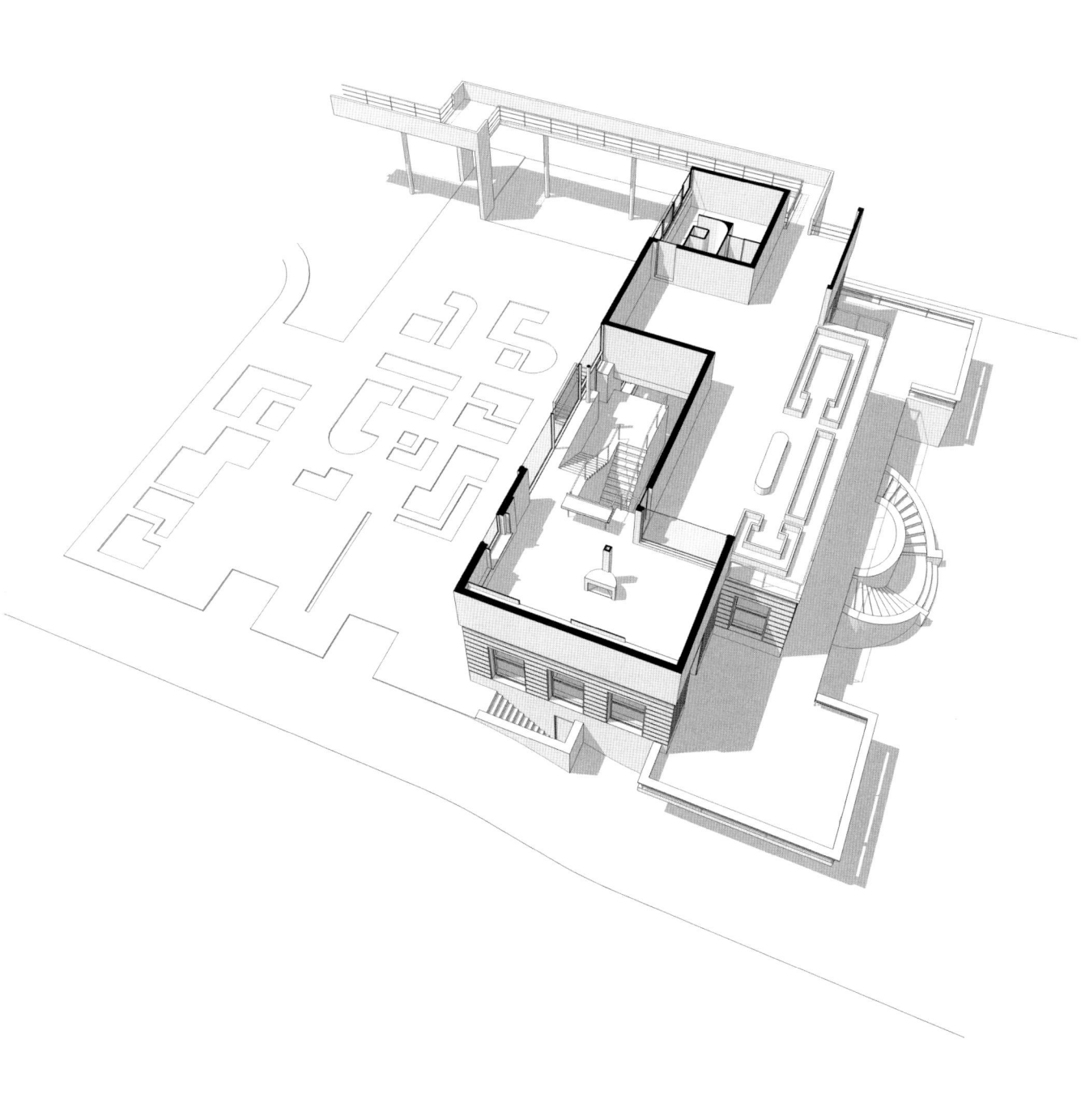

Second-floor planar perspective showing east elevation

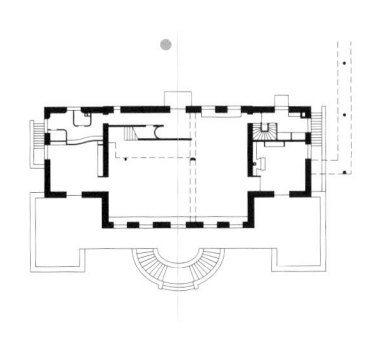

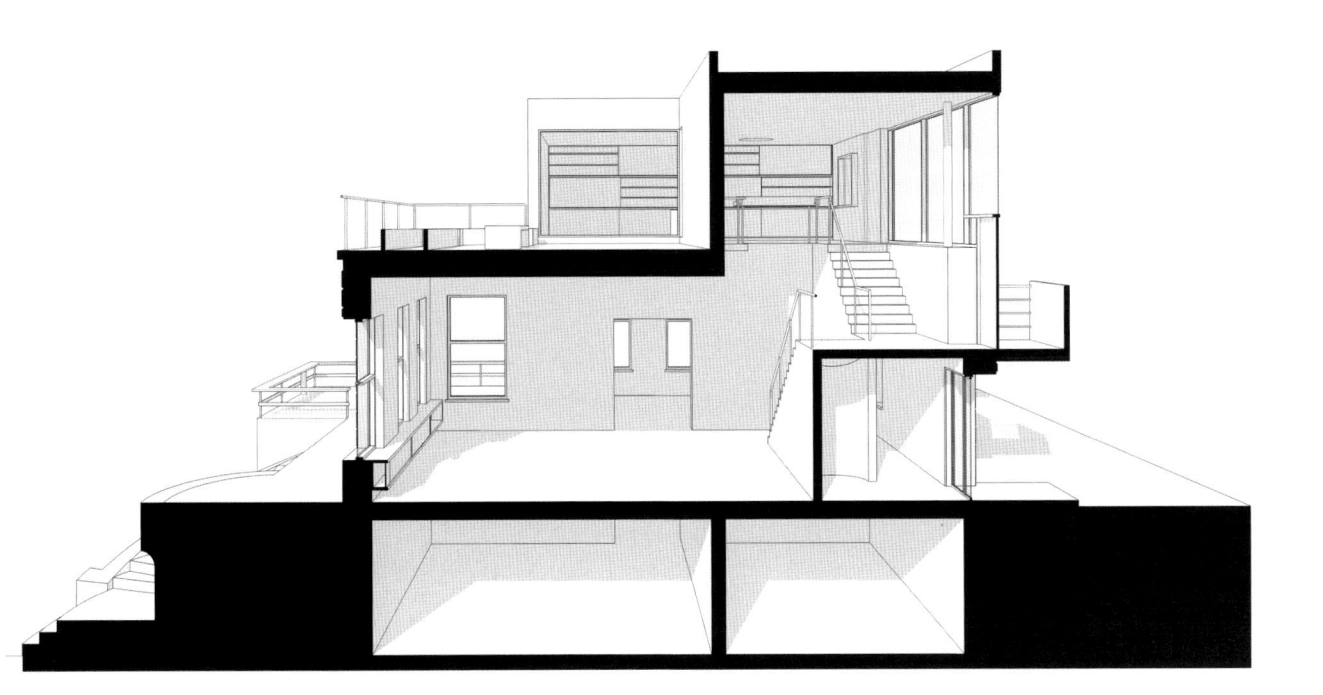

VILLA CHURCH NO. 2 — North–south sectional perspective at stairs

East–west sectional perspective at stairs

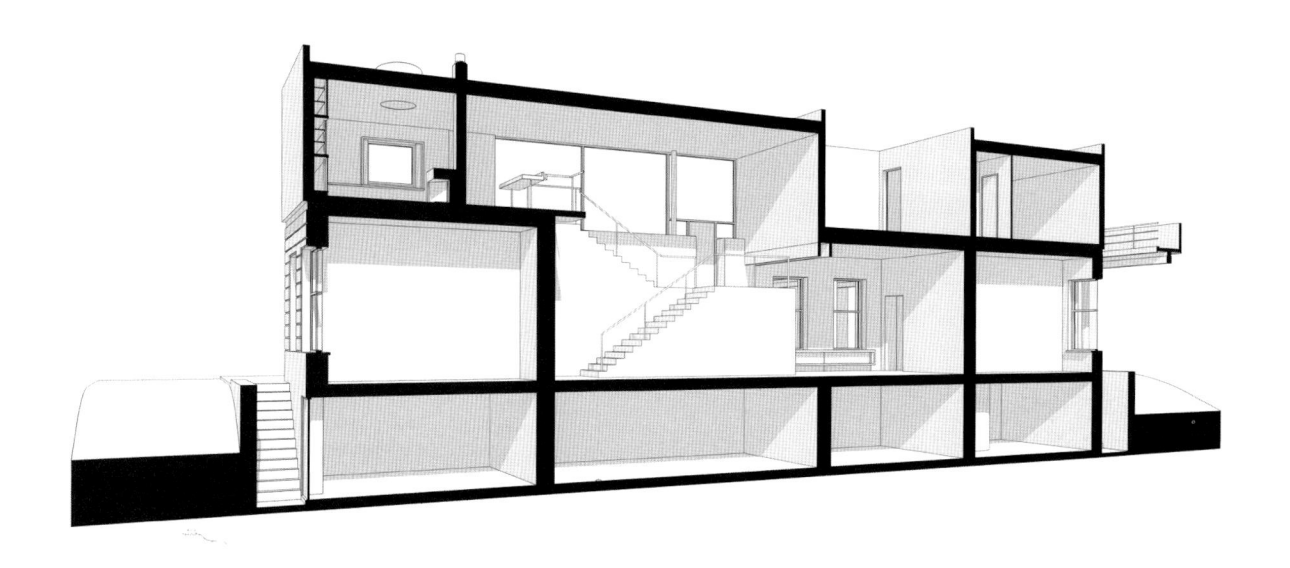

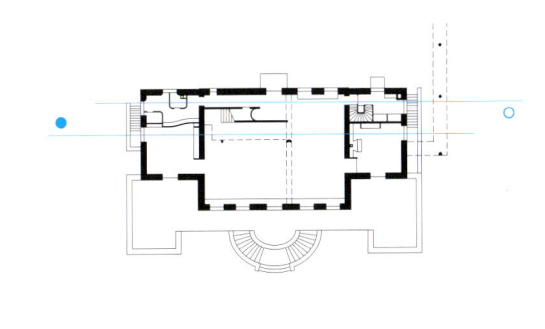

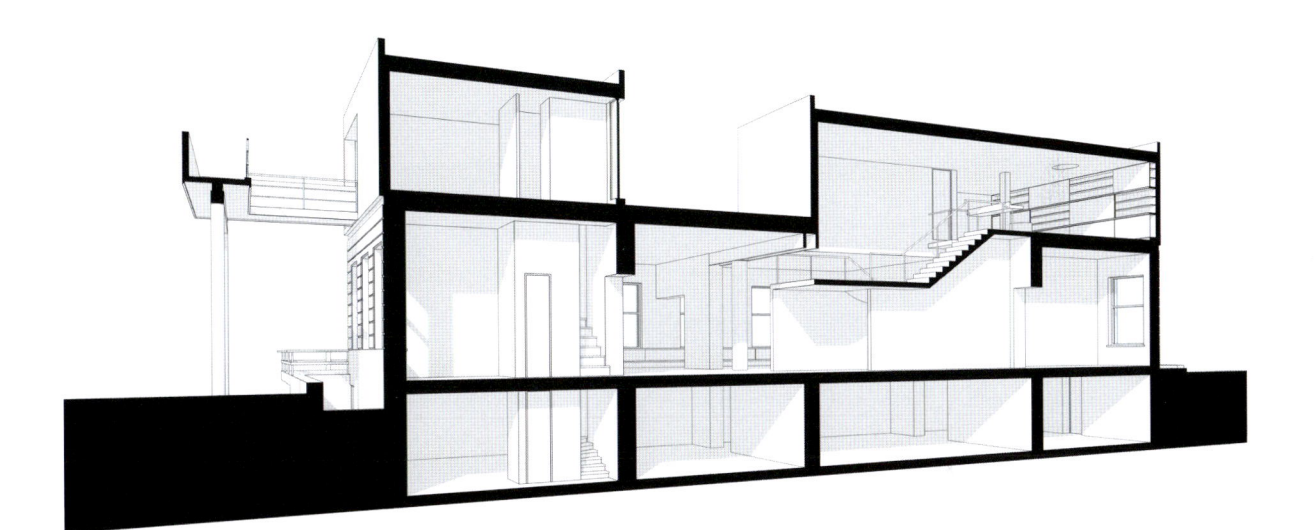

121 **VILLA CHURCH NO. 2**   O   West–east sectional perspective at stairs

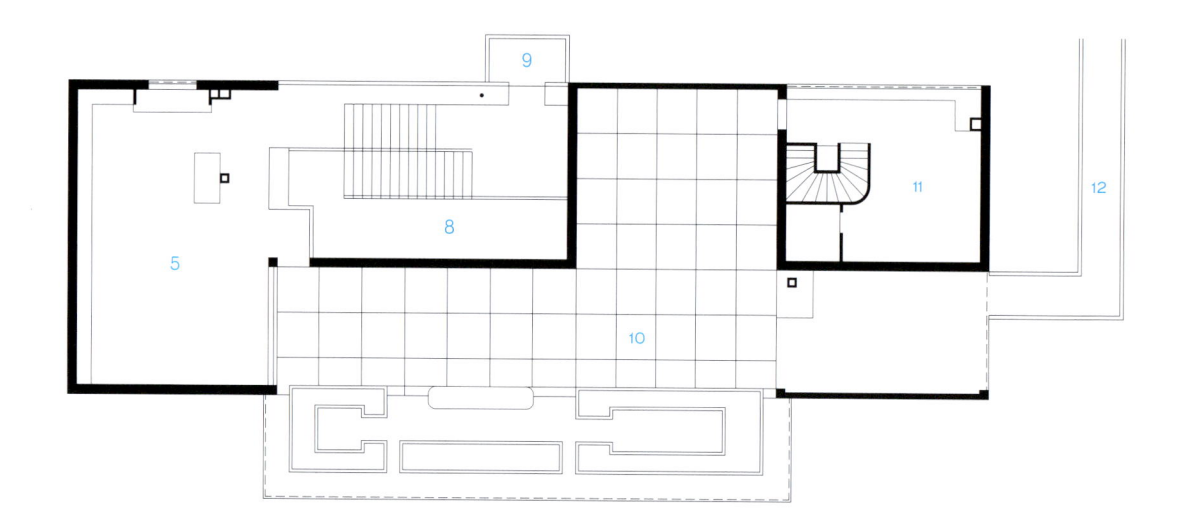

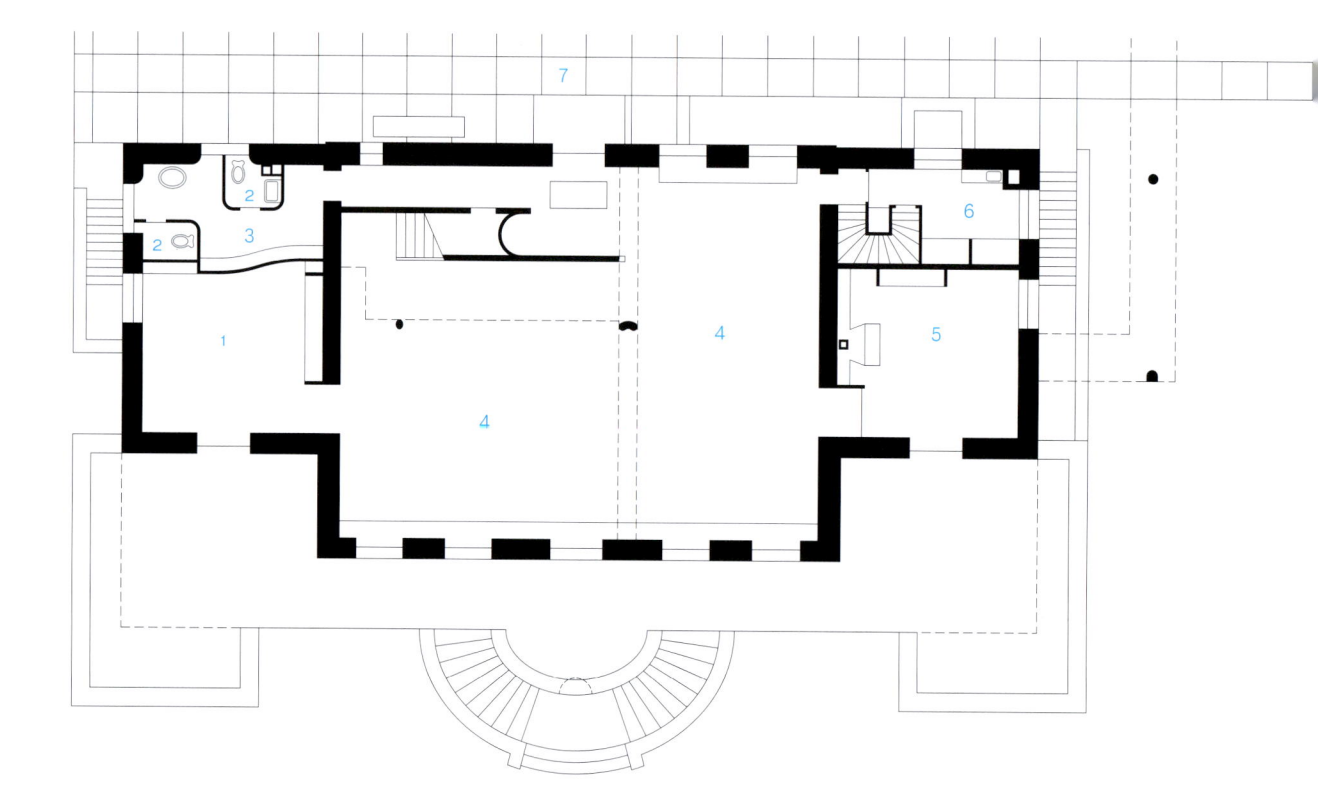

Second-floor plan
First-floor plan

1. Workroom
2. Toilet
3. Cloakroom
4. Music and dance hall
5. Library
6. Utility room
7. Garden
8. Open to below
9. Balcony
10. Roof terrace
11. Office
12. Bridge

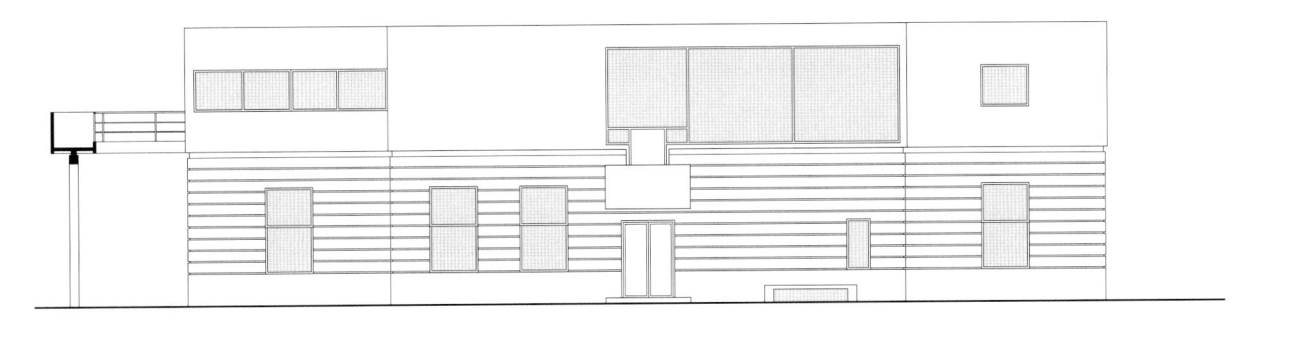

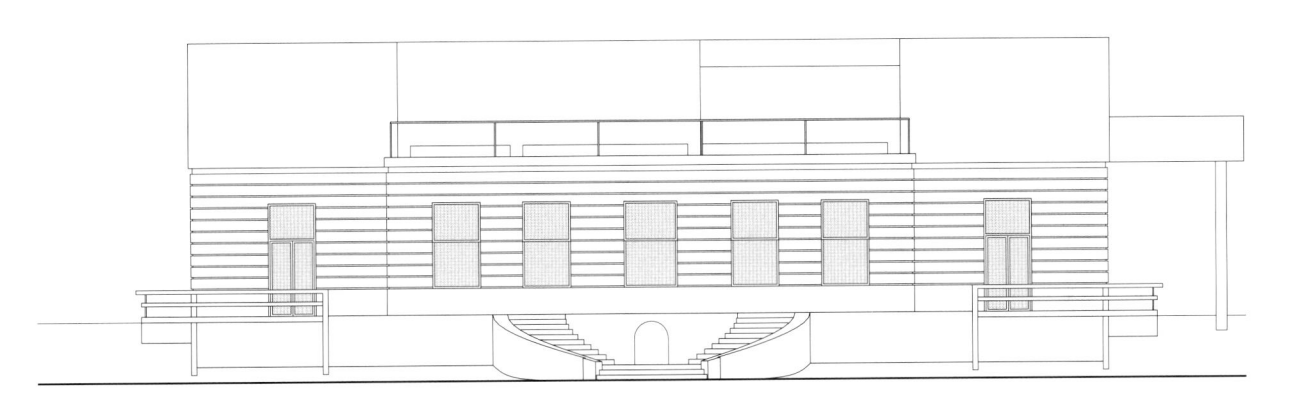

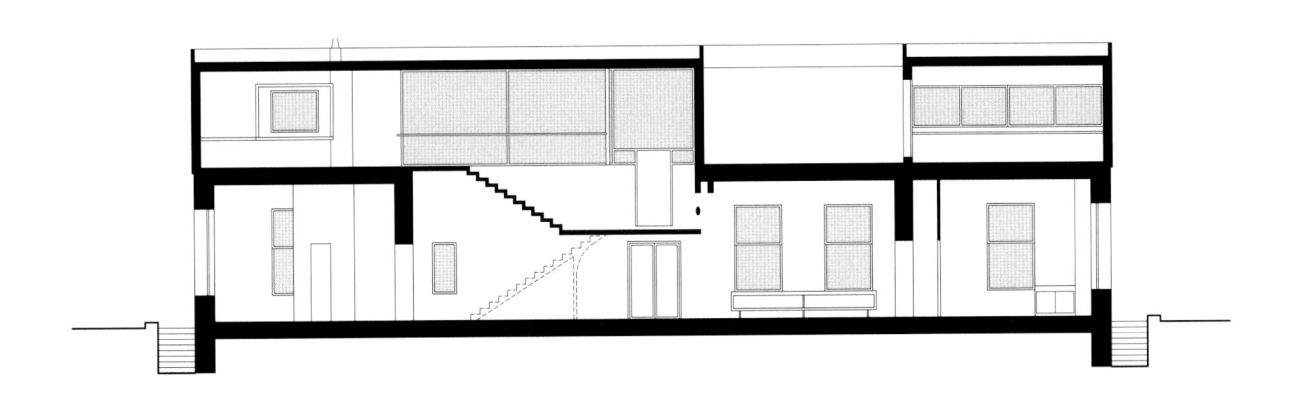

South elevation
North elevation
East–west section

14 WEISSENHOFSIEDLUNG VILLA NO. 1

LOCATION: Stuttgart, Germany
DATE: 1927

This is the first of two houses that Le Corbusier designed for the Weissenhofsiedlung (Deutscher Werkbund exhibition) in Stuttgart in 1927. At that time Mies van der Rohe was the exhibit director and president of the Werkbund, and he invited Le Corbusier to participate in the experimental modern housing development. Since Le Corbusier was considered a leading figure in the modernist movement by his international contemporaries, he was given a prominent site at the edge of the estate, overlooking the hill and city below.

Weissenhofsiedlung Villa No. 1 was designed as a single-family residence, and its significance derives from its strict formal adherence to Le Corbusier's Maison Citrohan housing prototype. Le Corbusier also took this opportunity to demonstrate again in full scale his Five Points of a New Architecture. Because the house was raised on *pilotis*, the outdoor garden on the ground level could flow around it, integrating the house with its surroundings. Although the overall massing of the residence is a simple cube, the design has a strong sense of diagonal movement created through offset internal circulation, an asymmetrical arrangement of interior spaces and windows, and simple yet important detailing such as a steel pipe at the roof that opens up a corner. The result is a dynamic and complex articulation of the basic cubic form.

CLIENT: Deutscher Werkbund
PROGRAM: Experimental housing prototype for a single-family residence
FEATURES: Adherence to the Five Points of a New Architecture, elements from the Maison Citrohan prototype

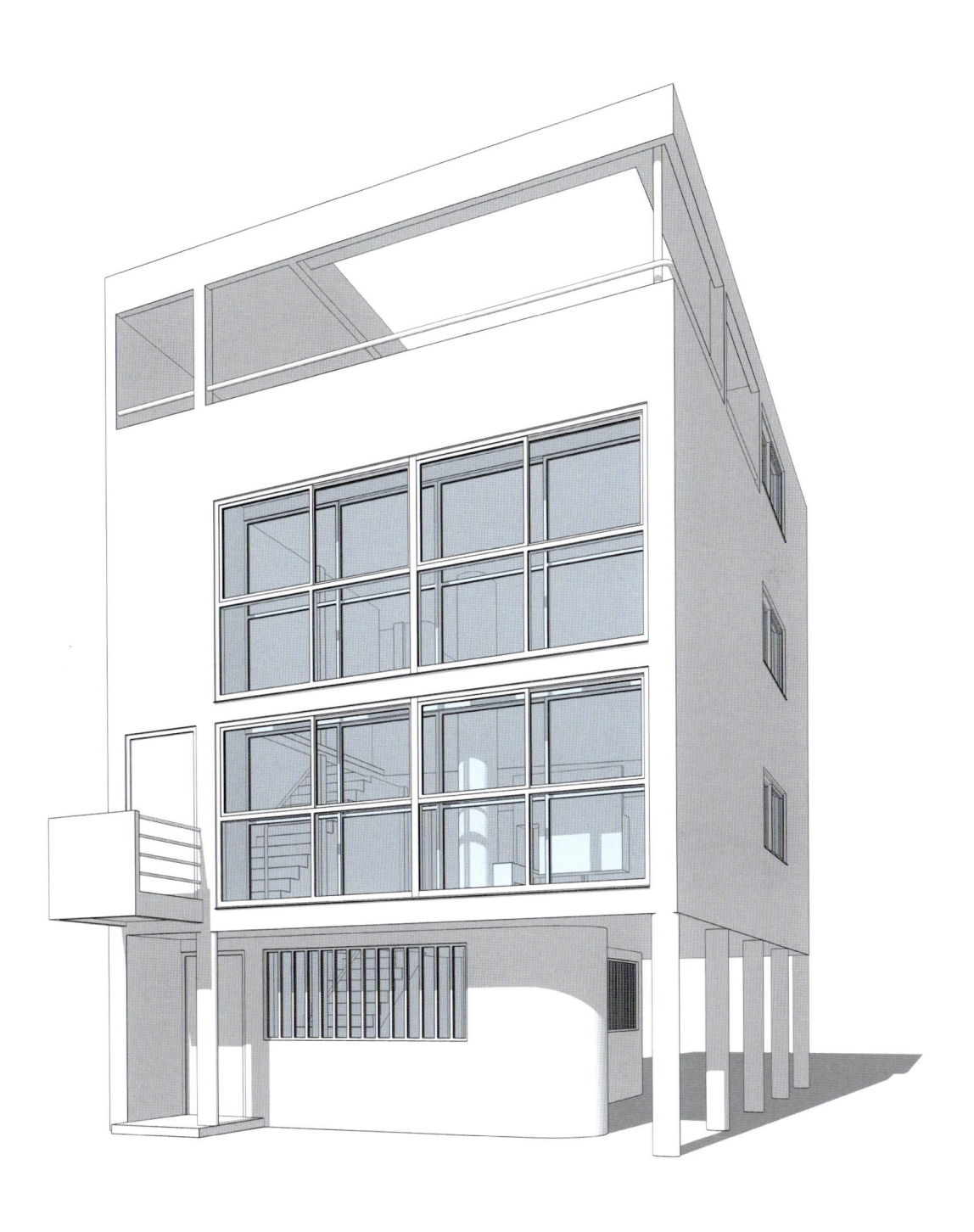

WEISSENHOFSIEDLUNG VILLA NO. 1 Exterior perspective, south elevation

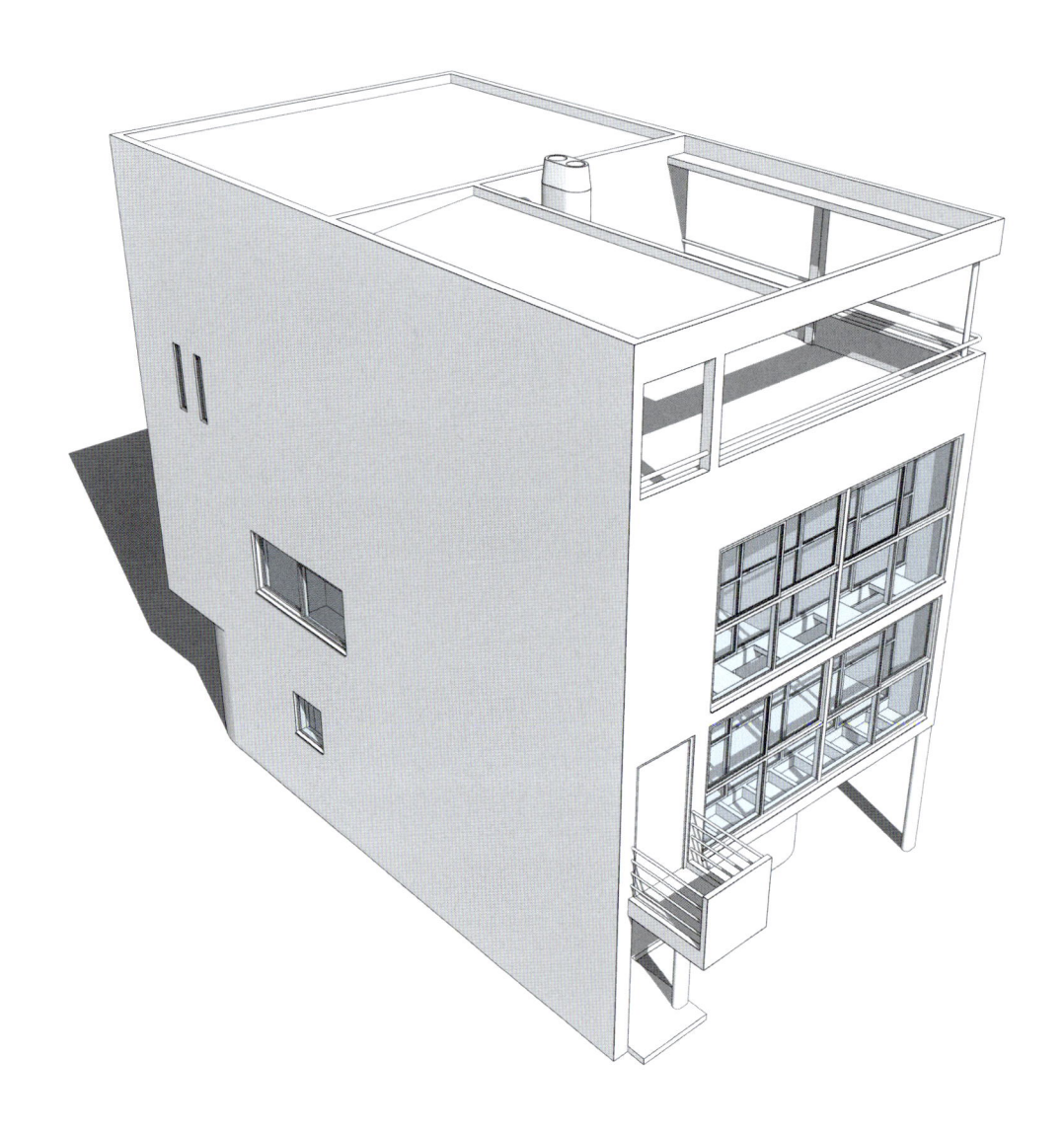

WEISSENHOFSIEDLUNG VILLA NO. 1   Aerial perspective, southwest corner

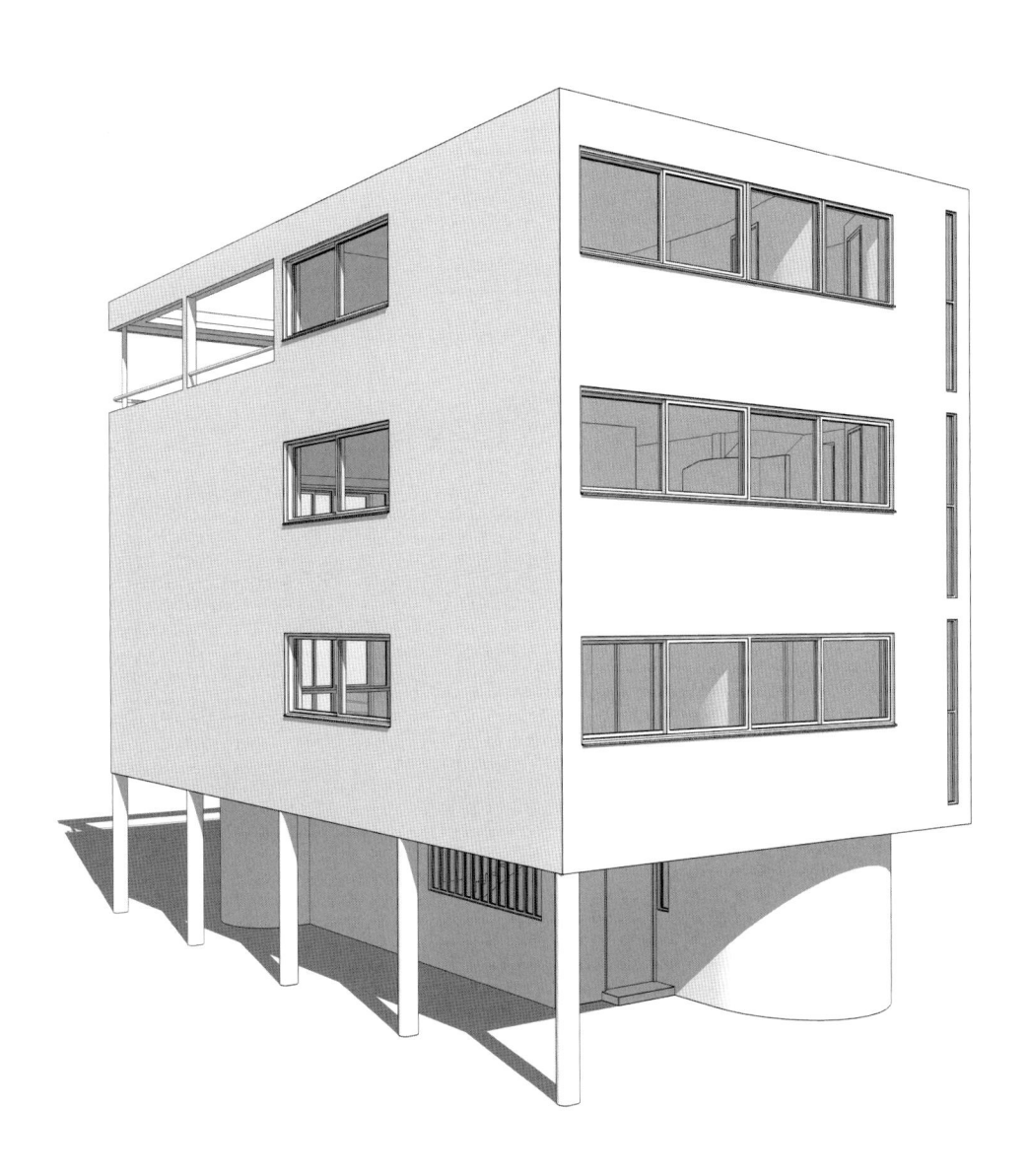

127 WEISSENHOFSIEDLUNG VILLA NO. 1 Exterior perspective, northeast corner

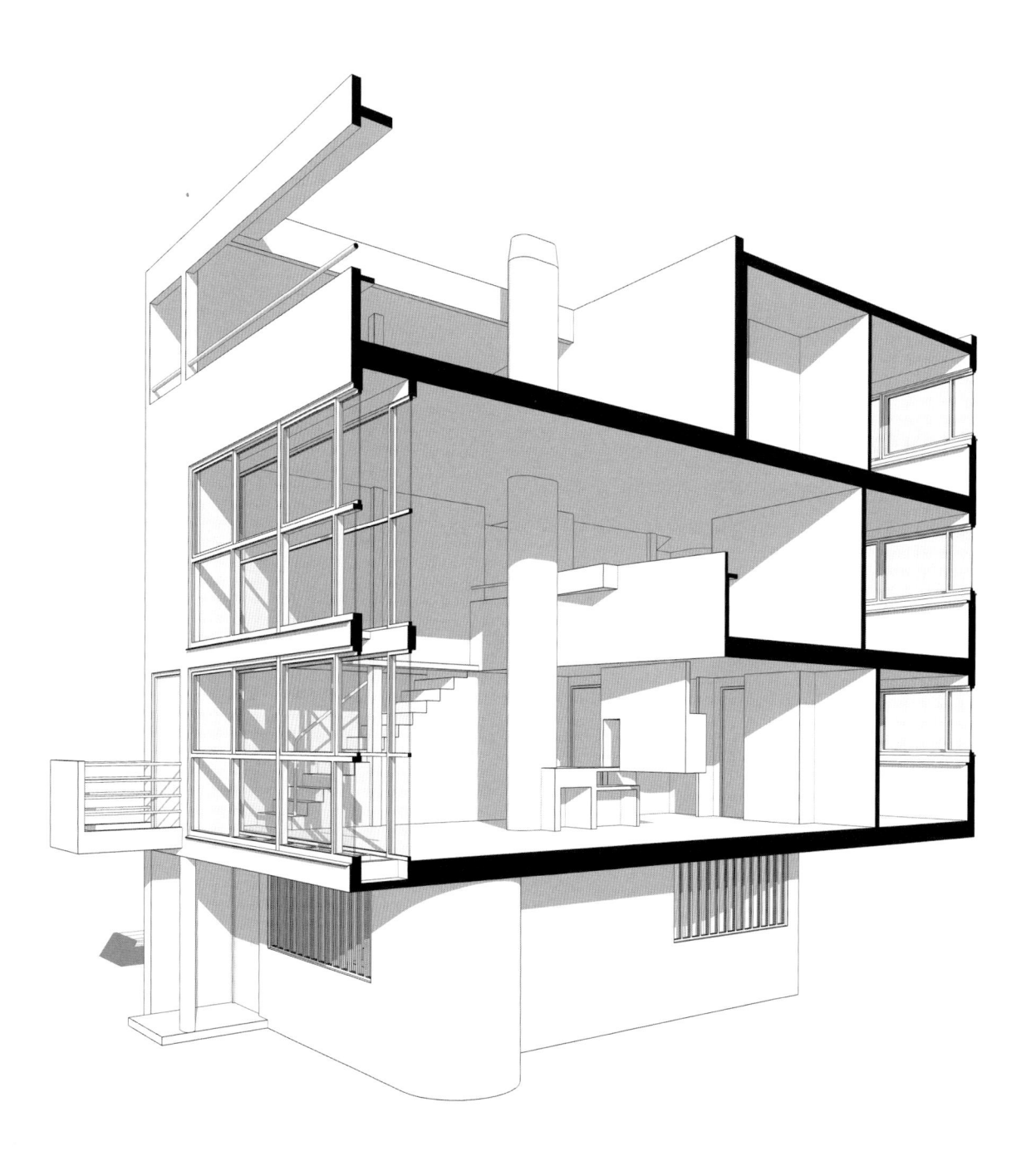

South–north sectional perspective at double-height living room

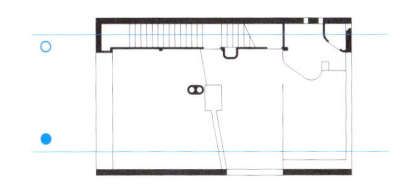

129　**WEISSENHOFSIEDLUNG VILLA NO. 1**　　North–south sectional perspective at stairs

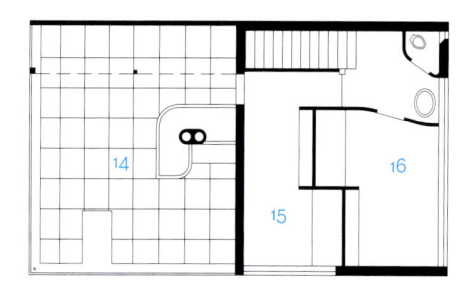

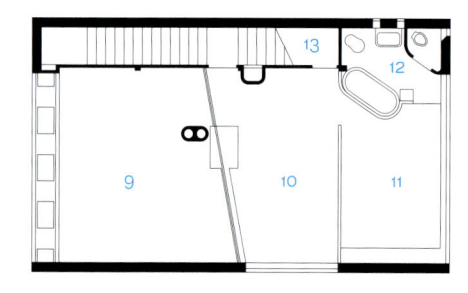

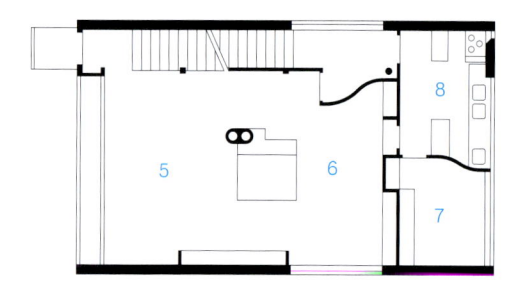

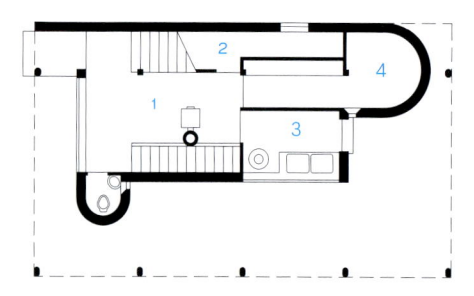

Fourth-floor plan
Third-floor plan
Second-floor plan
First-floor plan

1. Mechanical room
2. Coal storage
3. Laundry
4. Cellar
5. Living room
6. Dining room
7. Maid's room
8. Kitchen
9. Open to below
10. Sitting room
11. Bedroom
12. Bathroom
13. Storage
14. Roof terrace
15. Guest room
16. Children's room

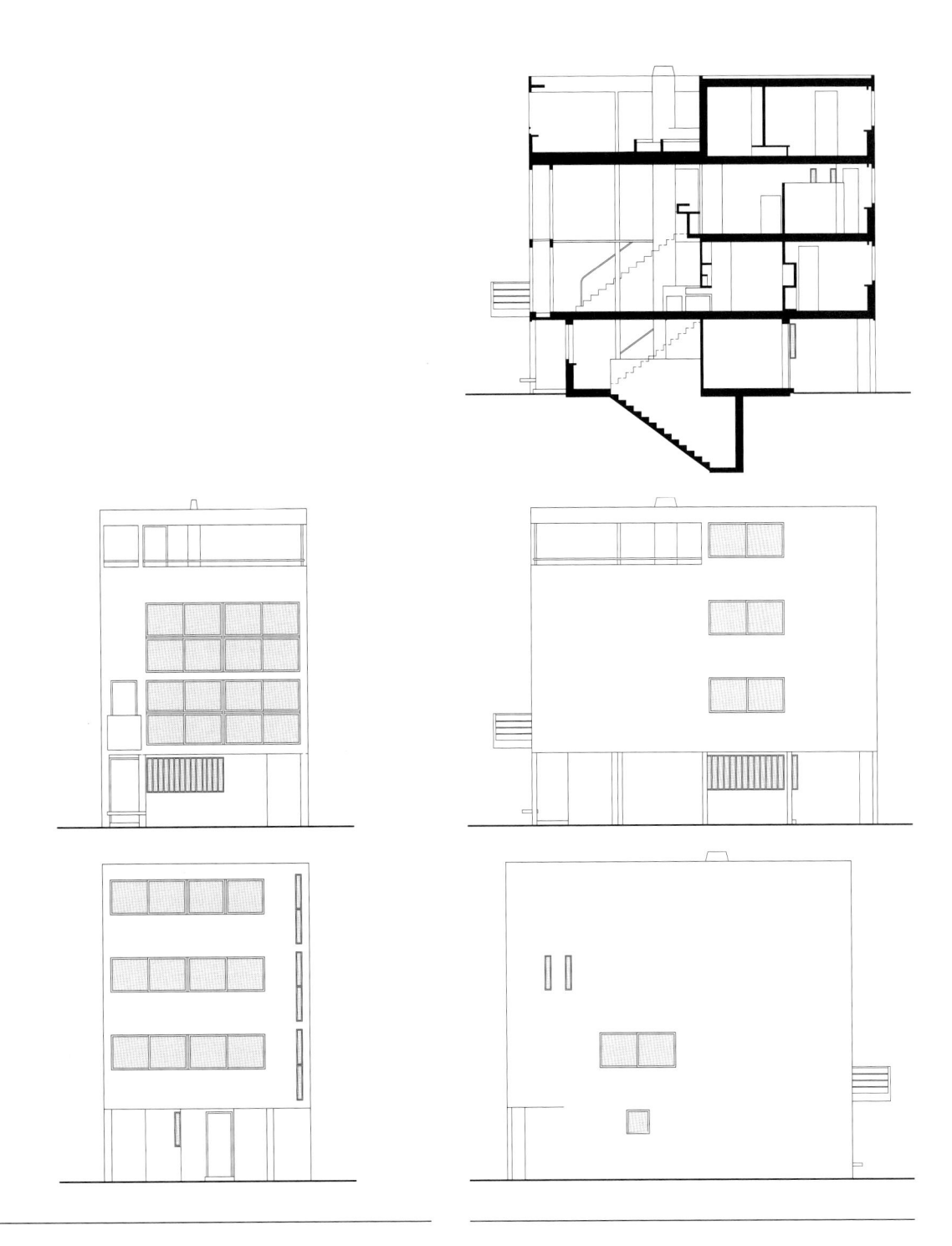

South elevation
North elevation

South–north section
East elevation
West elevation

15 WEISSENHOFSIEDLUNG VILLA NO. 2

LOCATION: Stuttgart, Germany
DATE: 1927

Based on Le Corbusier's low-cost housing prototype Maison Dom-ino of 1914, the duplex Weissenhofsiedlung Villa No. 2 was more progressive in its planning concept than the Villa No. 1. Interior planning was centered around a flexible space that was linearly arranged and could be subdivided with movable partitions into smaller rooms inspired by Pullman sleeping cars. There was no distinction between living areas and bedrooms; built-in cabinets were designed to conceal beds when they were not in use.

Spanning the width of each of the two units of the villa is a long corridor from which every subdivision of the central living space, as well as a shared kitchen and bathroom, can be accessed. The idea was so radical at the time that it was difficult for the sponsor to find tenants, and the duplex was later rented by a single tenant. In order to support the planning concept of transformable spaces, vertical circulation space is pushed off to one side. A strip window stretches across the entire width of the building, combining the two apartments as a unified whole and providing air, light, and views to every space housed within. At the roof terrace, a floating canopy whose horizontality mirrors that of the strip window below frames a view of the surrounding hills and city and formally integrates the outdoor roof terrace with the rectangular volume of living spaces. The columns of Villa No. 2 were made of steel rather than concrete in response to detailed instructions from Mies van der Rohe regarding materials and methods of construction.

CLIENT: Deutscher Werkbund
PROGRAM: Experimental housing prototype for a duplex residence
FEATURES: Adherence to the Five Points of a New Architecture, movable partitions inspired by Pullman sleeping cars

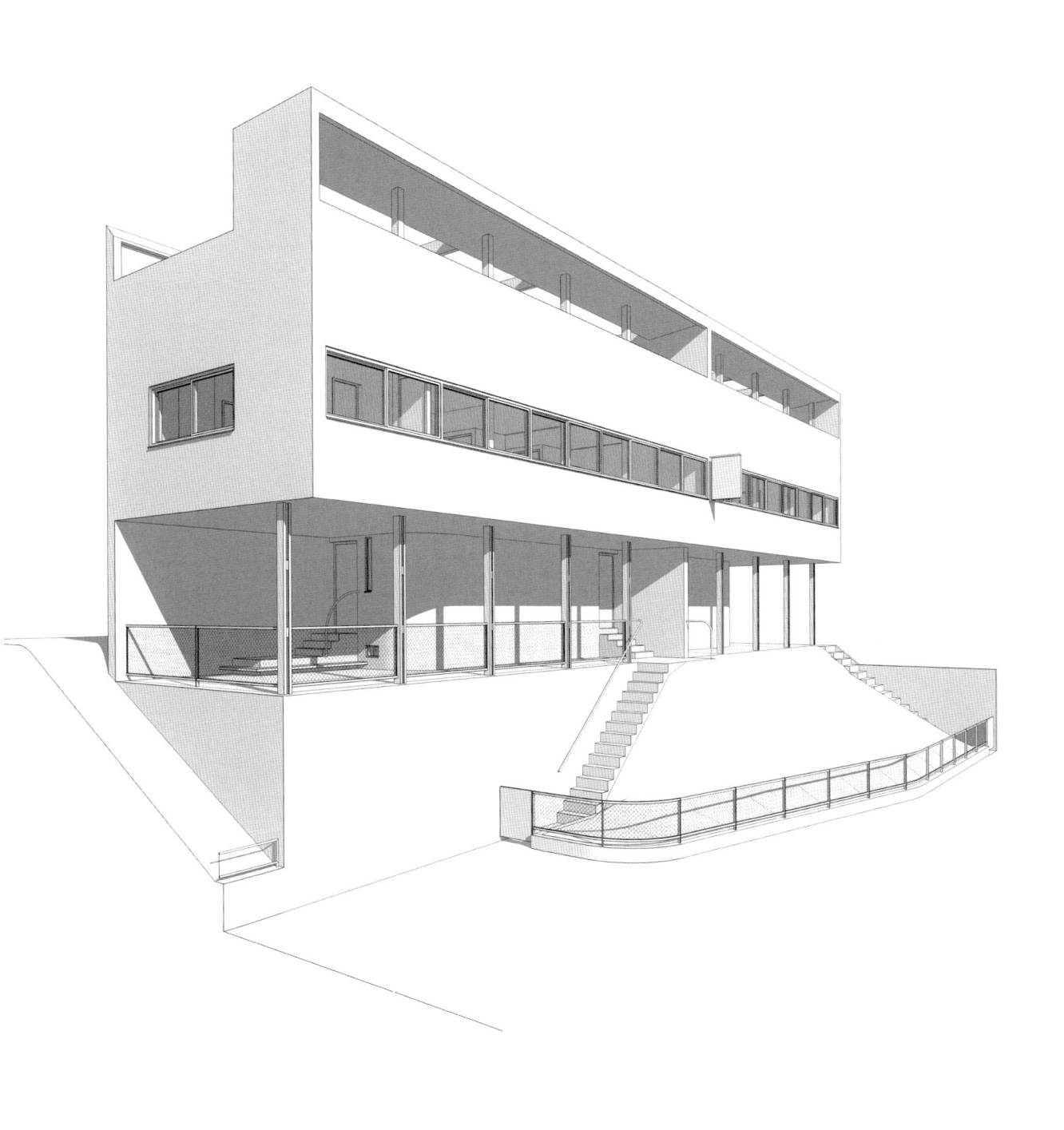

WEISSENHOFSIEDLUNG VILLA NO. 2 Exterior perspective, southeast corner

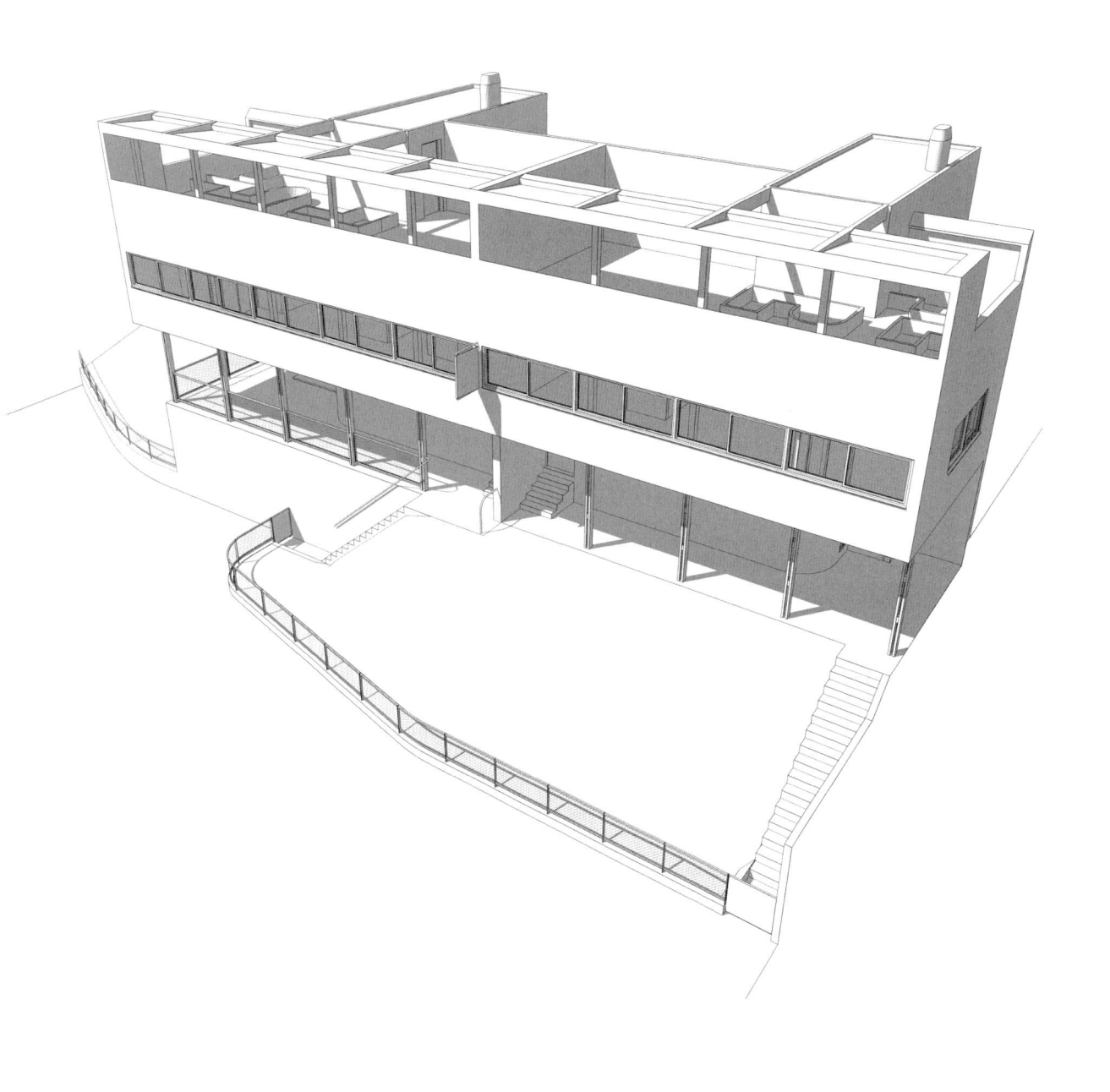

WEISSENHOFSIEDLUNG VILLA NO. 2 Aerial perspective, northeast corner

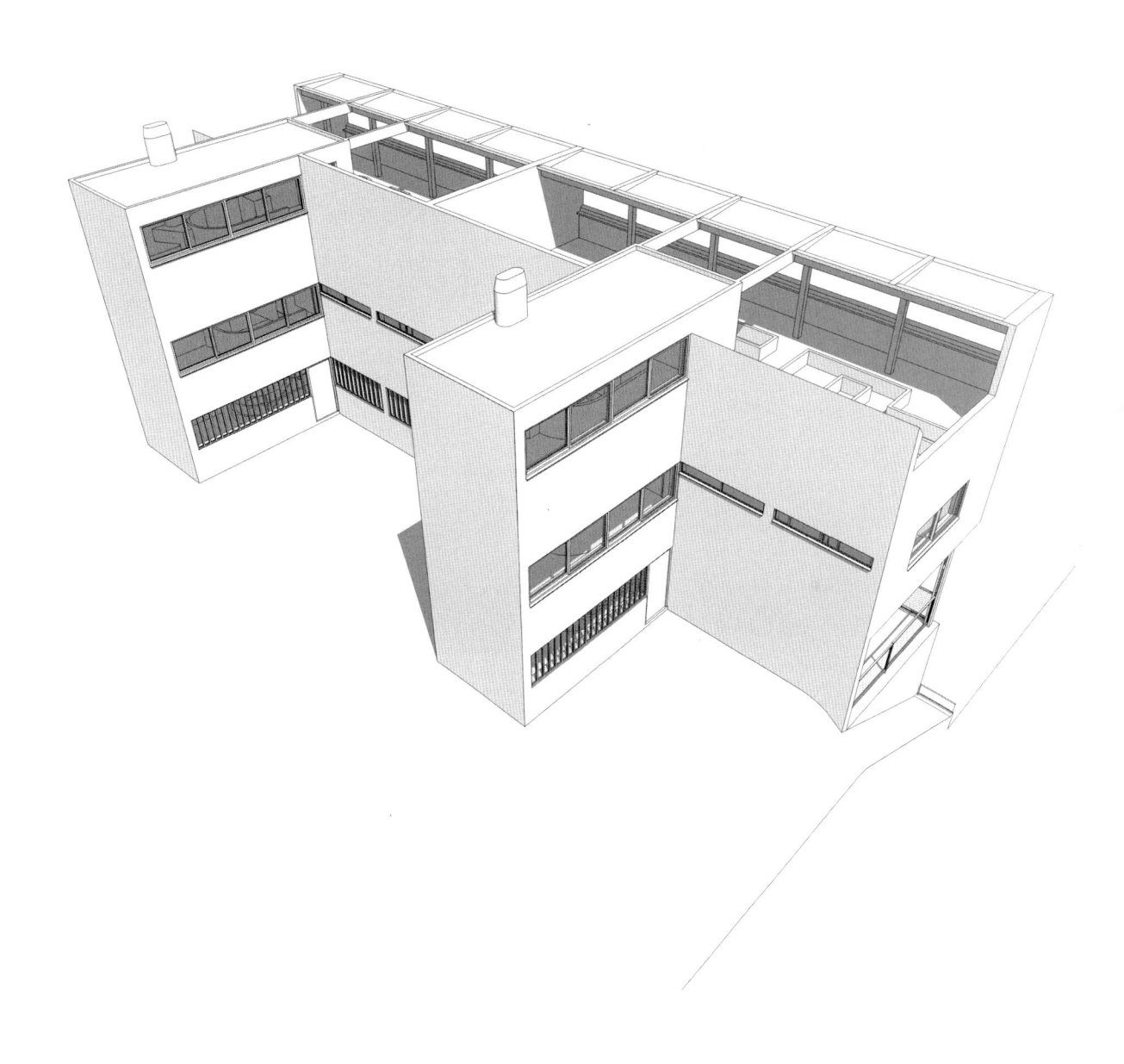

135 WEISSENHOFSIEDLUNG VILLA NO. 2 Aerial perspective, southwest corner

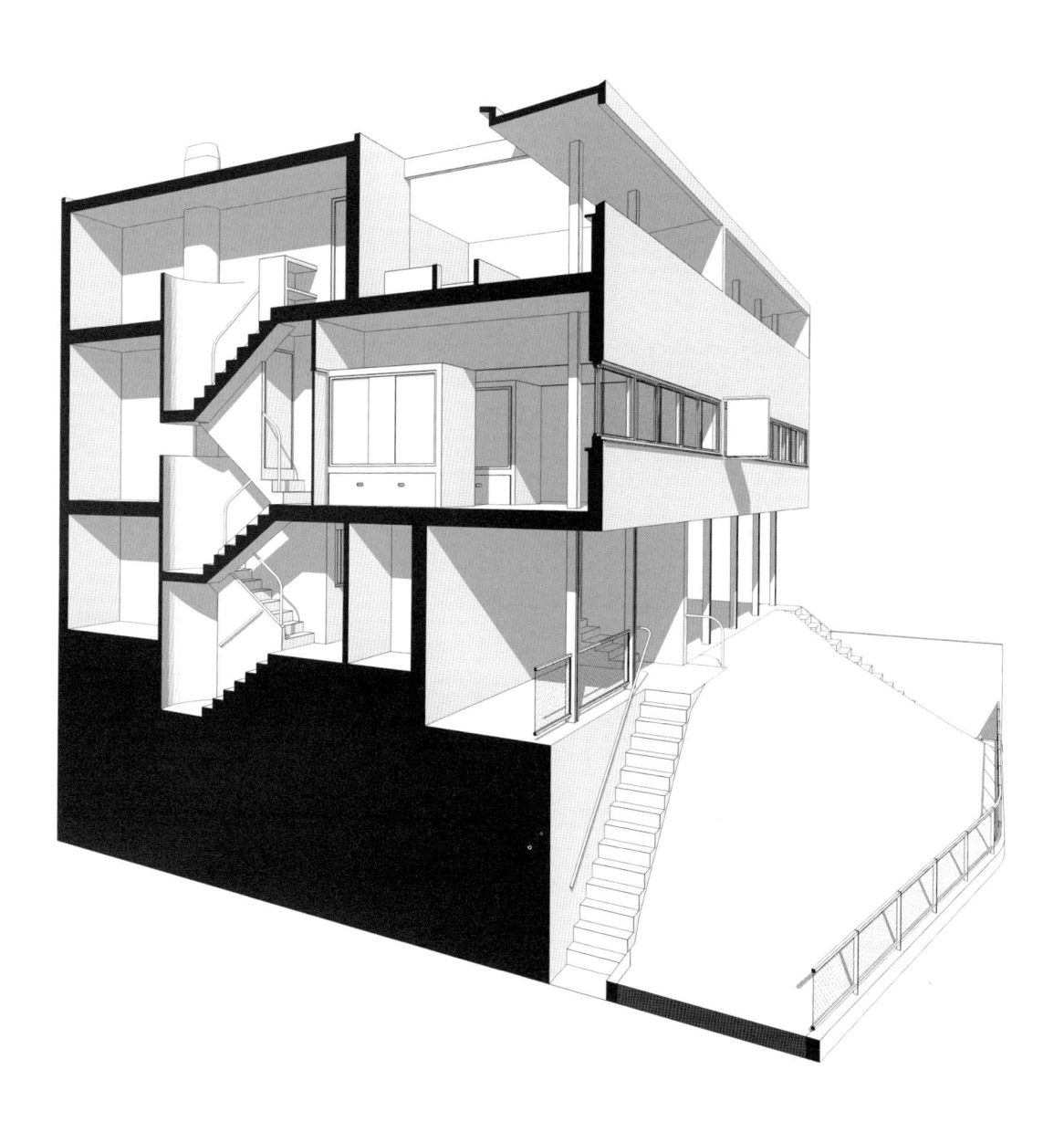

136　**WEISSENHOFSIEDLUNG VILLA NO. 2**　　●　West–east sectional perspective at stairs

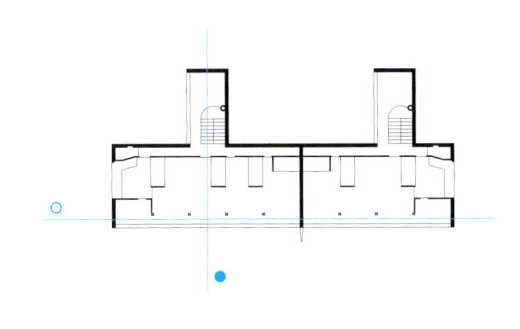

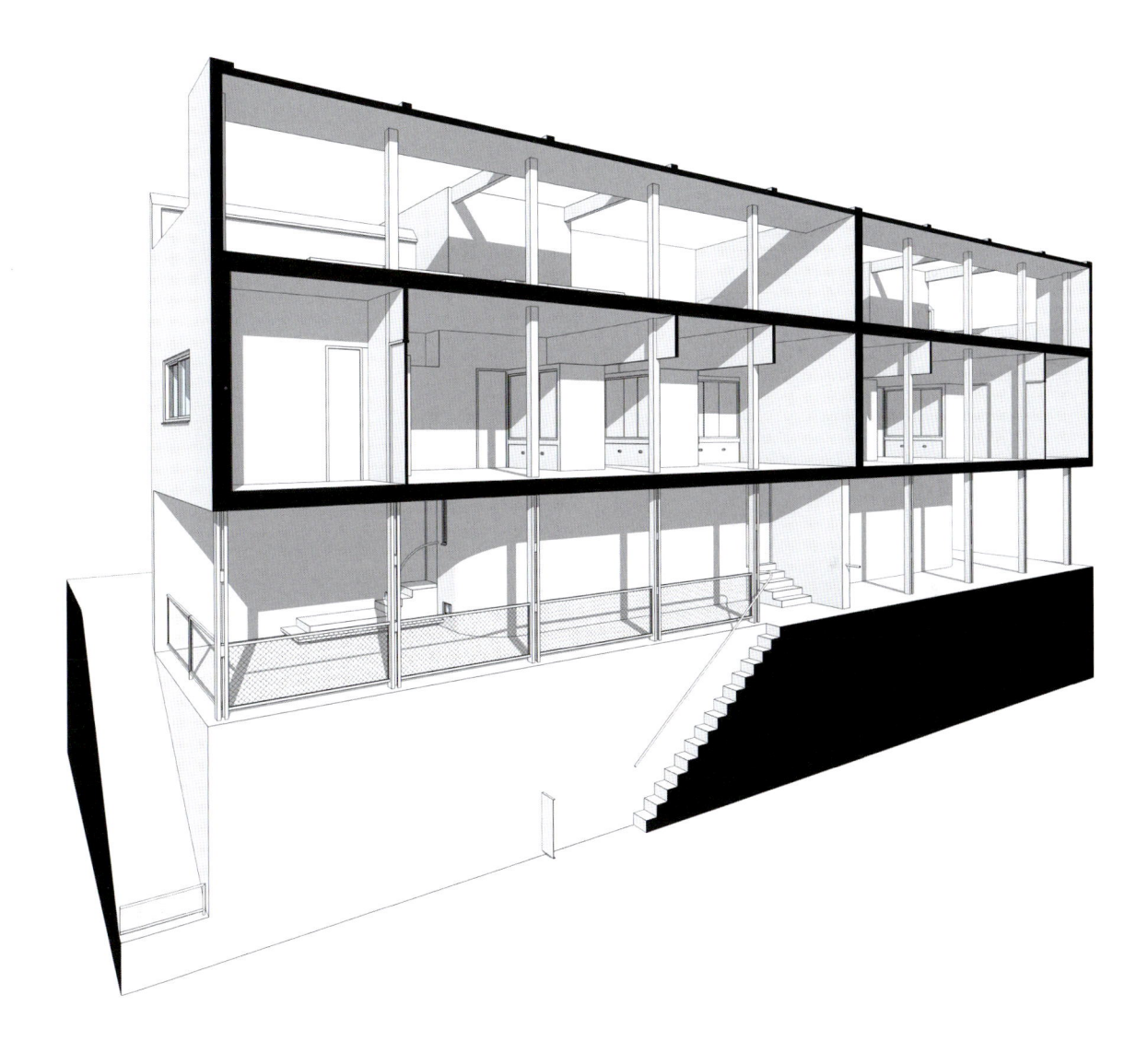

137 **WEISSENHOFSIEDLUNG VILLA NO. 2**   ○ South–north sectional perspective at flexible living space

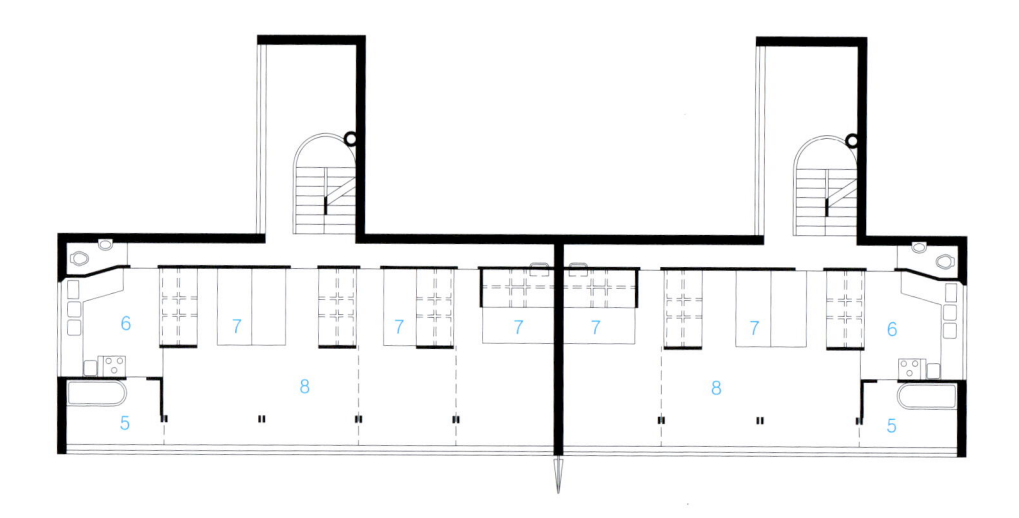

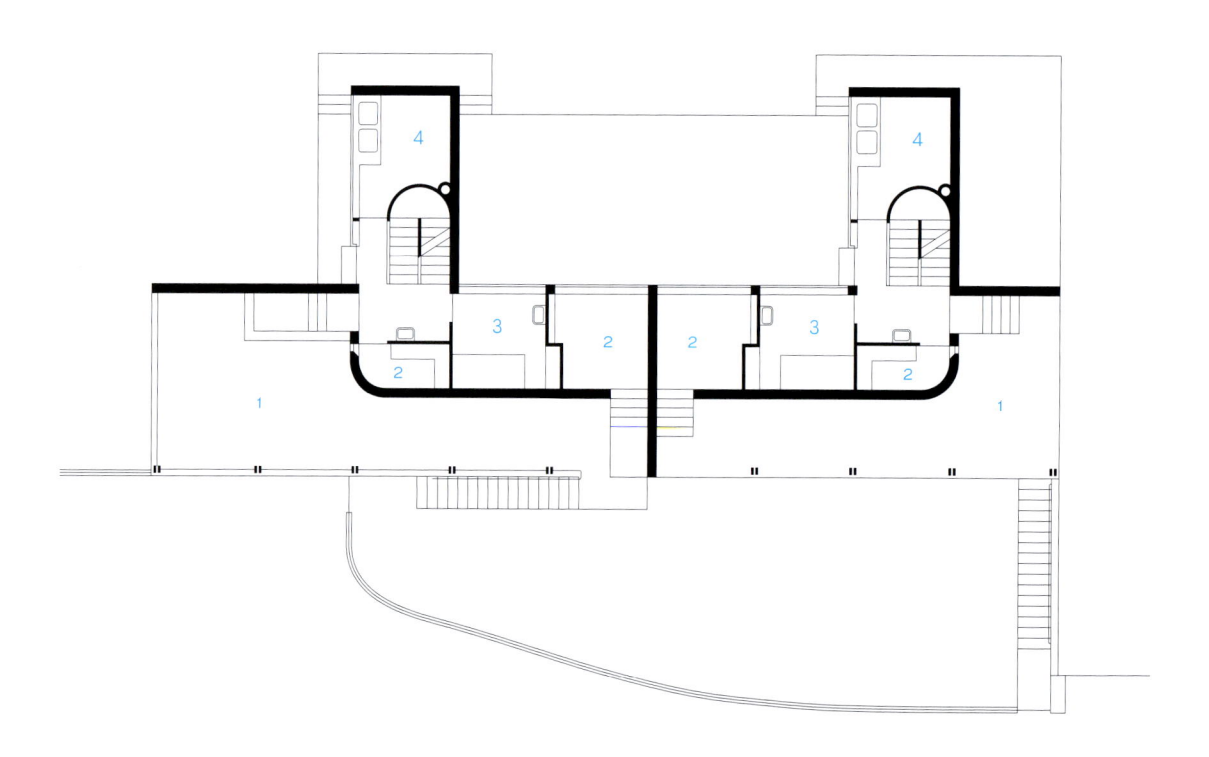

Second-floor plan
First-floor plan

1. Outdoor terrace
2. Storage
3. Maid's room
4. Laundry
5. Bathroom
6. Kitchen
7. Bedroom
8. Living room

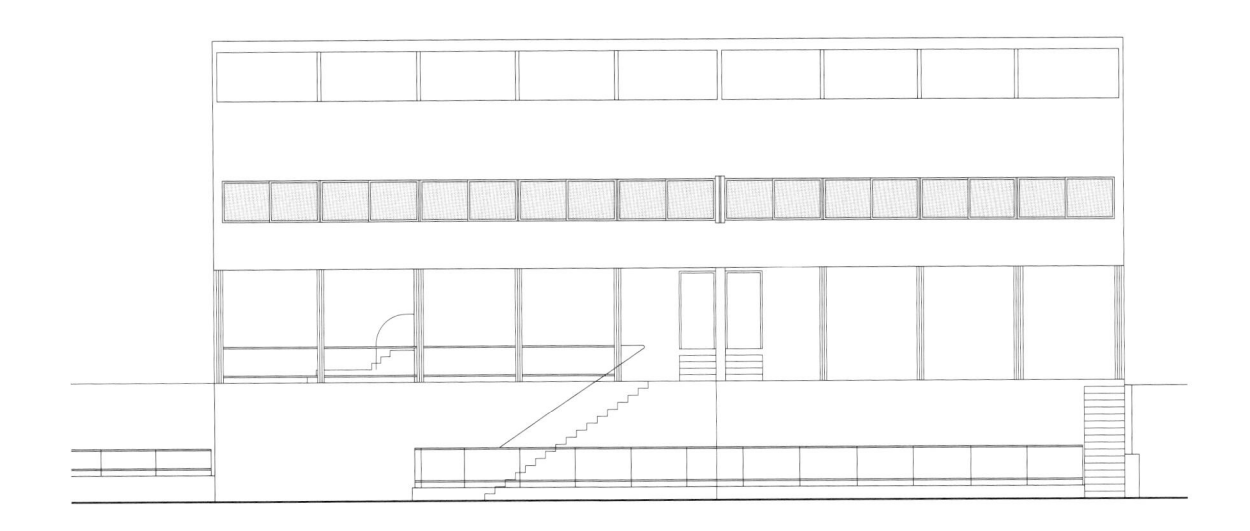

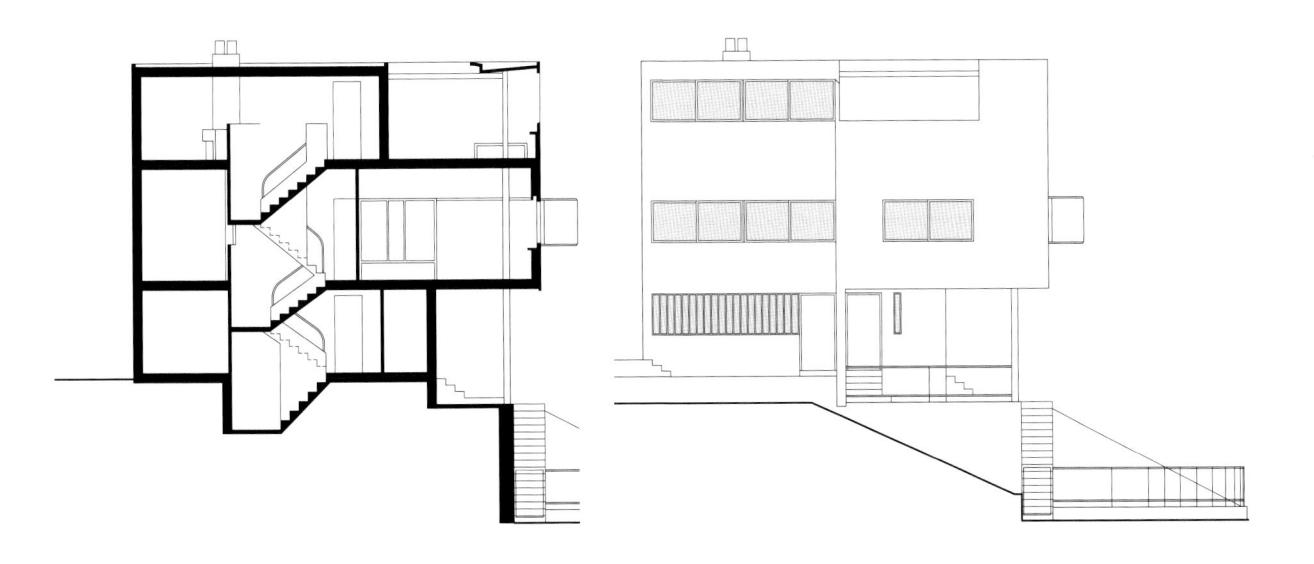

East elevation
West–east section

South elevation

139 **WEISSENHOFSIEDLUNG VILLA NO. 2**

16 VILLA BAIZEAU

LOCATION: Carthage, Tunisia
DATE: 1928

As the director of a Tunisian construction company, Lucien Baizeau had a keen interest in the latest housing concepts and building techniques. He commissioned Le Corbusier to apply the innovative principles demonstrated in the Weissenhofsiedlung villas to the design of a private house for Baizeau's family. In response to the client's demand that the house moderate the hot, humid climate of northern Africa, Le Corbusier initially designed it as a hybrid of the Maison Citrohan and Maison Dom-ino, with double-height, interlocking spaces and a roof parasol for cross-ventilation and solar shading. However, the client rejected the first two schemes and dictated the final design. A variation of the Maison Dom-ino, the as-built scheme features large cantilevered terraces, which act as horizontal shades and also catch the breeze. The architect never visited the site, and a local contractor hired by the client supervised the construction.

Some of the forms and concepts of the unrealized schemes reemerged in the designs of the Villa Shodhan and the Villa Sarabhai in India several decades later, adapted to the tropical climate. Villa Shodhan is similar formally to one of the unbuilt schemes for Villa Baizeau, with interlocking volumes and a floating roof parasol.

CLIENT: Lucien Baizeau
PROGRAM: Family residence
FEATURES: Elements from Maison Dom-ino design, cantilevered terraces

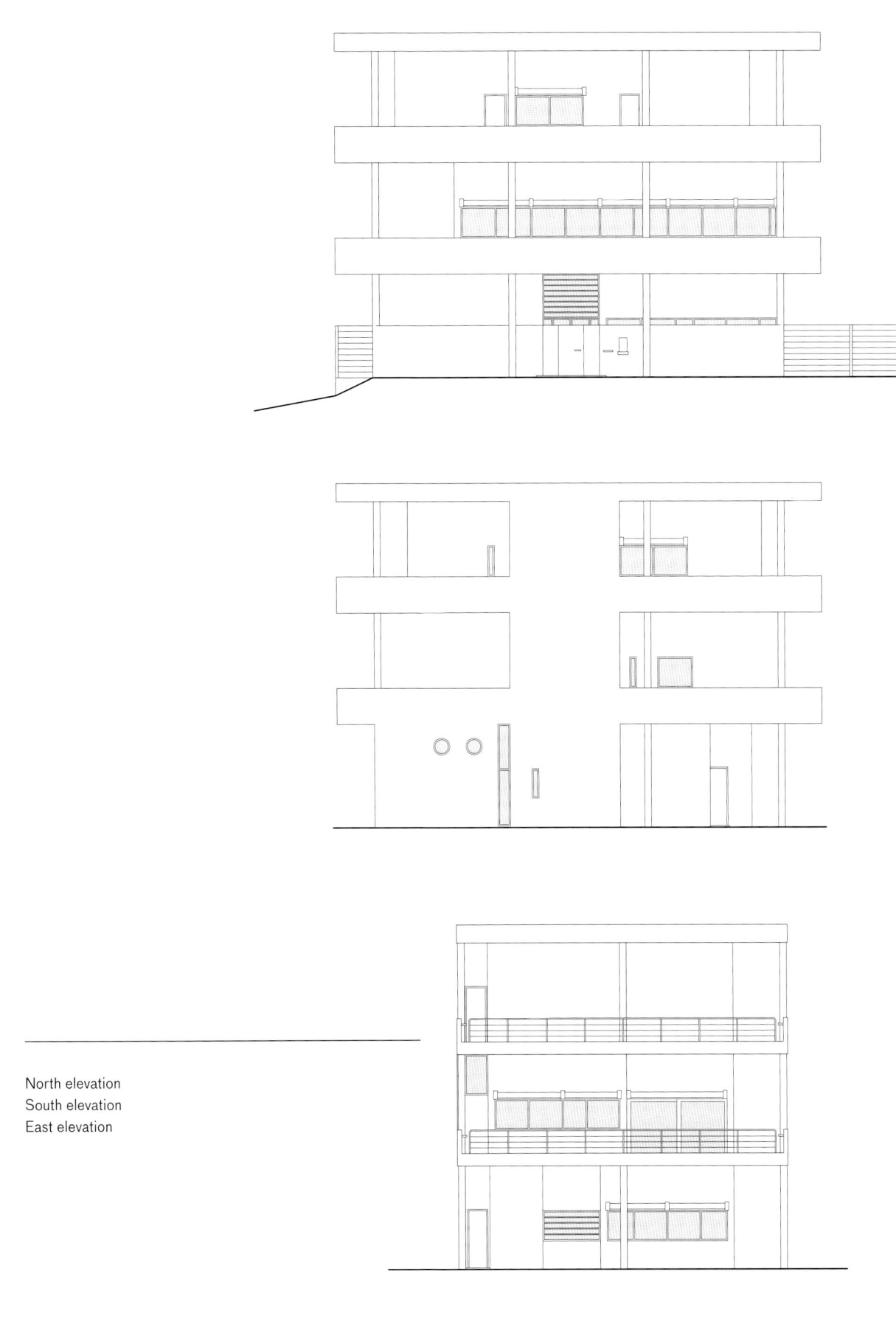

North elevation
South elevation
East elevation

141 **VILLA BAIZEAU**

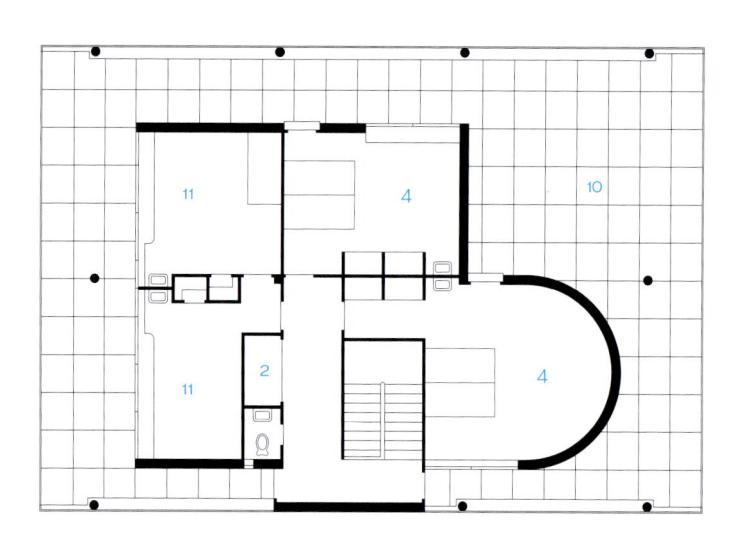

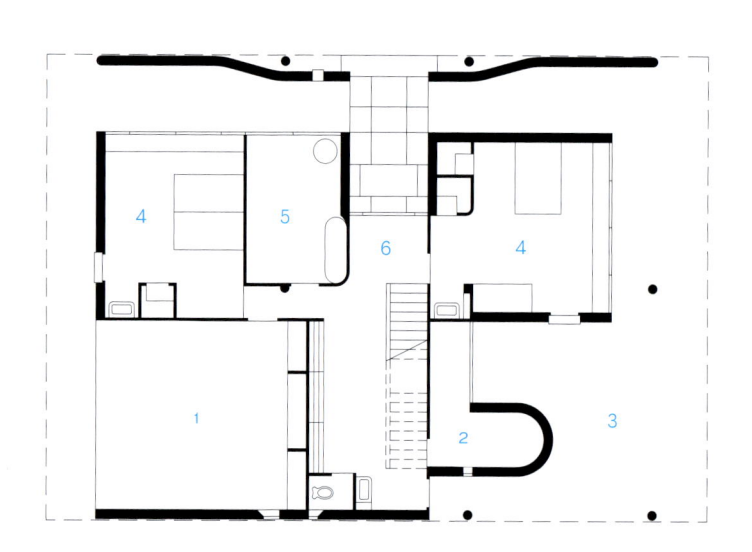

1. Garage
2. Storage
3. Covered patio
4. Bedroom
5. Bathroom
6. Vestibule
7. Living room
8. Pantry
9. Kitchen
10. Terrace
11. Maid's room

Third-floor plan
Second-floor plan
First-floor plan

142 **VILLA BAIZEAU**

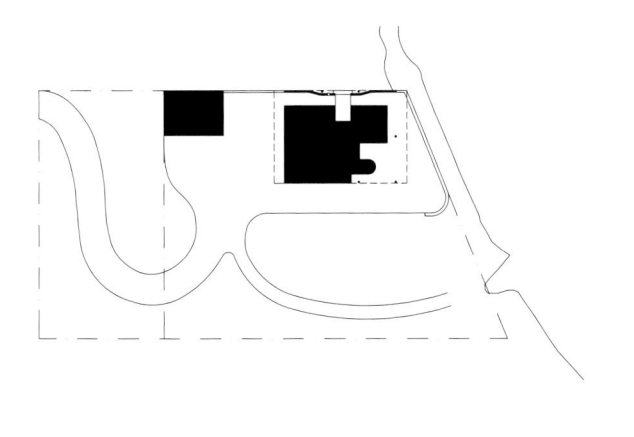

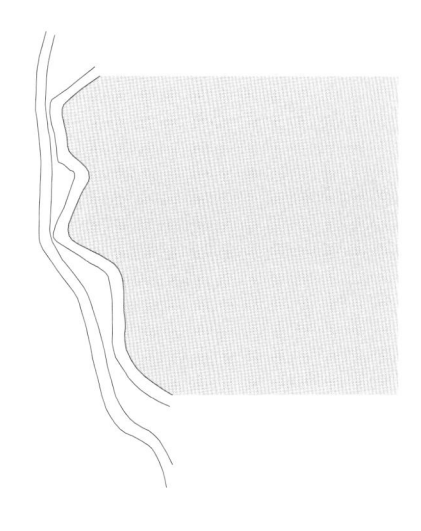

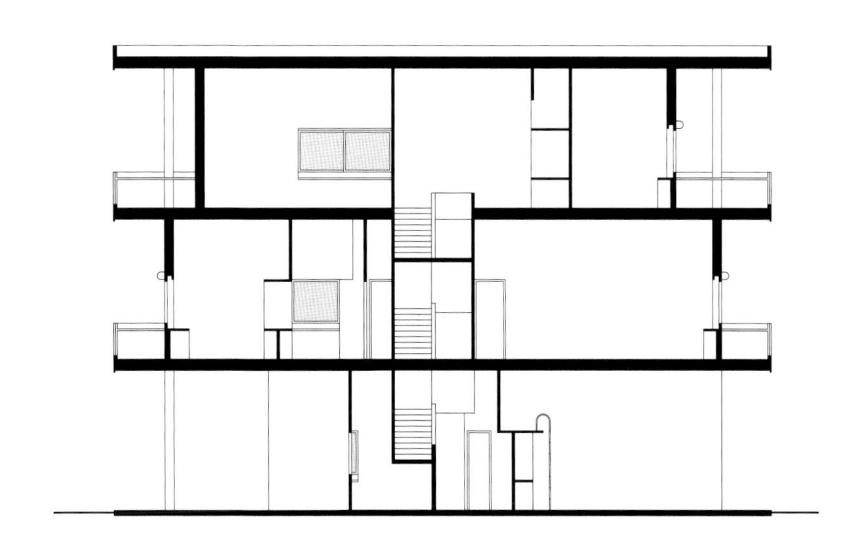

Site plan (1:1000)
East–west section
South–north section

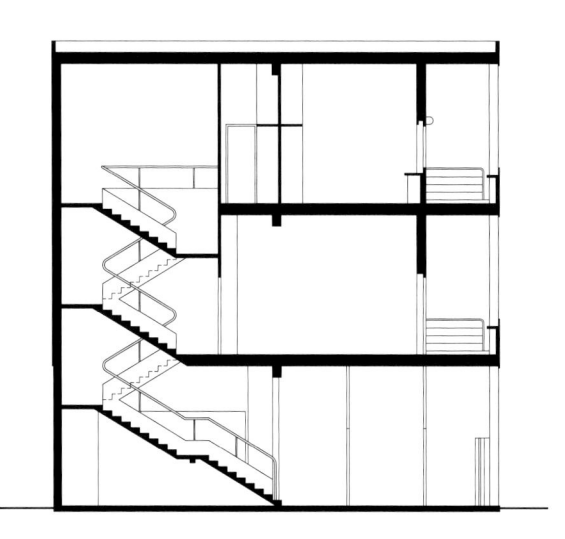

143 **VILLA BAIZEAU**

VILLA SAVOYE

LOCATION:	Poissy-sur-Seine, France
DATE:	1928

Villa Savoye was built as a weekend house for Pierre and Emilie Savoye, who wanted to escape the urban life of Paris and enjoy the rustic landscapes of Poissy-sur-Seine, a small town about an hour's ride from Paris. According to Le Corbusier, the couple had no preconceptions about the design of their house. Villa Savoye synthesized all of Le Corbusier's ideas to date about modern architecture. The pristine white box expresses the industrial machine aesthetic often associated with the modernist movement, and the house is raised on *pilotis*, freeing the ground floor for vehicular access. (The plan is shaped by the turning radius of a car.) At the center of the house, a ramp is an organizing element that both divides and connects different parts of the building.

Natural light guides the occupant's journey through the house, which ends at the rooftop solarium, where a picture window frames a view of what was then a pastoral landscape surrounding the house. Likewise, strip windows on all elevations frame views of the surroundings. The living room extends through a glass sliding door out to the roof garden, allowing a fragment of nature to enter in and become a part of the house.

Le Corbusier considered this particular house to be the result of a long process of refinement, and he intended it to be a standard model for suburban development, envisioning several identical villas Savoye.

CLIENTS:	Pierre and Emilie Savoye
PROGRAM:	Weekend house
FEATURES:	Ramp, spiral stairs, adherence to the Five Points of a New Architecture, planning based on the turning radius of a car

Exterior perspective, northeast corner

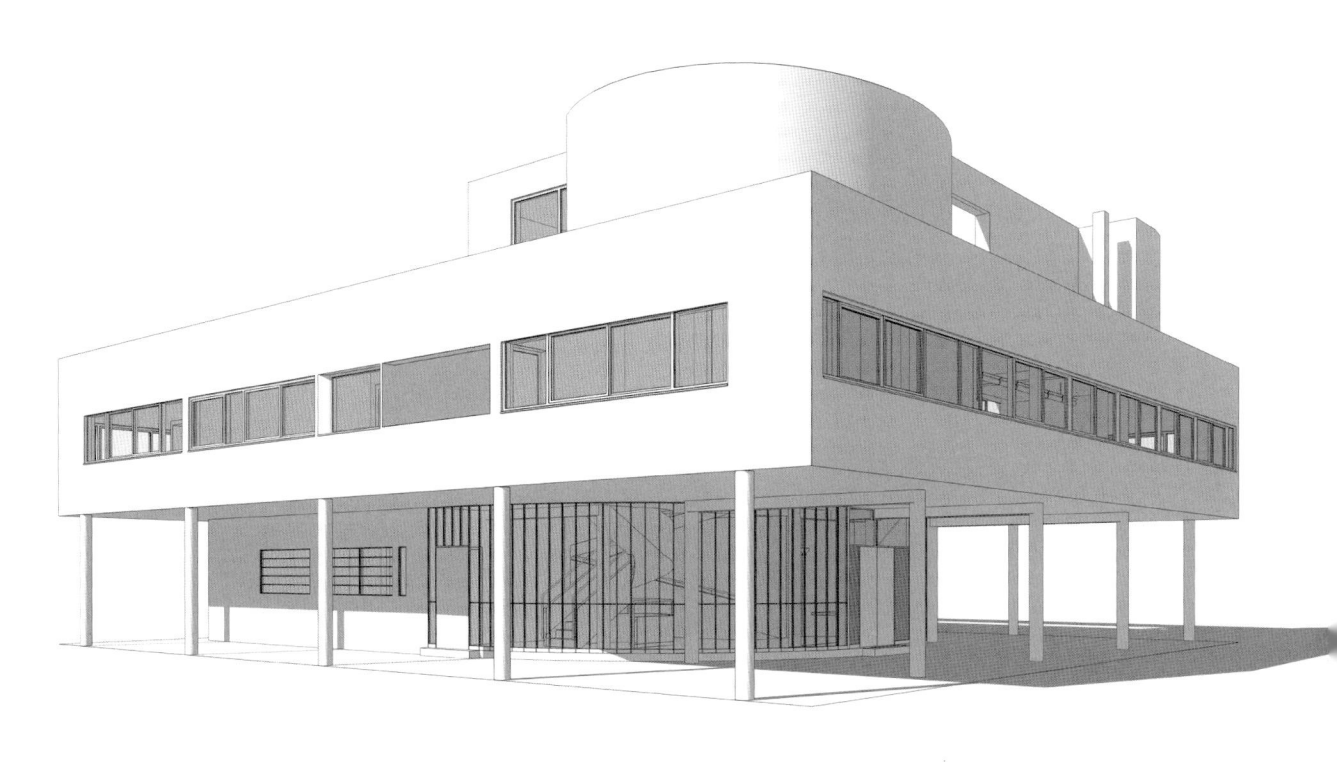

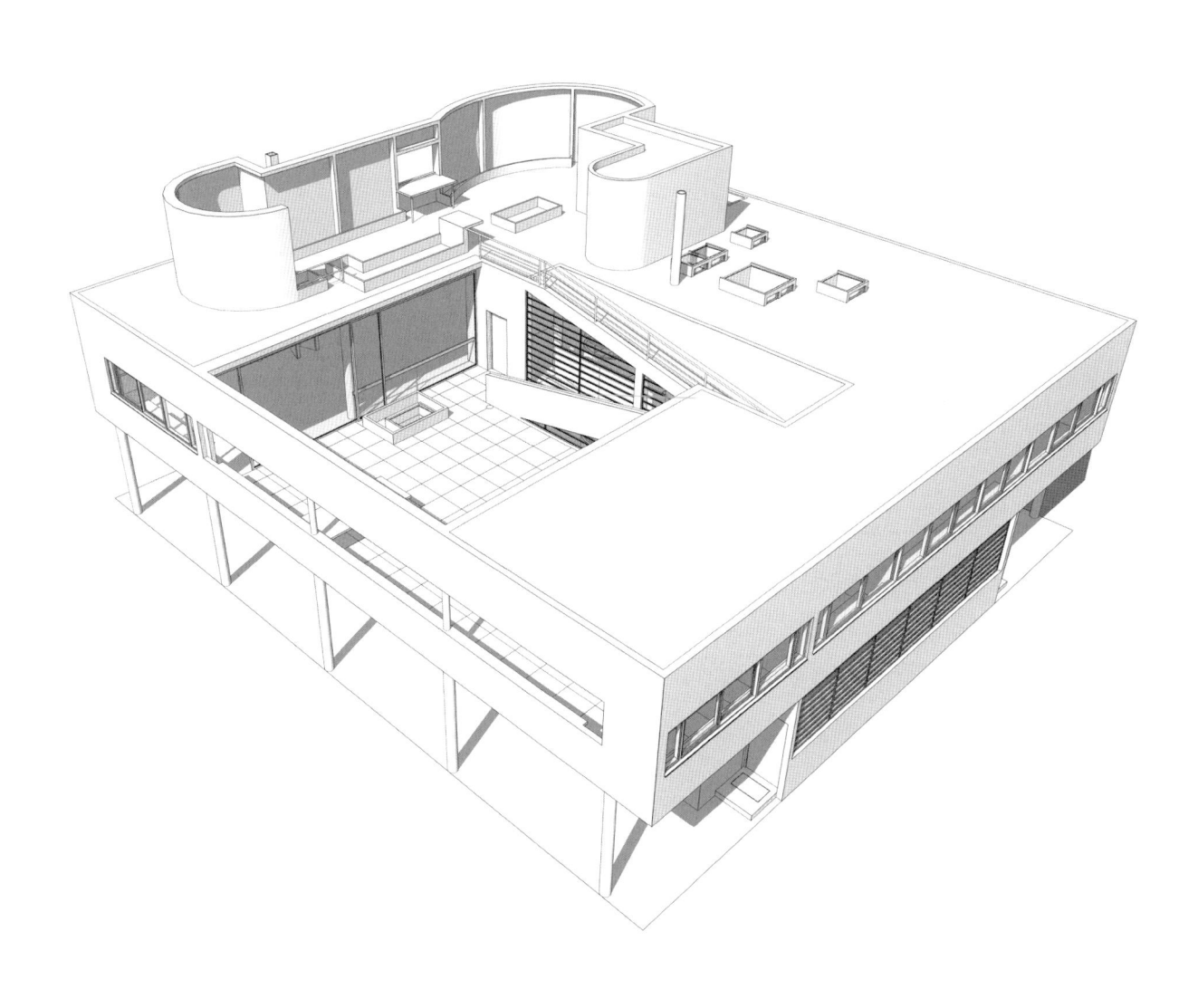

VILLA SAVOYE Aerial perspective, southwest corner, roof garden and solarium

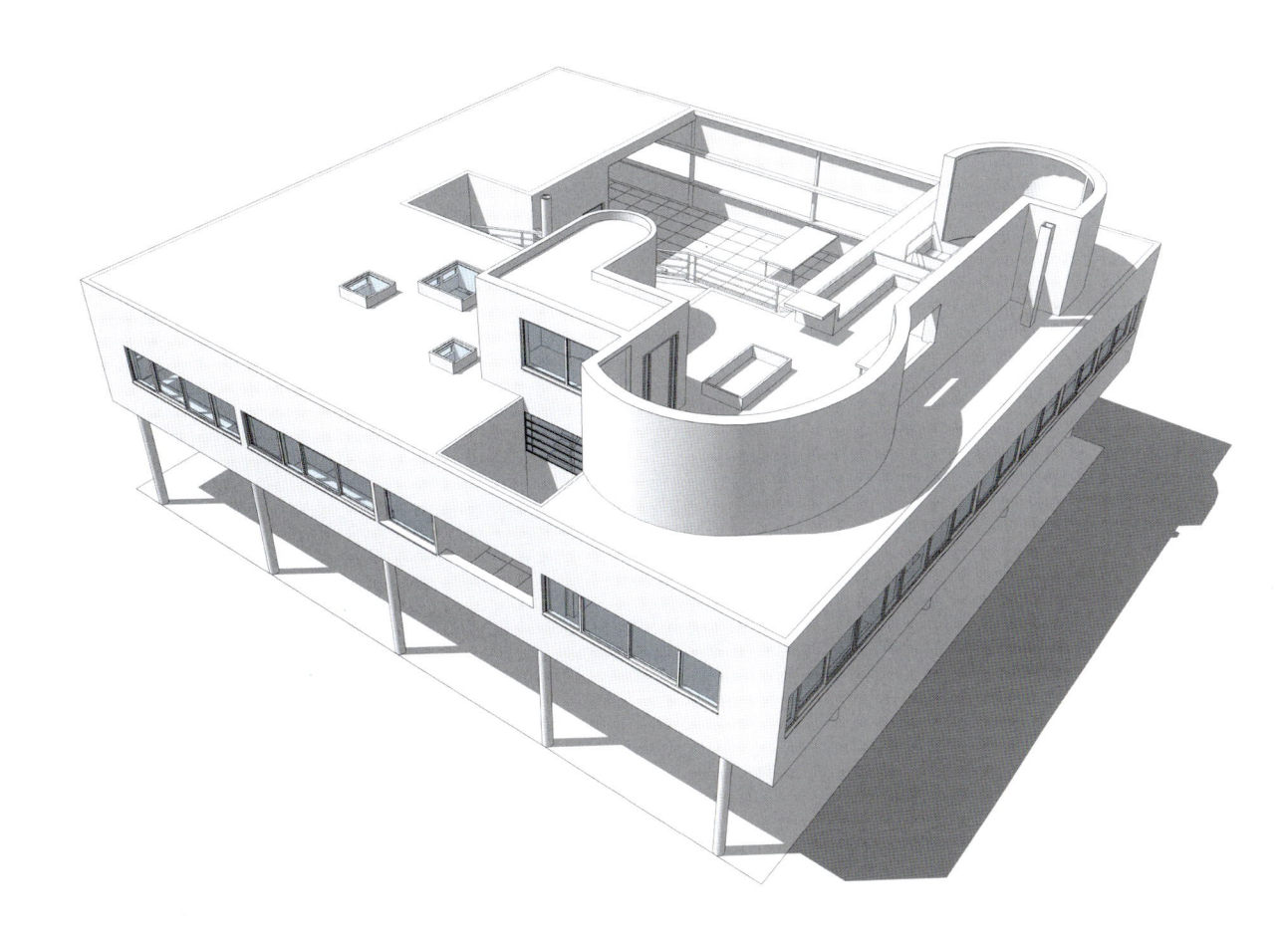

VILLA SAVOYE Aerial perspective, northeast corner, roof garden and solarium

North–south sectional perspective at ramp

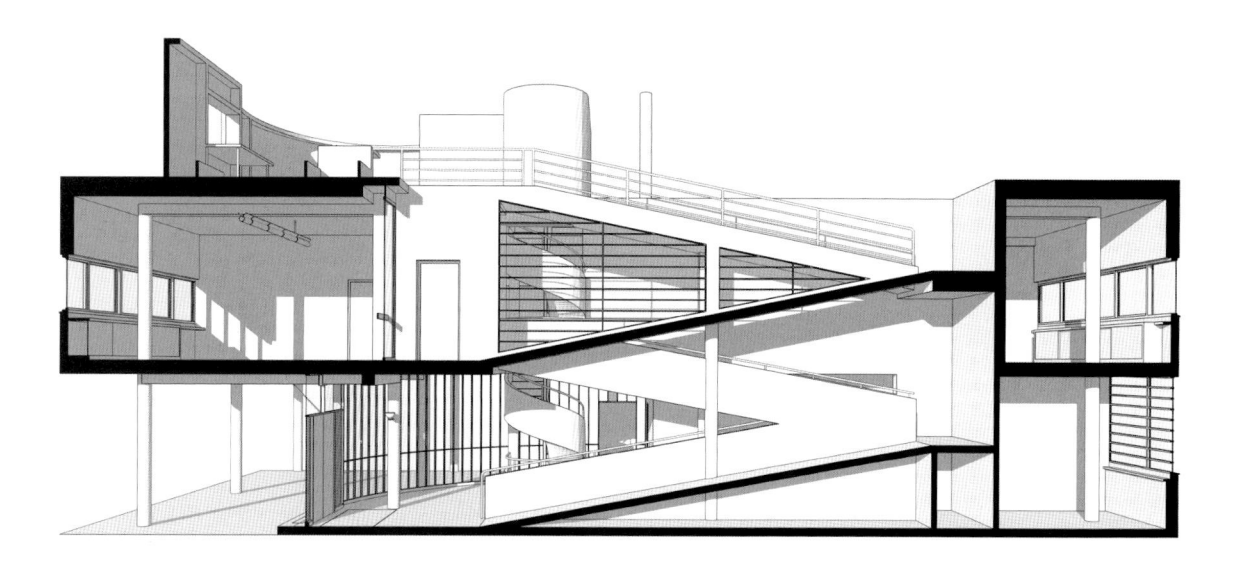

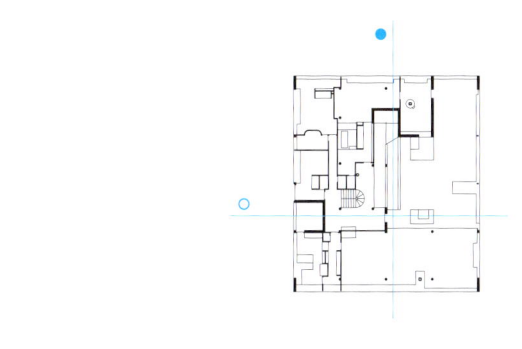

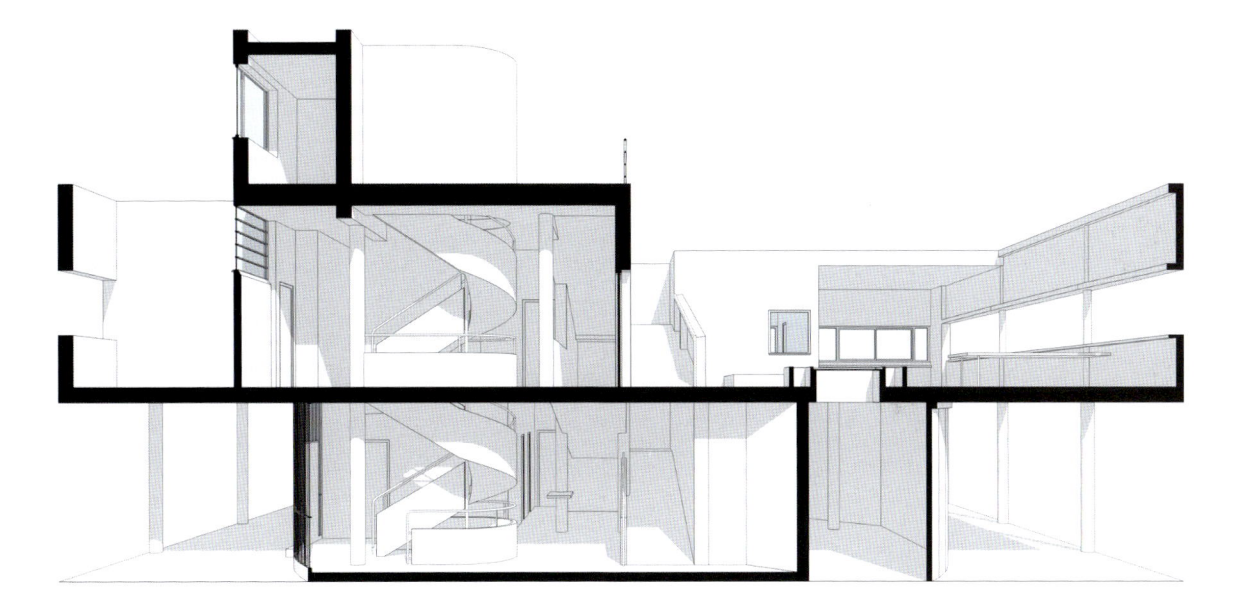

149 **VILLA SAVOYE**   East–west sectional perspective at entrance hall

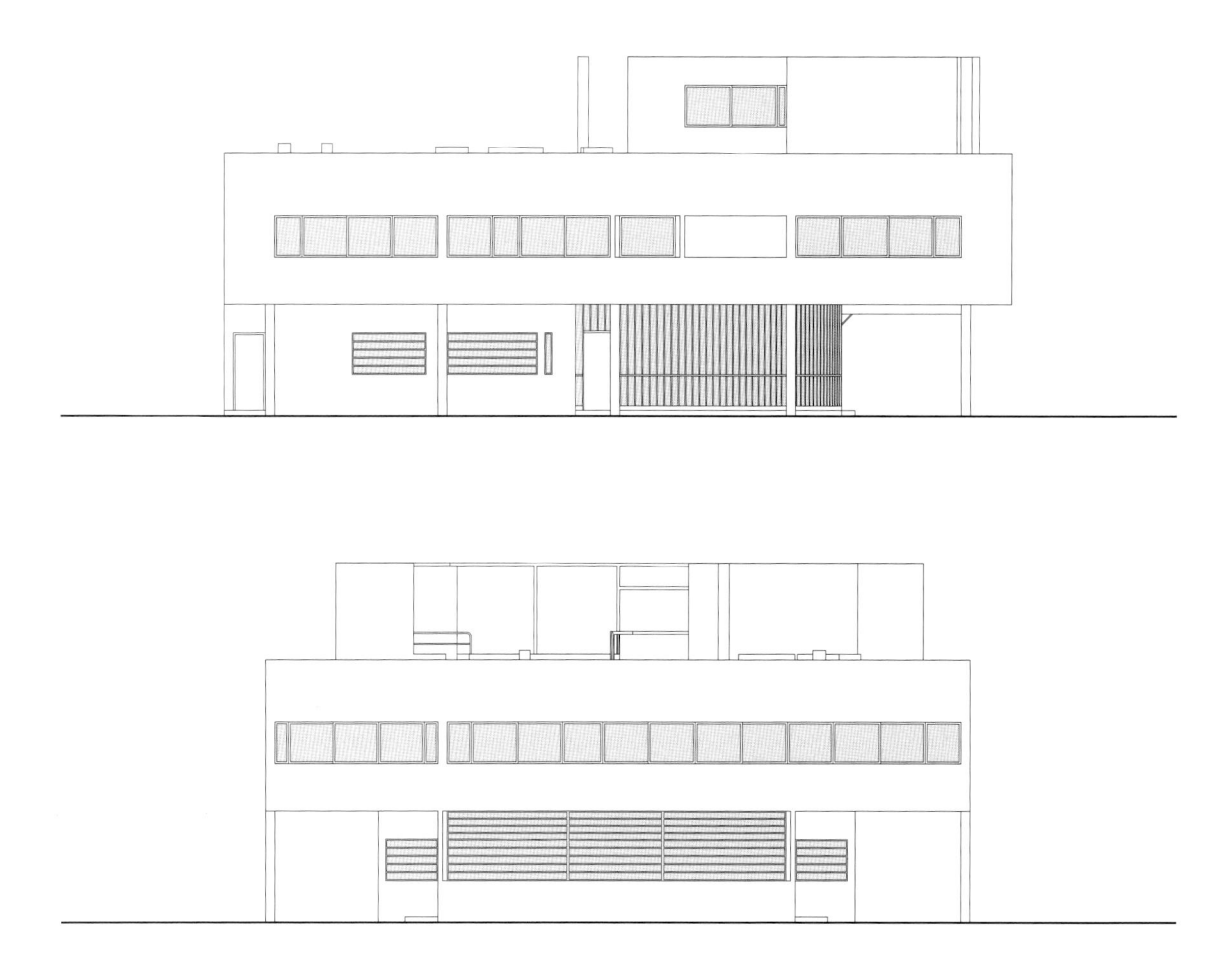

East elevation
South elevation

North elevation
West elevation
North–south section

VILLA SAVOYE

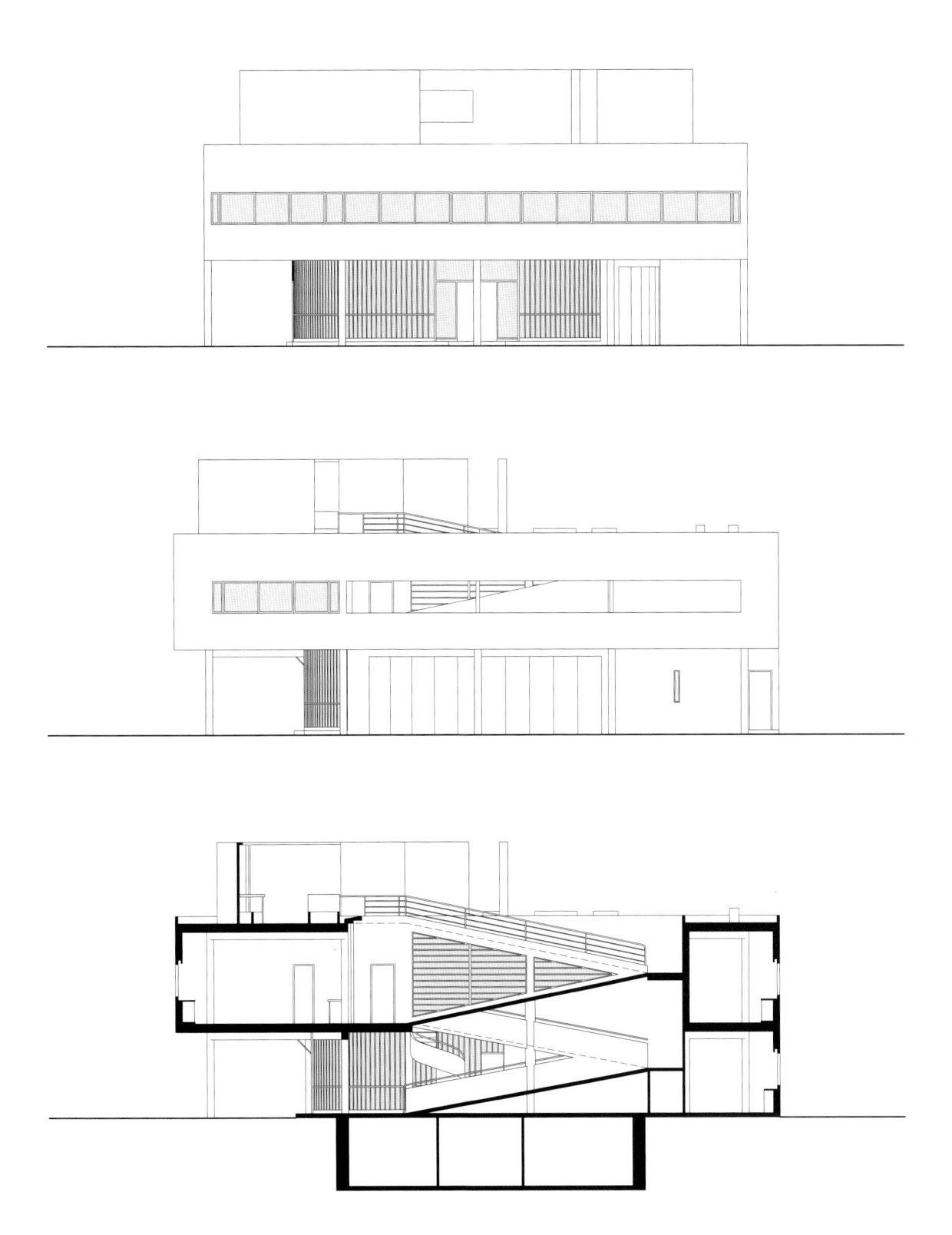

152 **VILLA SAVOYE**

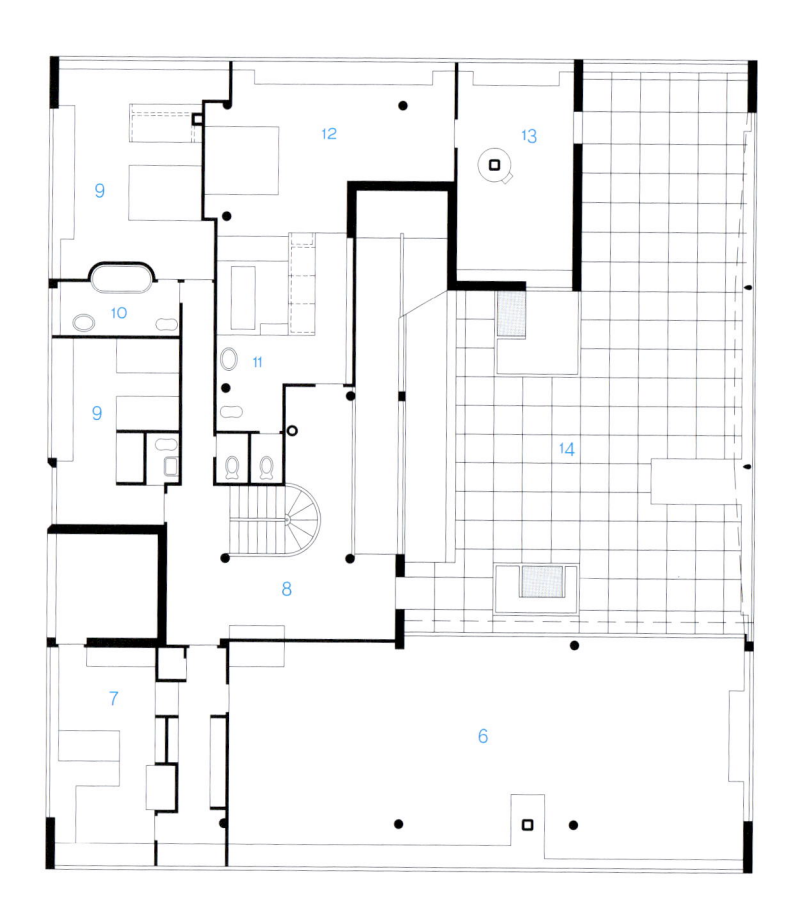

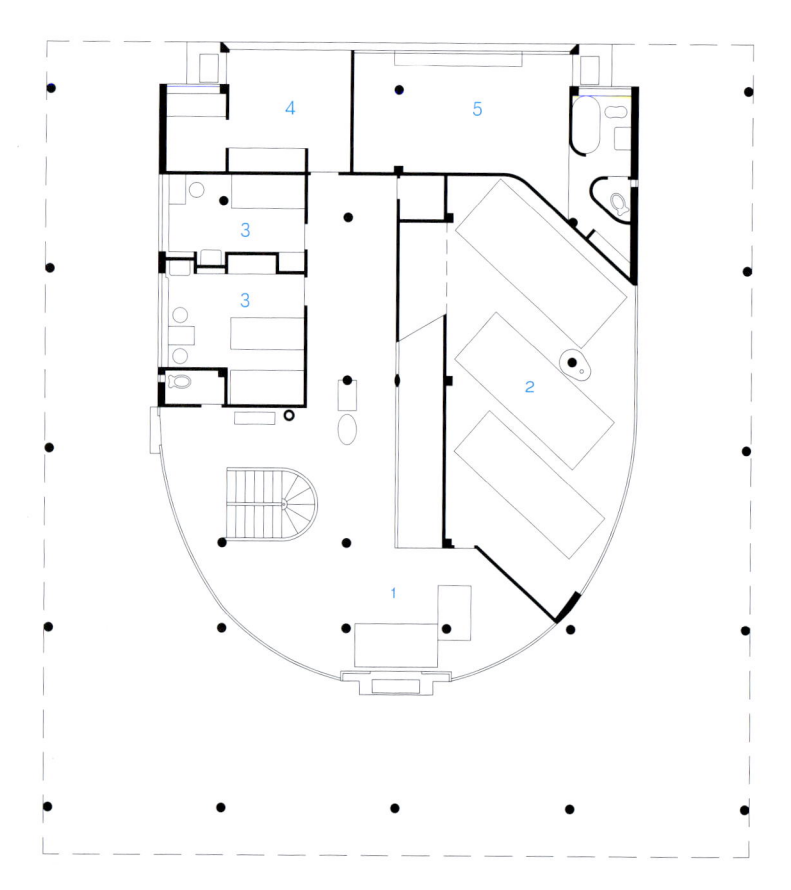

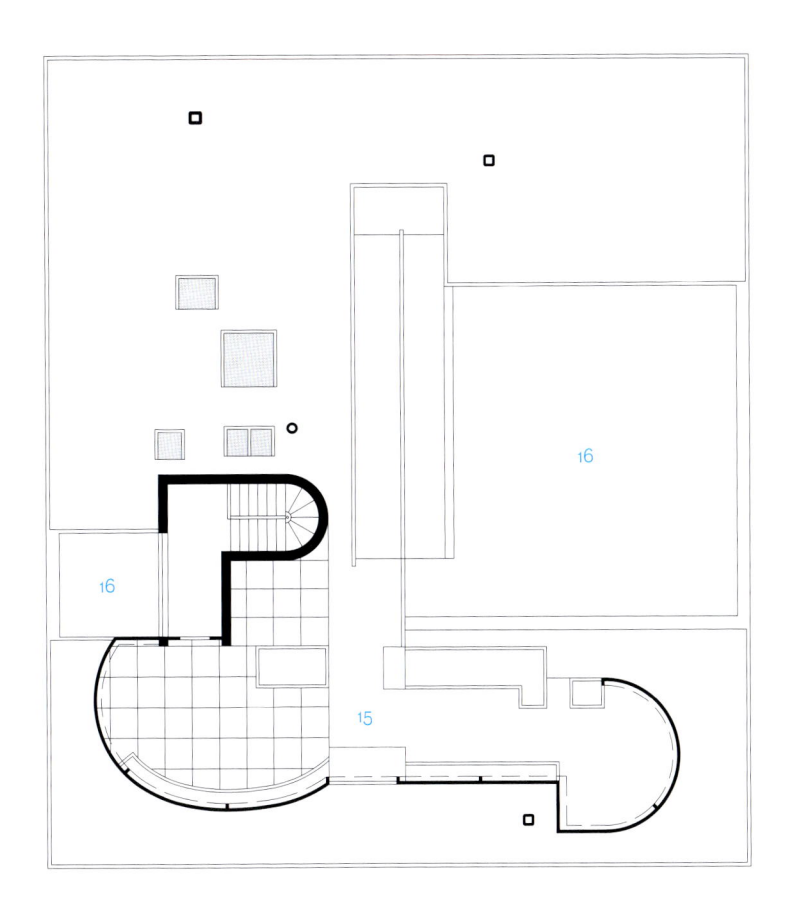

Second-floor plan Third-floor / roof terrace plan
First-floor plan

1	Entrance hall	9	Bedroom
2	Garage	10	Bathroom
3	Maid's room	11	Master bathroom
4	Laundry	12	Master bedroom
5	Chauffeur's room	13	Sitting room
6	Living room	14	Outdoor terrace
7	Kitchen	15	Solarium
8	Hall	16	Open to below

VILLA DE MANDROT

LOCATION: Le Pradet, near Toulon in the south of France
DATE: 1929

Designed as a vacation home for Hélène de Mandrot, the house is located outside Toulon in Le Pradet. It is Le Corbusier's first building that architecturally expresses the division and contrast between local materials and labor and industrialized construction materials and methods. This reflected his realization that the modern architecture of an industrialized society does not have to exclude or hide vernacular materials and methods of construction. The main building components of the house are load-bearing masonry walls made of locally available stone, poured-in-place concrete slabs and columns, and prefabricated steel windows. In addition to the use of local stone, the siting of the house reinforces its connection with its setting. The house rises naturally out of the site and is oriented to provide views of the surrounding Mediterranean landscape.

By bringing together old and new materials and methods of construction, Le Corbusier tried to maximize the architectural potential of each and achieve a timeless architecture that was contemporary yet rooted in local history. As an architectural statement of Le Corbusier's changing philosophy, the house was a success; however, it was so fraught with problems—mainly severe water leaks through the joints between masonry walls and steel windows—the client called it uninhabitable from the very first days.

CLIENT: Hélène de Mandrot
PROGRAM: Vacation house
FEATURES: Prefabricated steel windows, load-bearing masonry walls, courtyard, guesthouse

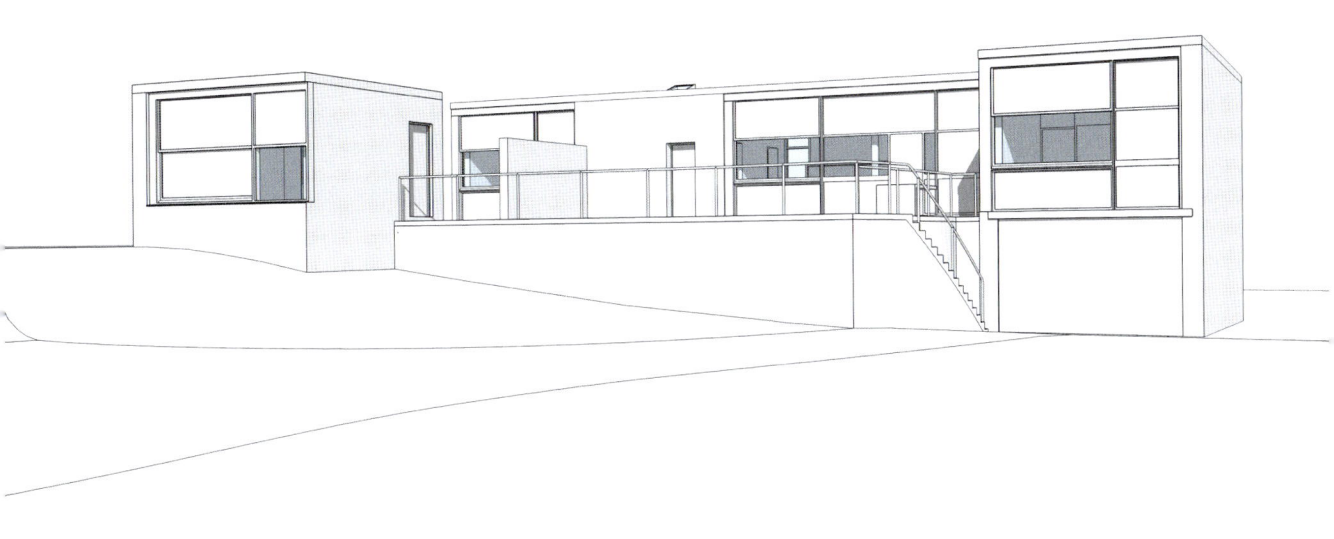

155 **VILLA DE MANDROT** Exterior perspective, south elevation

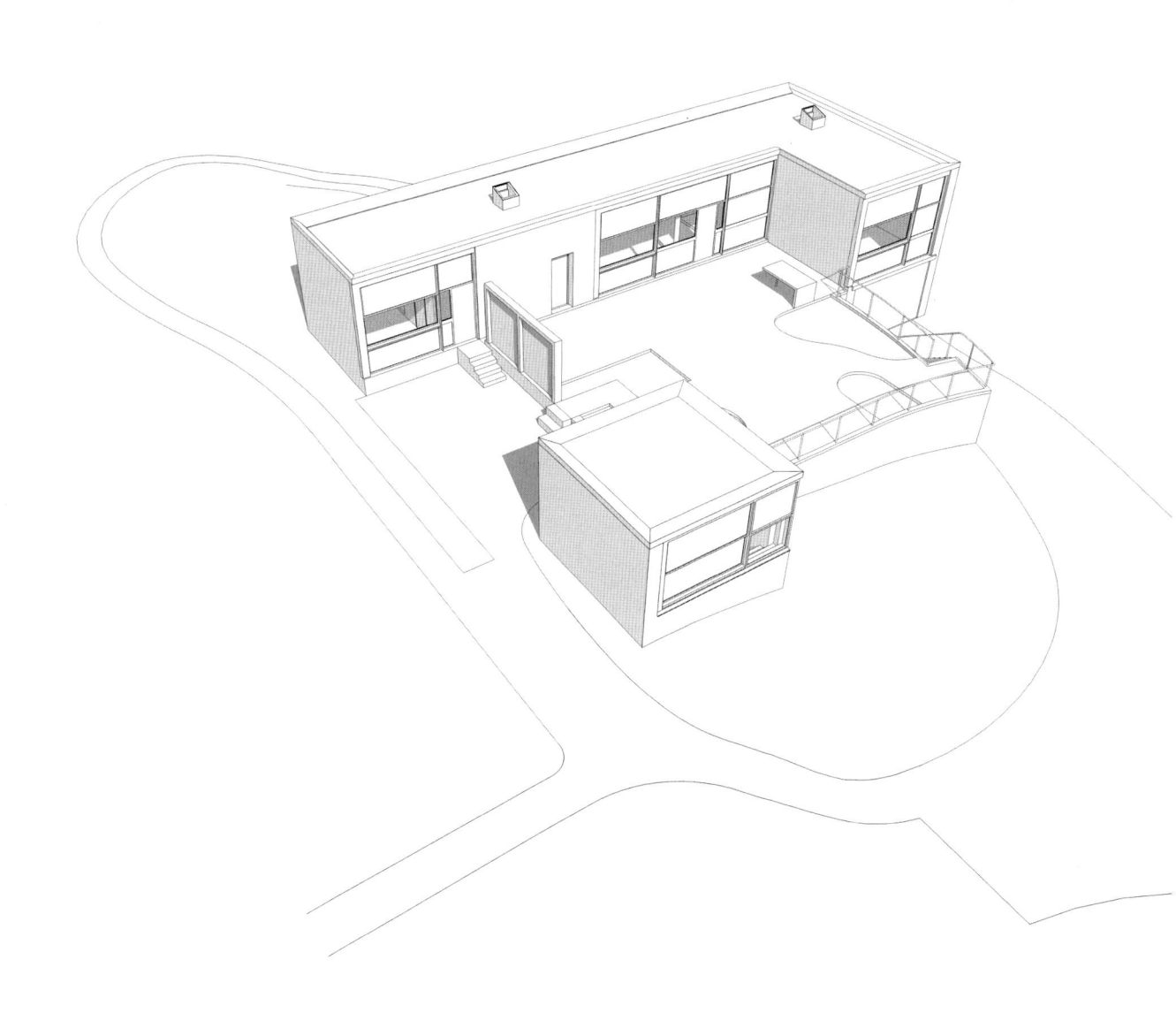

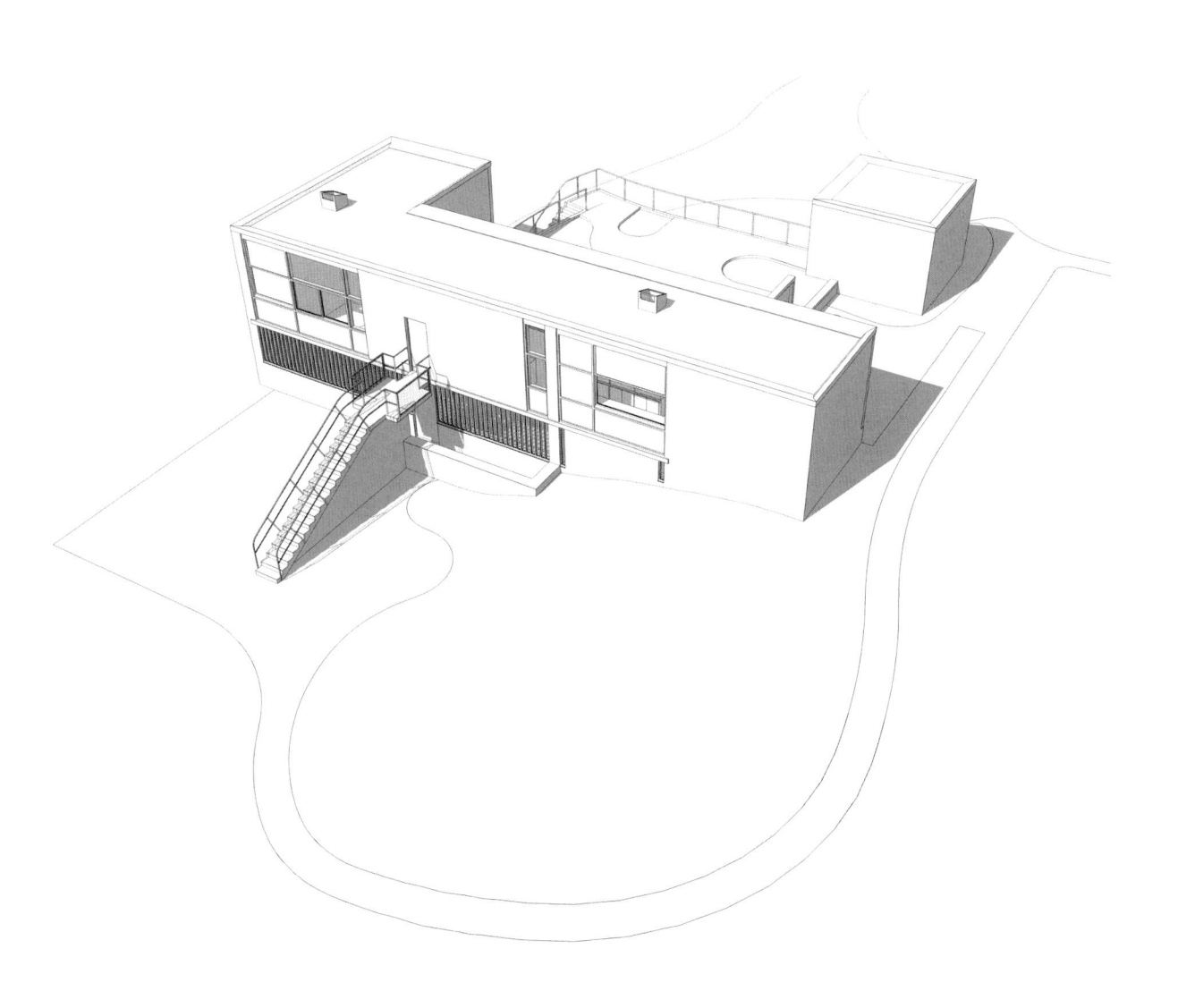

VILLA DE MANDROT Aerial perspective, northwest corner, backyard

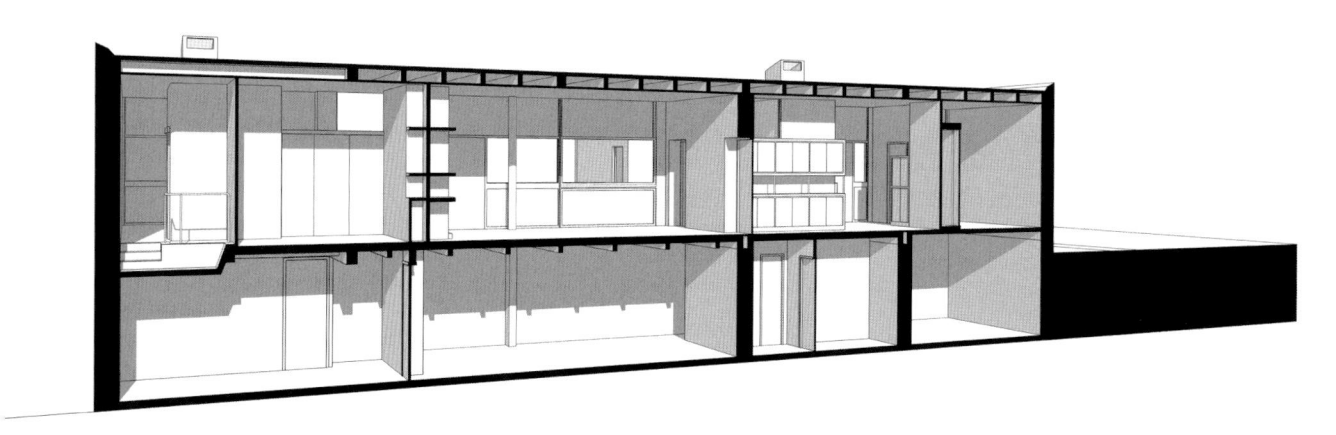

158 **VILLA DE MANDROT**   •   East–west sectional perspective

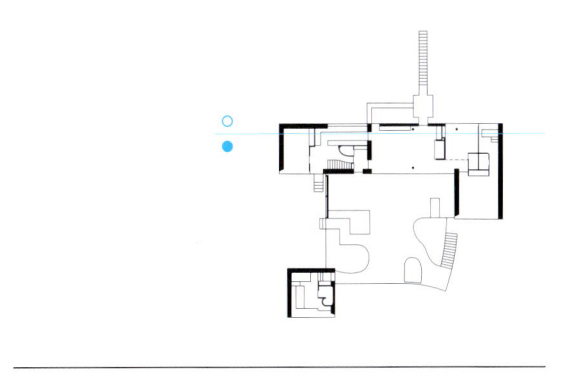

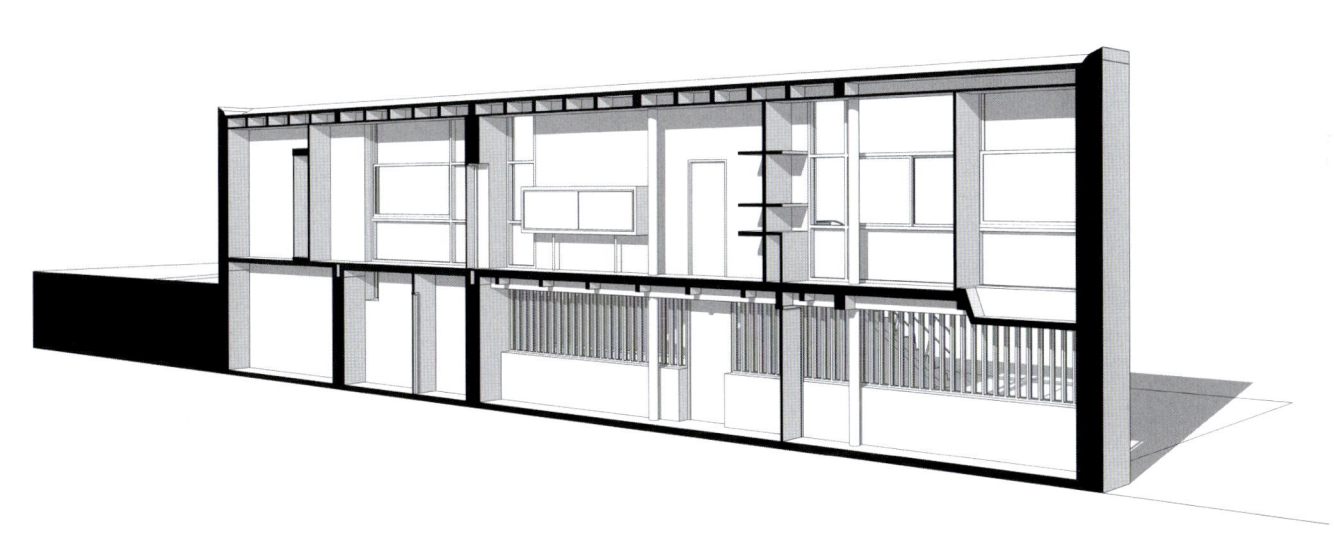

159 VILLA DE MANDROT ○ West–east sectional perspective

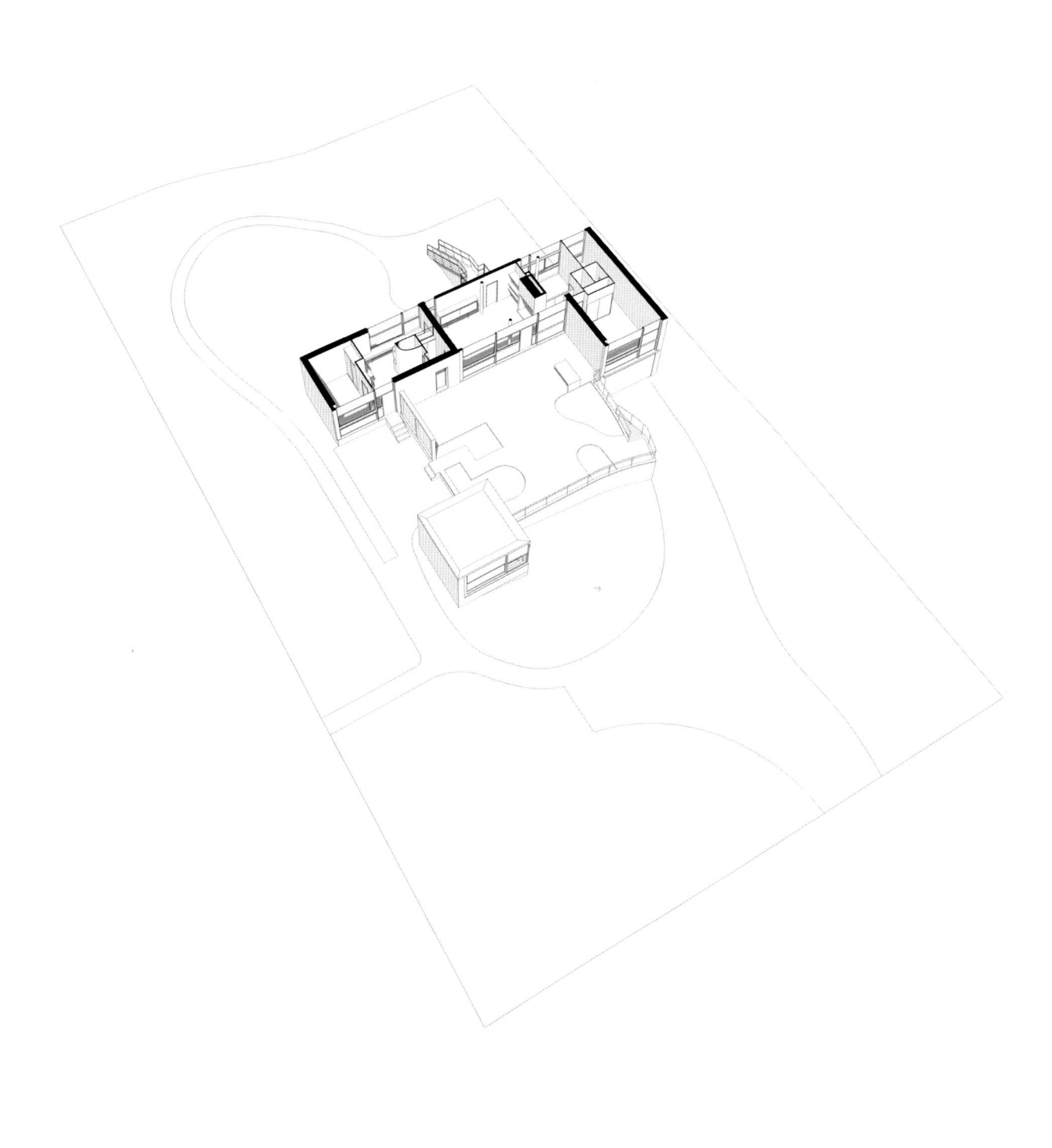

160 **VILLA DE MANDROT** Second-floor planar perspective, southwest corner

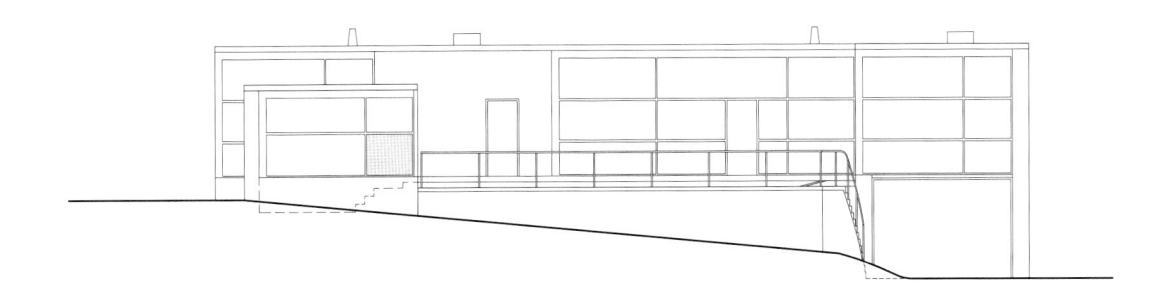

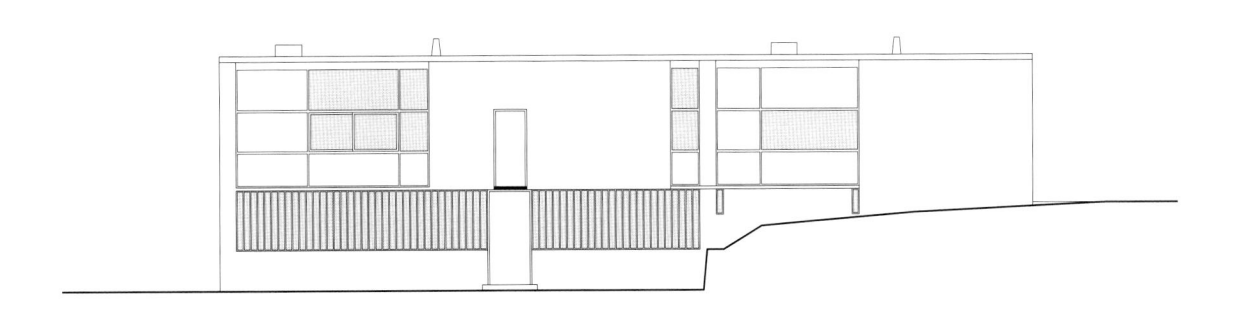

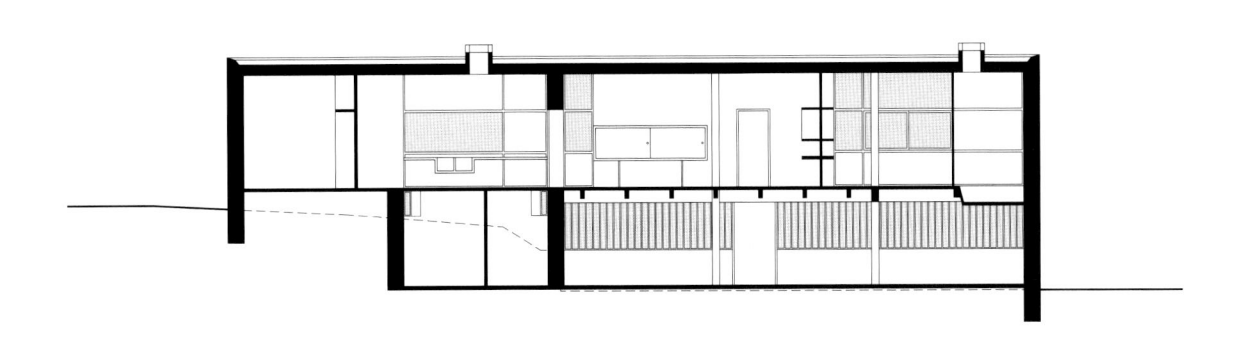

South elevation
North elevation
West–east section

First-floor plan
Site plan (1:500)

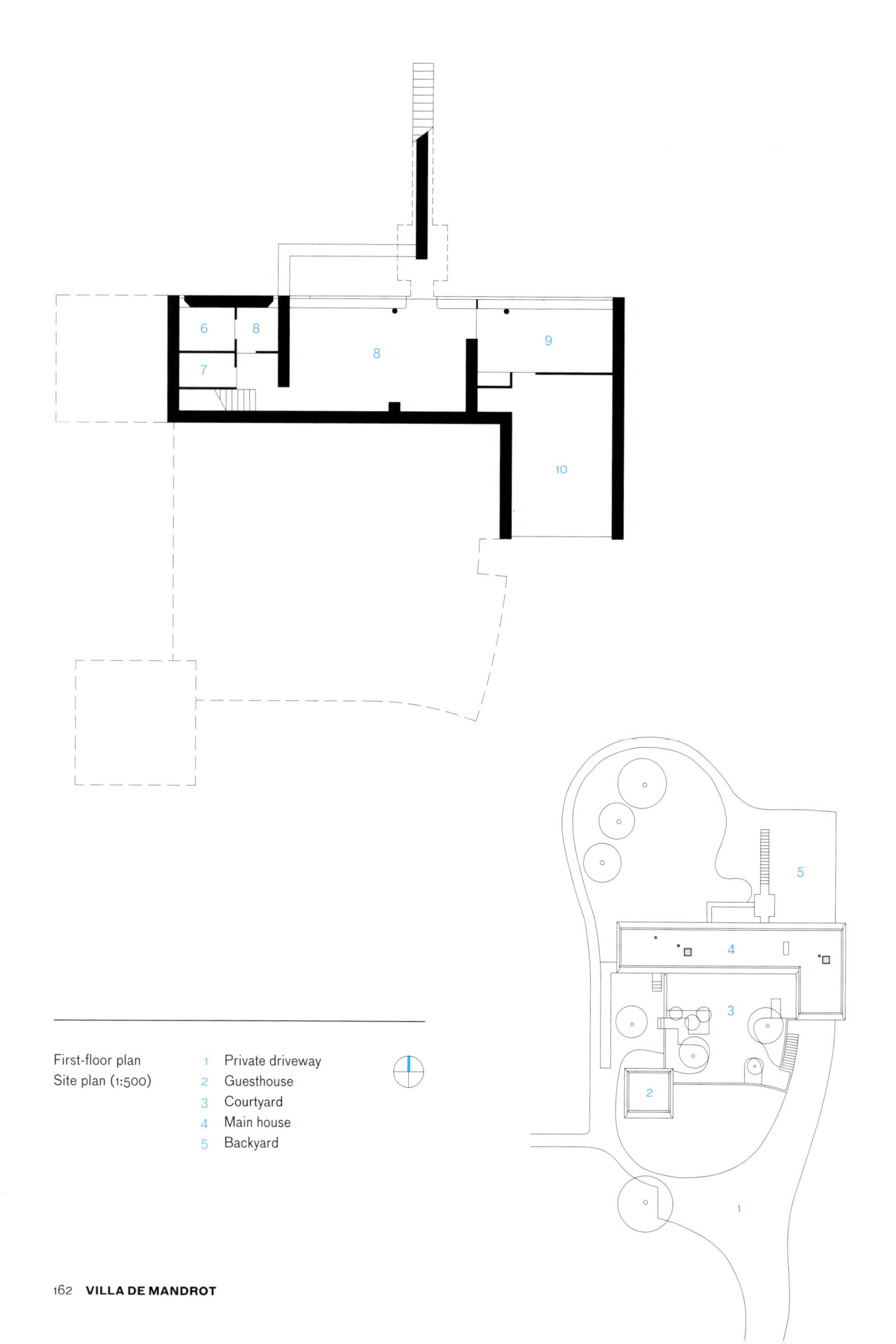

1. Private driveway
2. Guesthouse
3. Courtyard
4. Main house
5. Backyard

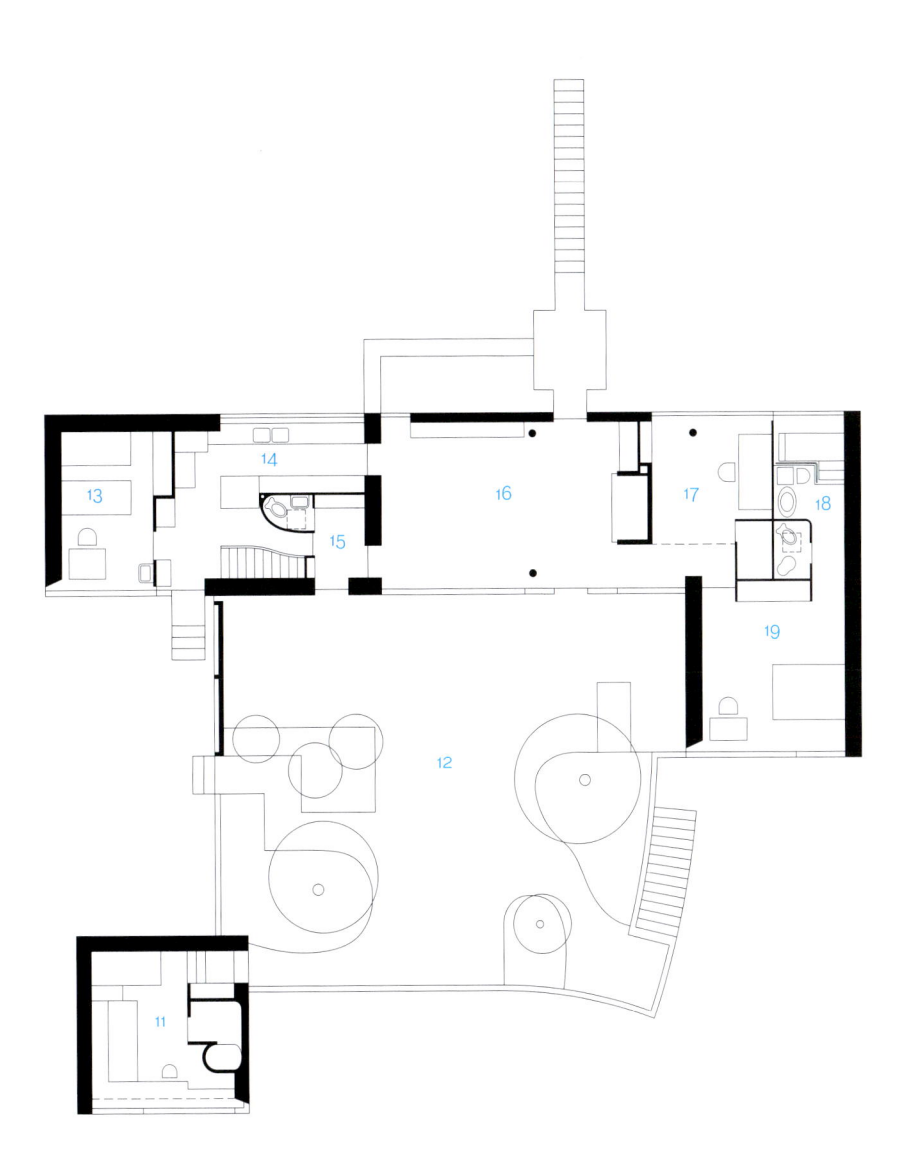

Second-floor plan

- 6 Cellar
- 7 Coal storage
- 8 Utility room
- 9 Workshop
- 10 Garage
- 11 Guesthouse
- 12 Courtyard
- 13 Bedroom
- 14 Kitchen
- 15 Entrance vestibule
- 16 Living and dining room
- 17 Study
- 18 Master bathroom
- 19 Master bedroom

MAISON DE WEEKEND (HENFEL)

LOCATION: La Celle-Saint-Cloud, a suburb near Paris, France
DATE: 1934

With the Maison de Weekend—as with villas le Sextant and de Mandrot—Le Corbusier began to move away from the streamlined forms of his purist, white villas of the 1920s, experimenting with traditional methods of construction and primitive forms of dwellings. The most distinctive feature of the house is the vaulted roof, which evokes not only industrial but also ancient architecture. The flexibility implied in the modular nature of the vaulted construction accommodates various planning arrangements, which are clearly demonstrated in the varying length of each bay of the roof and also in the independent single module of the vault in the garden.

Sectional perspectives show the privacy of the interior spaces; this privacy was the client's primary requirement. There is hardly any view to the outside, with the one exception of a floor-to-ceiling window.

Burying the house in the embankment and limiting the number and size of openings creates private interior spaces. Glass-block walls also ensure privacy while bringing in diffused light. Covering the house with a sod roof and using unfinished stone for the exterior wall visually integrates the building with the surrounding natural landscape.

However, the client's initial excitement for the house was later tempered when its cellar was flooded with water leaks through walls that were constantly damp.

CLIENT: Henri Félix
PROGRAM: Small weekend house
FEATURES: Concrete vaults, load-bearing masonry, sod roof

Exterior perspective, southwest corner

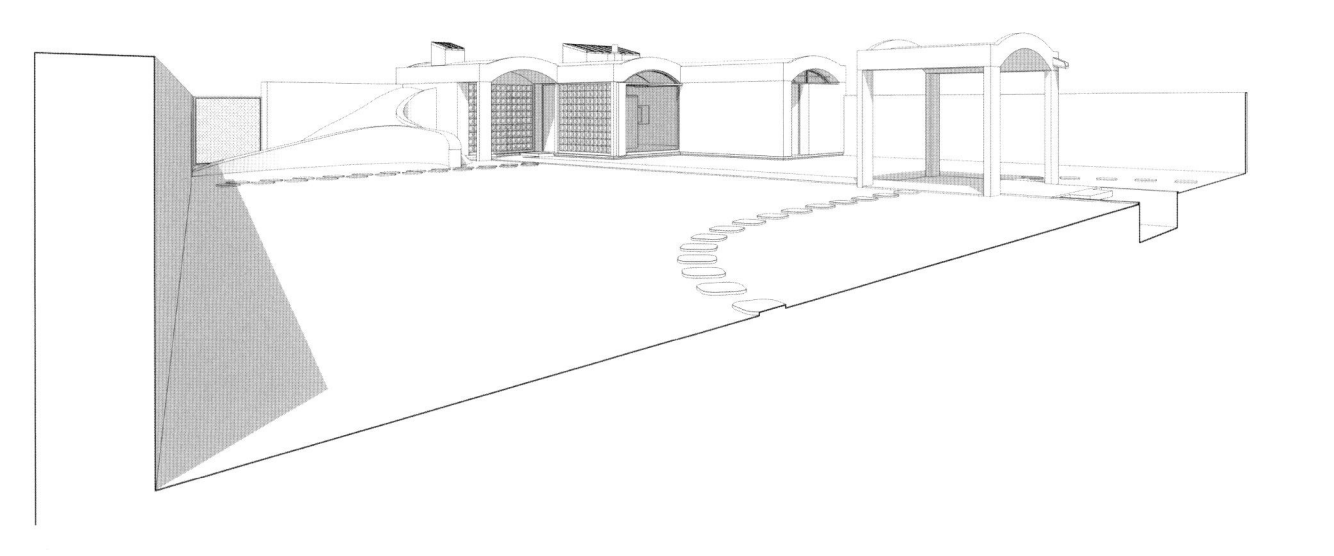

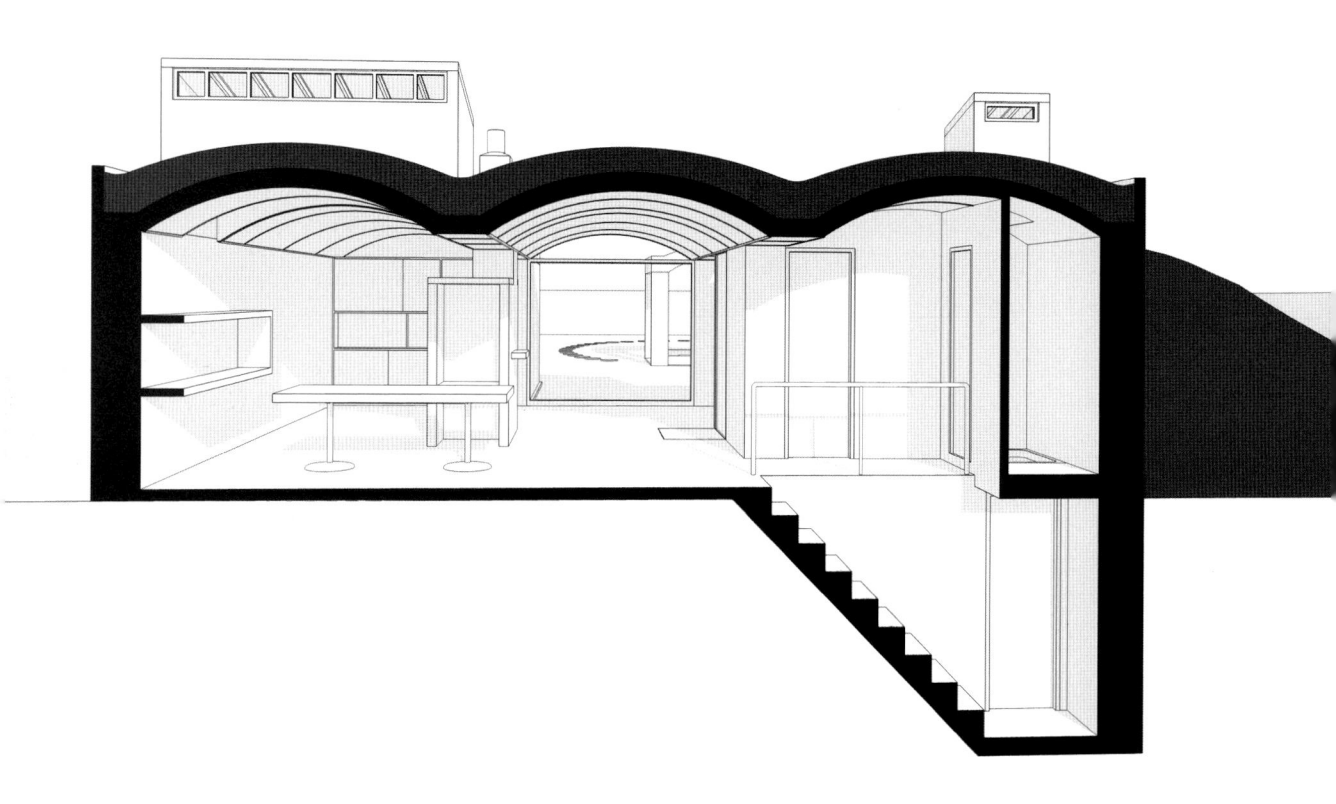

166 **MAISON DE WEEKEND**   •   East–west sectional perspective at stairs

East–west sectional perspective at skylights

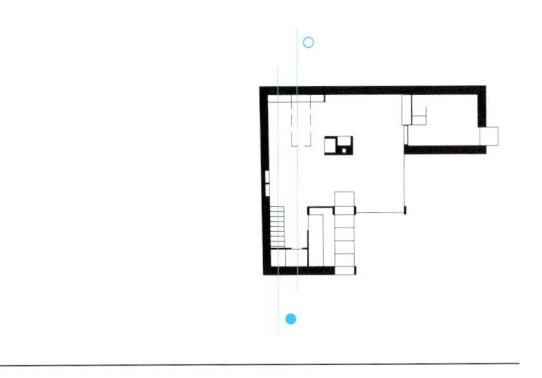

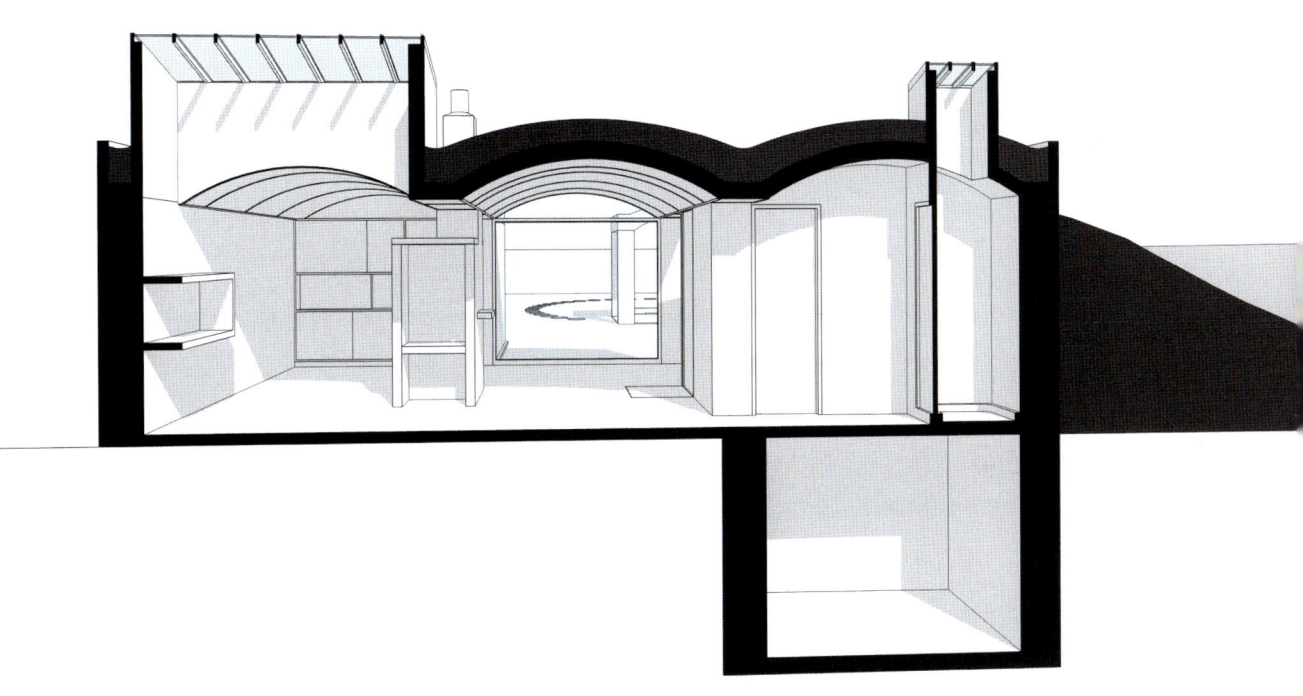

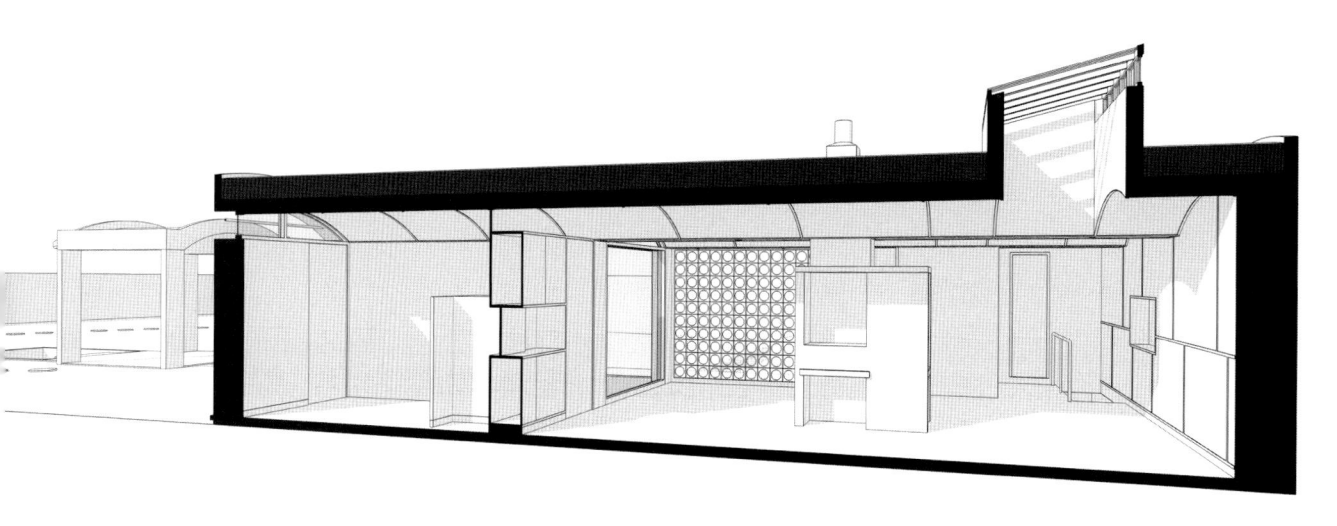

South–north sectional perspective at living and dining rooms

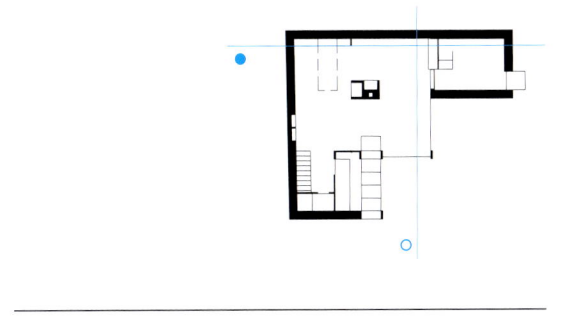

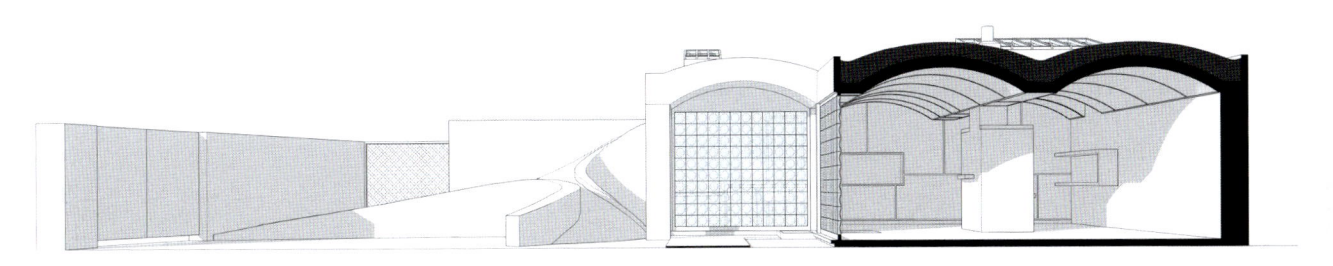

West–east sectional perspective at entrance hall

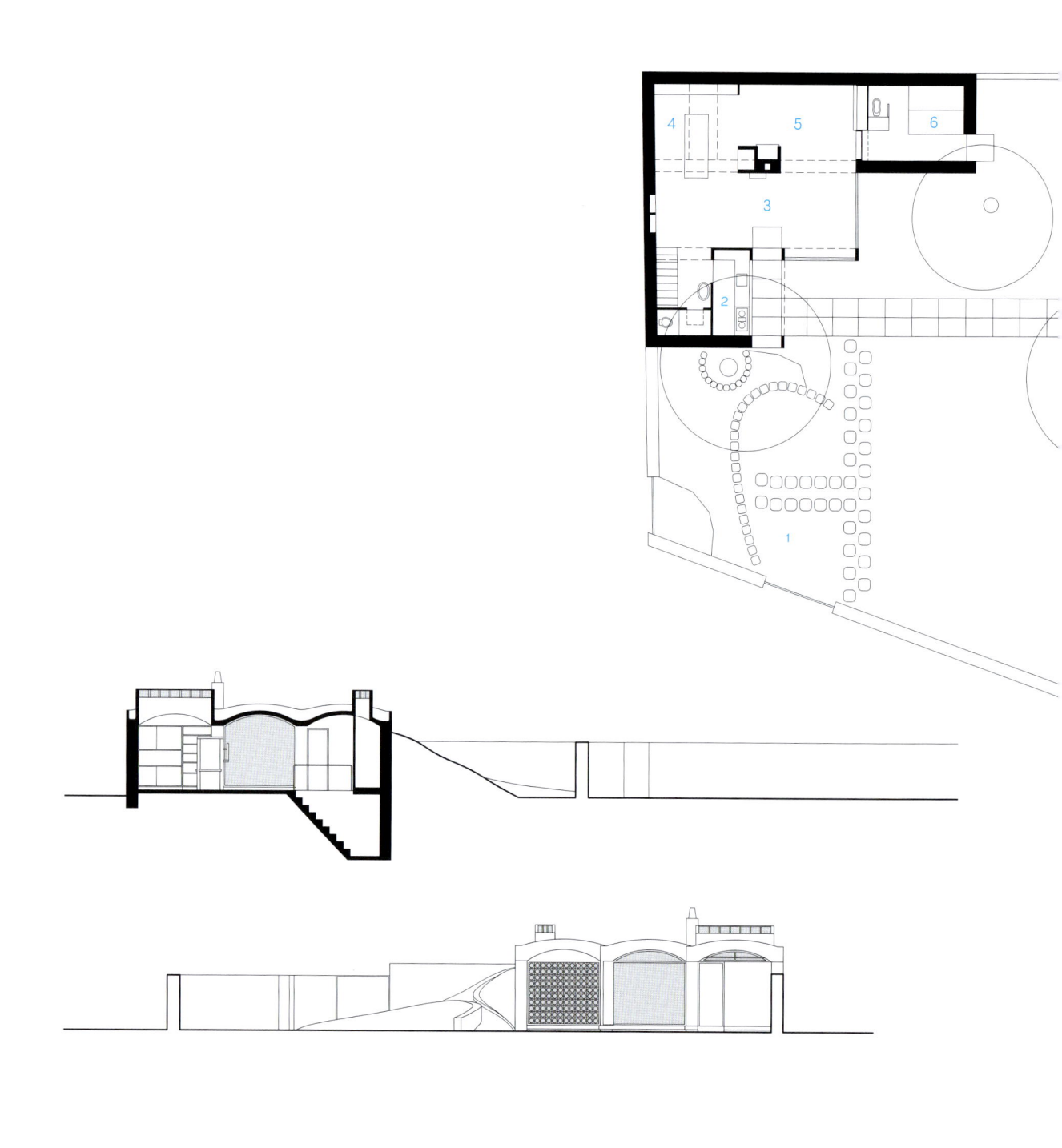

East–west section
South elevation

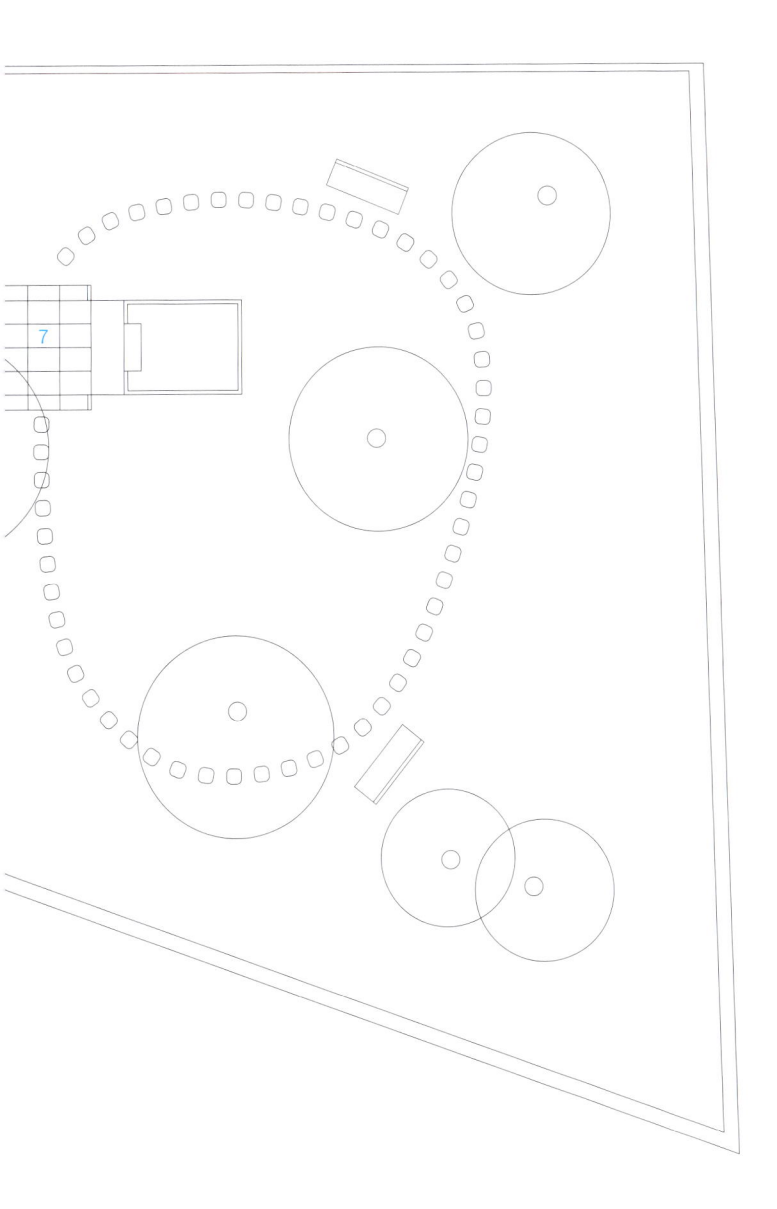

First-floor plan

1. Parking
2. Kitchen
3. Entrance hall
4. Dining room
5. Living room
6. Bedroom
7. Gazebo

171 **MAISON DE WEEKEND**

VILLA LE SEXTANT

LOCATION: Les Mathes, France
DATE: 1935

Villa le Sextant was designed for Albin Peyron, director of the Compagnie des Lampes and son of Colonel "Albin" Louis Octave Peyron, commissioner general of the French Salvation Army, for whom Le Corbusier had built Cité de Refuge (1929) in Paris. Because it was used only during the summer months, Villa le Sextant was built with the most economical means. Due to its limited budget, Le Corbusier planned the house in distinct components that could easily be constructed in separate successive phases by the local contractors without the architect's administrative support.

L-shaped, load-bearing masonry walls are oriented so that the private areas of the house face the ocean and the more public areas face the street. A V-shaped roof with a large gutter, downspouts, and scuppers at its center was designed to respond to the local climate, with its occasional downpours. The roof also reflects interior planning layouts. Constructional logic and building components—the scale and spacing of large masonry walls, primary girders, secondary beams, and rafters; the corrugated roof panels; and the oversized wooden guardrails—articulate the house.

Although the design may seem formally restrained, Le Corbusier succeeded in creating a residence that provides rich spatial experiences through his careful attention to siting, placement of windows, and construction details.

CLIENT: Albin Peyron
PROGRAM: Summer vacation house
FEATURES: Design expressive of the constructional logic

Exterior perspective, northeast corner

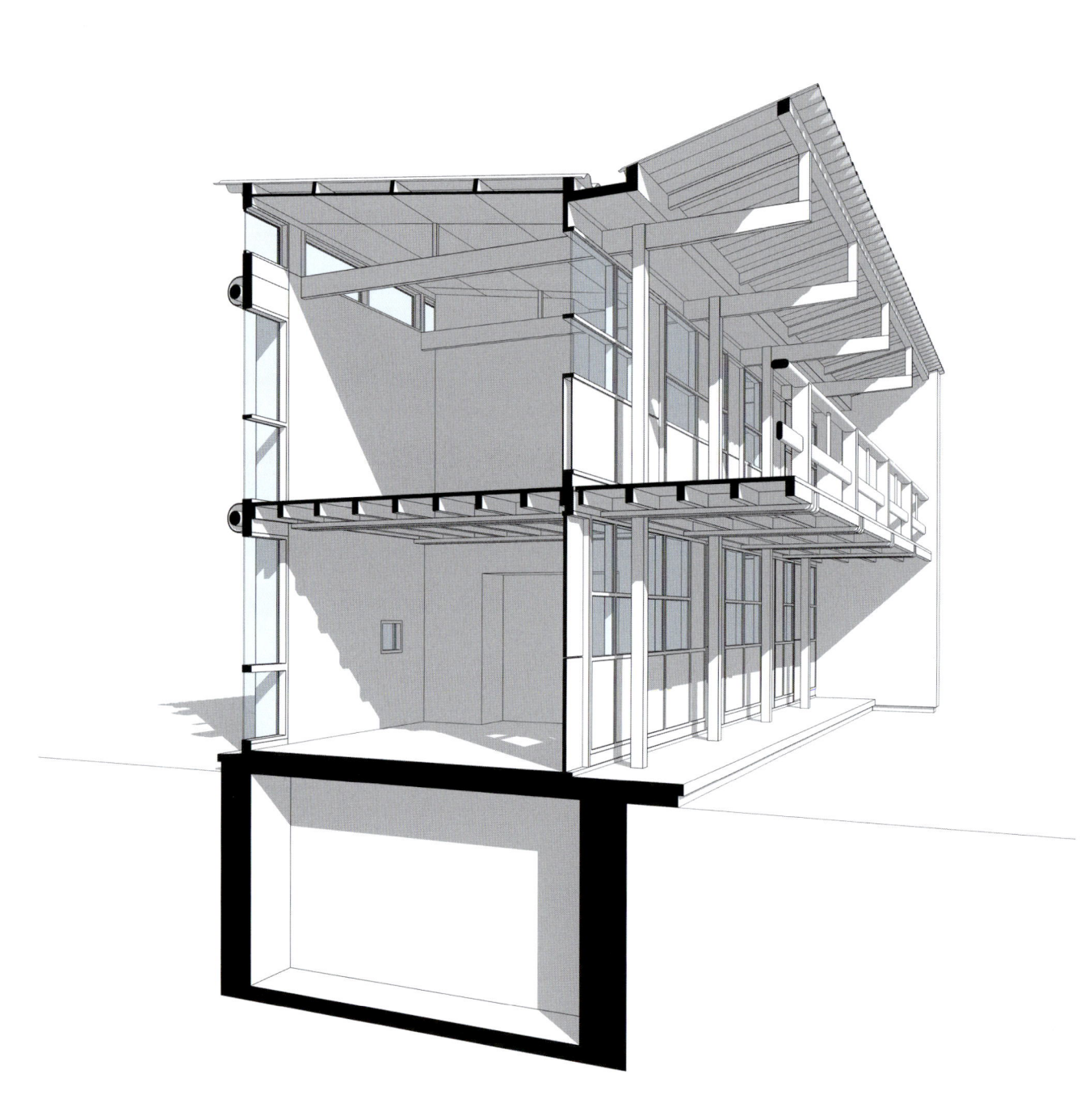

West–east sectional perspective at living room and kitchen

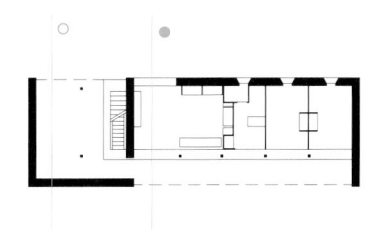

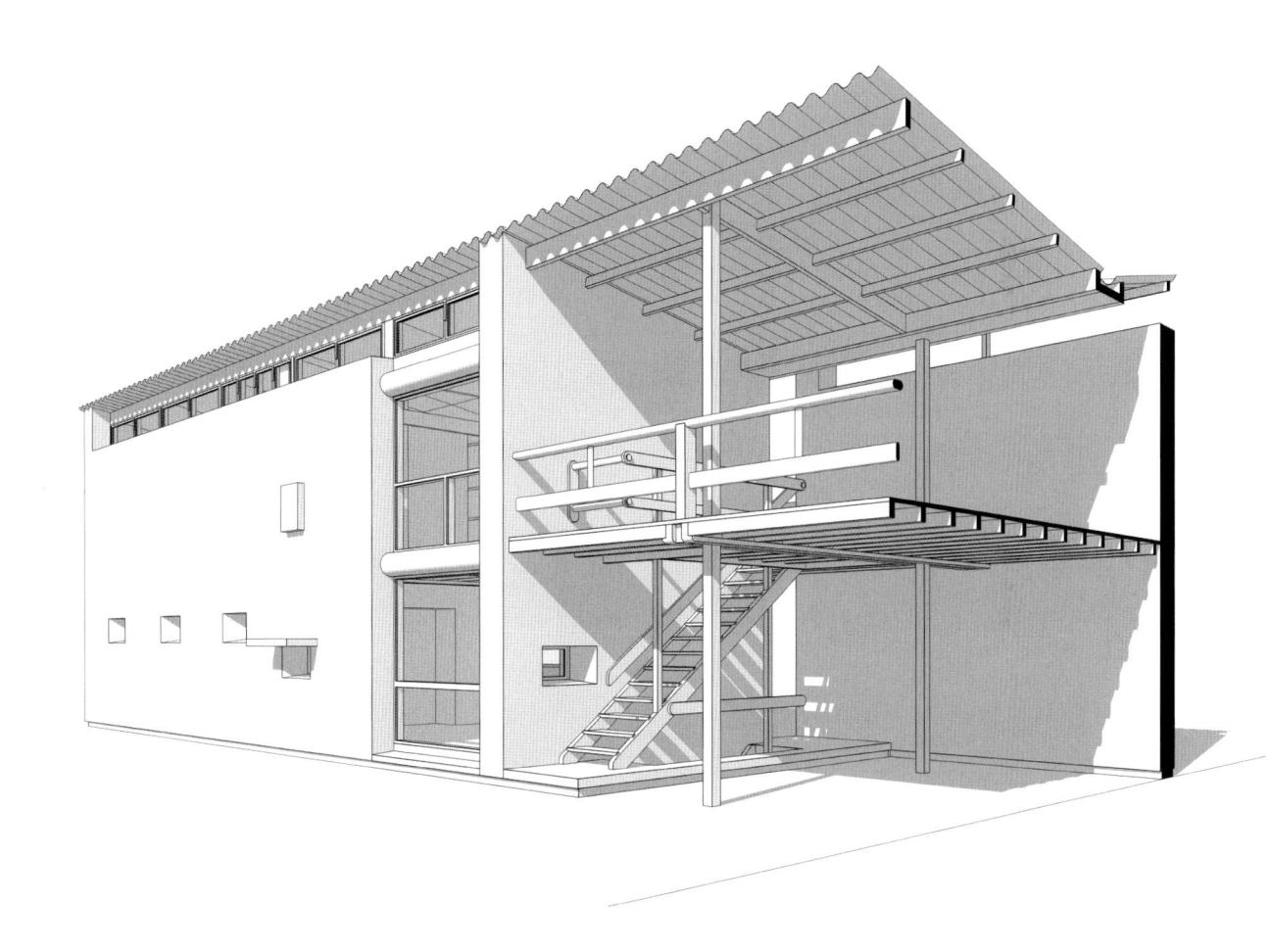

175 **VILLA LE SEXTANT** ○ West–east sectional perspective at terrace and covered patio

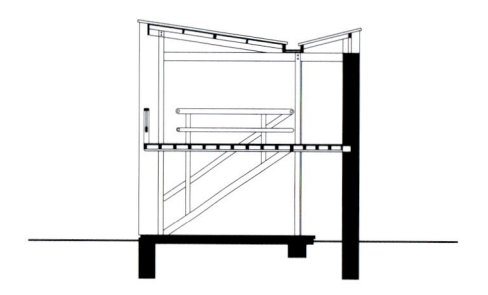

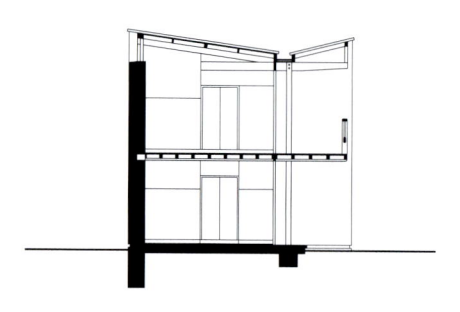

West–east sections
Second-floor plan
First-floor plan

1 Covered patio
2 Dining room
3 Kitchen
4 Bathroom
5 Bedroom
6 Terrace
7 Living room

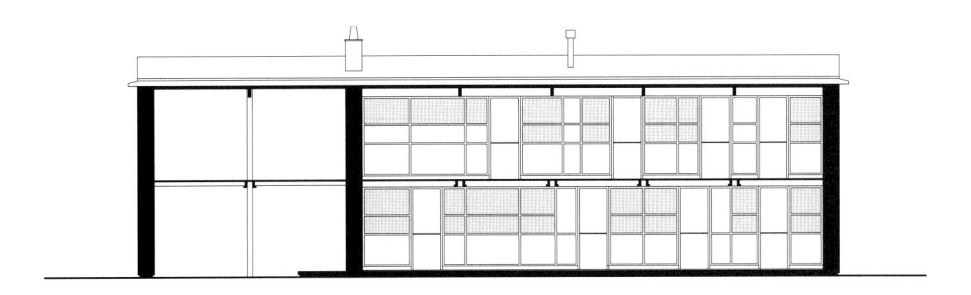

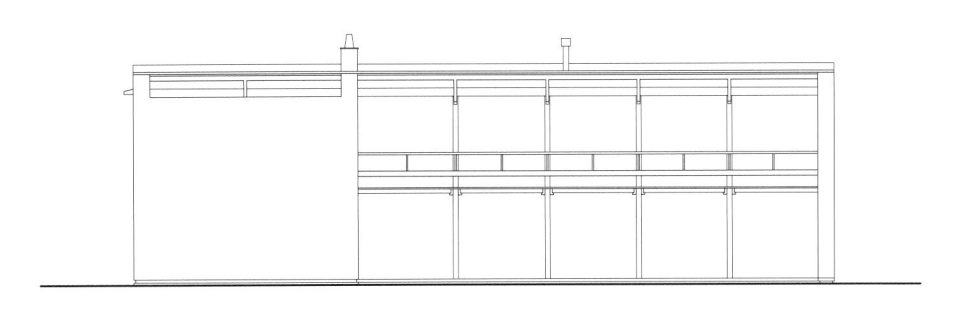

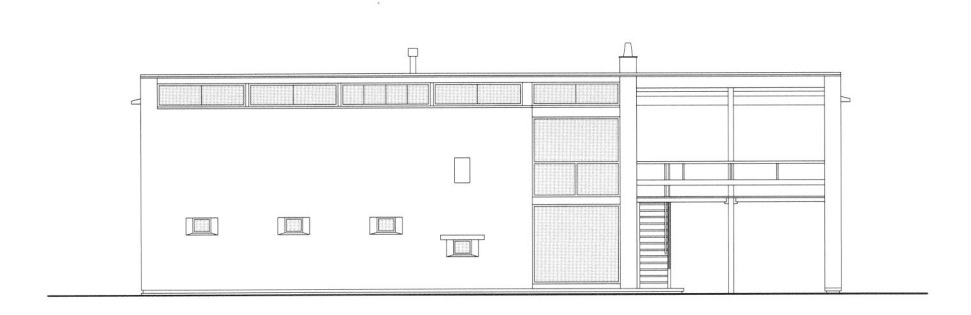

South–north section
East elevation
West elevation

21 MAISON CURUTCHET

LOCATION: La Plata, Argentina
DATE: 1949

Maison Curutchet is one of only two projects that Le Corbusier realized in the Americas. At the time of the commission, he was working on an urban plan for Buenos Aires that was being reviewed by the city government. Before this commission from Dr. Pedro Domingo Curutchet, Le Corbusier had designed two unexecuted projects in Argentina—Villa Ocampo and Villa Martinez.

Maison Curutchet was built on a narrow site with existing buildings on all sides but one, which is open to the Paseo del Bosque park across the street. Its program consists of a clinic and residence. Basing his design on his previously perfected Five Points of a New Architecture, Le Corbusier raised the building up on *pilotis* to free up space for courtyards to serve both the clinic and residence. The clinic is positioned in front, while the residence is in the back, with an exterior ramp and roof garden connecting the two.

Local architect Amancio Williams, whom Le Corbusier recommended to Dr. Curutchet, tried to retain as much of the original design as possible during detail development and the early stages of construction. Local contractor Simón Ungar, who was hired to keep the project under budget and on schedule, replaced Williams and made several changes to the design, such as lowering and raising wall heights, without Dr. Curutchet's approval.

A brise-soleil (a solar shading device) doubles as a formal element to integrate two separate and contrasting programs into one unified composition. The vertical projection of the brise-soleil above the roof terrace at the clinic aligns with the roof parapet of a neighboring building and corresponds to the scale of a second double-height brise-soleil at the residence. Facing the street and park, it is sized appropriately as an urban element. By conforming the shape of the house to an angled edge of the site and incorporating brise-soleils, Le Corbusier made a site-specific and climate-appropriate adaptation of his architectural ideas from the 1920s.

CLIENT: Dr. Pedro Domingo Curutchet
PROGRAM: Clinic and family residence
FEATURES: Adherence to the Five Points of a New Architecture, ramp, brise-soleil

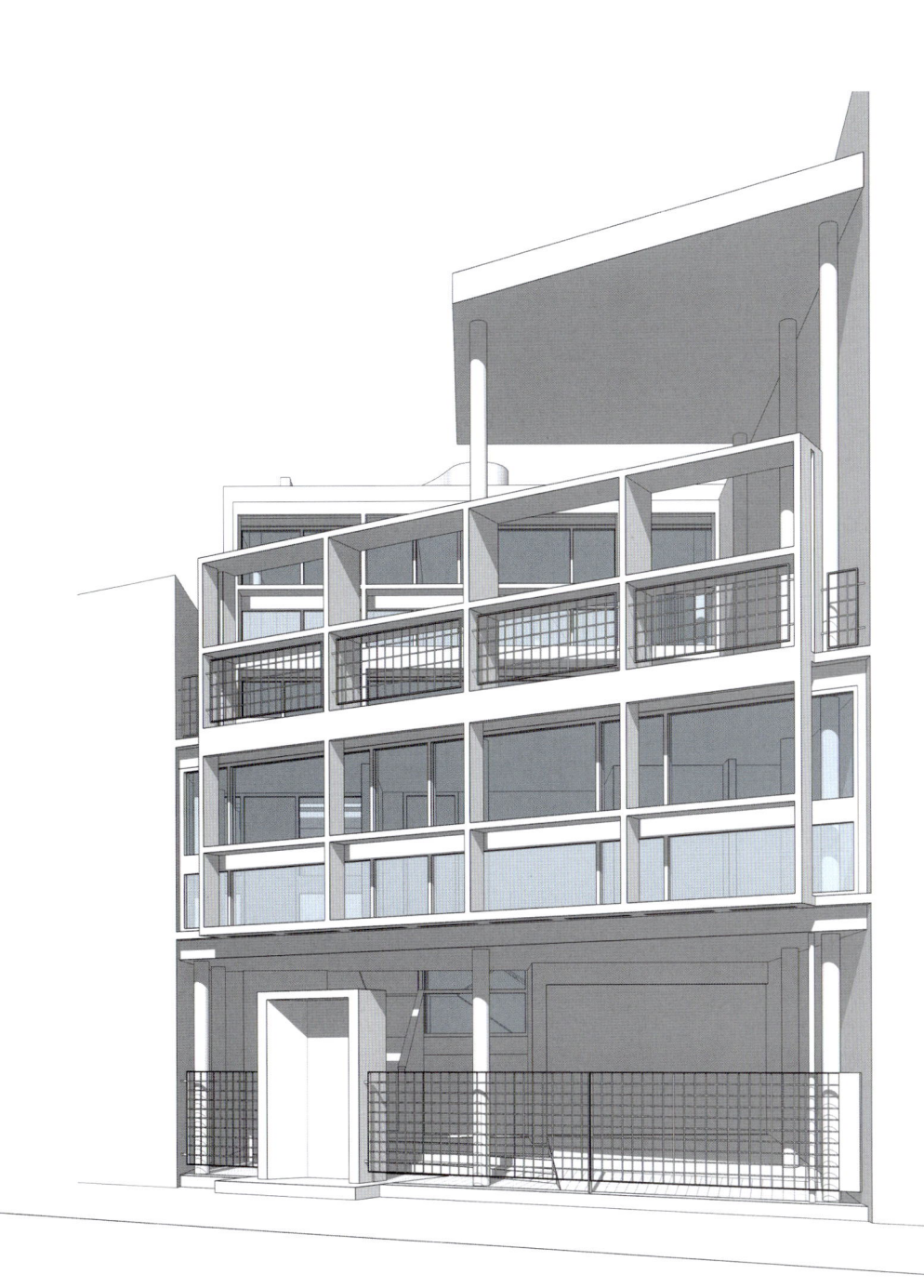

179 MAISON CURUTCHET — Exterior perspective, north elevation

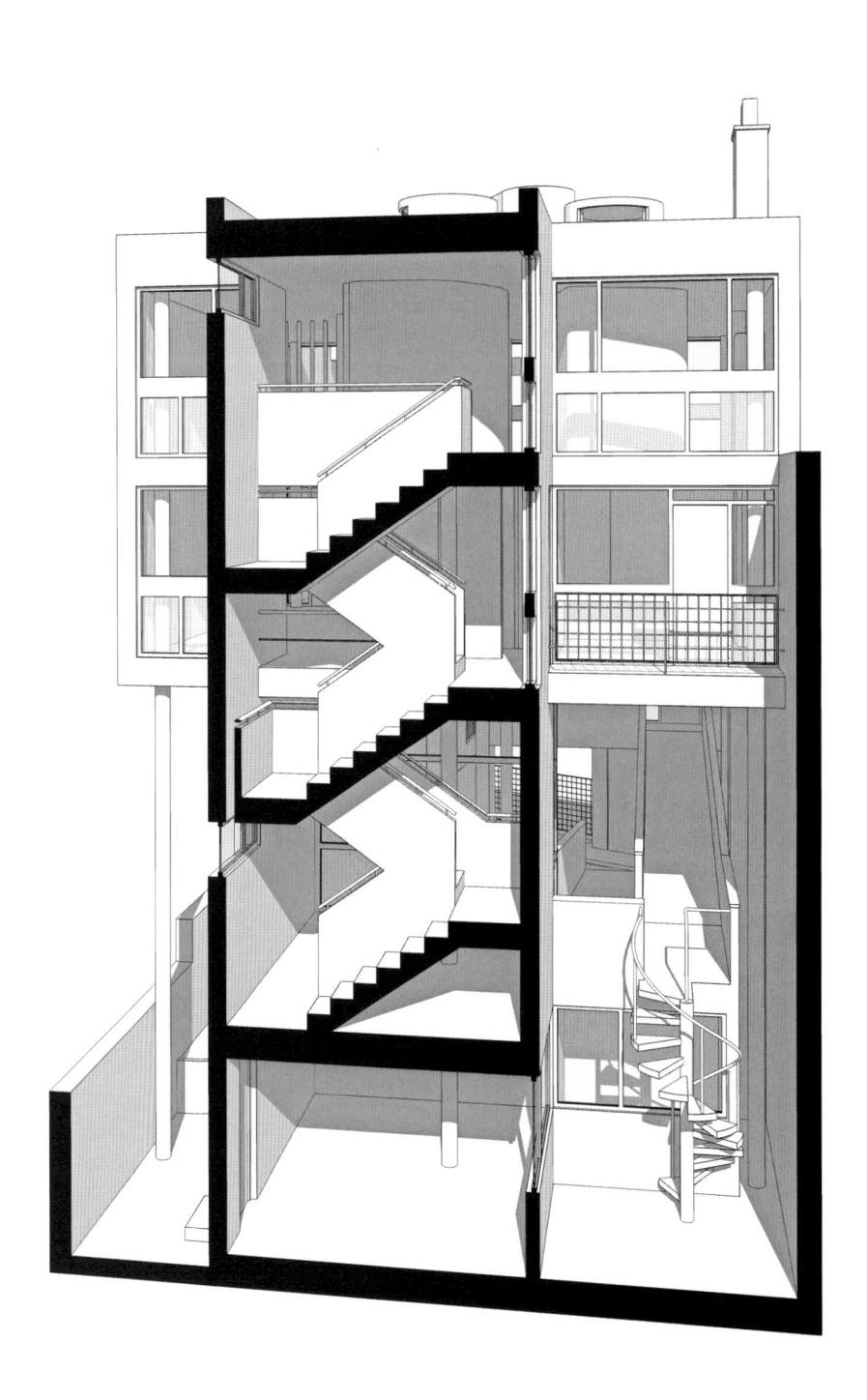

180 **MAISON CURUTCHET** ● West–east sectional perspective at stairs

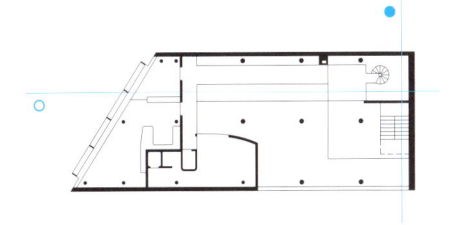

181 **MAISON CURUTCHET** ○ South–north sectional perspective at ramp

182 MAISON CURUTCHET

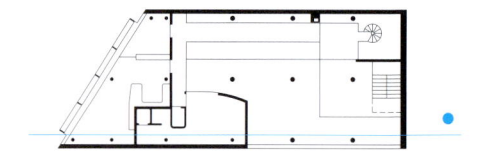

North–south sectional perspective at roof terrace

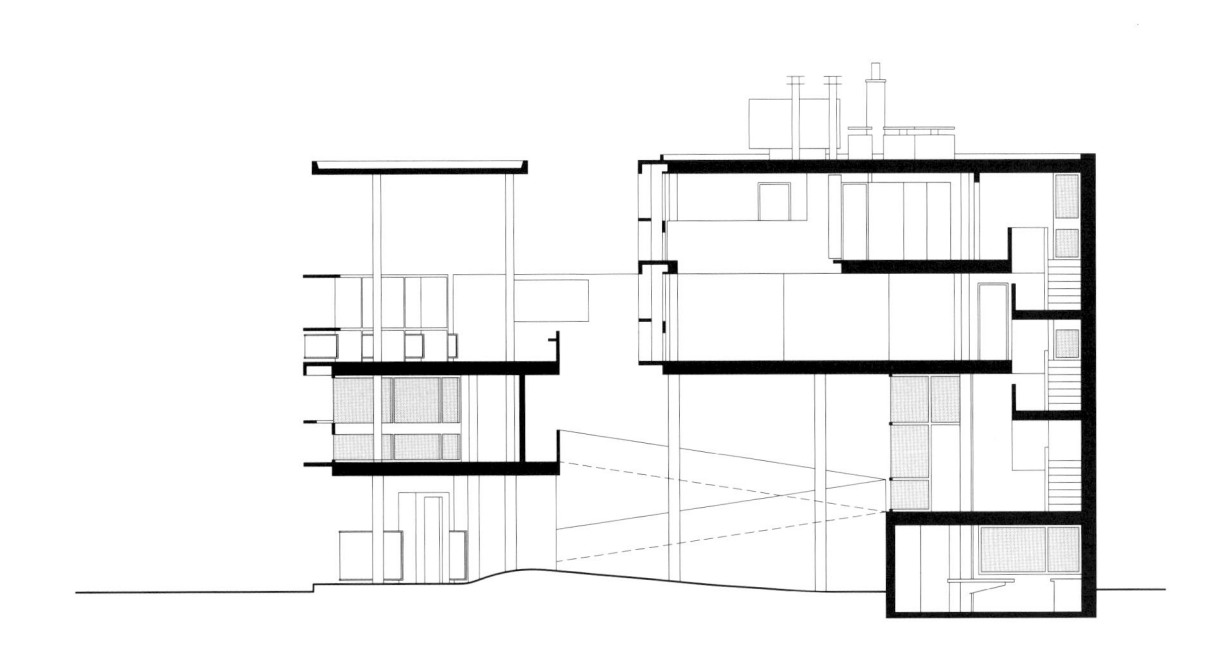

North–south section

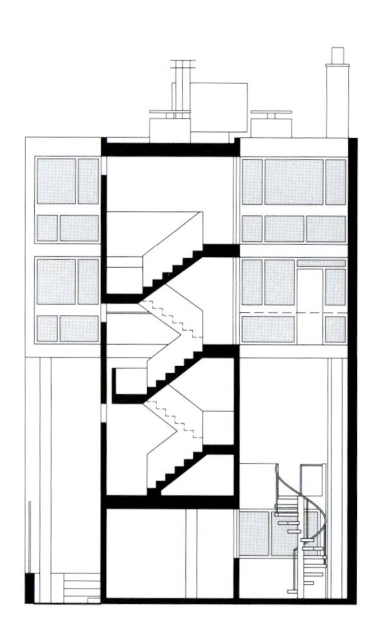

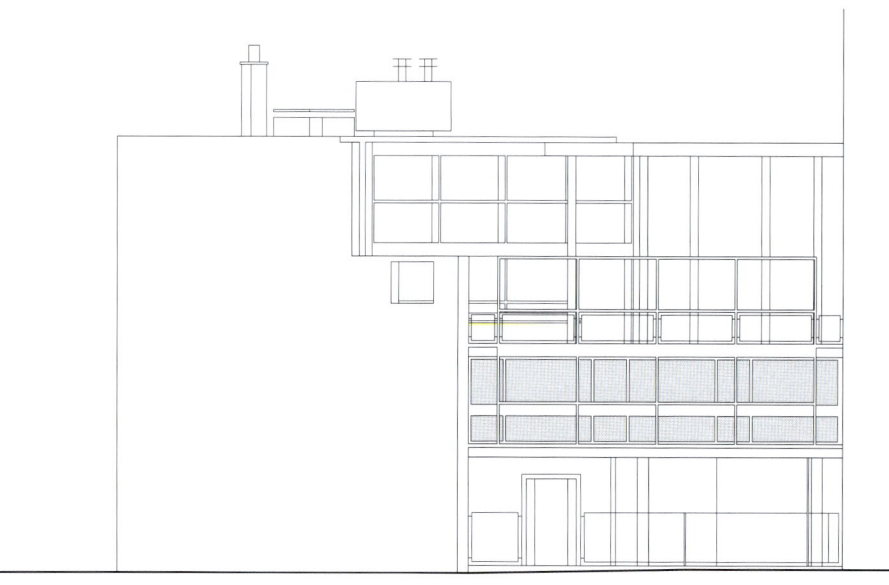

West–east section
North elevation

Fourth-floor plan
Third-floor plan
Second-floor plan
First-floor plan

1 Garage
2 Courtyard
3 Utility room
4 Boiler room
5 Waiting room
6 Clinic
7 Apartment
8 Open to below

9 House entrance
10 Roof terrace
11 Living room
12 Dining room
13 Pantry
14 Kitchen
15 Bedroom
16 Bathroom

MAISON CURUTCHET

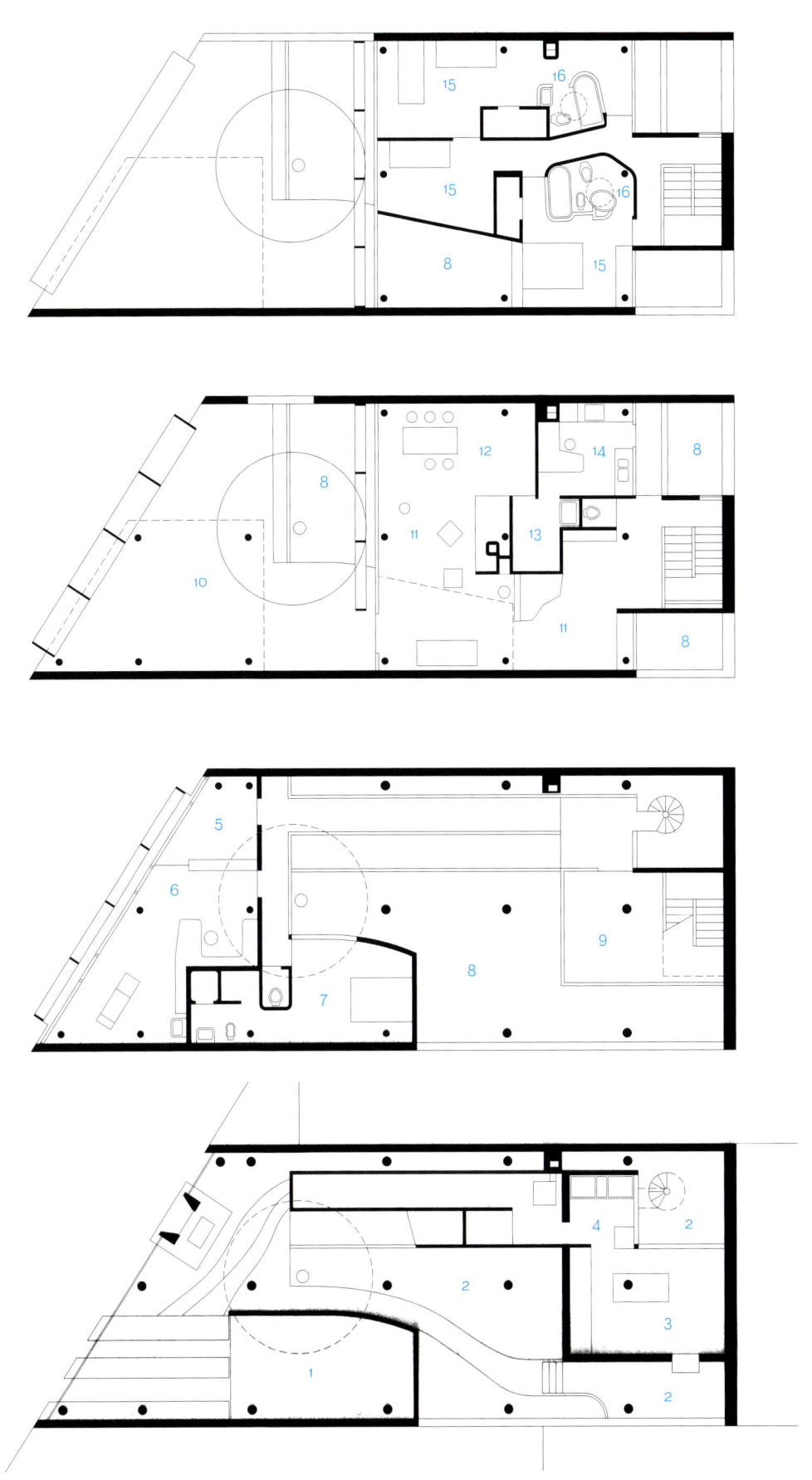

LE PETIT CABANON
LE CORBUSIER

LOCATION: Roquebrune-Cap-Martin, France
DATE: 1951

Sometime after the Second World War, Le Corbusier began spending the month of August in Roquebrune-Cap-Martin in the southeast of France. He dined frequently at a restaurant called l'Etoile de Mer and became friends with its owner, Thomas Rebutato. Rebutato brokered two commissions for the architect in Roquebrune-Cap-Martin: Rob (six holiday studios for artists) and Roq (a large-scale housing development meant to be a holiday village for tourists), neither of which were realized.

Le Corbusier designed a cabin to use as a temporary shelter during the completion of Rob, but since the project was never built, he decided to make the cabin his vacation home. It shares a party wall with Rebutato's restaurant on a narrow terraced lot on a steep slope running down to the Mediterranean Sea. The exterior walls of the cabin are finished with half-round logs, and the roof is covered with corrugated metal panels. The cabin was prefabricated in Corsica and was assembled on site in 1951. Le Corbusier himself applied the final finishes on the cabin over three years and made several on-site improvements. The plan is dimensioned according to the Modulor, a measuring tool that Le Corbusier invented based on mathematics and the proportions of the human body. Different functional zones within the one-room interior space are defined by built-in furniture and the locations of openings. One of the windows frames the bay of Monaco, where Le Corbusier drowned while swimming in 1965.

CLIENT: Le Corbusier
PROGRAM: Summer house
FEATURES: Plan dimensioned according to the Modulor, prefabrication and on-site assembly

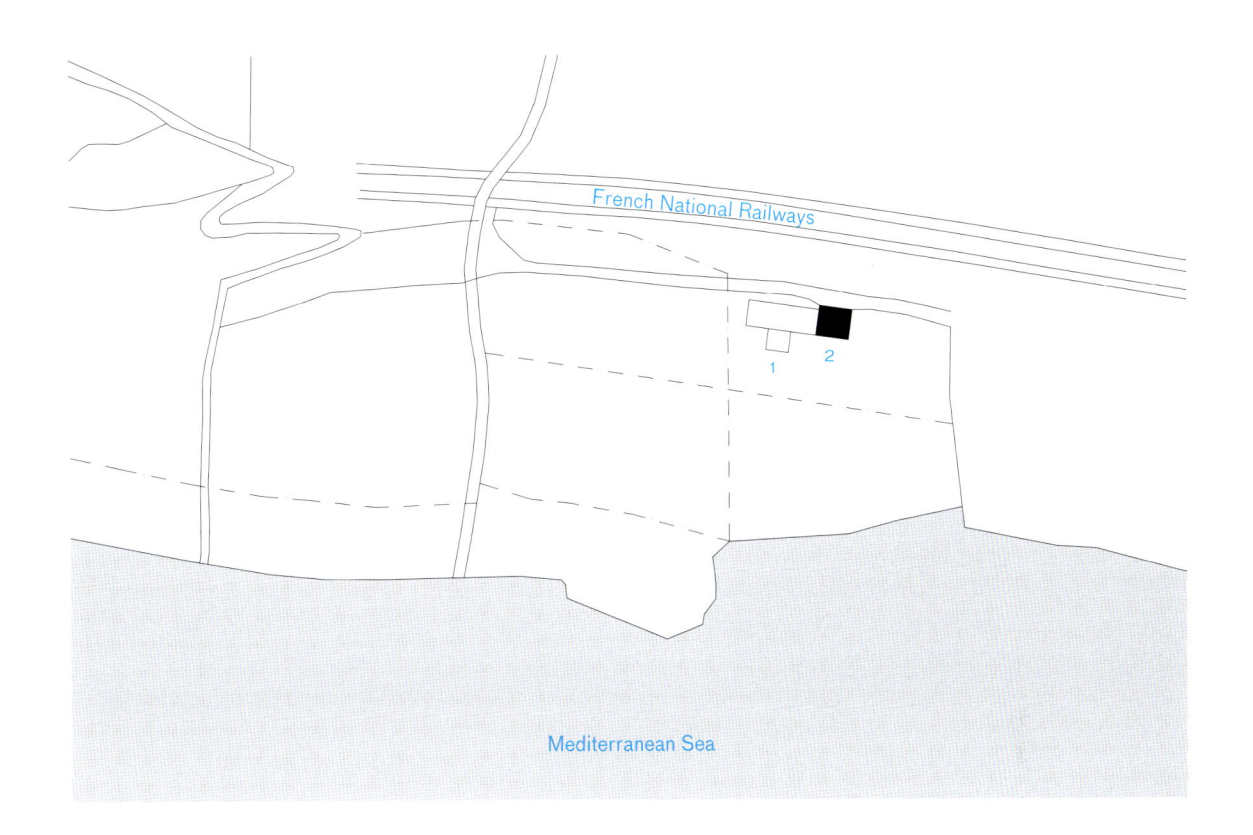

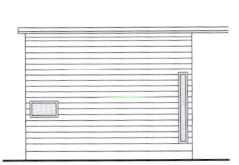

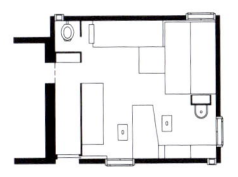

Site plan (1:1000)
1 L'Etoile de Mer restaurant
2 Le Petit Cabanon

South–north section, south elevation,
   east elevation, north elevation

First-floor plan

187 **LE PETIT CABANON LE CORBUSIER**

23 MAISONS JAOUL

LOCATION: Neuilly-sur-Seine, a western suburb of Paris, France
DATE: 1951

André Jaoul commissioned Le Corbusier to design houses for his family and his son's family. Early schematic-design options included a single structure to house both families. As built, Jaoul's residence, House A, is positioned parallel to and a short distance away from the street. House B is set perpendicular to House A. Together they divide the site into a front garden; a hard-surface public entrance court; and more-private, landscaped family gardens. A below-grade garage can be accessed by stairs from both houses.

Maisons Jaoul exemplified Le Corbusier's evolving ideas about the ideal house: from the white villas of the machine aesthetic in the 1920s through residences fabricated with hybrid constructional methods fusing primitive materials and advanced technologies in the 1930s and, finally, in the late 1940s, a new dwelling concept of reinterpreted ancient architecture.

Catalan vaults with brick tiles are the most distinctive feature of the interior spaces. The different sectional profiles of Catalan vaults along their primary and secondary axes create a varied spatial experience. The vaults evoke associations with primitive and ancient architecture, as do the heavy, load-bearing brick walls with rough joints and the monumental massing of the buildings. Roofs with plant materials bring these houses closer to primitive huts or cave dwellings than high-tech machines for living. Le Corbusier incorporated his architectural inventions: the *aérateur* (an operable vent with an insect screen) and *ondulatoires* (windows with dimensions based on the Modulor), the latter of which were the clearest expressions of the Modulor dimensions that were used throughout the buildings.

CLIENT: André Jaoul
PROGRAM: Two family residences
FEATURES: Catalan vault, sod roof, private gardens, double-height spaces, floating balcony, *aérateur, ondulatoires*

Exterior perspective, northwest corner

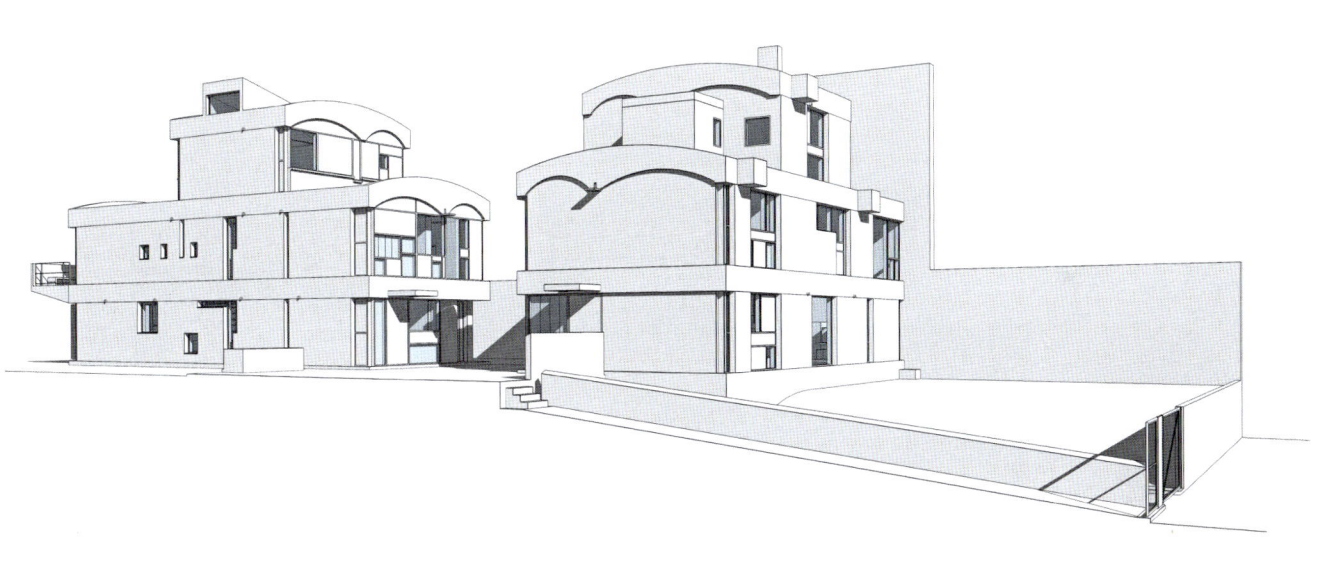

North–south sectional perspective at double-height living room

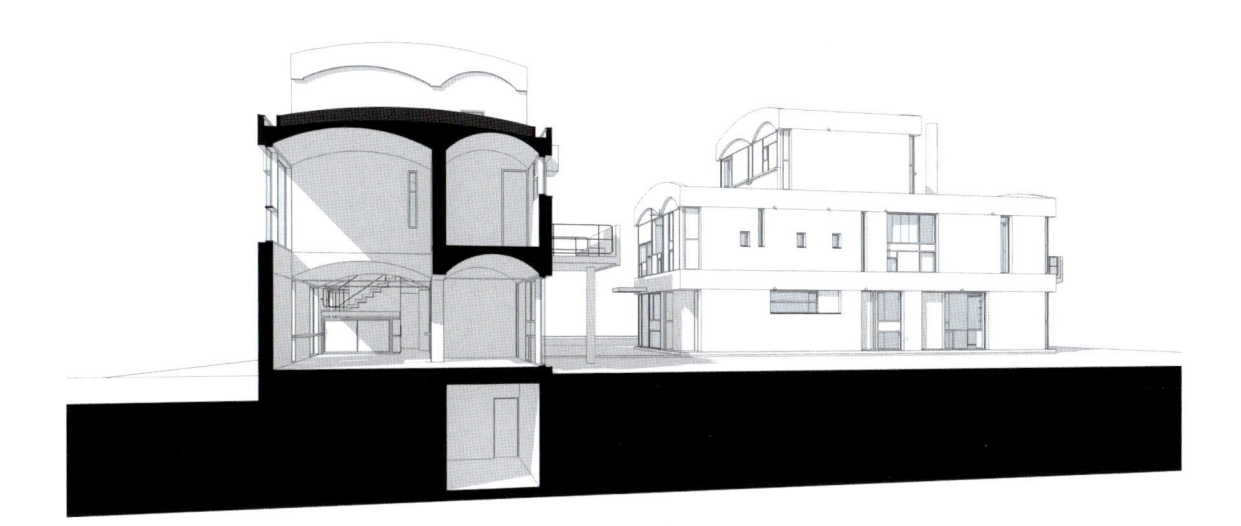

191 **MAISONS JAOUL**   ◯   West–east sectional perspective at double-height living room

East–west sectional perspective at stairs

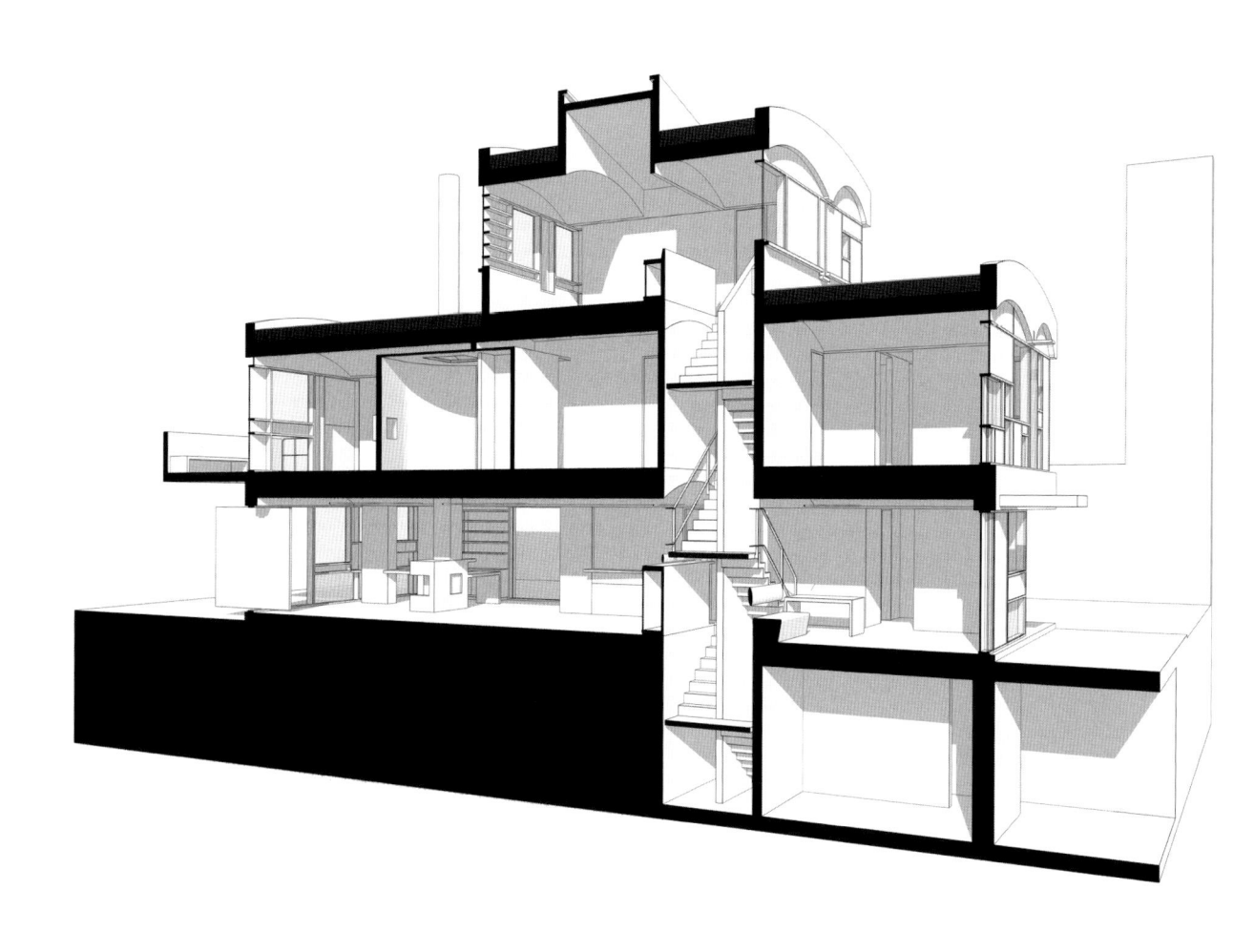

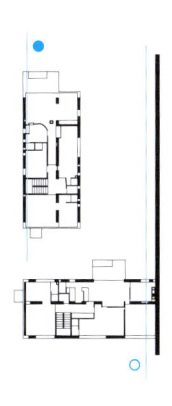

West–east sectional perspective at private garden

Subdivision plan (1:2000)

1 Lot for Maisons Jaoul

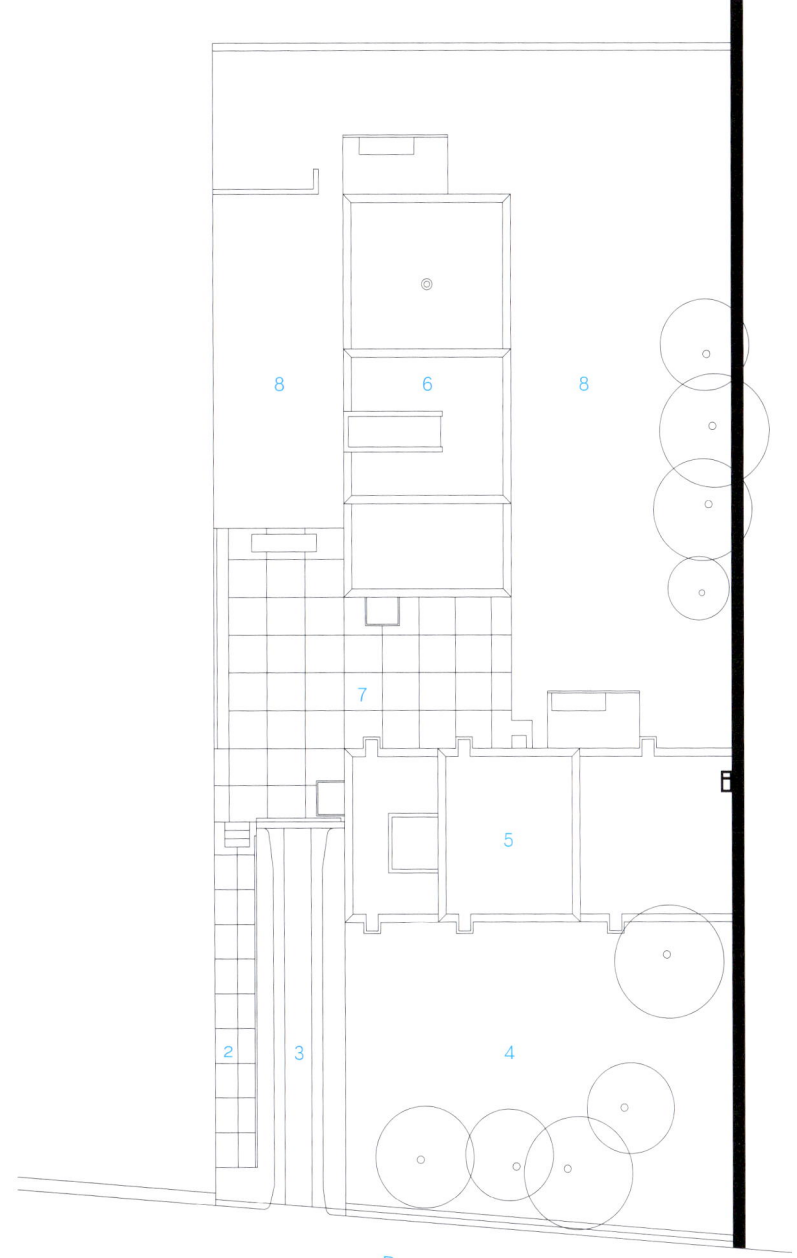

Site plan (1:300)

Rue de Longchamp

2 Entrance ramp
3 Driveway to underground garage
4 Front garden
5 House A
6 House B
7 Entrance court
8 Private garden

MAISONS JAOUL

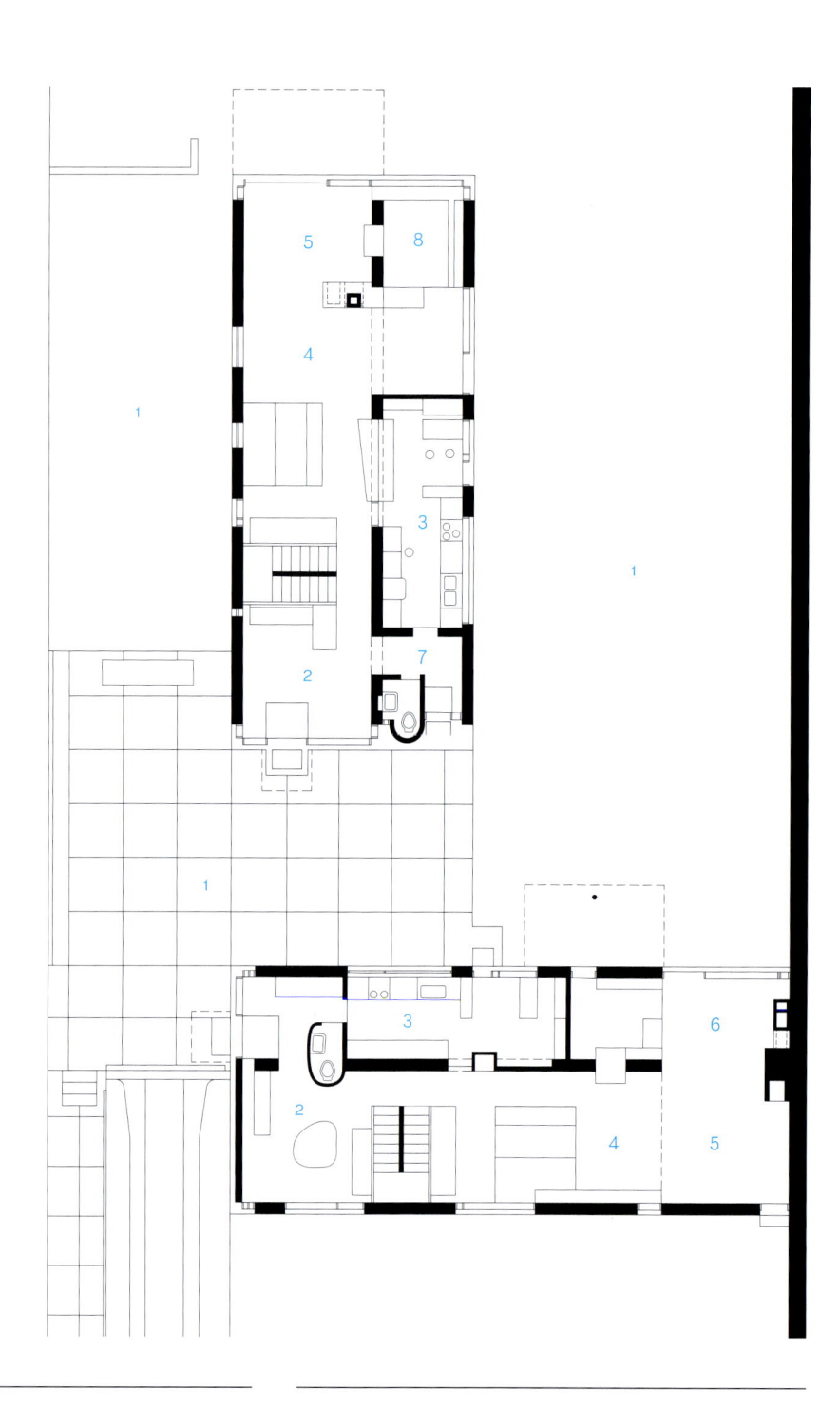

First-floor plan

1 Garden	8 Office
2 Entrance hall	9 Bedroom
3 Kitchen	10 Bathroom
4 Dining room	11 Chapel
5 Living room	12 Open to below
6 Study	13 Balcony
7 Service entrance	14 Green roof

Second-floor plan

Third-floor plan

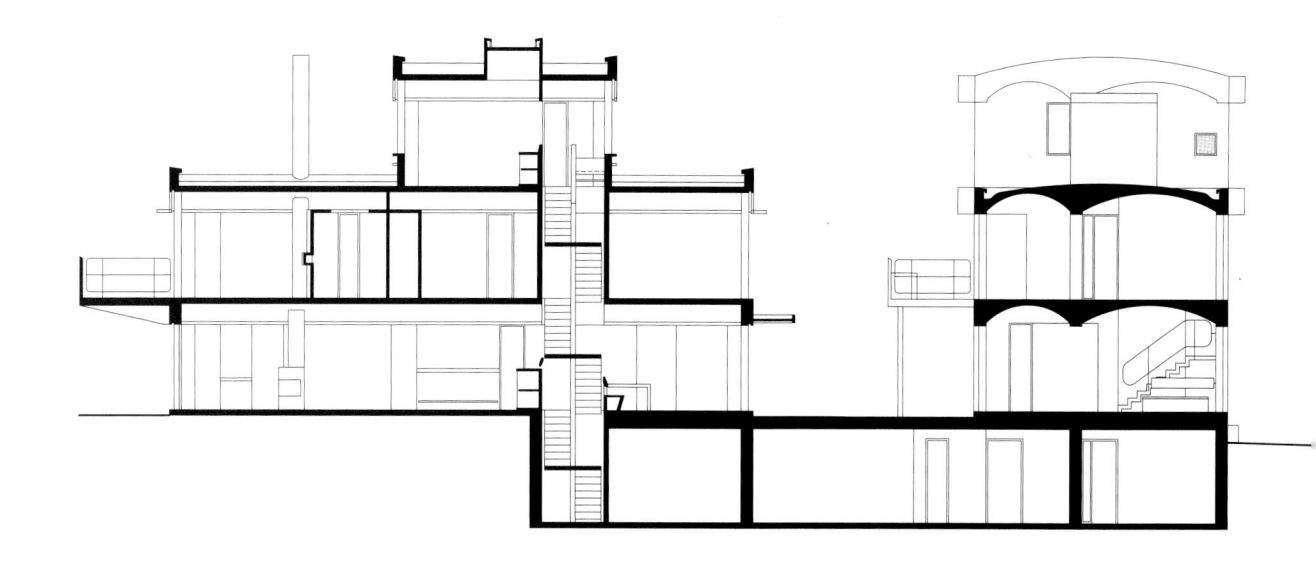

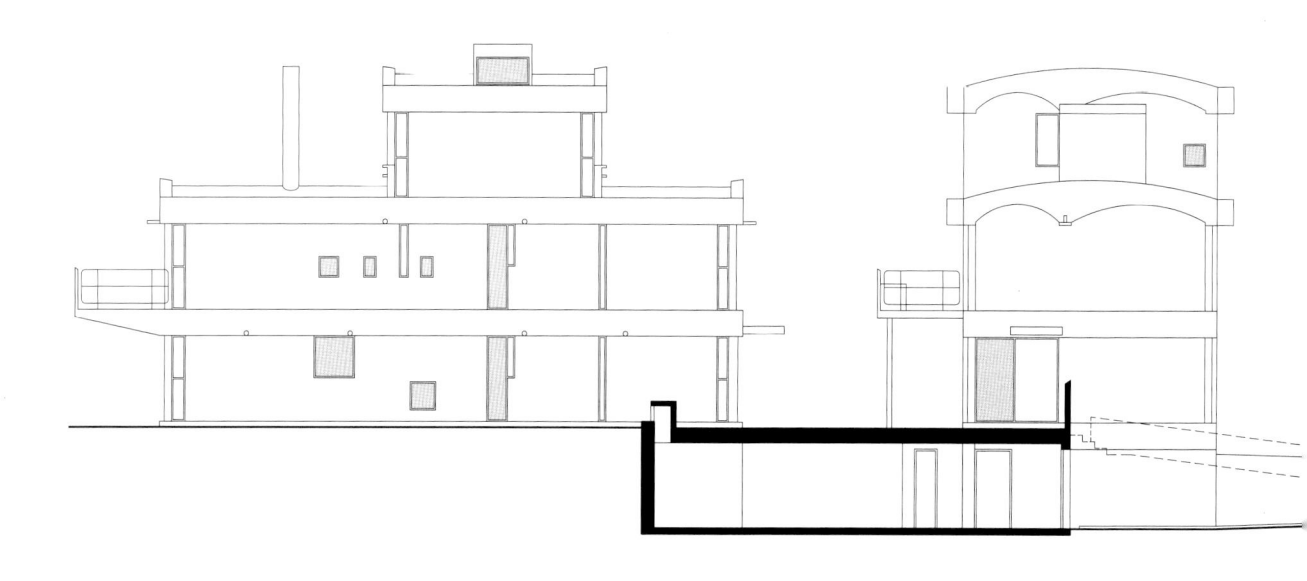

East–west section, Houses B & A
North elevation, Houses B & A
West elevation, House B

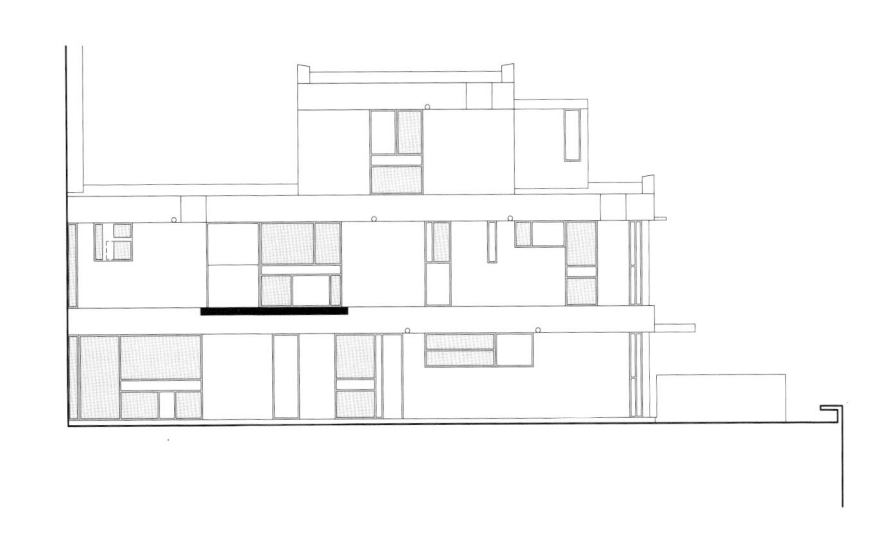

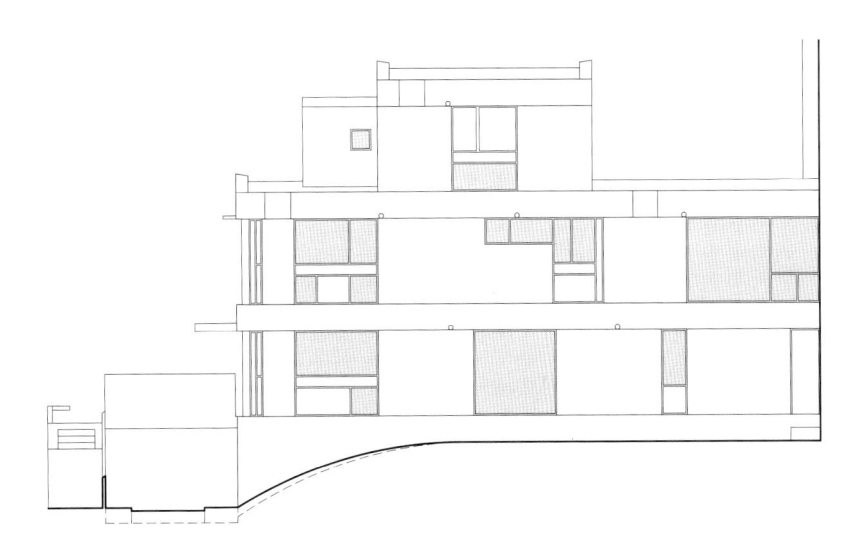

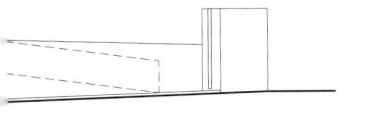

East elevation, House A
West elevation, House A

VILLA SHODHAN

LOCATION: Ahmedabad, India
DATE: 1951

This was the first of Le Corbusier's buildings in India, and he initially developed the plan of the house for Surottam Hutheesing, the secretary of the Millowners' Association. When Hutheesing abandoned the project, the plan was sold to another millowner, Shyamubhai Shodhan, who executed it on a different site without altering the plan.

Villa Shodhan is a compendium of Le Corbusier's earlier ideas, adapted to the Indian climate by providing protection from strong sun and heavy rain. The double-height living spaces and bedrooms are reminiscent of Maison Citrohan; the simple structural layout, Maison Dom-ino; cascading outdoor roof gardens, Villa Stein-de Monzie; interpenetrating spaces in section, the unbuilt schemes of the Villa Baizeau; an oculus in the roof parasol, Pavillon de l'Esprit Nouveau; the architectural promenade created by a ramp, Villa Savoye; and the brise-soleil, Maison Curutchet. Le Corbusier's conscious effort to experiment and develop different forms of ideal dwellings using primitive construction and a more naturalistic aesthetic, which started in 1930s, led to a complete synthesis in India. The Villa Shodhan is noteworthy because it is unique and yet closely related to his earlier projects—proof that his former concepts could be transformed easily to meet the requirements of widely differing clients and sites. The house is not a new prototype, not a new model, but a testament to the strength and validity of architectural principles that Le Corbusier had developed over more than forty years.

CLIENT: Shyamubhai Shodhan
PROGRAM: Family residence
FEATURES: Parasol, interlocking volumes of interior spaces, *aérateur*, *ondulatoire*, brise-soleil, ramp, exterior stair, oculus, outdoor terrace

201 **VILLA SHODHAN** Exterior perspective, southeast corner

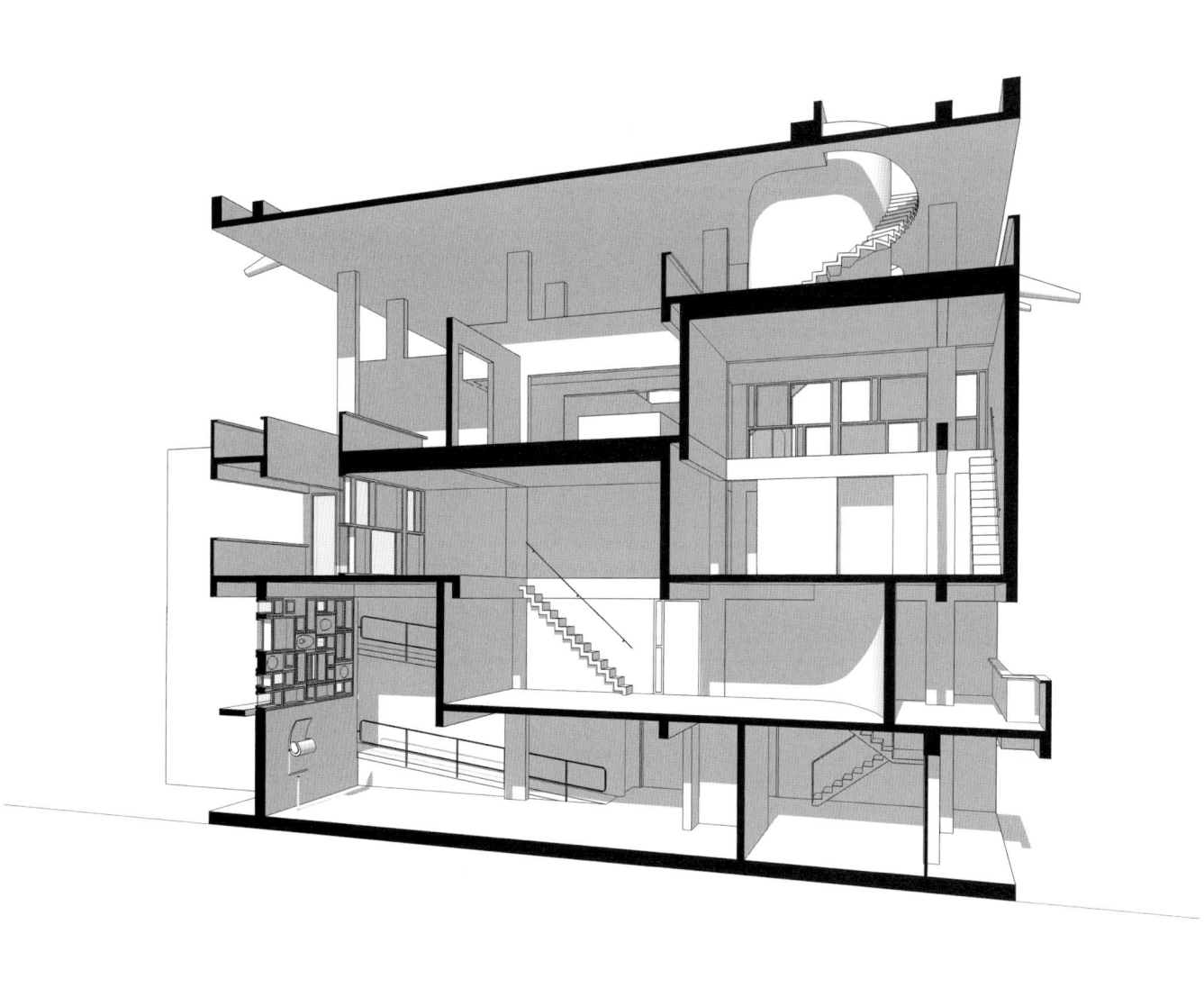

East–west sectional perspective at double-height entrance hall

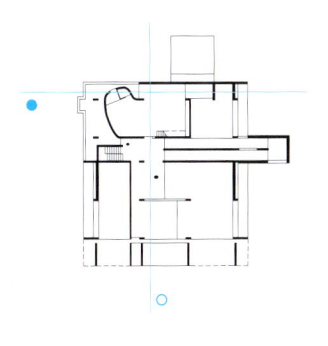

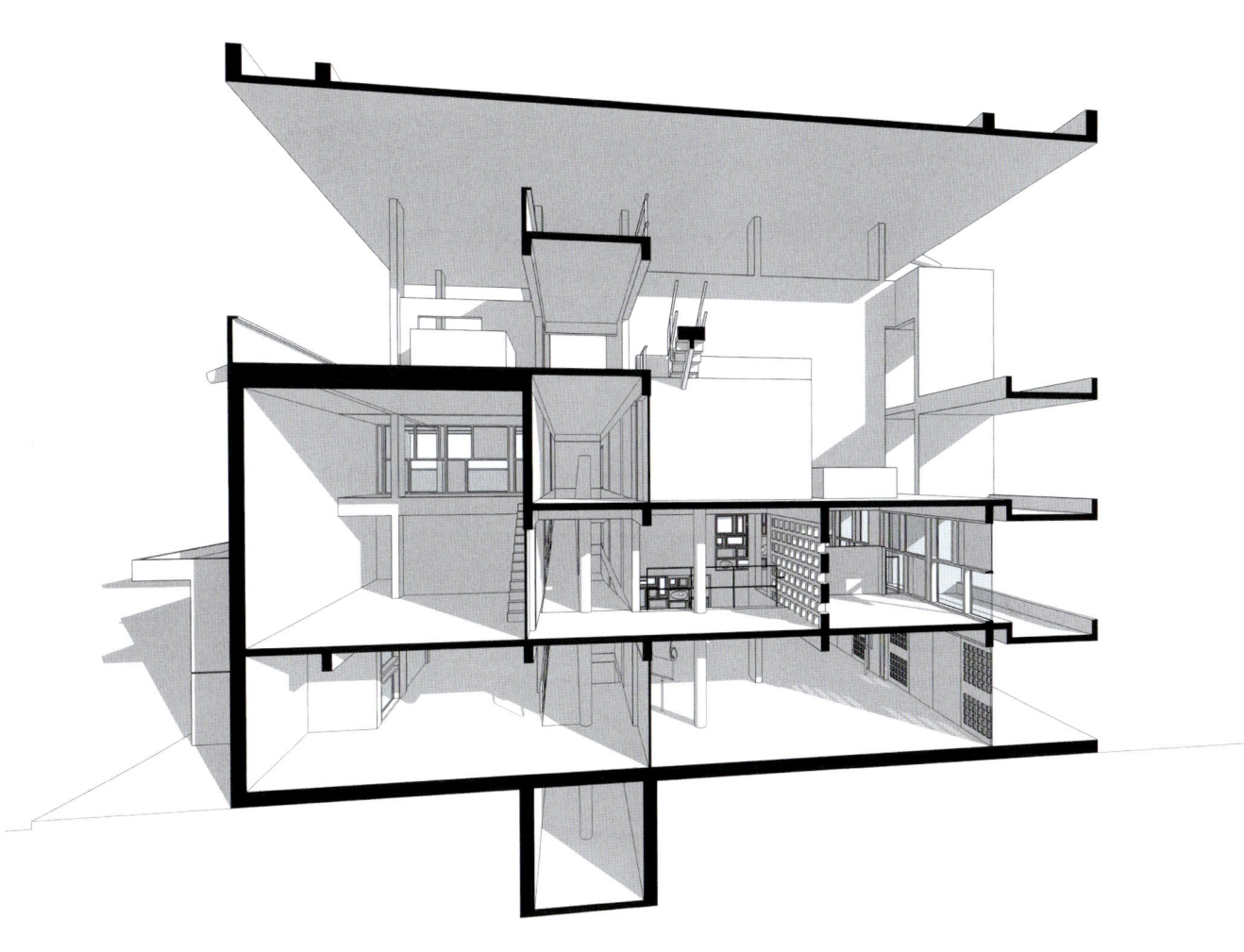

North–south sectional perspective at third-floor ramp

204 **VILLA SHODHAN**   West–east sectional perspective at third-floor outdoor terrace

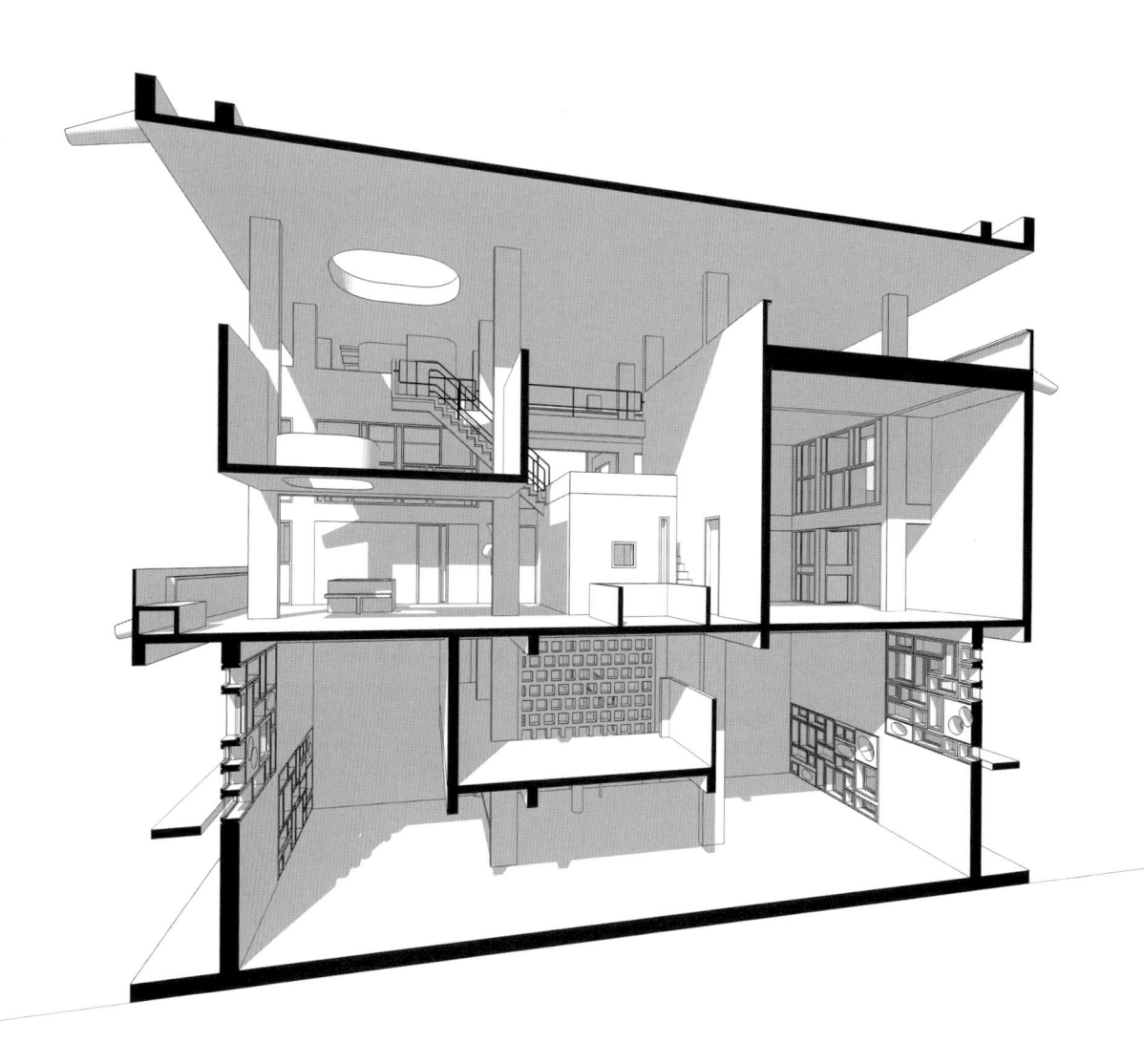

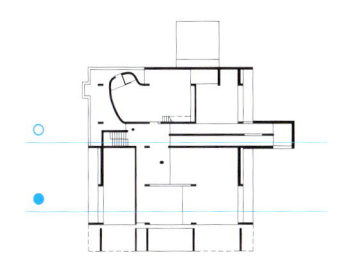

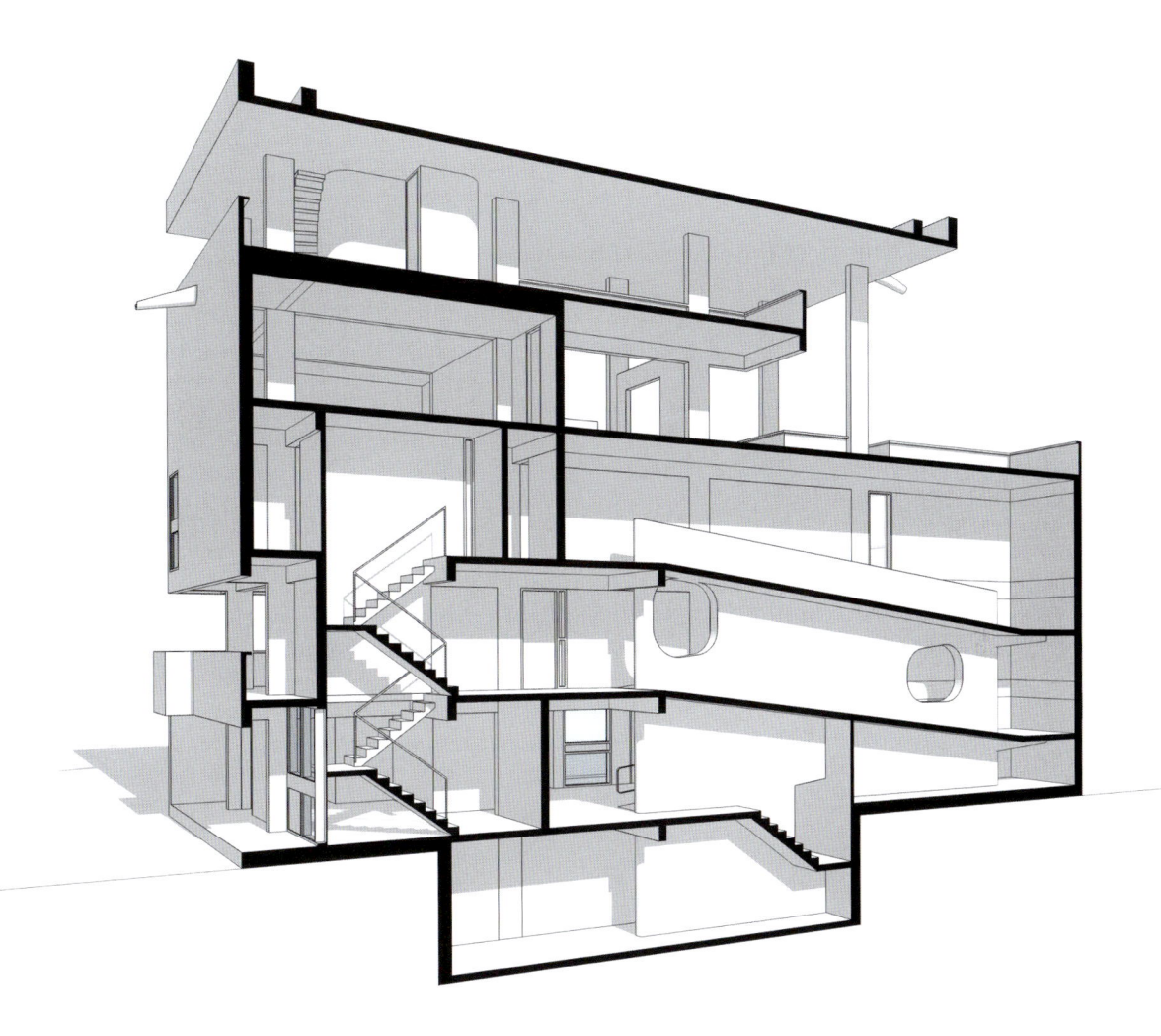

205 VILLA SHODHAN — West–east sectional perspective at ramp

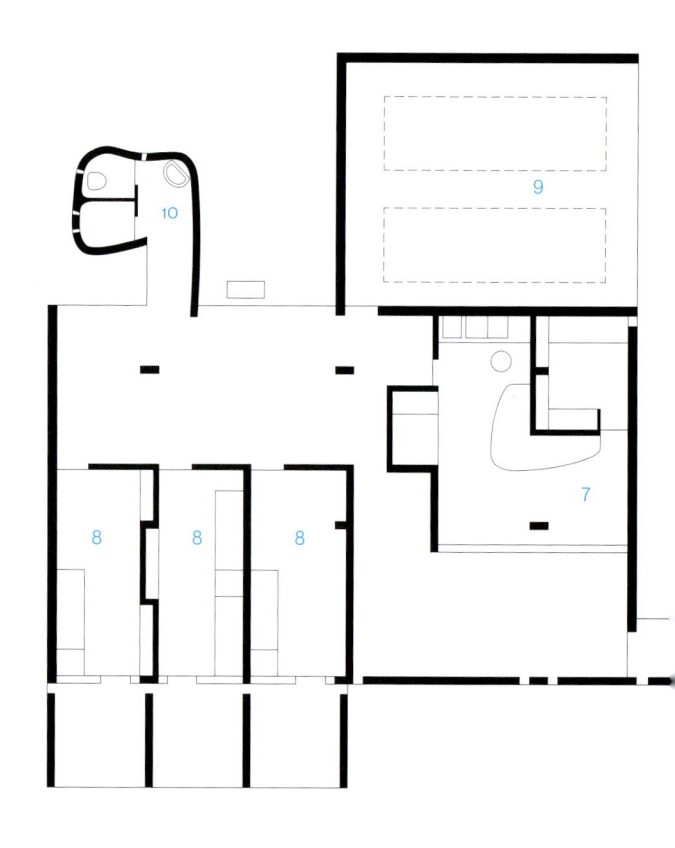

First-floor plan

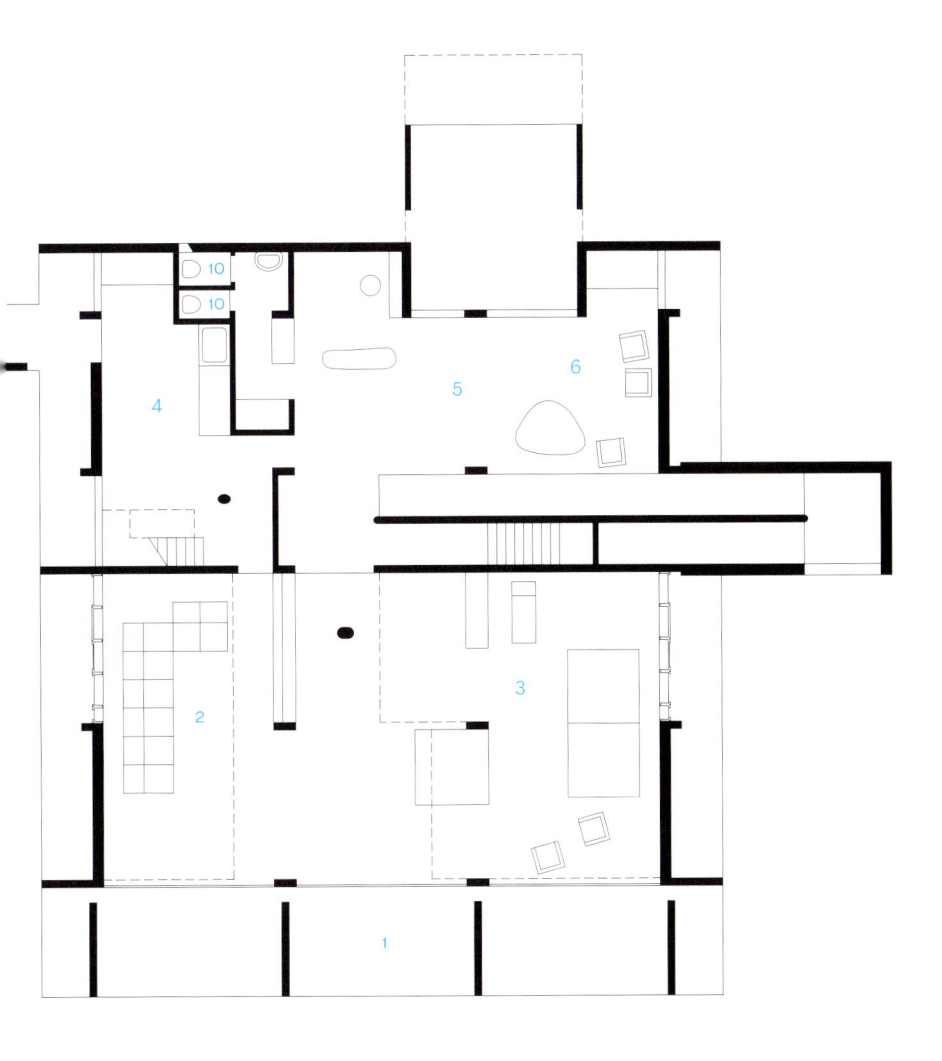

1 Veranda
2 Dining room
3 Living room
4 Pantry
5 Entrance hall
6 Waiting room
7 Kitchen
8 Maid's room
9 Garage
10 Toilet

208 **VILLA SHODHAN**

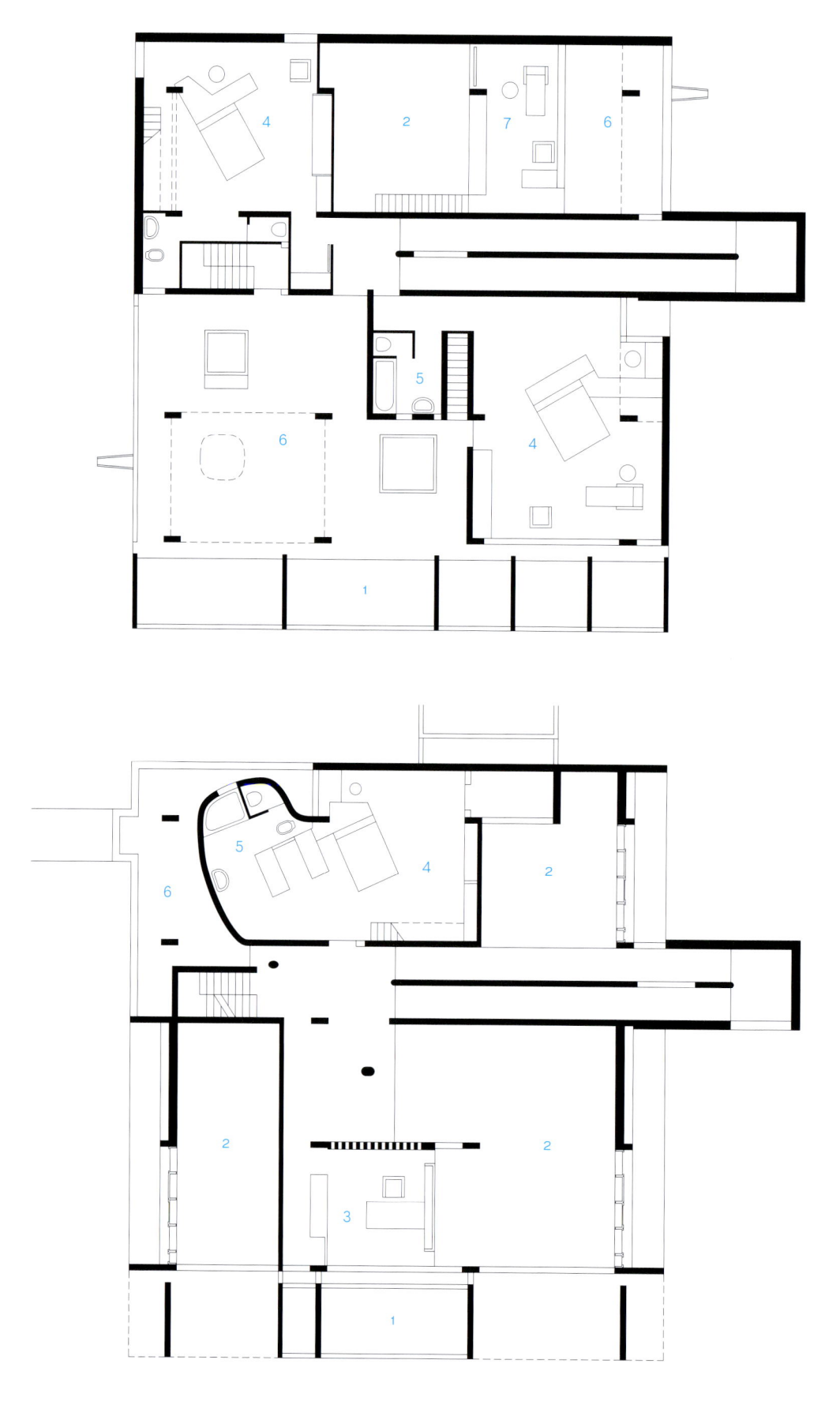

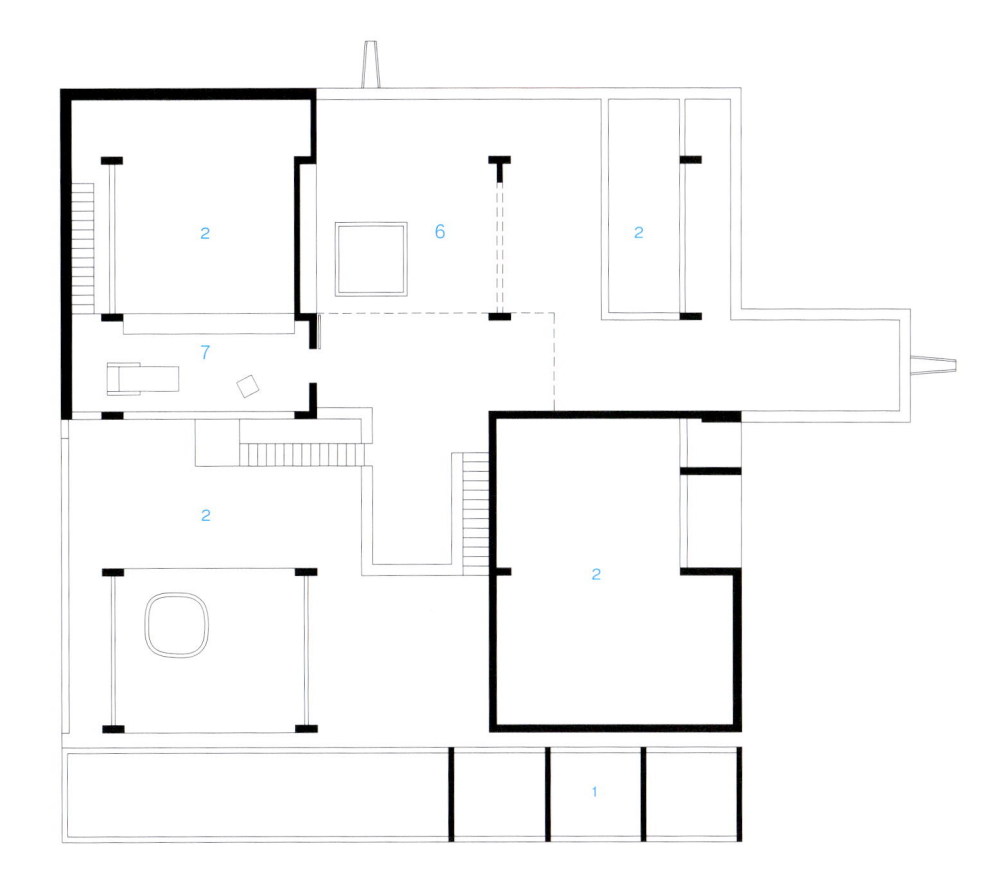

Third-floor plan   Fourth-floor plan
Second-floor plan

1 Veranda
2 Open to below
3 Study
4 Bedroom
5 Bathroom
6 Outdoor terrace
7 Gallery

210 VILLA SHODHAN

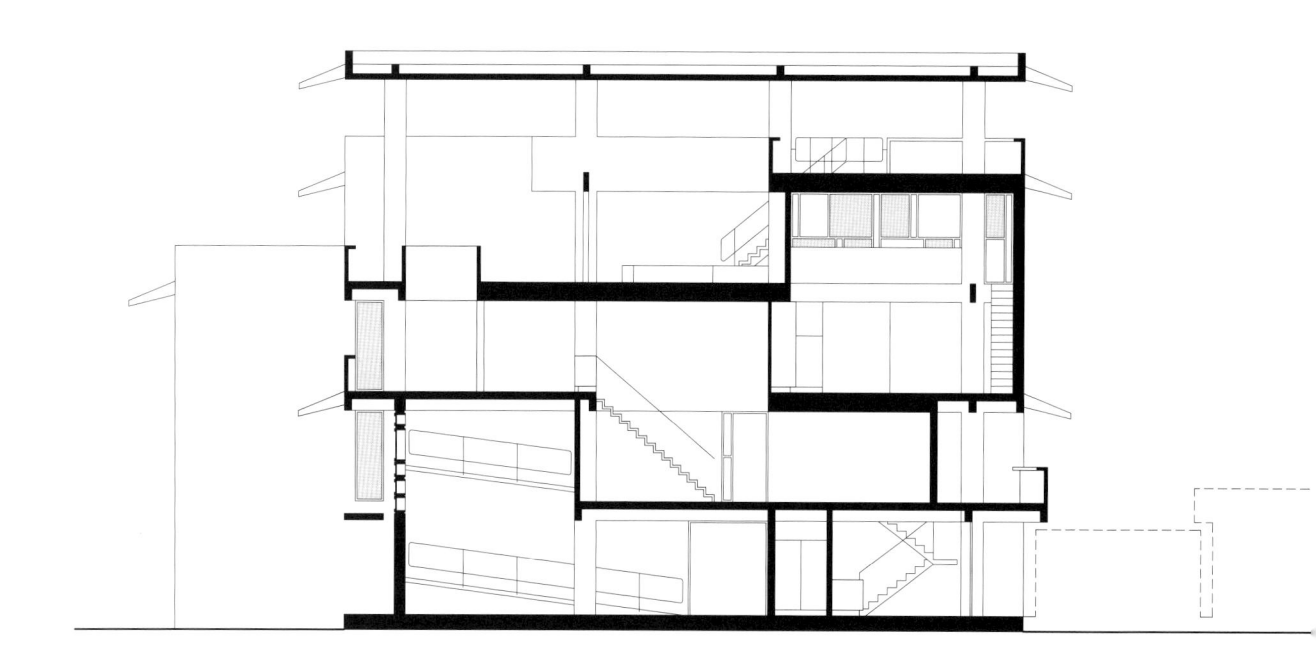

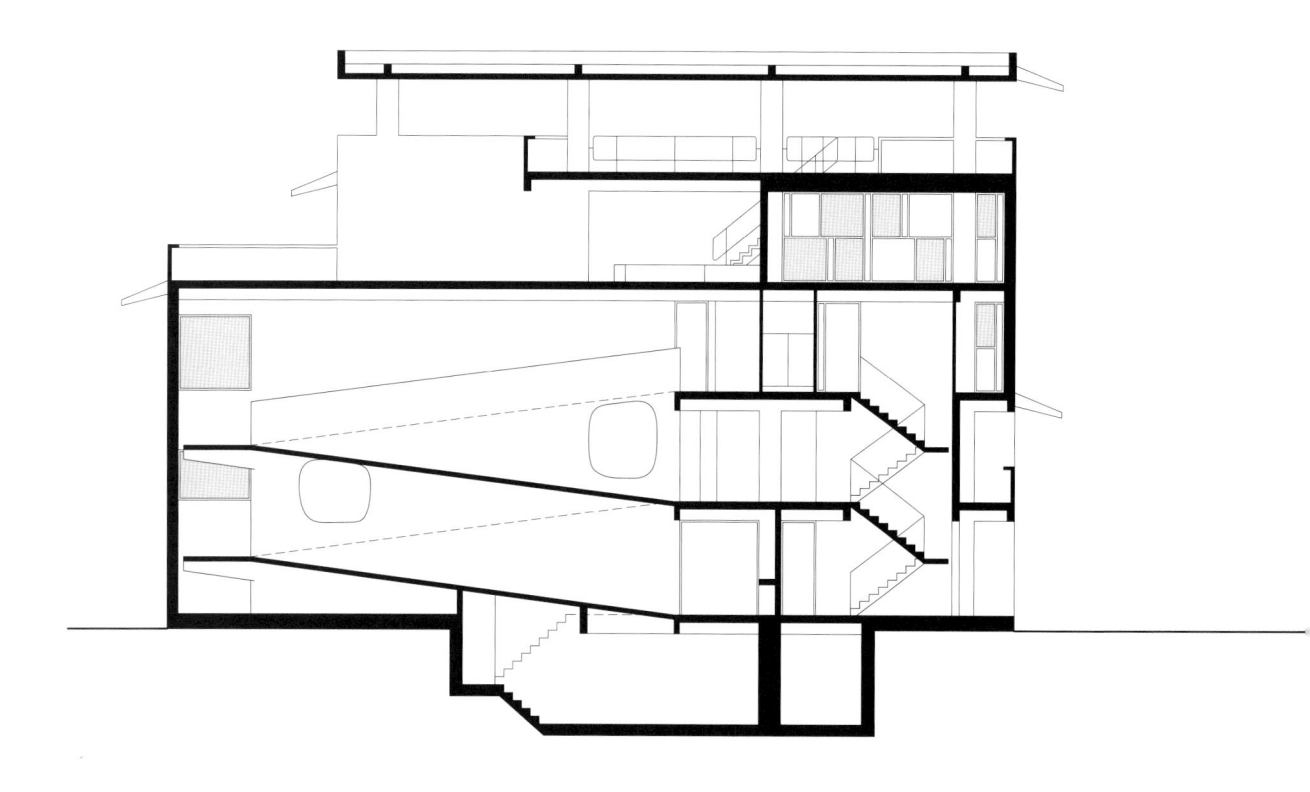

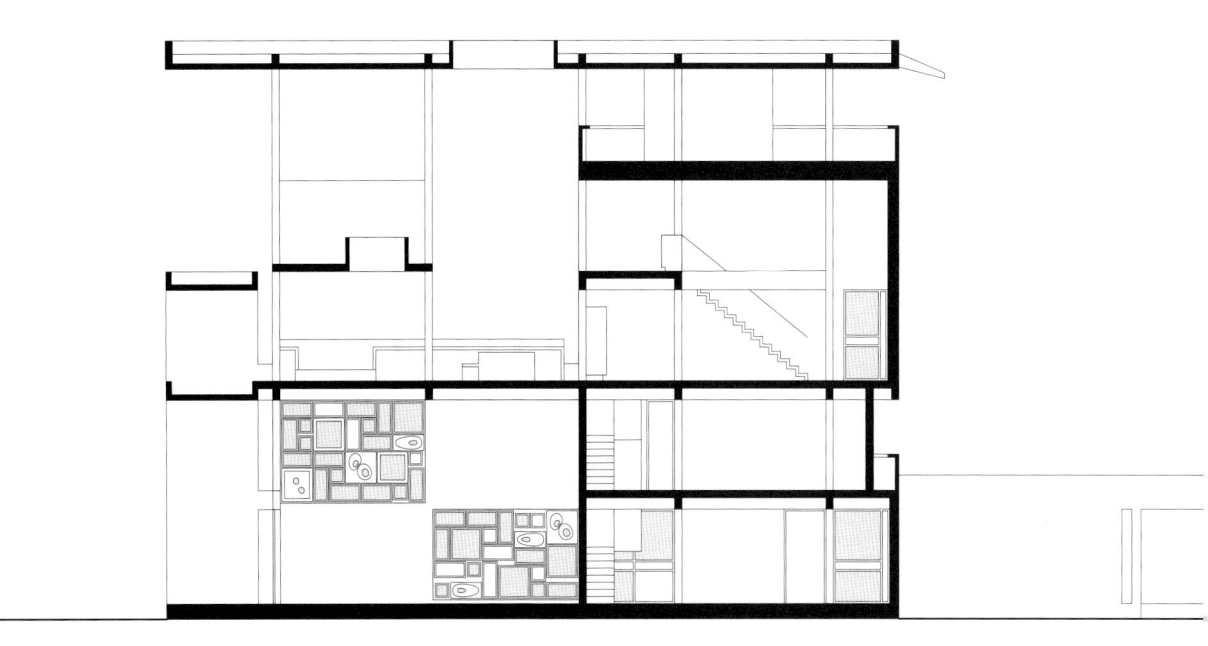

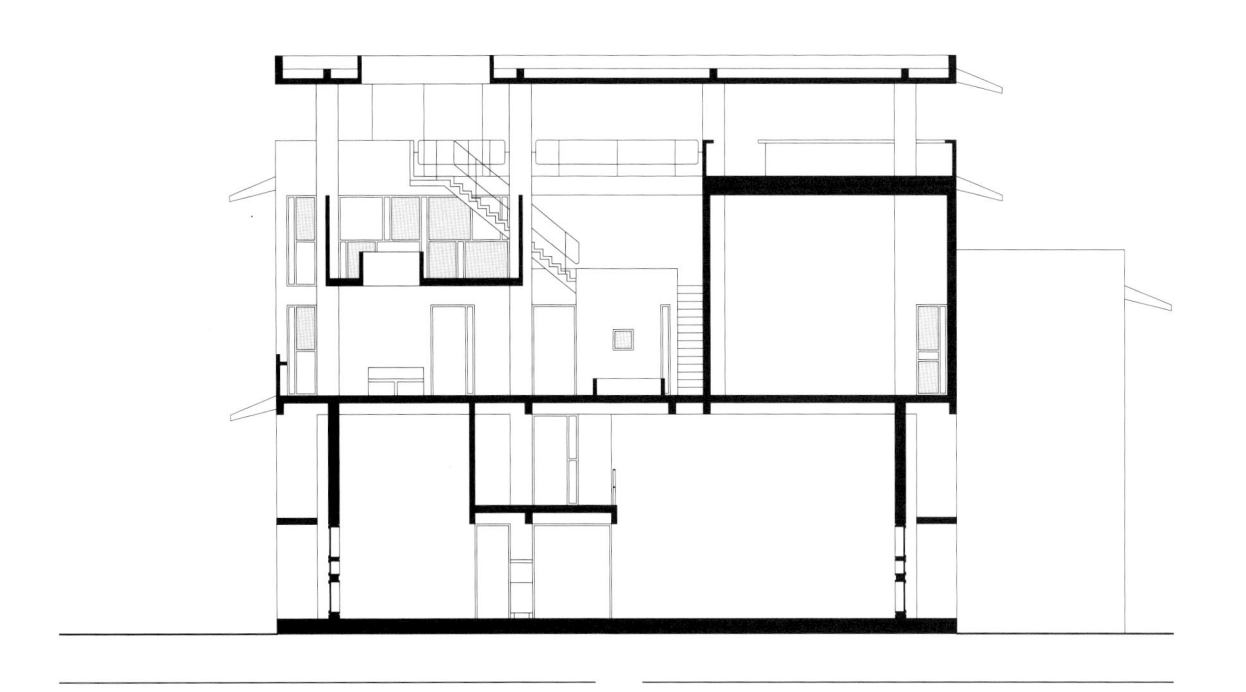

East–west sections

South–north section
West–east section

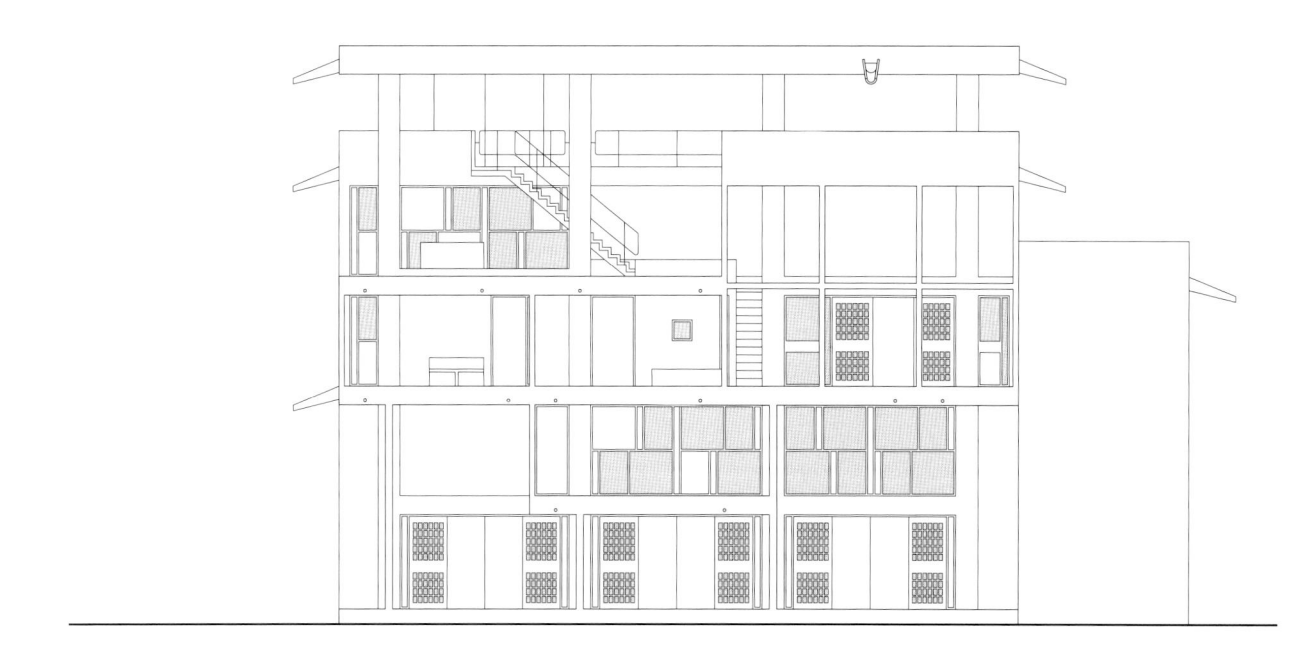

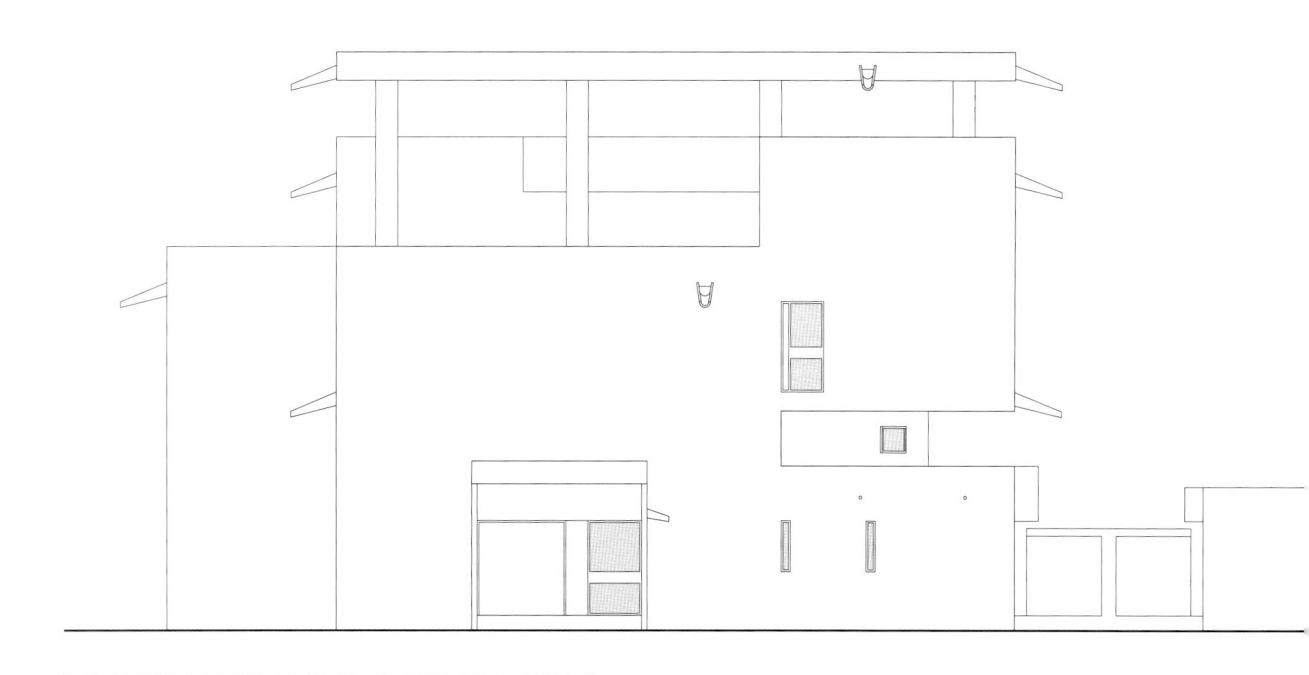

South elevation
North elevation

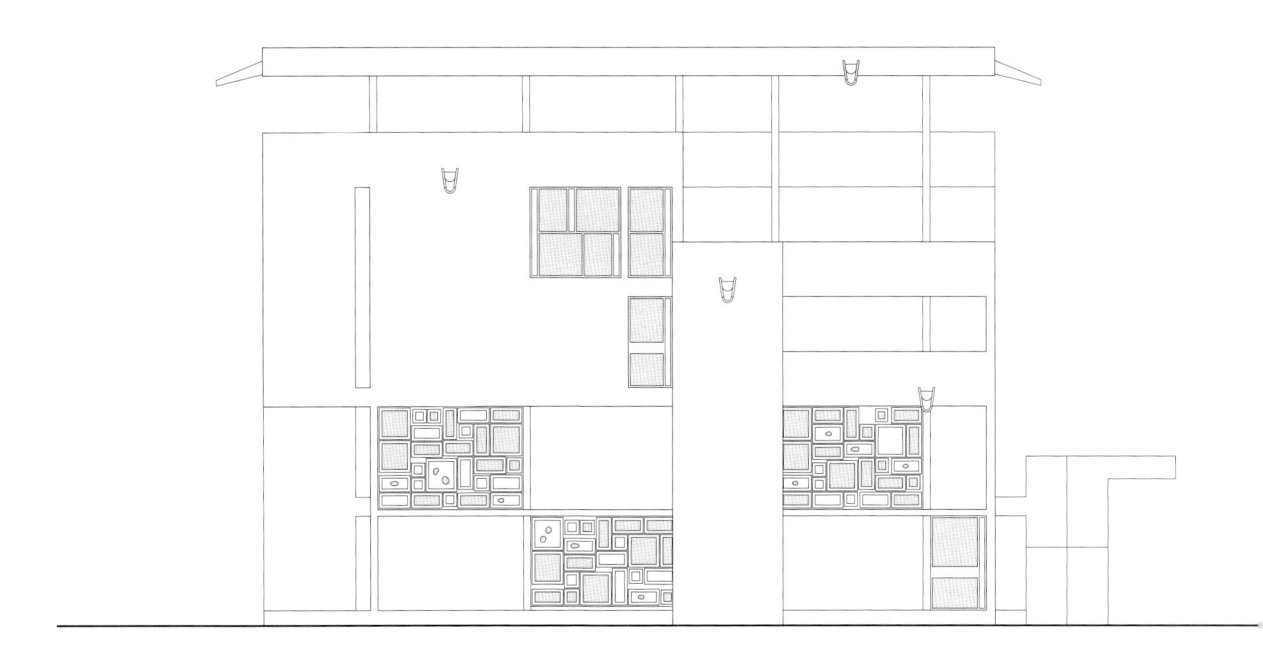

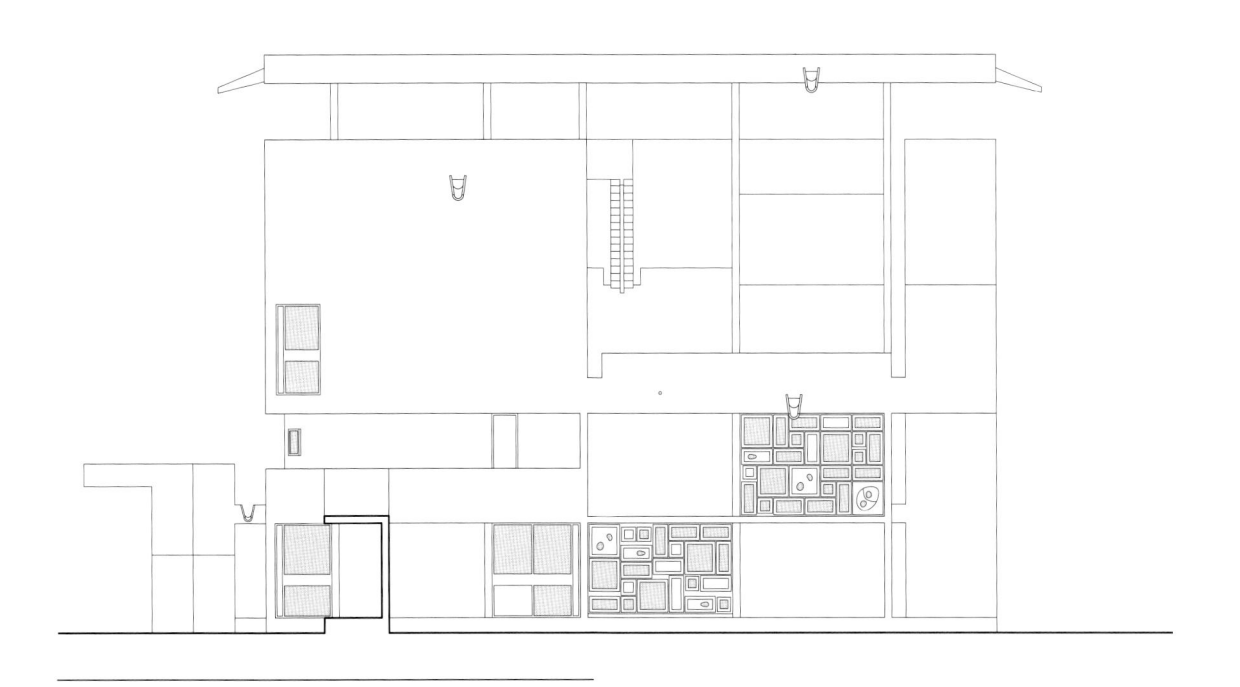

East elevation
West elevation

VILLA SARABHAI

LOCATION:	Ahmedabad, India
DATE:	1951

This house is a variation of the Maison Monol, a housing prototype with vaulted ceilings designed by Le Corbusier in 1919. In Maison Monol the sectional profiles of the vaults were expressed on the elevations, but here they are hidden behind a deep concrete fascia. (The client considered the expressed vault to appear too industrial.) Another difference from the Maison Monol is the structure of the vaults. Here, because the vaults are not supported directly by the load-bearing walls but rather carried by deep concrete beams, the walls could be more freely arranged, creating surprisingly complex and mysterious interior spaces within a simple, linear structural grid.

The regional climate influenced the choice of the site of Villa Sarabhai within a large compound owned by the family. The house was positioned to catch the summer breeze and low winter sun. When large, rotating doors are open, verandas create multifunction spaces that act as extensions of indoor areas. The sod roof further blurs the distinction between the house and its surrounding gardens while sheltering the house from the scorching summer sun. Large scuppers expressive of the rainy season articulate the elevations with their long shadows. They resemble ancient sundials, evoking the dimension of time. Although the Maison Monol prototype was originally developed to meet mass-housing needs in Europe after the First World War, it finds here in Ahmedabad a new expression as a form of dwelling unique to its context.

CLIENT:	Manorama Sarabhai
PROGRAM:	Family residence for a widow and her son
FEATURES:	Vaulted roof structure, roof garden, swimming pool, water slide, scupper, *aérateur*, *ondulatoire*

Exterior perspective, south elevation

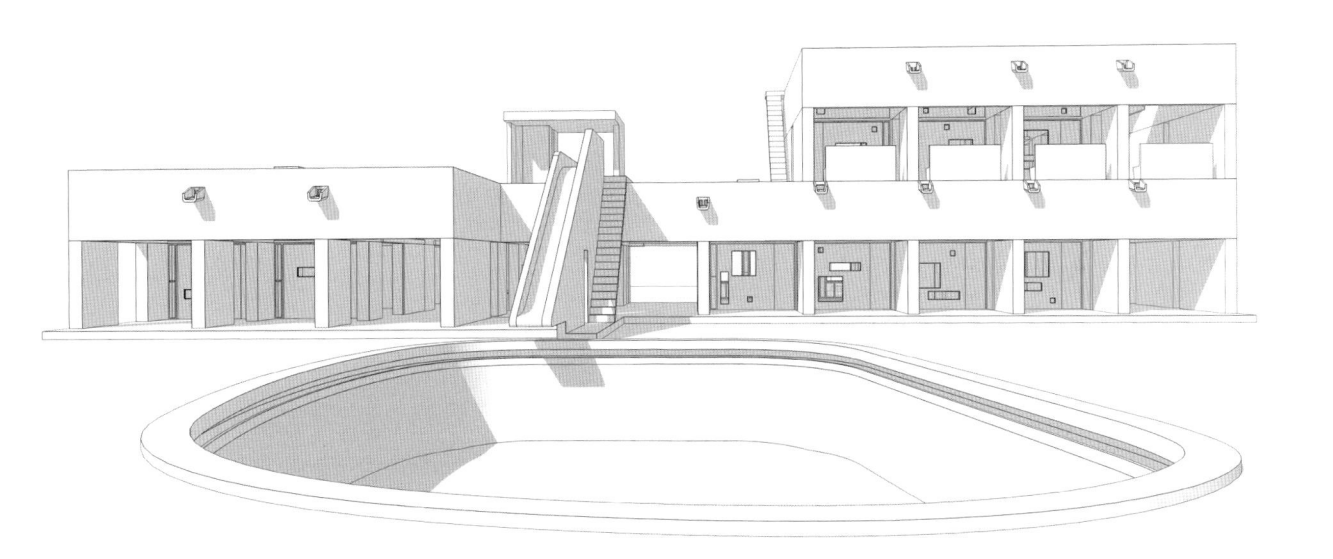

Aerial perspective, southwest corner

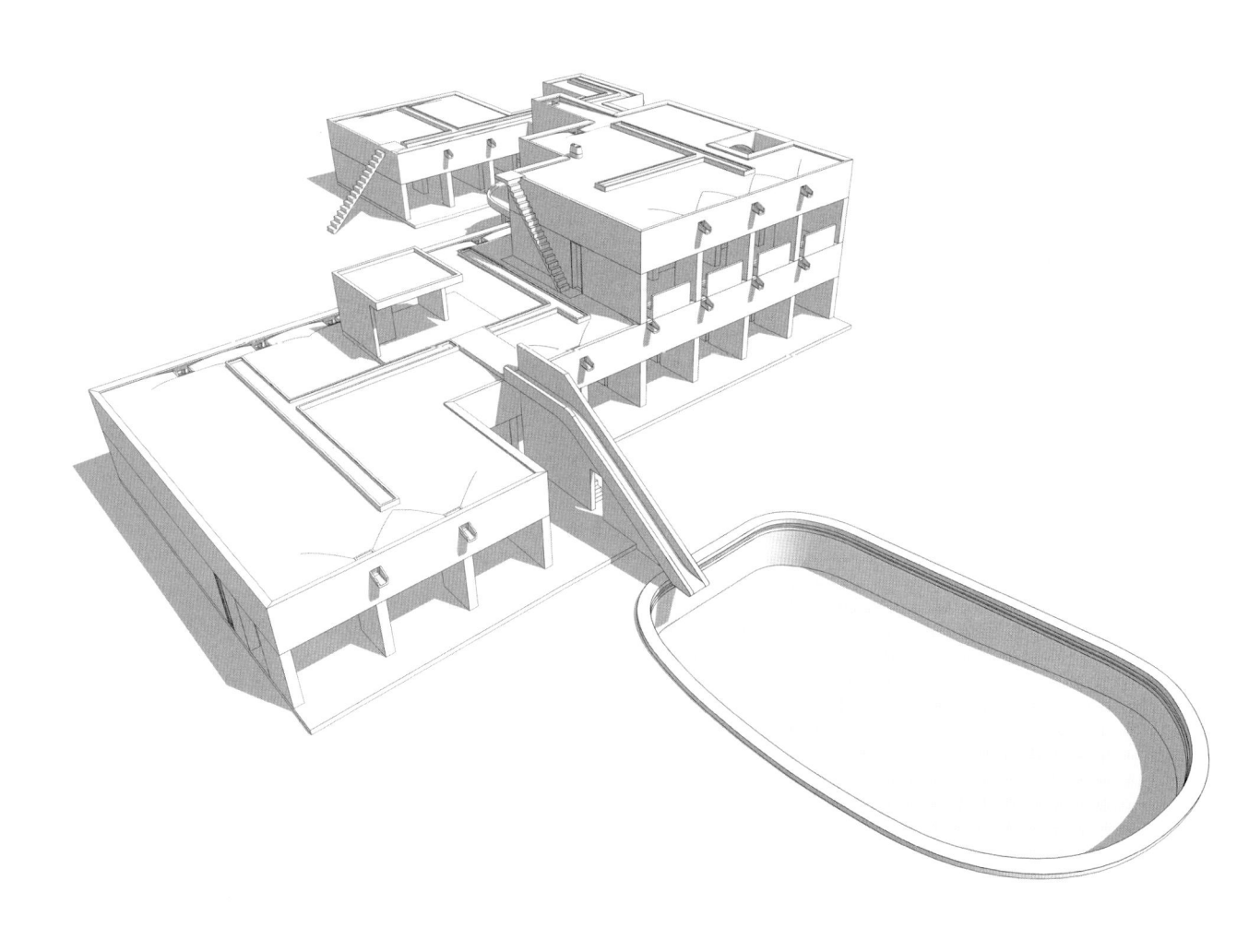

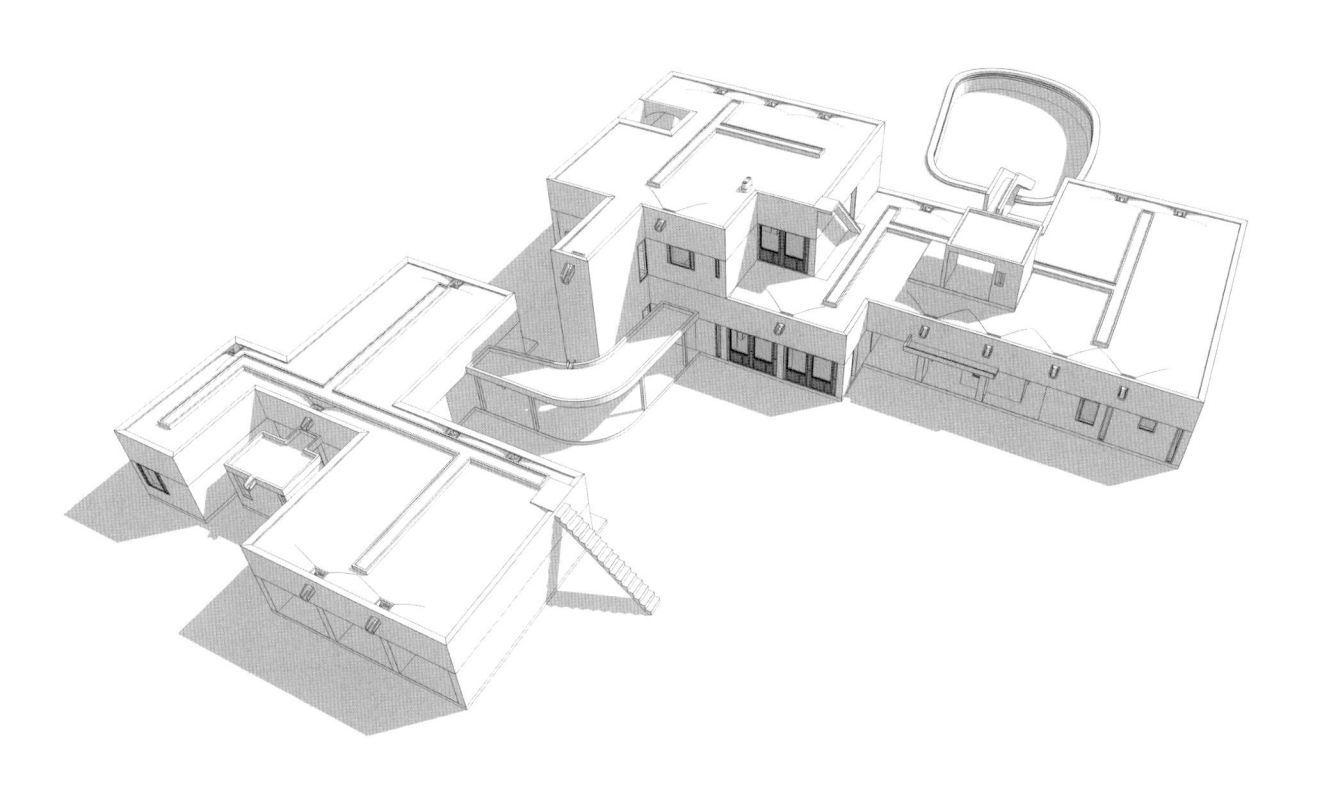

VILLA SARABHAI Aerial perspective, northwest corner

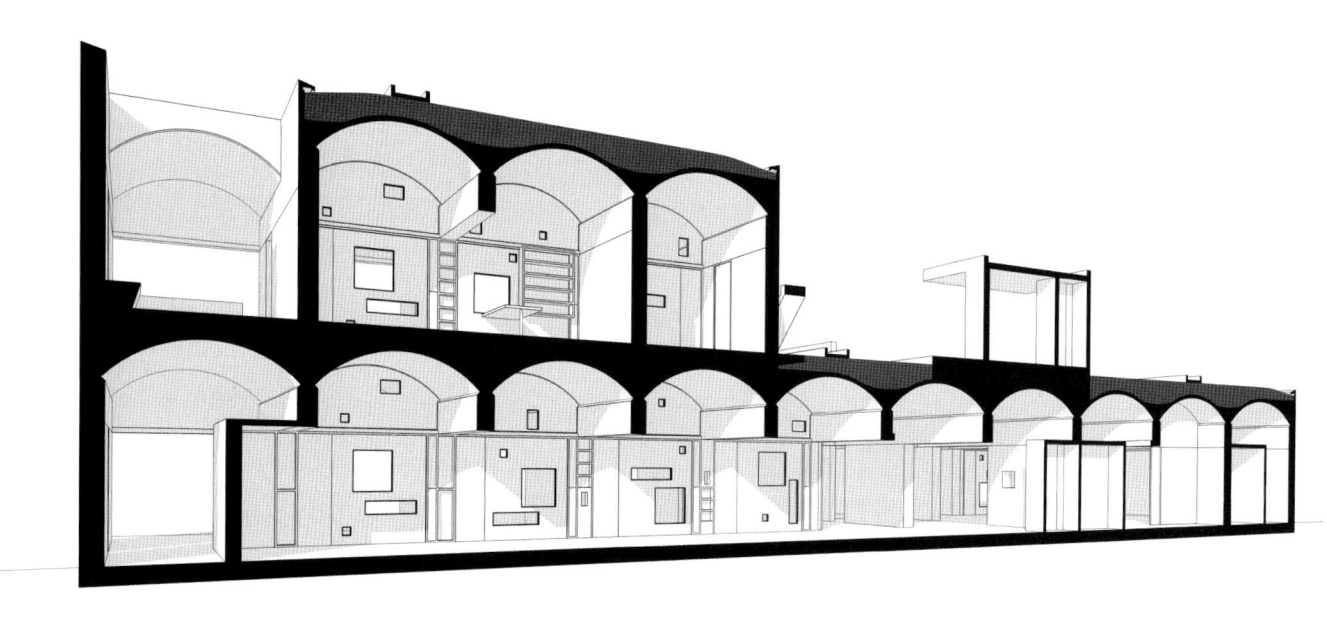

East–west sectional perspective at living and dining room

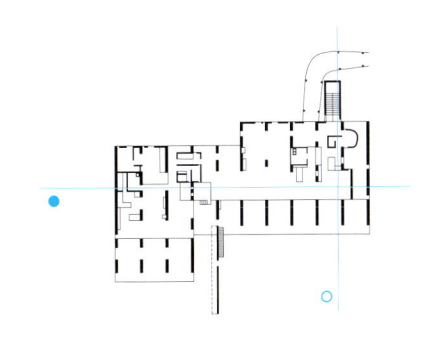

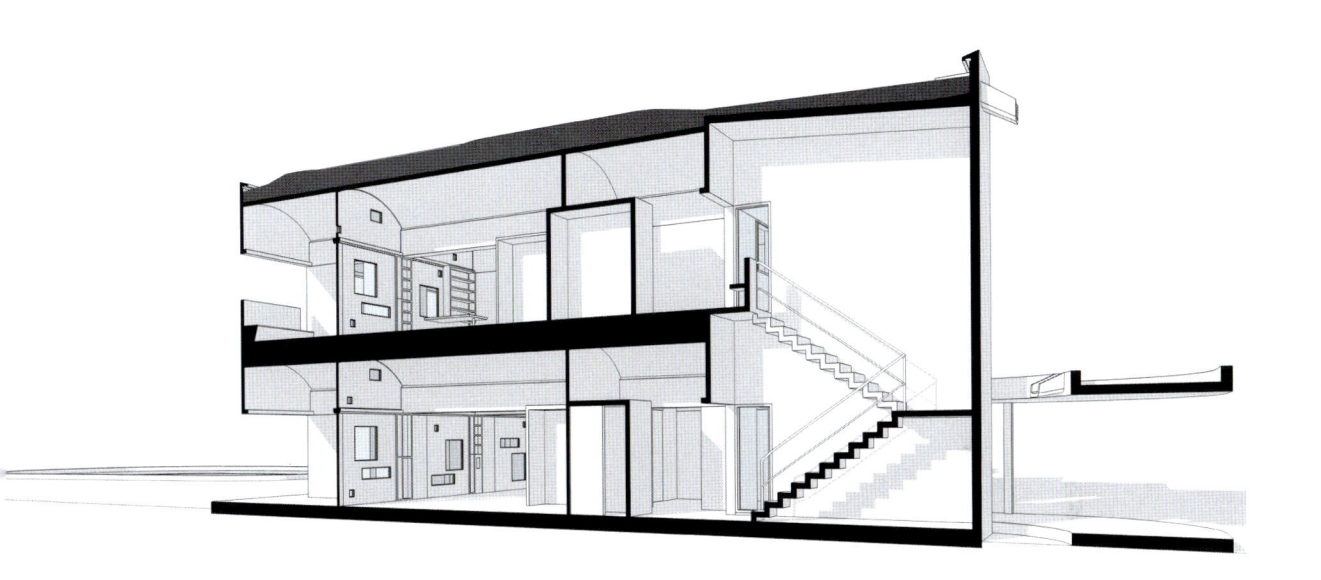

219 **VILLA SARABHAI**   South–north sectional perspective at stairs

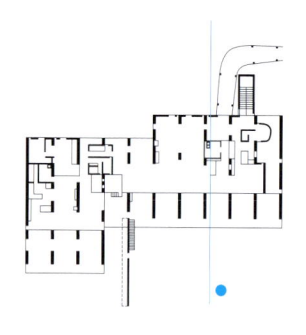

220 **VILLA SARABHAI** ● North–south sectional perspective at mechanical room

First-floor planar perspective from northeast corner

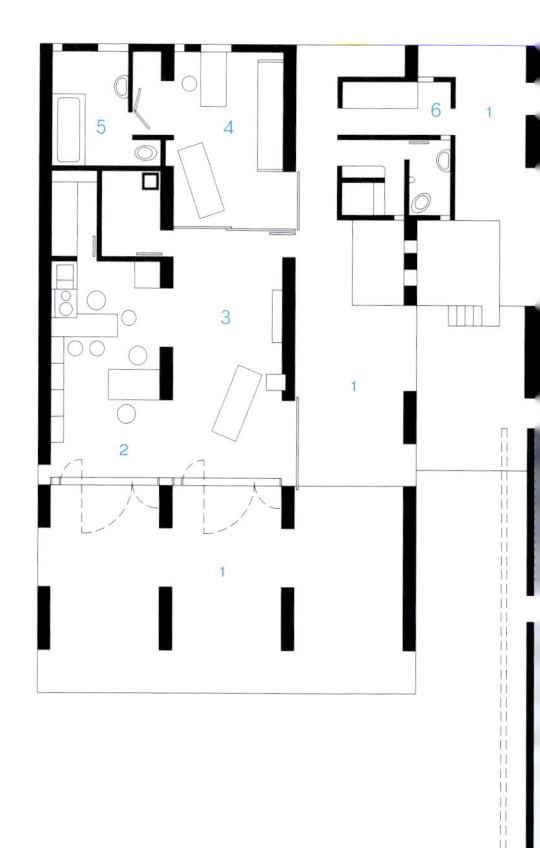

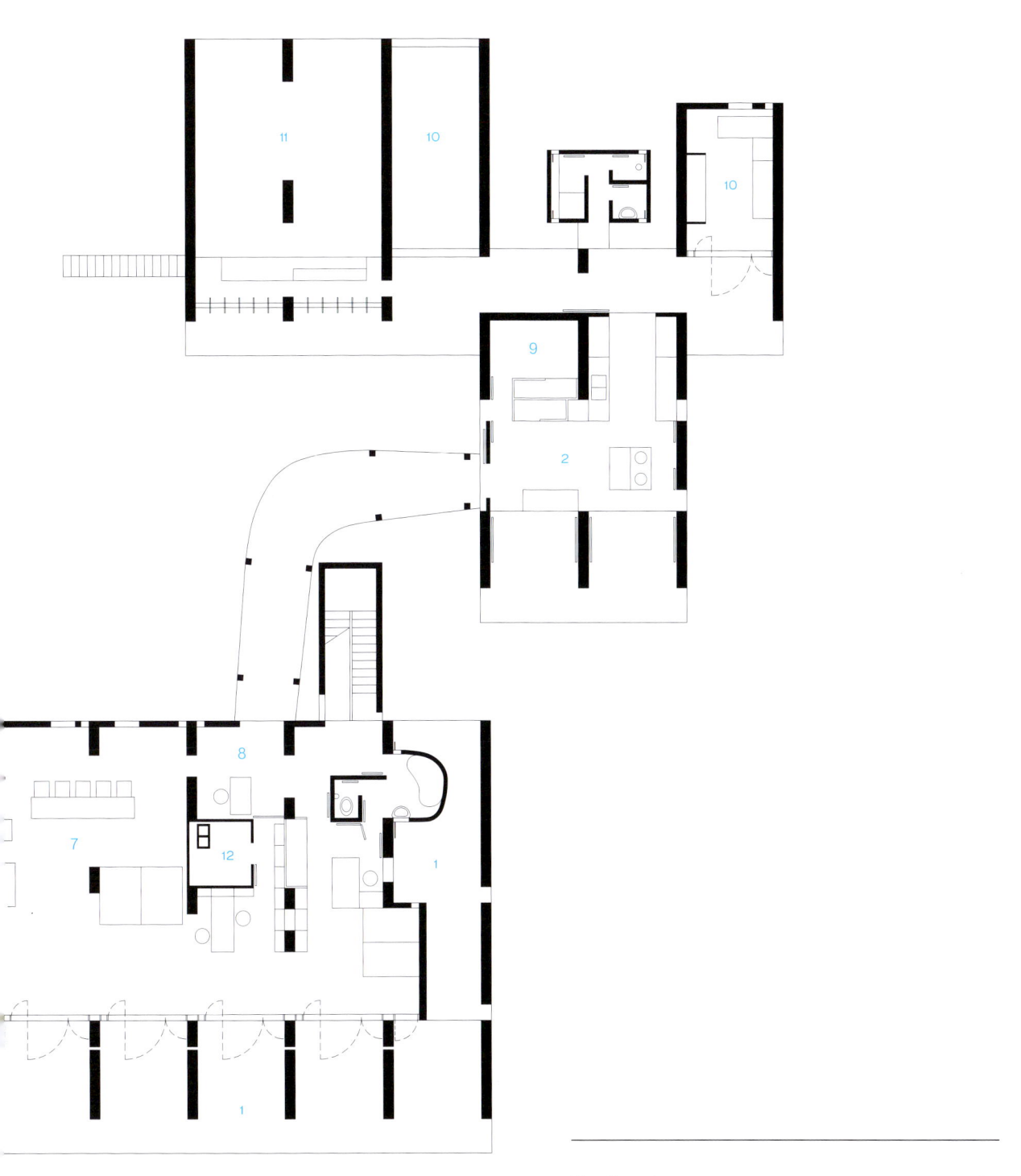

First-floor plan

1. Veranda
2. Kitchen
3. Studio
4. Bedroom
5. Bathroom
6. Caretaker's room
7. Living and dining room
8. Study
9. Pantry
10. Maid's room
11. Garage
12. Mechanical room

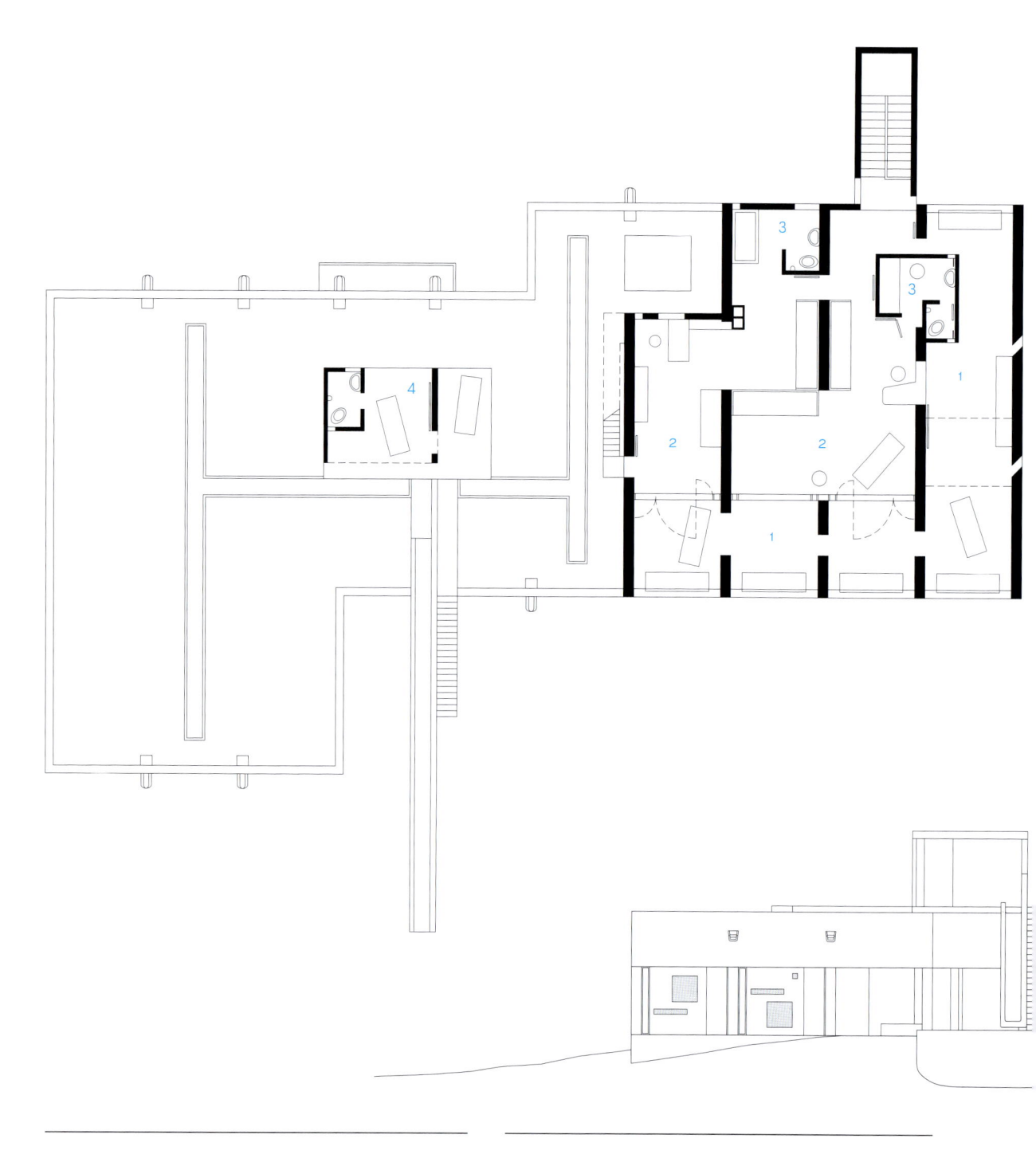

Second-floor plan

1. Veranda
2. Bedroom
3. Bathroom
4. Gazebo

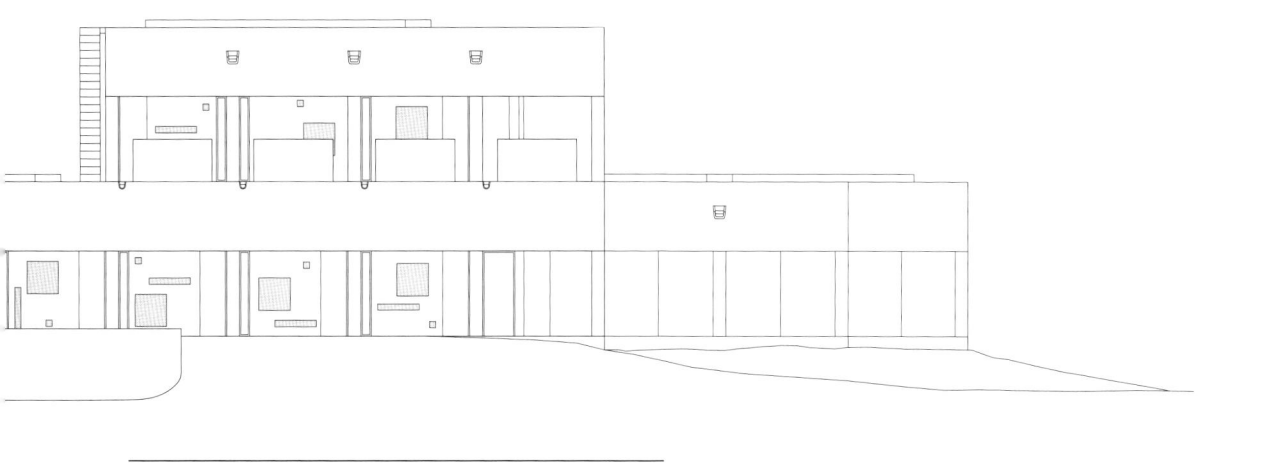

South elevation

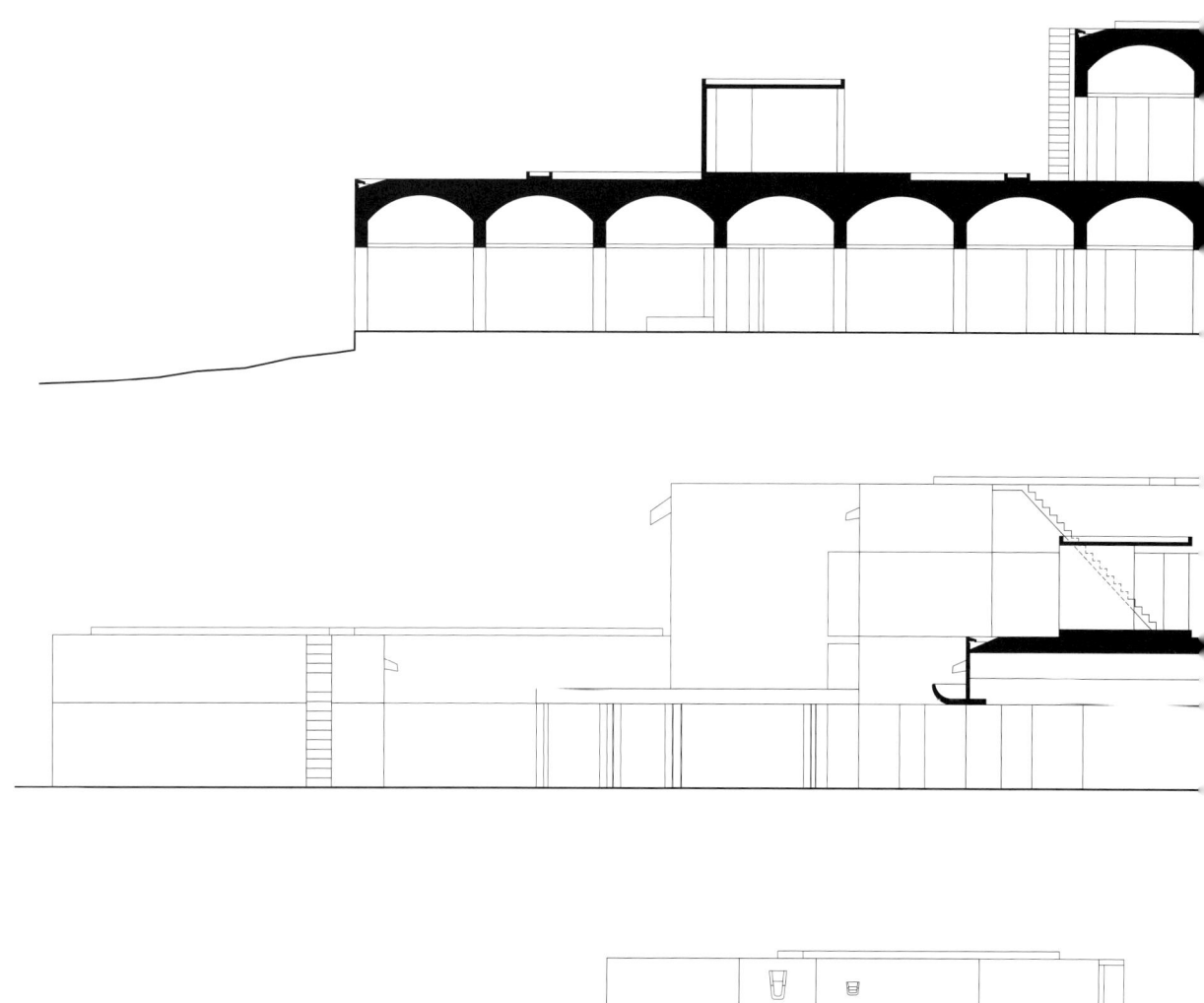

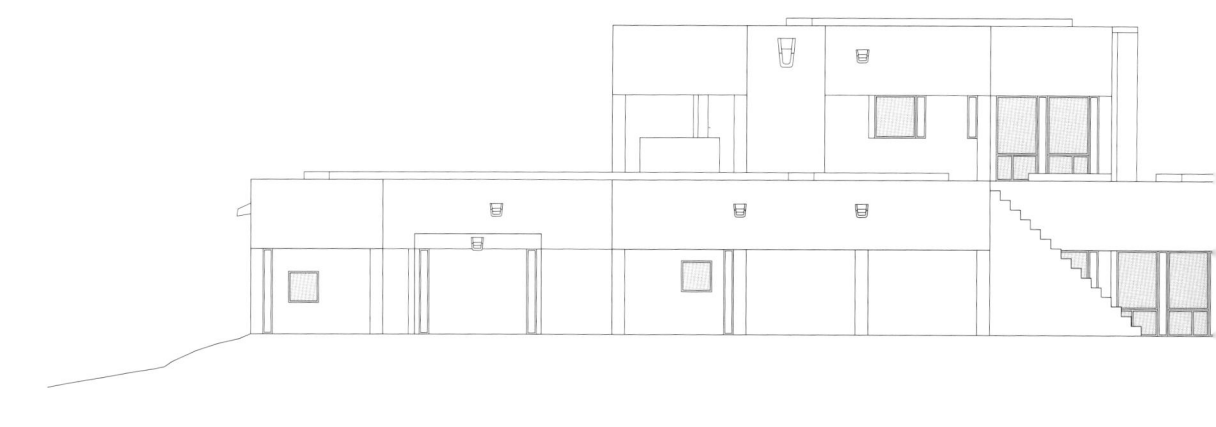

West–east section
North–south section
North elevation

VILLA SARABHAI

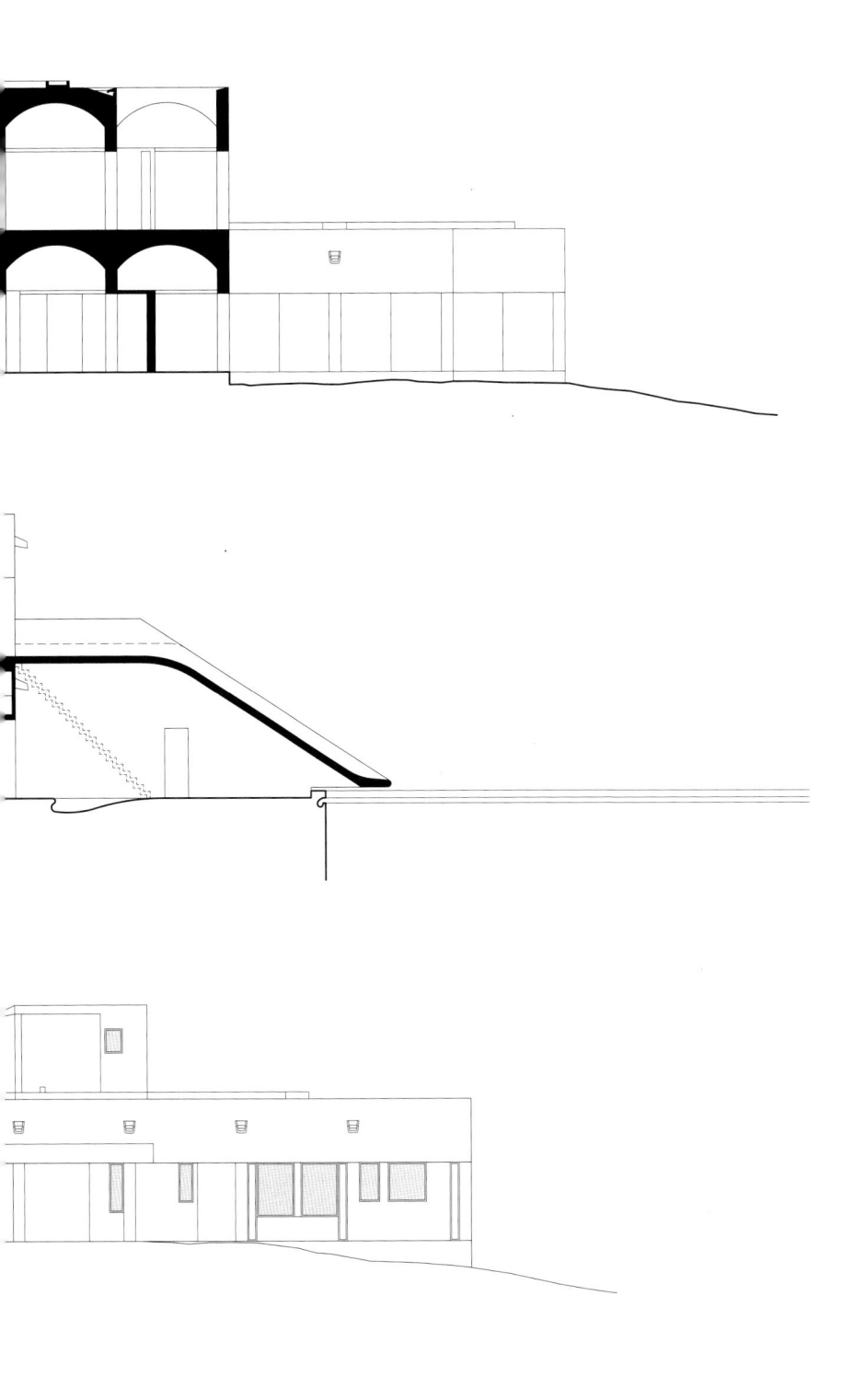

MAISON DE L'HOMME

LOCATION: Zurich, Switzerland
DATE: 1963

The last building that Le Corbusier designed, Maison de l'Homme, was completed posthumously. It now serves as a museum and visitors' center for showcasing the architect's paintings.

The Maison de l'Homme was Le Corbusier's only built structure that employed the Le Brevet system. (It had earlier been explored in projects that were not realized, such as Rob and Roq at Roquebrune-Cap-Martin.) Developed by Le Corbusier and Jean Prouvé, Le Brevet is a modular system based on a cubic frame, each side measuring 226 centimeters, built with standard angles. Each module is bolted to another; theoretically, the system is infinitely expandable horizontally (although its vertical growth is limited by the strength of a typical standard angle). Infill panels can be designed to suit various needs. (Five different exterior panels are used in Maison de l'Homme.)

Despite the house's large number of vertical columns—an inevitable outcome of using a modular system with relatively small dimensions—its interior spaces are surprisingly open and fluid. This is due to not only the slender sectional profile of these columns but also intelligent planning, with provisions for unobstructed diagonal views across different spaces that open directly to the outside. Sectional perspectives clearly show that rich and dynamic spaces can easily be achieved with a standard modular system, despite its repetitive nature. The house's most notable feature, a floating parasol, is a simplified, faceted version of the hyperbolic-paraboloid saddle structure, built with flat sheets of steel and reinforcing struts in standard sections. The exterior concrete ramp projects out to counterbalance the predominantly rectangular base building of the Le Brevet system.

CLIENT: Heidi Weber
PROGRAM: Museum for Le Corbusier's paintings
FEATURES: Parasol, Le Brevet modular construction system, *aérateur, ondulatoire*, ramp

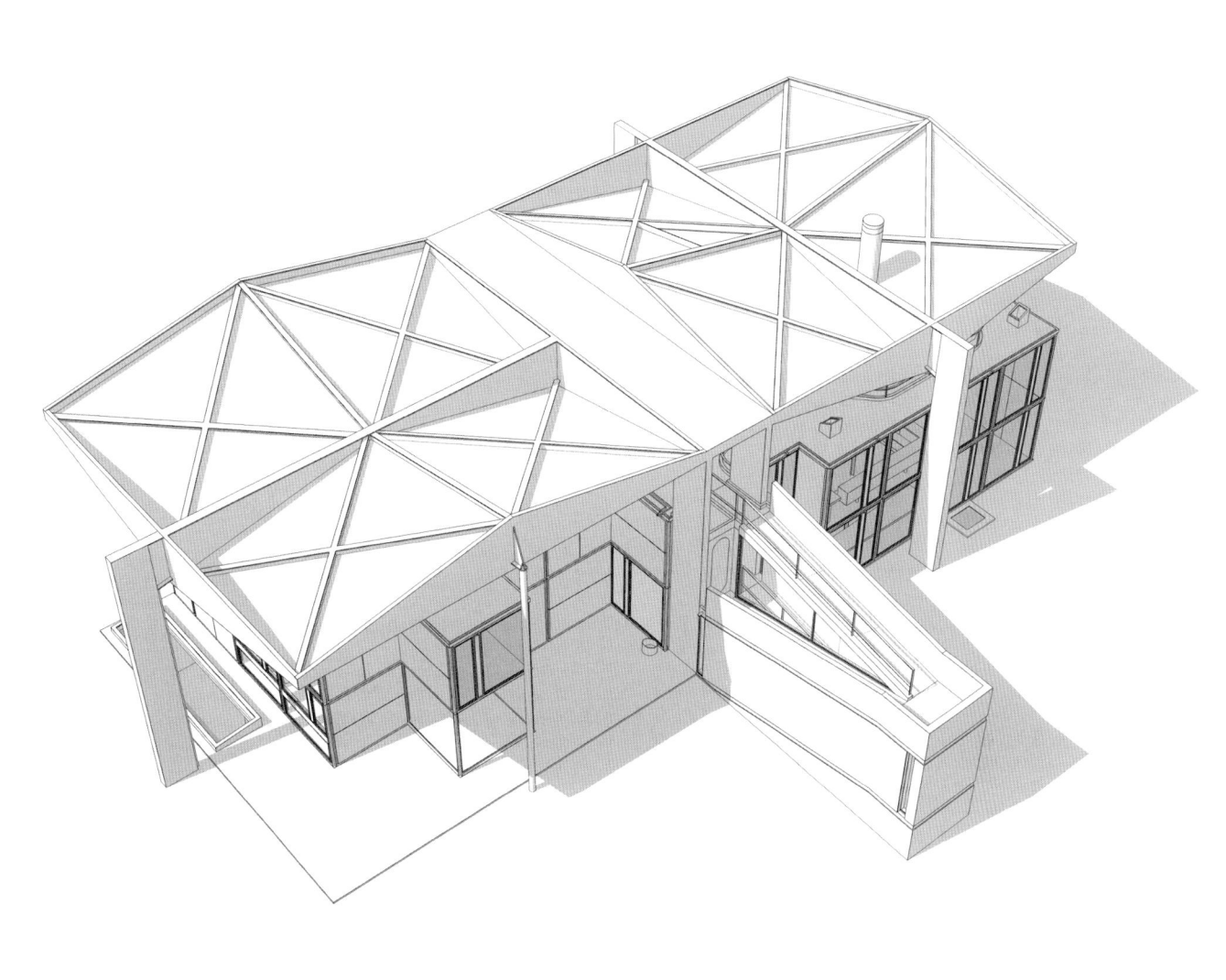

229 **MAISON DE L'HOMME** Aerial perspective, northeast corner

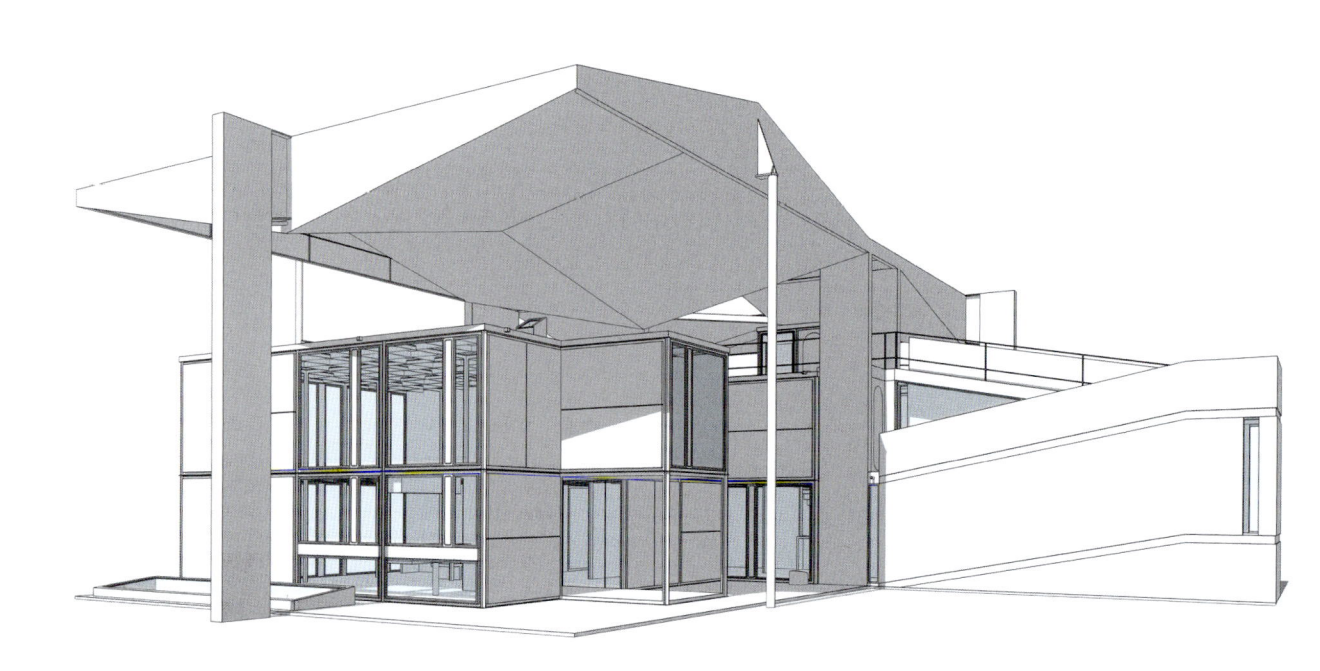

Exterior perspective, northeast corner, exterior ramp

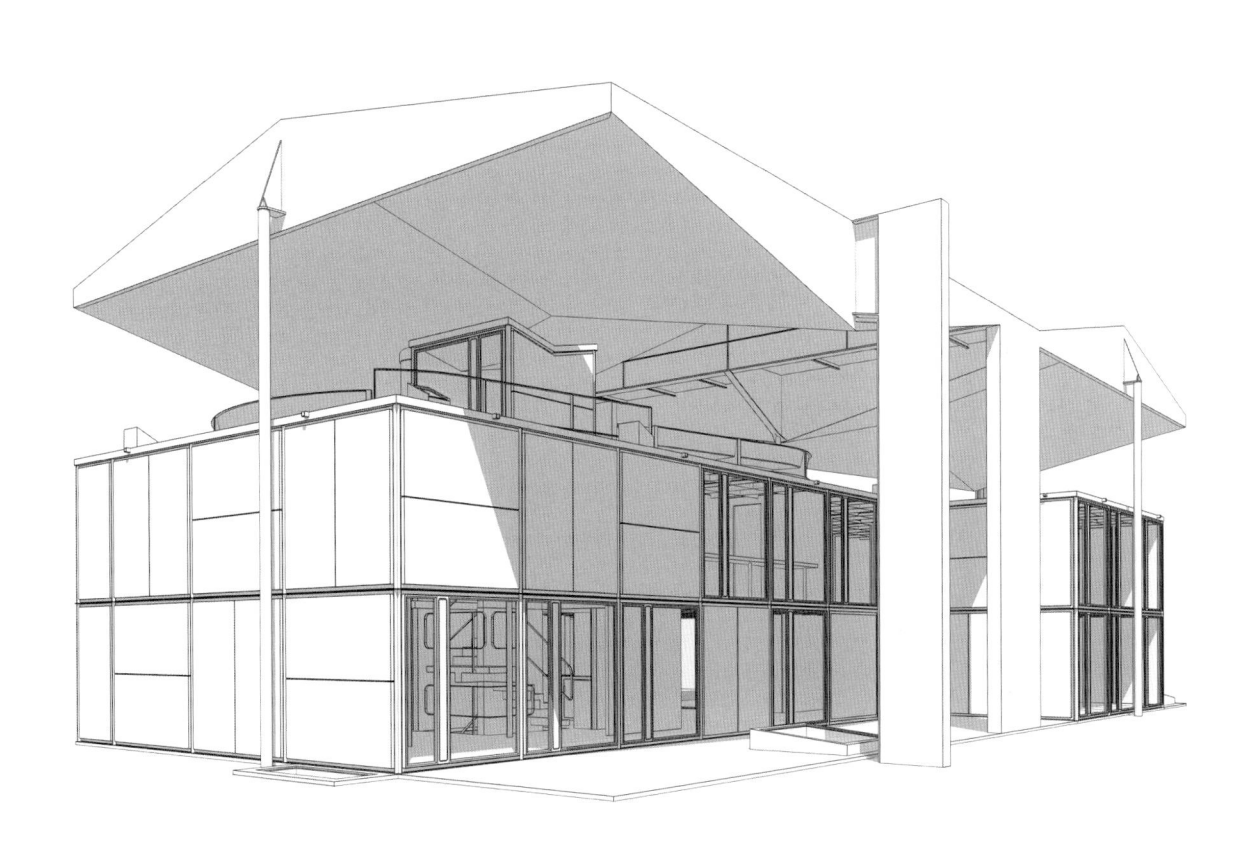

231 **MAISON DE L'HOMME** — Exterior perspective, southwest corner, outdoor terrace

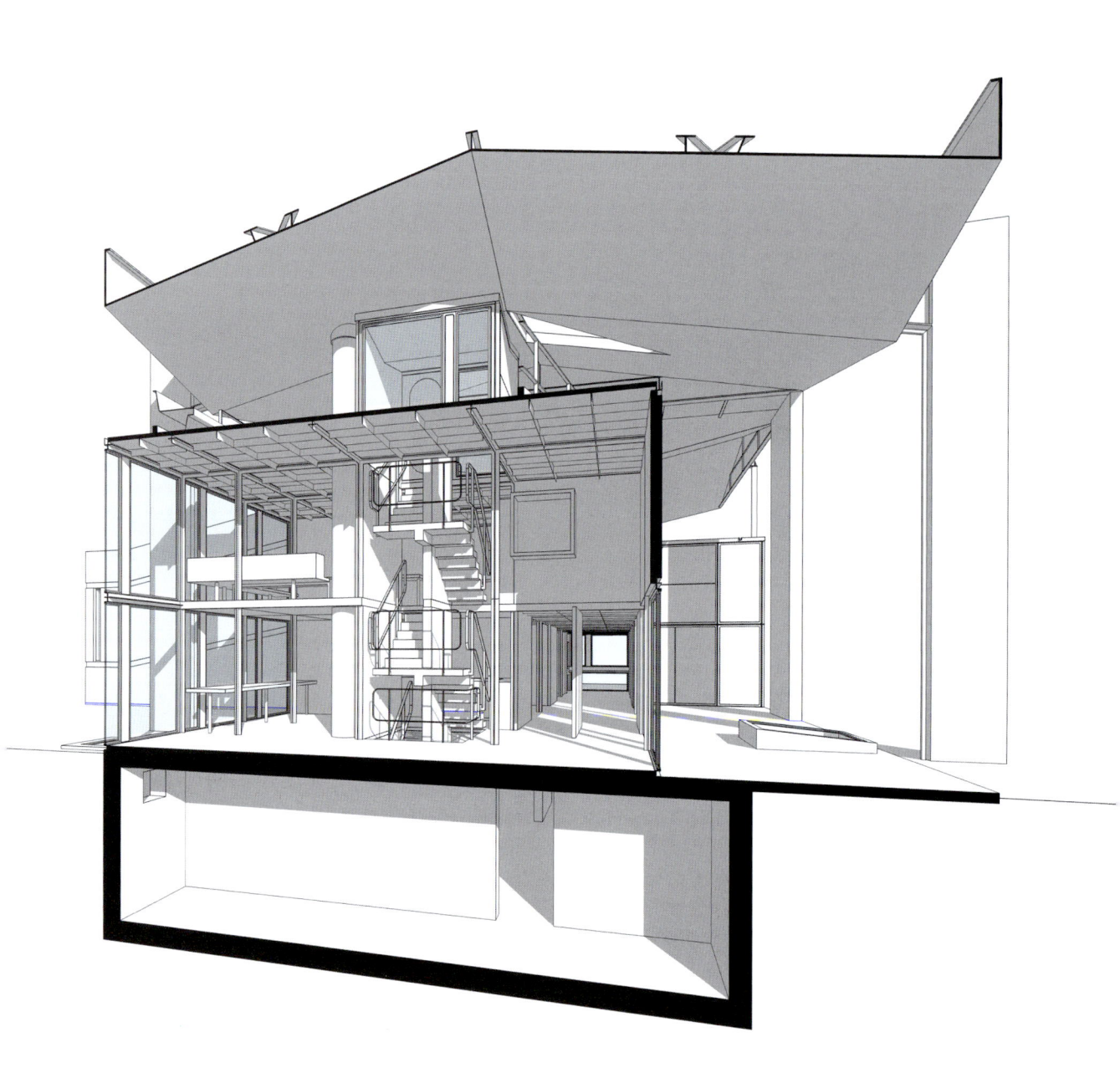

232 **MAISON DE L'HOMME** • North–south sectional perspective at double-height space

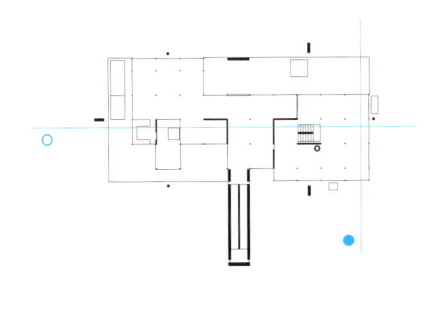

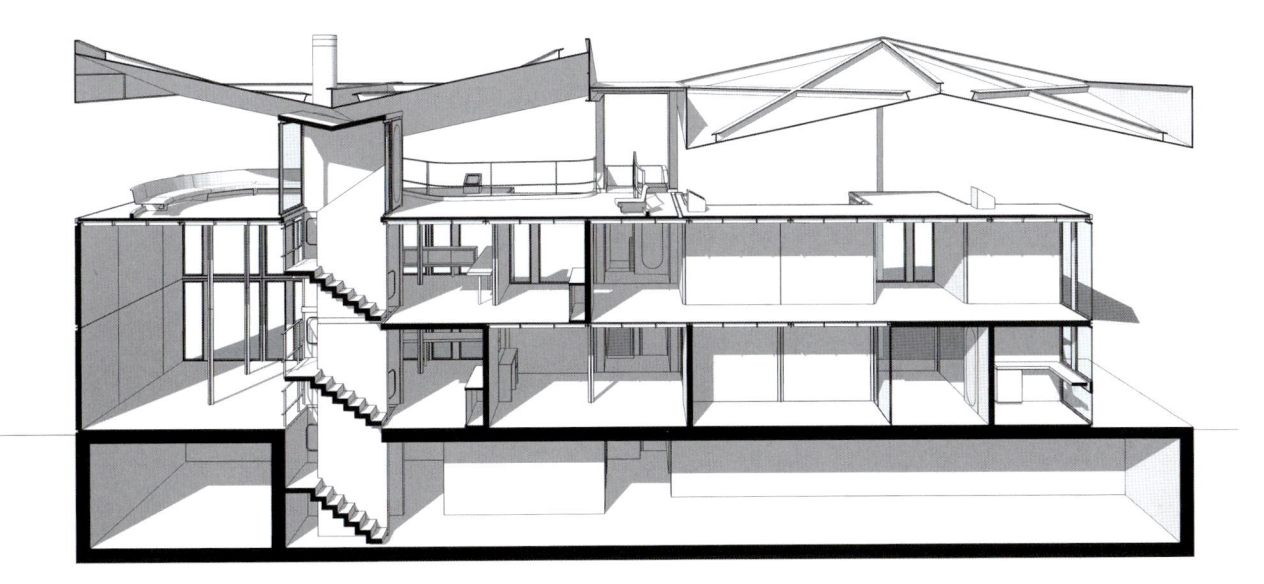

233 **MAISON DE L'HOMME**   ○   West–east sectional perspective at stairs

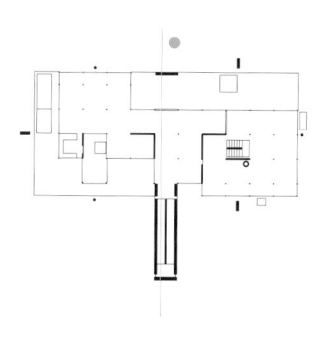

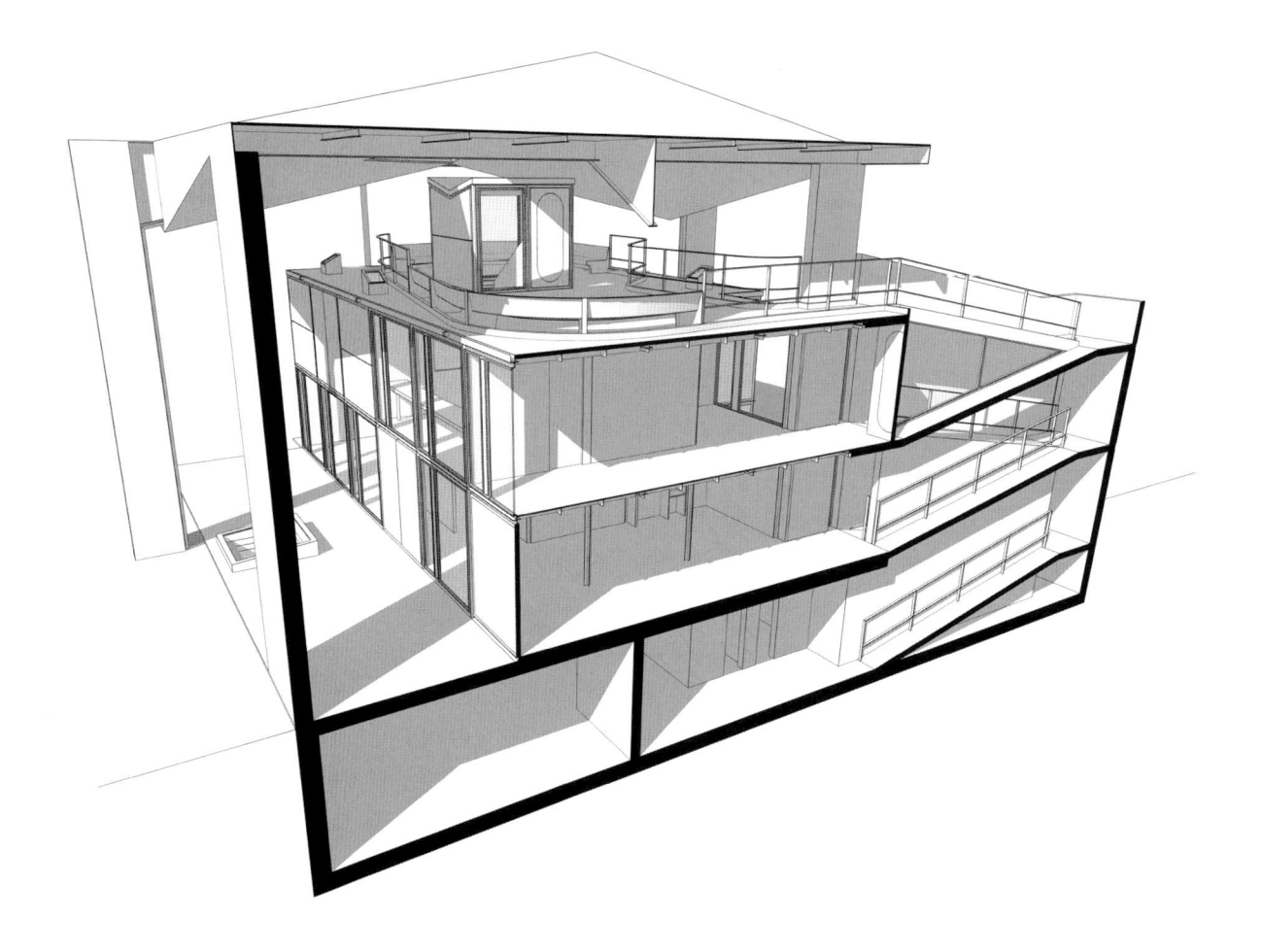

South–north sectional perspective at ramp

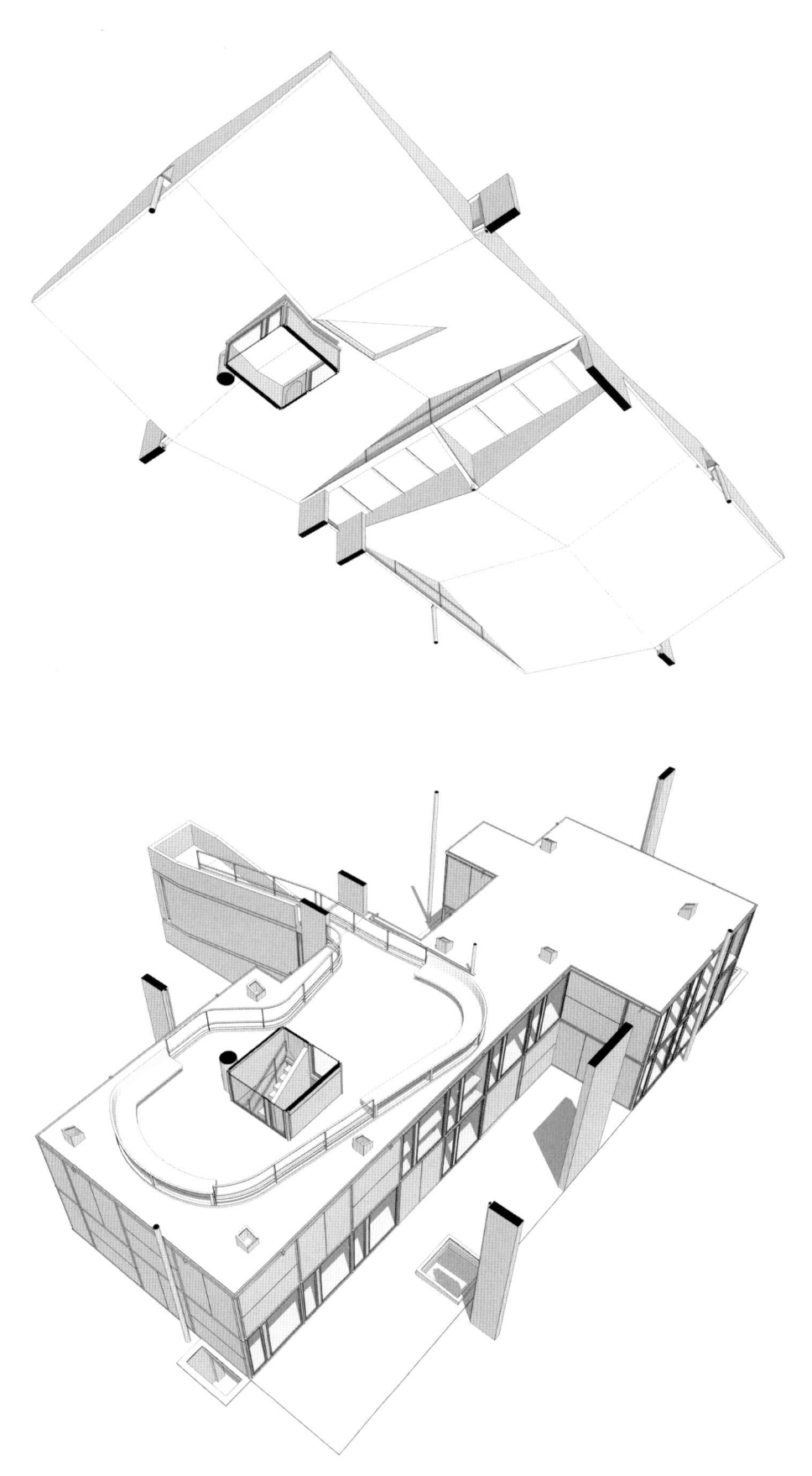

Worm's-eye perspective showing underside of canopy and aerial perspective showing roof terrace

235 **MAISON DE L'HOMME**

236 MAISON DE L'HOMME

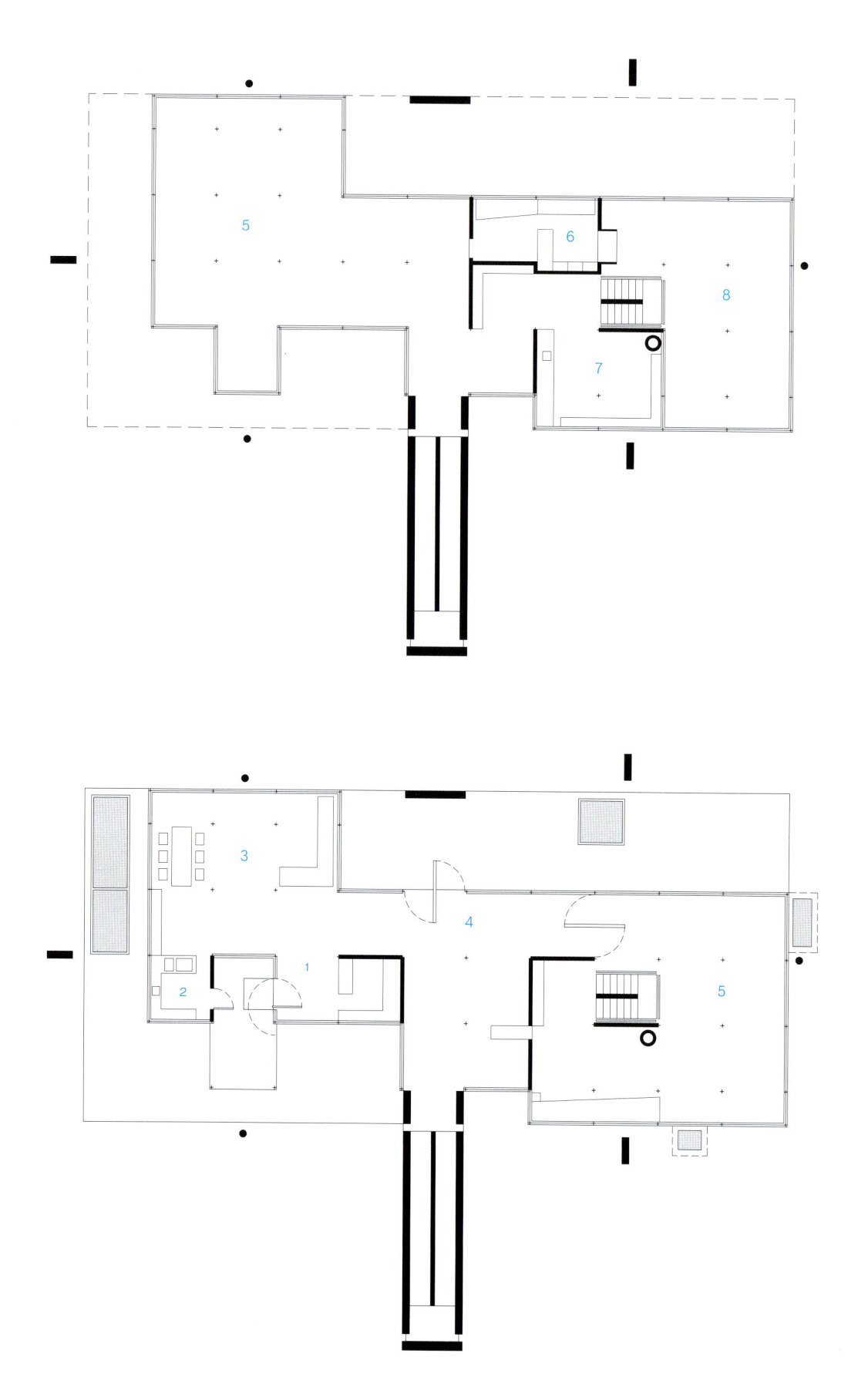

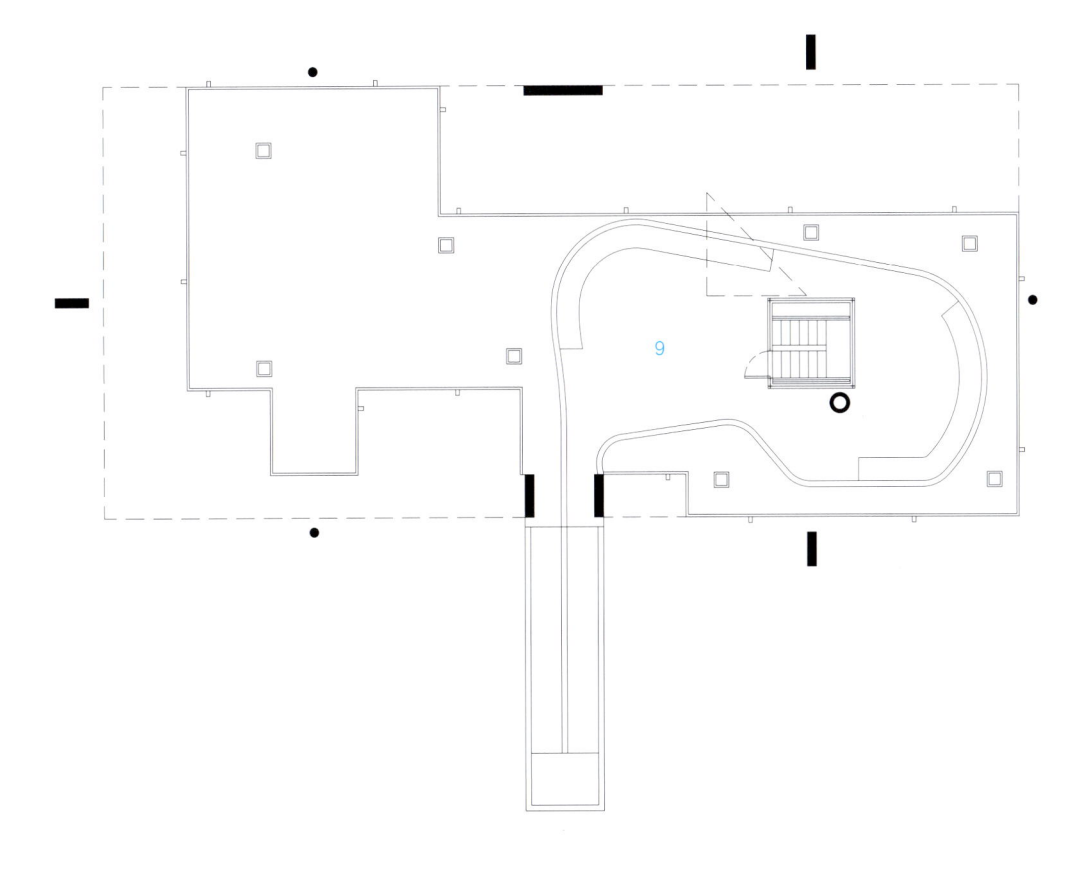

Second-floor plan   Third-floor / roof terrace plan

First-floor plan

1 Entrance hall
2 Kitchen
3 Dining and living room
4 Gallery
5 Exhibition hall
6 Library
7 Study
8 Open to below
9 Roof terrace

237 **MAISON DE L'HOMME**

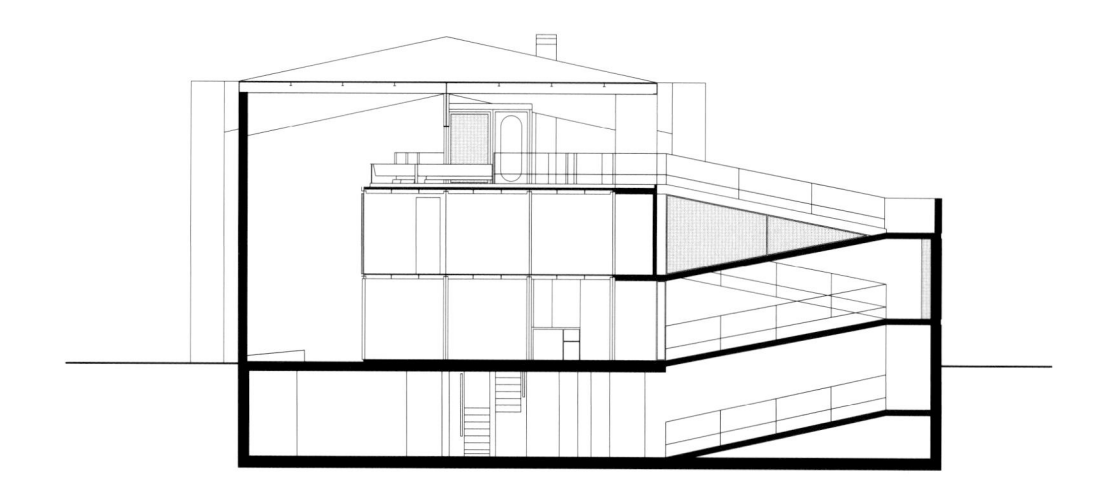

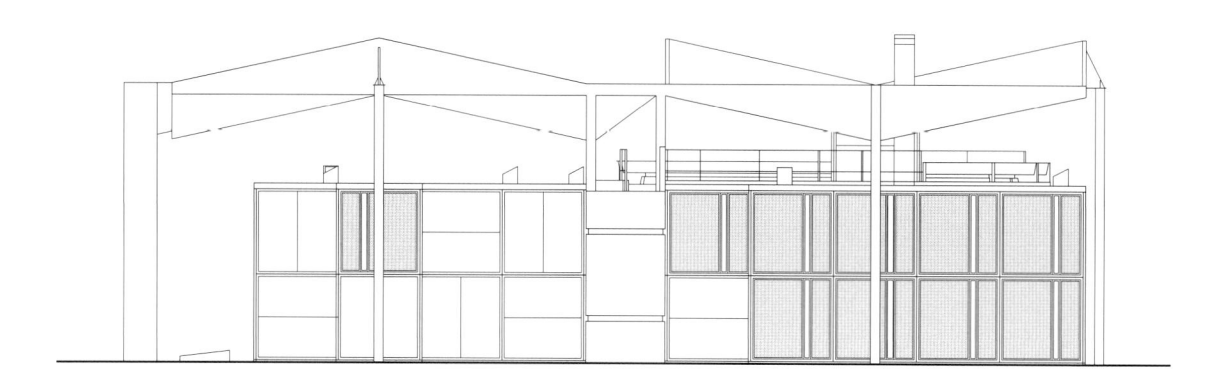

South–north section
North elevation

West–east section
West elevation
South elevation

238 MAISON DE L'HOMME

239 **MAISON DE L'HOMME**

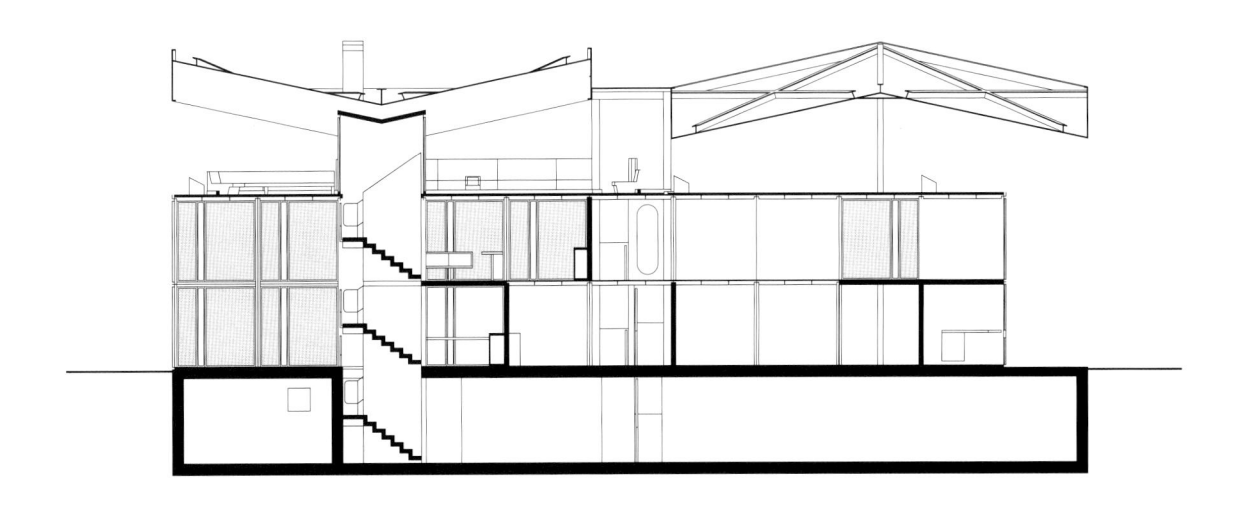

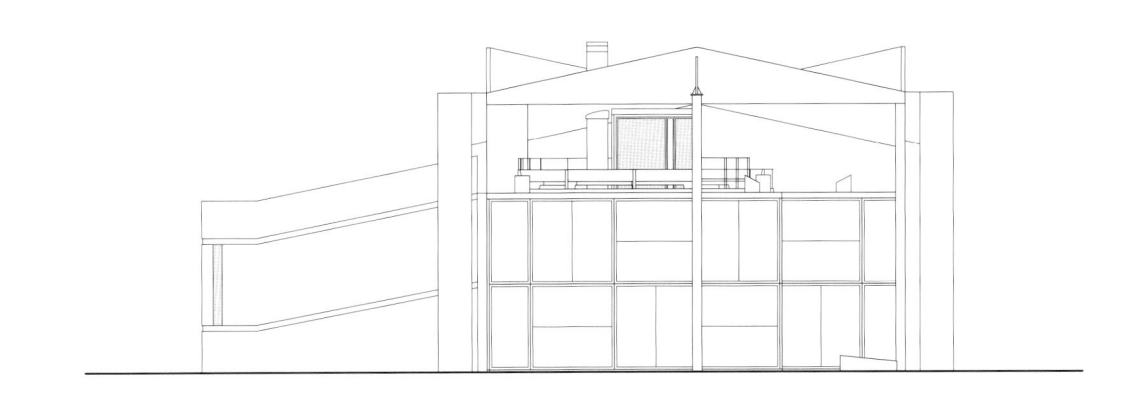

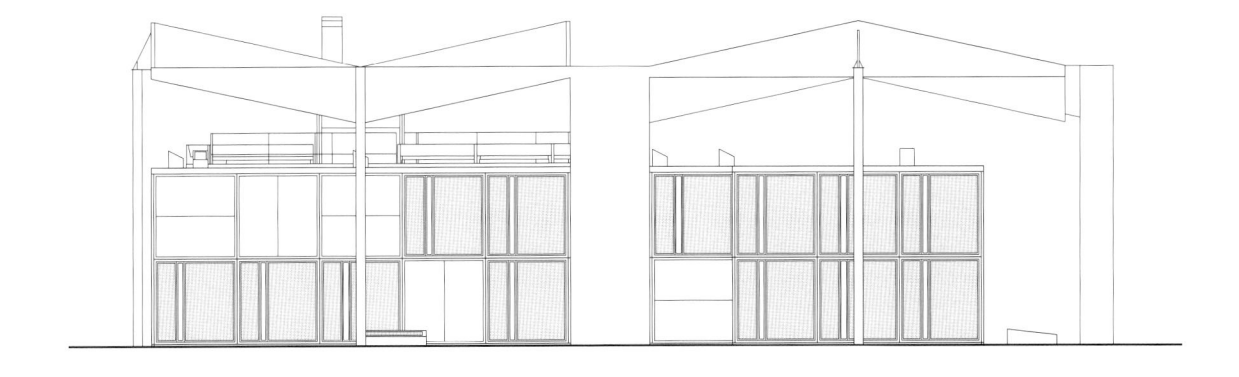

BIBLIOGRAPHY

Baker, Geoffrey H. *Le Corbusier: An Analysis of Form*. New York: Taylor & Francis, 2001.
Blake, Peter. *Le Corbusier: Architecture and Form*. Baltimore: Penguin Books, 1966.
Baltanás, José. *Walking through Le Corbusier: A Tour of His Masterworks*. New York: Thames & Hudson, 2006.
Benton, Tim. *The Villas of Le Corbusier and Pierre Jeanneret 1920–30*. Basel: Birkhäuser, 2007.
Boesiger, Willy, ed. *Le Corbusier*. New York: Praeger, 1972.
Boyer, M. Christine. *Le Corbusier: Homme de Lettres*. New York: Princeton Architectural Press, 2011.
Brooks, H. Allen, ed. *Le Corbusier*. Princeton: Princeton University Press, 1987.
Curtis, William J. R. *Le Corbusier: Ideas and Forms*. Oxford: Phaidon, 1986.
———. *Modern Architecture Since 1900*. Upper Saddle River, NJ: Prentice Hall, 1996.
Frampton, Kenneth. *Le Corbusier: Architect and Visionary*. London: Thames & Hudson, 2001.
———. *Le Corbusier: Architect of the Twentieth Century*. New York: Abrams, 2002.
———. *Modern Architecture: A Critical History*. New York: Thames & Hudson, 1992.
———. *Studies in Tectonic Culture: The Poetics of Construction in Nineteenth and Twentieth Century Architecture*. Edited by John Cava. Cambridge, MA: MIT Press, 1995.
Futagawa, Yukio, ed. *Le Corbusier—Sarabhai House, Ahmedabad, India, 1951–55. GA: Residential Masterpieces* 10. Tokyo: A.D.A. Edita, 2011.
Gans, Deborah. *The Le Corbusier Guide*. New York: Princeton Architectural Press, 2000.
Jencks, Charles. *Le Corbusier and the Tragic View of Architecture*. Cambridge, MA: Harvard University Press, 1973.
Kurrent, Friedrich, ed. *Scale Models: Houses of the 20th Century*. Basel: Birkhäuser, 1999.
Lapunzina, Alejandro. *Le Corbusier's Maison Curutchet*. New York: Princeton Architectural Press, 1997.
Le Corbusier. *Creation is a Patient Search*. New York: Praeger, 1960.
———. *The Final Testament of Père Corbu: A Translation and Interpretation of* Mise au point *by Ivan Žaknic*. New Haven: Yale University Press, 1997.
———. *Oeuvre complète*. 8 vols. Zurich: Les Éditions d'Architecture, 1946–1970.
———. *Sarabhai House, Ahmedabad, India, 1955: and Shodhan House, Ahmedabad, India, 1956. GA 32*. Tokyo: A.D.A. Edita, 1964.
———. *Le Corbusier Talks with Students*. New York: Princeton Architectural Press, 1999.
———. *Villa Savoye, Poissy, France, 1929–31*. Tokyo: A.D.A. Edita, 1972.
———. *Modulor 1 and 2*. Cambridge, MA: Harvard University Press, 1980.
Le Corbusier Foundation. *Le Corbusier Plans*. Paris: Codex Images International, 2005.
———. *Le Corbusier Archive*. New York: Garland, 1982.
Lyon, Dominique. *Le Corbusier Alive*. Paris: Vilo, 2000.
Maniaque Benton, Caroline. *Le Corbusier and the Maisons Jaoul*. New York: Princeton Architectural Press, 2009.
Mori Art Museum. *Le Corbusier: Art and Architecture–A Life of Creativity*. Tokyo: Remixpoint, 2007.
Pawley, Martin and Yukio Futagawa. *Le Corbusier*. New York: Simon & Schuster, 1970.
Rüegg, Arthur, ed. *Polychromie architecturale: Le Corbusier's Color Keyboards from 1931 to 1959*. Basel: Birkhäuser, 1997.
Samuel, Flora. *Le Corbusier and the Architectural Promenade*. Basel: Birkhäuser, 2010.
———. *Le Corbusier in Detail*. Burlington, MA: Architectural Press, 2007.
Sbriglio, Jacques. *Le Corbusier & Lucien Hervé: A Dialogue between Architect and Photographer*. Los Angeles: Getty, 2011.
———. *Le Corbusier: Les Villas La Roche-Jeanneret*. Basel: Birkhäuser, 1997.
Shodan Basu, Manisha. *Le Corbusier's Villa Shodhan: A Personal Look at his Final Work of Residential Architecture*. Copenhagen: Royal Danish Academy of Fine Arts, School of Architecture Publishers, 2008.
von Moos, Stanislaus. *Le Corbusier: Elements of a Synthesis*. Rotterdam: 010, 2009.
Weber, Heidi. *Heidi Weber: 50 Years Ambassador for Le Corbusier, 1958–2008*. Zurich: Heidi Weber Museum, Centre Le Corbusier, 2009.
Wogenscky, André. *Le Corbusier's Hand*. Cambridge, MA: MIT Press, 2006.